More Praise for *The American Miracle*

"This is a brisk, joyous romp through some of the most critical providential moments that made America an exceptional nation, told by a Yale-trained historian . . . who writes with brio and conviction."

—Karl Rove, senior advisor to President George W. Bush

"If you love reading American history, or any history written like a page-turning novel . . . or just love great writing—the artistry of words that often read more like poetry than prose—you will love this book. The fact that Michael Medved gives the reader all of these makes this a must-read."

—Lanny J. Davis, former special counsel to
President Clinton; author of *Truth to Tell*

"Michael Medved has written an engaging, affectionate, and historically compelling book about America. *The American Miracle* is a source of knowledge, a source of comfort, a source of inspiration. After reading it, you'll know America better and treasure her more."

—Peter Wehner, White House aide to Presidents George Bush
and George W. Bush; senior fellow, Ethics and Public Policy Center

"Michael Medved has written a timely study of the centrality of faith and providence in the American story, challenging Americans to reaffirm the religious ideals on which their nation was founded. Read it and be inspired."

—Rabbi Lord Jonathan Sacks, former chief rabbi of the United Hebrew
Congregations of the Commonwealth; author of *Not in God's Name*

"Michael Medved chronicles in intriguing detail how America's unlikely founding and enduring success can't be explained by luck or coincidence but only one thing: divine providence. After reading this book, even the toughest skeptics will be hard pressed not to believe that God had a role in America's fortune."

—Bill Bennett, secretary of education under President Reagan;
author of *America: The Last Best Hope*

"Medved speaks truth boldly and reasons carefully . . . and he is also a most gifted writer. In *The American Miracle* he reminds us that there once was a day when Americans knew the history of our country as a story of promise and providence, and he is confident that Americans can learn that story again."

—R. Albert Mohler Jr., president, Southern Baptist Theological Seminary

Also by Michael Medved

The 5 Big Lies About American Business:
Combating Smears Against the Free-Market Economy (2009)

The 10 Big Lies About America:
Combating Destructive Distortions About Our Nation (2008)

Right Turns: Unconventional Lessons from a Controversial Life (2004)

Hollywood vs. America: Popular Culture
and the War on Traditional Values (1992)

Hospital: The Hidden Lives of a Medical Center Staff (1983)

The Shadow Presidents: The Secret History of the
Chief Executives and Their Top Aides (1979)

with Diane Medved, PhD

Saving Childhood: Protecting Our Children from the
National Assault on Innocence (1998)

with Harry Medved

Son of Golden Turkey Awards (1986)

The Hollywood Hall of Shame: The Most Expensive Flops
in Movie History (1984)

The Golden Turkey Awards: Nominees and Winners—
the Worst Achievements in Hollywood History (1980)

with Harry Medved and Randy Dreyfuss

The Fifty Worst Films of All Time (1978)

with David Wallechinsky

What Really Happened to the Class of '65? (1976)

~ THE ~

American Miracle

Divine Providence in the
Rise of the Republic

Michael Medved

CROWN
FORUM
NEW YORK

Crown Forum with colophon is a registered trademark of
Penguin Random House LLC.

Library of Congress Cataloging-in-Publication Data
Names: Medved, Michael, author.
Title: The American miracle / Michael Medved.
Description: First edition. | New York : Crown Forum, 2016. | Includes
bibliographical references and index.
Identifiers: LCCN 2016023658 | ISBN 9780553447262 (hc) |
ISBN 9780553447279 (eISBN)
Subjects: LCSH: United States—History—Religious aspects—Christianity.
Classification: LCC E179 .M483 2016 | DDC 277.3—dc23
LC record available at https://lccn.loc.gov/2016023658

ISBN 978-0-553-44726-2
eBook ISBN 978-0-553-44727-9

Printed in the United States of America

Jacket design by Ervin Serrano
Jacket images: Illustration by Archive Images/Alamy stock photo; texture
by SuriyaPhoto/Shutterstock and MaxyM SuriyaPhoto/Shutterstock;
sunburst graphic by Artnis/Shutterstock

10 9 8 7 6 5 4 3 2 1

First Edition

For Diane
My own American miracle

Contents

1: THE GLORIOUS FOURTH   *1*
Dedication, Death, and Fifty Years of Miracles

2: BLOWN BLESSEDLY OFF COURSE   *27*
The Mayflower Pilgrims Find Their Place

3: REVOLUTIONARY REVELATIONS   *49*
Timely Rescues from an Unseen Ally

4: INDISPENSABLE, INDESTRUCTIBLE   *73*
The Illogical Survival of George Washington

5: "AN ASSEMBLY OF DEMIGODS"   *89*
Confrontation, Compromise, and a Miraculous Convention

6: PROVIDENTIAL PURCHASE   *123*
Disconnected Developments Double America's Size

7: AMERICAN AGINCOURT   *149*
Astonishing Victory, Answered Prayers

8: "BIG DRUNK" AND LONE STAR LUCK   187
*A Broken Marriage, an Indian Exile,
and a Scrap That Changed History*

9: GOLDEN TIMING   233
*Defying a President, Detaching California,
and Discovering Gold*

10: THE MIRACLE OF LINCOLN   265
*America's Most Unlikely President
and His Supernatural Success*

11: WAITING FOR A SIGN   301
Lost Orders and Found Faith

12: THE MESSENGER AND HIS MESSAGE   325
Lincoln's Vision, Death, and Destiny

13: "THIS FAVORED LAND"   359
America Is No Accident

With Gratitude . . .   375

Sources   379

Index   393

"I have lived, Sir, a long time, and the longer I live, the more convincing proofs I see of this truth—that God governs in the affairs of men. And if a sparrow cannot fall to the ground without his notice, is it probable that an empire can rise without his aid?"

—Benjamin Franklin, remarks to the
Constitutional Convention, June 28, 1787

"No people can be bound to acknowledge and adore the Invisible Hand which conducts the affairs of men more than those of the United States. Every step by which they have advanced to the character of an independent nation seems to have been distinguished by some token of providential agency."

—George Washington, first Inaugural Address, April 30, 1789

"You have the highest of human trusts committed to your care. Providence has showered on this favored land blessings without number, and has chosen you as the guardians of freedom, to preserve it for the benefit of the human race. May He who holds in His hands the destinies of nations, make you worthy of the favors He has bestowed, and enable you, with pure hearts and hands and sleepless vigilance, to guard and defend to the end of time the great charge He has committed to your keeping."

—President Andrew Jackson, "Farewell Address," March 4, 1837

"It is the object of the present work to explain the steps by which a favoring providence, calling our institutions into being, has conducted the country to its present happiness and glory."

—George Bancroft, opening declaration of his
History of the United States, 1876

"Intelligence, patriotism, Christianity, and a firm reliance on Him who has never yet forsaken this favored land are still competent to adjust in the best way all our present difficulty."

—Abraham Lincoln, first Inaugural Address, March 4, 1861

THE
American Miracle

LINKED IN DEATH AS WELL AS LIFE: John Adams (second president of the United States) and Thomas Jefferson (third president, who defeated Adams in his bid for reelection).

"Jefferson survives." —Reported last words of John Adams, July 4, 1826

"Let the annual return of this day forever refresh our recollection of these rights." —Thomas Jefferson, June 24, 1826, ten days before his death on July 4

1

THE GLORIOUS FOURTH

Dedication, Death, and Fifty Years of Miracles

Coincidence alone could never explain it: that much seemed obvious to Americans of 1826, just as it does to citizens of today. The eerie events of that epochal Independence Day suggested the intervention of supernatural forces, mixing death and dedication in such powerful ways that observers of all faiths, and of no faith, saw evidence of destiny's direction in American affairs. Even now, after nearly two hundred years of turbulent history, recollections of that "Glorious Fourth" can compel the most skeptical scholars to acknowledge weird, wonderful aspects in the rise of the Republic, and to reconsider the disconcerting old idea that God shows special tenderness toward the American experiment.

On the occasion of the fiftieth Fourth of July, such confidence in providential protection seemed not only logical but unavoidable. After all, the older citizens of the federal Union had already witnessed a half century of miracles, highlighted by the new nation's prodigious growth and unprecedented prosperity. Americans viewed themselves as a chosen people, selected for special responsibilities to accompany their special blessings, and so looked to biblical references to establish the proper context for major public celebrations.

The preparations for the anniversary repeatedly invoked the Old Testament notion of jubilee, citing a well-known verse in Leviticus:

"And ye shall hallow the fiftieth year and proclaim liberty throughout all the land and unto all the inhabitants thereof; it shall be a jubilee unto you" (25:10). After all, a portion of this same verse had been inscribed onto the Liberty Bell itself—already a cherished national icon just two generations after it reputedly rang out in Philadelphia's Independence Hall to celebrate signing of the Declaration.

A half century later, leaders in every corner of the country arranged for pealing bells in cities, villages, and crossroads churches, in recognition of the breathtaking growth of the young Republic. The most recent census showed almost twelve million inhabitants—nearly five times the population that had launched a world-changing revolution. Even more dramatic, a loose coalition of thirteen thinly settled colonies, clinging to a relatively narrow band of territory at the edge of the Atlantic, had given way to twenty-four flourishing states with plausible dreams of an American empire someday reaching all the way to the Pacific.

In the midst of this dizzying change, Americans of the era clung to their precious remaining connections to the nation's heroic origins, expressing special gratitude for the unlikely survival of the two titans who had played the most prominent roles in declaring independence. At a time when male life expectancy barely reached forty years, John Adams, the "Atlas of Independence" and the second president of the United States, had passed his ninetieth birthday with his faculties and health remarkably intact. From his ancestral home outside of Boston, he watched with passionate engagement as his oldest son (and intellectual soul mate) presided over the government in faraway Washington as the sixth president. In fact, one of the former chief executive's doctors reported that the inauguration of his son in 1825 actually enhanced the old man's strength and vitality. "But physicians do not always consider how much the powers of the mind, and what is called good spirits, can recover the lost energies of the body," wrote Benjamin Waterhouse to President John Quincy Adams. "I really believe that your father's revival is mainly owing to the demonstration that his son has not served an ungrateful public."

Six hundred miles away, at the elegant hilltop plantation house he had designed for himself, Adams's old friend (and sometime bitter rival) Thomas Jefferson also defied the actuarial tables. At eighty-three, the third president struggled with various digestive and urinary tract afflictions, but he received frequent visitors and maintained a prolific correspondence, commenting eloquently on current affairs. He told his grandson that "I am like an old watch, with a pinion worn out here, and a wheel there, until I can go no longer." He also carefully prepared for his own demise, penning a valedictory poem to his adored surviving daughter, enclosing it in a simple, elegant box she opened only after his death:

> *Then farewell, my dear, my lov'd daughter, adieu!*
> *The last pang of life is in parting from you!*

Yet even with his intensifying focus on his own mortality, Jefferson expressed a fierce determination to survive one more Fourth of July so that "he might breathe the air of the Fiftieth Anniversary."

As the great day approached, organizers of the elaborate public festivities in all of the nation's most important cities turned their attention to Adams and Jefferson as potential guests to lend historic weight to their celebrations. In the Continental Congress of 1776, it had been Adams who led the relentless fight for independence and who, once he had succeeded, recommended his young friend Jefferson to draft the declaration that would explain the decision to a wondering world. Now, of the fifty-six patriots who had affixed their signatures to that final document, only these two and one more—eighty-eight-year-old Charles Carroll of Maryland—were alive to see the half-century commemoration of their handiwork.

Despite pleas from every corner of the country, frail health and the rigors of travel made the journey unthinkable for each of the old men. Adams would have dearly loved to join his son at the White House to preside together over the capital's Grand Jubilee, but a journey to Washington would have consumed more than five days, rattling over rough roads in stiflingly hot stagecoaches and making brief water passages on belching, filthy steamboats.

Instead, he received visitors in the sprawling, comfortably cluttered two-story Quincy residence, Peacefield, he had called home since 1788. He had inhabited the house for the quarter century since disillusioned voters turned him out of the White House after his single term, following an exceptionally nasty and painfully personal campaign waged against him by followers of Jefferson, his old friend. Adams and his wife, Abigail, first acquired the structure and its forty acres of verdant fields and orchards at the conclusion of his diplomatic service in Europe following the Revolution; it stood just down a country road from the modest saltbox home in which he had been born and raised, and from the similarly unassuming neighboring structure in which his son John Quincy first opened his eyes to the New England sunlight. The old man still owned both buildings and hoped to keep them in the family for perpetuity. His beloved Abigail had left him a widower eight years before with her reported last words, "Do not grieve, my friend, my dearest friend. I am ready to go. And John, it will not be long." She rested now in the local churchyard, where her husband of fifty-four years meant to join her when his time came.

Leaders from Boston hoped to lure the old lion to the festive commemorations they had planned in the nearby city, but Adams declined to make the ten-mile trip. He even turned down the local Independence Day committee from Quincy, though he provided them with a sharply worded letter they could read aloud at the upcoming anniversary. He wrote: "My best wishes, in the joys, and festivities, and the solemn services of that day on which will be completed the fiftieth year from its birth, of the independence of the United States: a memorable epoch in the annals of the human race, destined in future history to form the brightest or the blackest page, according to the use or the abuse of those political institutions by which they shall, in time to come, be shaped by the human mind."

The committee of his neighbors, perhaps hoping that the great man would reconsider his participation in commemorations so close to his home, came calling at Peacefield a few days later. They asked Adams to suggest a toast that could be presented in his honor on the holiday. "I will give you," he said without hesitation, "INDEPENDENCE FOREVER."

After a moment of silence, his respectful visitors asked if he might consider adding something further. He leaned on his cane and scowled back at them from under his halo of white hair. "Not a word," he crisply replied.

"RAYS OF RAVISHING LIGHT AND GLORY"

His friend Thomas Jefferson felt no similar reluctance to discourse at length. When Mayor Roger Weightman of Washington, D.C., invited all living former presidents—Adams, Jefferson, James Madison, and James Monroe—to attend the festival planned for the seat of government, each respectfully declined, citing the infirmities of age. The "Sage of Monticello," however, carefully composed a public response that promptly appeared in newspapers around the country and created a national sensation in the weeks before the holiday. He wrote at a desk in his sun-dappled chamber, where a plaster bust of Adams rested on a shelf and overlooked his colleague's work with assumed approbation. Jefferson wrote:

> I should, indeed, with peculiar delight, have met and exchanged there congratulations, personally, with the small band, the remnant of that host of worthies who joined with us on that day, in the bold and doubtful election we were to make, for our country, between submission and the sword; and to have enjoyed with them the consolatory fact that our fellow citizens, after half a century of experience and prosperity, continue to approve the choice we made. May it be to the world, what I believe it will be, (to some parts sooner, to others later, but finally to all) the signal of arousing men to burst the chains, under which monkish ignorance and superstition had persuaded them to bind themselves, and to assume the blessings and security of self-government. The form which we have substituted restores the free right to the unbounded exercise of reason and freedom of opinion. All eyes are opened or opening to the rights of men. The general spread of the light of science has already laid open to every view the palpable truth, that the mass of mankind has not been born with saddles on their backs, nor a favored

few, booted and spurred, ready to ride them legitimately, by the grace of God. These are grounds of hope for others; for ourselves, let the annual return of this day forever refresh our recollection of these rights, and an undiminished devotion to them.

With this elegantly crafted testament of faith in the work of his own Revolutionary cohort, Jefferson managed, as he always did, to upstage his old friend. Even John Adams's son, the president of the United States, read Jefferson's words and pronounced himself impressed by the elderly Virginian's vigor of language and clarity of mind.

But it had been the elder Adams, not the more effusive Jefferson, who first predicted the way a grateful nation would come to rejoice over their bold gamble on nationhood. In an exultant letter to his wife, Abigail, back home in Boston, the irascible and tireless patriot had described a fateful day of decision at the Continental Congress in Philadelphia in 1776 and then recorded an uncanny burst of prophecy, shockingly typical of our founding fathers. The delegate from Massachusetts declared that the second day of July, when his congressional colleagues first voted to authorize permanent separation from the mother country, would become known as

the most memorable epocha in the history of America. I am apt to believe that it will be celebrated by succeeding generations as the great anniversary festival. It ought to be commemorated as the day of deliverance, by solemn acts of devotion to God Almighty. It ought to be solemnized with pomp and parade, with shows, games, sports, guns, bells, bonfires and illuminations from one end of this continent to another, from this time forward forevermore. You will think me transported with enthusiasm but I am not. I am well aware of the toil and blood and treasure it will cost us to maintain this Declaration and to support and defend these states. Yet through all the gloom, I can see rays of ravishing light and glory.

REJECTING MR. JEFFERSON'S "SEDITIOUS PAPER"

Unfortunately, it took more than a generation for those rays to shine in a healing, benevolent fashion on the implacably warring factions that afflicted the new nation. To a startling extent, partisanship undermined the development of a national holiday and even spoiled appreciation of the Declaration, which was indelibly associated with its principal author, Jefferson, a profoundly controversial figure for most of his political career. The Federalists who controlled the national government between 1789 and 1801 felt no inclination to honor Jefferson's masterpiece, considering its language too explicitly anti-British and suspiciously, if vaguely, pro-French. On July 4, 1800, two ministers ostentatiously walked out of a public worship service honoring independence when one of their young students insisted on reading aloud from Mr. Jefferson's "seditious paper."

Within a year, one of the most vitriolic elections in American history brought the Jeffersonians into full control in the capital. The new president delivered a famously conciliatory inaugural address, attempting to defuse wild talk of disunion and resistance from some of the indignant Adams loyalists. "Every difference of opinion is not a difference of principle," Thomas Jefferson declared. "We have called by different names brethren of the same principle. We are all Republicans, we are all Federalists." Nevertheless, his triumphal followers displayed a fervent determination to exclude their vanquished foes from their strictly partisan Fourth of July balls and banquets, much as they themselves had been excluded in previous years.

Only with the presidency of James Monroe (1817–25) did the nation finally welcome the "Era of Good Feelings," in which even the most strident politicos could put aside contempt for the opposition long enough to jointly fire cannon, march in flag-waving parades, gorge themselves at public banquets, and toast the Republic with brimming silver bowls of rum in community-wide celebrations of Independence Day. In part, this development reflected the disappearance of the most divisive issue of America's early years: the ongoing world war between

Britain and France in which competing U.S. factions took opposite sides. With Napoleon's definitive defeat in 1815, the old Federalists and their heirs had no more reason to fear the rampages of imperial or revolutionary France, just as Jefferson's Democratic-Republican minions felt less inclination toward bitterness against the globally victorious British Empire they had battled in both a bloody revolution and the War of 1812. Monroe won reelection with no organized opposition, and during his second term even aging political warriors, most notably Adams and Jefferson, began to embrace the idea that their common values and shared experiences counted for more than ideological distinctions or colliding ambitions

After all, the most discerning among them understood that the rising Republic faced more dangerous divisions than the wearying resentments between the fading Federalists and the ruling Republicans. Though himself a lifelong slaveholder, Jefferson displayed prophetic foresight in predicting the way that raging arguments over the extension of slavery to not yet settled territories posed a lethal threat to the cause of national union. In a startling 1820 letter, Jefferson wrote from Monticello about the national debate surrounding the Missouri Compromise and the admission to the Union of a new slave state. "This momentous question, like a fire bell in the night, awakened and filled me with terror," he lamented to his friend John Holmes, congressman from anti-slavery Massachusetts and later a senator from Maine. "I considered it at once as the knell of the Union. It is hushed indeed for the moment. But this is a reprieve only, not a final sentence. A geographical line, coinciding with a marked principle, moral and political, once conceived and held up to the angry passions of men, will never be obliterated; and every new irritation will mark it deeper and deeper." In the midst of his long retirement, more than eleven years after leaving the tumult of Washington, the then seventy-seven-year-old Jefferson foresaw the long, tortured process that led in four decades to secession, civil war, and the most prodigious bloodletting in the nation's history. "I regret that I am now to die in the belief that the useless sacrifice of themselves, by the generation of '76, to acquire self government and happiness to their country, is to be thrown away by the unwise and unworthy passions of their sons, and that my only consolation is to be that I live not to weep over it."

"JUST AS I WISHED"

Six years later, despite his failing health and disastrous finances (he had fallen deeply into debt with no hope of satisfying his creditors), Jefferson managed to put aside such concerns for the sake of the Grand Jubilee. The scholarly former president, who relaxed by reading Aeschylus, Sophocles, and, increasingly, Scripture, surely understood that the biblical jubilee (*yovayl*, in Hebrew) had also led to the English word "jubilation"—connected to wild shouts of joy comparable to the sounding ram's horns prescribed in Leviticus. Jefferson declined the chance to bring himself close to the expected noise and exultation and elected to pass up the five-mile carriage ride to the town of Charlottesville, in the valley beneath his mountaintop retreat. But he understood that he and his family would hear the pealing bells from every steeple in the town, set to celebrate the half-century survival of the United States. Determined to conserve his strength in advance of the great day, President Jefferson took to his bed on July 2. With a great-granddaughter at his bedside, he cited Luke's Gospel, "Lord, now lettest thou thy servant depart in peace." He assured the attending physician that "a few hours more, Doctor, and it will be all over."

Yet he lingered, with an obsessive desire to hang on to life until the actual anniversary of his most significant achievement. On the night of the third, at 7:00 p.m., he awoke from fitful slumber and asked, "Ah, Doctor, are you still there? Is it the Fourth?"

"It soon will be," the physician assured him.

But three hours later, still short of the stroke of midnight, the former president roused himself again and asked once more, "This is the Fourth?"

This time Nicholas Trist, who much later played a prominent, providential role in acquiring California and the Southwest for the United States, sat at the old man's bedside in the dim candlelight.

Married to Jefferson's granddaughter Virginia and acting as the old man's personal secretary, he refused to answer the inquiry, reluctant to disappoint his revered mentor in what could be his final moments of consciousness. The former president, however, could not be deterred.

"This is the Fourth?" he insisted, summoning his remaining force.

This time Trist nodded wordlessly, giving Jefferson the assurance that he craved without giving voice to an outright lie. "Ah," sighed the dying sage. "Just as I wished."

He continued breathing heavily and remained unconscious as the clock above his bed clanged twelve times to signal the midnight hour, officially welcoming the Glorious Fourth. His eyes opened again at four in the morning and he managed to summon his household slaves, who entered the bedroom in weeping, sniffling awe. Jefferson said farewell to each of them, then declined a doctor's offer of more laudanum to ease his discomfort. "No more," the great man rasped.

He uttered no further comprehensible words, but he had unequivocally achieved his ardent desire: living through more than half of his cherished nation's sacred day, finally expiring on Tuesday, the Fourth of July, at ten minutes before one o'clock in the afternoon. The celebratory bells had already begun ringing in the valley below, unaware of the loss of the local and international eminence.

Also unaware, John Adams stubbornly clung to life at Peacefield. Early in the oppressively humid summer morning of Tuesday, July 4, as the first celebratory cannon began blasting in the distance, the former president arose and demanded assistance to place himself in his favorite armchair in the second-floor study, looking out the window toward the town. Reverend George Whitney arrived for a holiday visit but sadly concluded that "the old gentleman was drawing to his end. Dr. Holbrook was there and declared to us that he could not live more than through the day." Adams's youngest son, Thomas, dispatched an urgent letter to Washington to alert the president, his brother, that their father neared the end of his course.

By midday, the weather darkened with an impending storm, and relatives and friends returned Adams to his bedchamber, watching the great man's labored breathing. As they shifted his position to improve his comfort, the former president awoke and blinked at the familiar surroundings. Reminded it was the Fourth of July, he lifted his head from the pillow and declared in a strong, clear voice: "It is a great day. It is a *good* day."

With more cannon barking out their salutes in the nearby village, afternoon thunder and lightning offered "the artillery of heaven," as subsequent observers described the dramatic scene. Adams lay back on his bedding, silently watching and listening, with his mind clear, according to those who waited with him. Toward evening, with a gentle rain falling, he breathed his astonishing last words in an effortful gasp that was still clear enough to be understood. "Thomas Jefferson survives," he managed. The breathing stopped shortly after six o'clock, with a resounding clap of thunder at the very moment of the great man's passing. Witnesses insisted that at the same instant, a sudden burst of light from the declining sun pushed through the looming clouds and spilled into the upstairs room like a benediction.

"PALPABLE MARKS OF DIVINE FAVOR"

In an era when news traveled no faster than the speed of a galloping horse, no one immediately understood the sad irony of Adams's final gasp, or the startling reality that the twin heroes of independence had died on the same landmark Independence Day.

President John Quincy Adams had spent the national holiday participating in a large parade, riding in a carriage surrounded by volunteer military companies, and then making his way to the Capitol to listen to long, windy speeches and a ceremonial reading of the Declaration. He learned of Jefferson's passing only on July 6, when the secretary of war informed him that the former president had expired at midday on the Fourth, at the very moment jubilee celebrations had reached their peak of intensity. That evening, President Adams described this news in his diary as "a strange and very striking coincidence," though he had not yet learned of his own father's passing.

He received letters two days later from his brother and others in Quincy that described his father's deteriorating condition, so he set off at five in the morning on the blistering Sunday of July 9 to make it to the family home before the end. A rider from Baltimore intercepted the president's carriage on his way to tell him it was already too late, but Adams nonetheless persisted in the arduous journey to Massachusetts to express proper respect for the passing of the patriarch.

On the way, he celebrated his own fifty-ninth birthday, adding to his mournful and fatalistic mood. He had already largely accepted the fact that, like his father before him, he would earn only one term in the presidency. After going through the home that his parents had owned for thirty-eight years, he wrote to his wife, Louisa: "Though it will bring me heavily in debt, I cannot endure the thought of the sale of this place. Should I live through my term of service, my purpose is to come and close my days here, to be deposited with my father and mother." Describing his tour of the familiar rooms, left painfully empty by recent events, the bookish and usually reserved president became unapologetically emotional. "Everything about the house is the same. I was not fully sensible of the change till I entered his bed-chamber," he wrote. "That moment was inexpressibly painful, and struck me as if it had been an arrow to the heart. My father and mother have departed. The charm which has always made this house to me an abode of enchantment is dissolved; and yet my attachment to it, and to the whole region round, is stronger than I ever felt it before."

Later, he ruminated on the larger meaning of his father's death, and the haunting timing that sent him out of the world on the same great, glorious day as Jefferson. It could not be mere coincidence, John Quincy Adams declared in his diary, but rather "visible and palpable marks of Divine Favor, for which I would humble myself in grateful and silent adoration before the ruler of the universe."

In every corner of the country, preachers, politicians, and professors expressed strikingly similar sentiments. "Was not the hand of God most affectingly displayed in this event, as if to add another to the multiplied proofs of His special superintendence over this happy country?" wrote B. L. Rayner, author of the first best-selling Jefferson biography, *The Life of Thomas Jefferson, with Selections from the Most Valuable Portions of His Voluminous and Unrivalled Private Correspondence* (1834). "The extraordinary coincidence in the death of these great men is without parallel in the records of history. . . . Heaven itself mingled visibly in the jubilee celebration of American Liberty, hallowing anew the day by a double apotheosis."

Massive crowds paid tribute to the two Revolutionary heroes. In Baltimore, more than twenty thousand assembled in a natural amphitheater to hear eulogies from dignitaries in Congress and the military. There Senator Samuel Smith attributed the timing of the deaths to an "all-seeing Providence, as a mark of approbation of their well-spent lives." In Salem, Massachusetts, newspaperman Joseph Sprague concluded: "Could they have chosen the day of their death, it would have been the one decreed by Providence."

Daniel Webster, at the time a rising congressman from Massachusetts and the most admired orator of his day, delivered his own celebrated memorial on August 2 to a weeping crowd that jammed Boston's Faneuil Hall, the "Cradle of Liberty," inescapably associated with the Revolution. In an address lasting more than two hours, the booming voice of the "godlike Daniel" so moved the gathered throng, and so effectively summarized the collision of joy, mourning, and gratitude associated with the most unforgettable Fourth, that its published and leather-bound commemorative text became an instant bestseller. "On our fiftieth anniversary, the great day of national Jubilee, in the very hour of public rejoicing, in the midst of echoing and reechoing voices of thanksgiving, while their own names were on all tongues, they took their flight together to the world of spirits," Webster thundered.

Like all his prominent contemporaries, the eloquent statesman saw an unavoidable message in the simultaneous passing of the two great men, a miraculous blessing in the remarkable fact that "on the day which had fast linked forever their own fame with their country's glory, the heavens should open to receive them both at once. As their lives themselves were the gifts of Providence, who is not willing to recognize in their happy termination, as well as in their long continuance, proofs that our country and its benefactors are objects of His care?"

To Webster, the manner in which Adams and Jefferson ascended to immortality made all the more unassailable his certainty that the Almighty had dictated "our position and character among the nations of the earth. It cannot be denied, but by those who would dispute against the sun, that with America, and in America, a new era commences in human affairs."

In his oration, memorized by several generations of schoolboys for its patriotic uplift, Webster emphasized the solemn responsibility associated with the undeniable gift of Divine favor: "America, America, our country, fellow citizens, our own dear and native land, is inseparably connected, fast bound up, in fortune and by fate, with these great interests. If they fall, we fall with them; if they stand, it will be because we have maintained them."

"THE GODLIKE DANIEL": Daniel Webster (1782–1852), Massachusetts congressman (and later senator and secretary of state).

He delivered a celebrated tribute to Adams and Jefferson in Boston, suggesting that their simultaneous passing offered "proofs that our country and its benefactors are objects of His care."

"BEYOND THE SCOPE OF
RATIONAL EXPLANATION"

The task of maintaining Webster's "great interests" has become more difficult due to spreading skepticism over divine involvement in American affairs. Even in the Republic's early, miraculous years, a few cynical visitors sniffed at the idea of some covenantal relationship between the Almighty and his favored flock in the United States. The brilliant British geologist, surveyor, and frontier explorer George William Featherstonhaugh lived in America for thirty-two years but never felt comfortable with the notion of some distinctive American destiny decreed from on high. After returning to England in 1838, he described such suggestions as nothing more than patriotic piffle, intended to "stimulate that national vanity and self-sufficiency which are often so conspicuous in young countries, and to cherish in his fellow-citizens that inflated feeling of superiority over other nations."

Nearly two centuries later, sophisticated sensibilities echo Featherstonhaugh's dismissive attitude far more closely than they reflect the reverence of his more celebrated contemporaries such as Daniel Webster and John Quincy Adams. From a globalist perspective that equally honors every culture, the very idea that the United States enjoys and deserves a special "position and character among the nations of the earth" seems not only dubious but dangerous.

Within sixty days of assuming the presidency, Barack Obama expressed his own skepticism when he attended a NATO meeting in Strasbourg, France, and received an uncomfortable query from a reporter for Britain's *Financial Times*. "Could I ask you whether you subscribe, as many of your predecessors have, to the school of American exceptionalism that sees America as uniquely qualified to lead the world," asked Ed Luce, "or do you have a slightly different philosophy?"

President Obama's response became notorious for fudging the question. "I believe in American exceptionalism," he declared, "just as I suspect that the Brits believe in British exceptionalism and the Greeks believe in Greek exceptionalism." In other words, America didn't count as exceptional at all: just one more deluded, atavistic nation-state besotted with exaggerated notions of its own grandeur and unique status—notions the president might tolerate but pointedly refused to endorse. The belief that fate, or providence, has selected the United States for special purposes and prominence can hardly coexist with the assumption that we are no more "exceptional" than belea-guered Greece. No matter his nation's illogically rapid rise to world dominance in the course of its brief history, and despite abundant evidence of the Republic's abiding good fortune, the forty-fourth pres-ident declined to discern in these developments the "visible and pal-pable signs of divine favor" that his predecessor John Quincy Adams recognized so readily in the far less imposing United States of 1826.

"75 TIMES EASIER TO BE DEALT A ROYAL FLUSH"

In fact, the axiomatic denial of any predestined role for America or a supernatural design in the nation's development makes it devilishly difficult for contemporary historians to account for haunting patterns in our history. One scholarly 2005 effort from an academic at the Uni-versity of Utah offers six tortured theories to explain the simultaneous passing of Adams and Jefferson, including the possibility that the sec-ond and third presidents deliberately arranged to die on the same day. "Of course, causing oneself to die need not carry the pejorative label suicide," writes Professor Margaret P. Battin. "It can be seen, rather, as a matter of self-deliverance in preference to the sufferings and indigni-ties of protracted dying."

In her fascinating monograph "July 4, 1826: Explaining the Same-Day Deaths of John Adams and Thomas Jefferson," she also en-tertains the possibility that they had been "caused to die by others," or "were simply hanging on, waiting for the same important anniversary." She dismisses, however, the possibility of divine intervention or mere chance: "The coincidence is too great," she writes and declares that "divine intervention requires background theological assumptions be-yond the scope of rational explanation."

And where do modern Americans typically turn if all attempts at "rational explanation" seem to fail? To conspiracy theories, of course. Professor Battin asks: "Could their families and caregivers have lied about the precise dates of their deaths, seeking to lend their demises a greater grandeur? Or was there a more orchestrated plan here, known only to these two men or to their physicians and families, that accounts for the extraordinary 'coincidence' or 'grand design' of their deaths?"

Considering the well-documented and pained reaction of Adams's son, the president of the United States, who displayed both surprise and emotion on the occasion of his father's passing, and in view of the number of people who crowded around Jefferson and reported his comments in his final hours, it's preposterous to suggest a closely coordinated secret scheme to fudge death details or, more malevolently, to arrange them.

Observers in 1826 most certainly saw an "orchestrated plan" at work, but they instinctively identified the orchestrator as the Sovereign of the Universe. "It was indeed a fit occasion for the deepest public feeling," wrote B. L. Rayner. "Happening singly, each of these events was felt as supernatural; happening together, the astonishment which they occasioned was general and almost overwhelming."

Margaret Battin struggles with that same astonishment in writing off the tendency to attribute the timing to chance or "intriguing coincidence." If so, she writes, "it is a coincidence of considerable magnitude, since it involves three distinct components: same day, same significant date (July 4, Independence Day), and same history anniversary (fifty years). . . . The fact that the death dates for both Adams and Jefferson fell on an historic anniversary—the 50th anniversary, not the 49th or 51st—may seem to stretch beyond the point of sheer plausibility the claim that this was mere coincidence."

To this day, Adams and Jefferson remain the only two presidents to have expired on the same day. And only one other president had the honor of dying on the Glorious Fourth: James Monroe, fifth president of the United States, wounded veteran of the Revolutionary War, and a close colleague of both Jefferson and Adams. He succumbed to heart failure at 3:15 in the afternoon of July 4, 1831, exactly five years after the Grand Jubilee. The stunned public could only marvel at the exceedingly odd fact that three of the first four presidents to die all perished on the same deeply significant calendar date, lending further support to perceptions of providential participation in the favored nation's development.

Mark Grant, whose *Macronicity* blog seeks obscure, mystical numerological significance in such perplexing occurrences, carefully calculates the odds of three presidents all dying on the same national holiday and suggests that the chances against such a pattern recurring stand at approximately fifty million to one. "It would be about 75 times easier to be dealt a Royal Flush in a poker game with five cards (which we should see once every 649,740 hands)," he writes. "Many readers can easily imagine how impressed poker players would be to see a hand like that dealt just once."

A RIGGED GAME?

America, on the other hand, has drawn just such remarkable hands again and again—giving rise to widespread suspicions of a rigged game.

If a single player wins an ongoing contest with maddening consistency, his frustrated rivals will inevitably accuse him of cheating. Our new nation's shockingly rapid rise to world dominance counts as so illogical, so utterly unforeseen, that many mystified observers have determined that the only rational explanation involves a shameful record of American greed, ruthlessness, and immorality. Given recent themes in our educational system, every schoolchild has heard about national guilt for cruel treatment of Native Americans, brutal exploitation of African slaves, and imperialist interference with less fortunate societies around the world. According to this logic, the United States' rise to international eminence can be explained by the rapacity of our political, business, and military leadership.

The great weakness in this understanding of American success involves its lack of context. Nearly all competing powers in the last three hundred years compiled histories regarding indigenous populations, slavery, and imperialism that count as far more problematic, and never more honorable, than the imperfect record of the United States. Yet none of these other societies, however disturbing and vile their abuses of power, managed to replicate America's triumphs for its own population or in global affairs. In fact, some of the worst offenders in terms of slavery, exploitation, and colonialism endured the opposite trajectory achieved by the United States: for Spain, Portugal, Belgium, and the Netherlands, bloody imperialist adventures corresponded with the loss of world power status, not its attainment.

Those who reject the trendy argument that America's unique good fortune stems from the nation's uniquely bad behavior tend to turn to "happy accidents" as the most convenient explanation for our disproportionate blessings. This reasoning cites the abundant resources of the North American continent, favorable patterns of immigration, the absence of contiguous rival powers, the edge provided by access to both the Atlantic and the Pacific Oceans, and a multitude of other seemingly random factors to explain the dynamism and dominance of the United States. Without question, America's advantages owe a great deal to coincidence and circumstance that no human being or group of people managed to arrange.

But a pattern of happy accidents still constitutes a pattern—an indication of something more than chance at work. To return to the poker analogy: if a player enjoys a particularly profitable night and wins most of the hands, it's sensible to credit the power of good luck. Yet if the same competitor achieves similar success over a period of years and decades, the other gamblers will come to assume that some other factor has determined the consistent outcome of their games.

Could it be a matter of superior skill on the part of the winning player? When applied to the United States, this notion emphasizes the sheer brilliance and dazzling competence of some of the nation's most conspicuous leaders.

In other words, it's not a rigged game—there's no need to reference divine providence—if you can cite the superior abilities of American leaders as a means to rationalize the freakishly durable winning streak of the United States. The most common deployment of this argument makes reference to the amazing talents of the Revolutionary generation: a rustic collection of loosely connected colonies somehow produced Jefferson, Hamilton, Madison, Washington, Adams, and Franklin, who managed to work together to make miracles happen.

But doesn't the simultaneous presence of leadership of this quality, arising at the same moment of history, in the same remote corner of the globe, constitute a miracle in its own terms?

Moreover, every one of the founding fathers, including those of decidedly unconventional religious faith, believed profoundly that divine providence directed their revolution. If we accord the founders so much insight and wisdom that we explain the nation's rise with reference to their abilities, then why should we reject their unanimous conclusion that a higher power steered their affairs?

"A FAVORING PROVIDENCE, CALLING OUR INSTITUTIONS INTO BEING"

Nor did this assumption expire with the founding generation. Fifty years after the Declaration, the haunting events of the Glorious Fourth in 1826 only served to certify what most Americans already believed concerning the Almighty's intimate involvement with the new nation.

In fact, all of the most significant leaders of the United States have spoken movingly of godly favor on their country: from John Adams to Abraham Lincoln, George Washington to Woodrow Wilson, Theodore Roosevelt to Dr. Martin Luther King Jr. In the twentieth century, the most cherished icons of left and right—FDR, JFK, and Ronald Reagan—all invoked divine providence as a factor in leadership at the highest level.

The nineteenth century's most eminent and influential historian, George Bancroft, captured the mainstream of national thought with his magisterial, ten-volume *History of the United States of America*, centered on the idea of the nation's heaven-ordained destiny. In his introduction to this once ubiquitous series of tomes, embraced by every university, secondary school, and public library in the country, Bancroft declared: "It is the object of the present work to explain how the change in the condition of our land has been accomplished; and, as the fortunes of a nation are not under the control of a blind destiny, to follow the steps by which a favoring providence, calling our institutions into being, has conducted the country to its present happiness and glory."

Few thinkers or politicians bothered to question the seemingly self-evident truth that "God shed his grace" on America the Beautiful, as Katharine Lee Bates (another college professor) proclaimed in her beloved 1893 song. As recently as 1925, the popular Jazz Age president Calvin Coolidge emphasized the religious nature of the national mission in his inaugural address. "America seeks no earthly empire built on blood and force," the newly reelected chief executive proclaimed. "No ambition, no temptation, lures her to thought of foreign domination. The legions which she sends forth are armed, not with the sword, but with the cross. The higher state to which she seeks the allegiance of all mankind is not of human, but of divine origin. She cherishes no purpose save to merit the favor of Almighty God."

None of these leaders doubted the role of destiny and divine power in producing and protecting the Republic that they served. This sense of a master plan, an unread but pre-plotted script that cast their nation in history's lead role, removed all need to characterize fellow citizens as either especially saintly or particularly sinful. As the patriotic hymn suggests, "God shed his grace" on America not as reward for distinctively righteous behavior but as an exercise of his inscrutable will. The Calvinists who helped shape the earliest stages of the American idea insisted that the predestined favor of heaven demanded that they make every effort to prove themselves worthy of that election, not that their own worthy behavior forced the inexplicable gift of divine favor.

The same instinct that led our forefathers to credit God for America's emergence allowed their more critical colleagues to blame God for the nation's shortcomings, misdeeds, and misfortunes. Either way, the politically incorrect notion that a higher power guided and nourished the American experiment enabled previous generations to appreciate their blessings without incessant argument over whether the citizens of the prodigiously successful Republic qualified as distinctively great or distinctively guilty.

Even today, most Americans can't seem to shake the traditional idea that the Almighty cares deeply and permanently about what happens to their country. Some twenty-first-century polling suggests that majorities now perceive a nation in decline and assume that life for our descendants will prove even more daunting than our challenges today. Undoubtedly, some of this pessimism originates with religious believers who view providential punishment as the unavoidable consequence of society's moral shortcomings.

This concept of one nation-state alternatively protected or penalized by the Lord of Creation relates only imperfectly to the biblical "chosen people" concept—the notion of a singular tribe with an unshakably significant status based on heritage alone. Lincoln slyly referred to his countrymen as the "almost chosen people" since American nationality from the beginning amounted to a fusion of self-selecting immigrant waves; we prefer to see ourselves as "one nation, indivisible" despite the undeniable diversity of our origins.

But the essence of that nationhood stresses shared ideas more than shared inheritance. And those ideas have given rise to a choosing nation as much as a chosen nation, but a distinctive state nonetheless selected by fate for important purposes, performing fateful missions and achieving world leadership through the startling history of the last two centuries. Even at times of national danger and distress—or, perhaps, especially at those times—the American people hold fast to the notion that their national destiny will play a decisive role in some grand, eternal scheme.

"THE CENTRAL EVENT OF THE PAST FOUR HUNDRED YEARS"

This conviction has always been widespread, but never close to unanimous. In every era, some skeptics gleefully deride claims as to the greatness, significance, or even uniqueness of the United States. In an angry piece in *Politico* in 2010, columnist Michael Kinsley condemned "American exceptionalism" as the loathsome "theory that Americans are better than everybody else." Contrary to this common caricature, arguments for the nation's distinctiveness, and for its world-changing destiny ordained by some higher power, don't assume that every decision or direction undertaken by the United States will be benevolent or right. But these traditional attitudes do recognize that everything our country does will prove deeply consequential. Foreign scoffers may join home-grown sophisticates in dismissing this vision of God's involvement in American affairs as idiotic and indulgent, but they will be hard-pressed to provide a more plausible explanation for the utterly unanticipated transformation of a disconnected cluster of remote wilderness outposts into a formidable nation-state that became the most formidable force in modern history.

To put the startling, unanticipated nature of that development in context, historian Walter A. McDougall of the University of Pennsylvania invokes the world as it was immediately prior to the British settlement of North America. At the opening of his indispensable three-volume history of the United States, he flatly declares:

> The creation of the United States of America is the central event of the past four hundred years. If some ghostly ship, some Flying Dutchman, were transported in time from the year 1600 into the present, the crew would be amazed by our technology and the sheer numbers of people on the globe, but the array of civilizations would be recognizable. There is today, as there was then: a huge Chinese empire run by an authoritarian but beleaguered bureaucracy; a homogeneous, anxious, suspicious Japan; a teeming crazy quilt of Hindus and Muslims in India attempting to make a state of themselves; an amorphous Russian empire pulsing outward or inward to proportion to Muscovy's projection of force; a vast Islamic crescent hostile to infidels but beset by rival centers of power; a dynamic, more-or-less Christian civilization in Europe aspiring to unity but vexed by its dense congeries of nations and tongues; and finally an Iberian/Amerindian culture in South America marked by relative poverty and strategic impotence. The only continent that would astound the Renaissance time-travelers would be North America, which was primitive and nearly vacant as late as 1607, but which

today hosts the mightiest, richest, most dynamic civilization in history—a civilization, moreover, that perturbs the trajectories of all other civilizations just by existing.

Any open-minded account of the astonishing emergence of this world-transforming civilization must consider elements beyond chance, acknowledging a role for fate as well as good fortune. With all respect to religious sensibilities and the timeless significance of the Bible, the story of America stakes its own powerful claim as the greatest story ever told. The leading contributors to that story nearly all sensed a supernatural element in the events in which they participated.

This book will make the case that the founders and their successors who perceived a providential role in the nation that they shaped weren't ignorant simpletons with delusions of grandeur. It wasn't superstitious or irrational for the greatest minds of two hundred years ago, giants such as John Quincy Adams and Daniel Webster, to seek a deeper meaning in the nearly simultaneous death of the two authors of independence on the Grand Jubilee celebrating the fiftieth anniversary of their achievement. The perception of higher purposes and grand plans in that case, as in so many others, counts as appropriate, even necessary.

The chapters that follow advance no grand, overarching theological theory and offer no bold prophecies, either reassuring or alarming, for the nation's future. They mean, rather, to recapture some of that same sense of wonder—and gratitude—that swept the nation following the Glorious Fourth of 1826. In addition to conspicuous turning points considered from a providential perspective, these accounts will also include little-known tales of storms, epidemics, unlikely survivals, mislaid battle plans, desperate duels, shabby political deals, foreign adventures, well-timed slave rebellions, bureaucratic insubordination, failed assassinations, meteor showers that lit the skies, reckless gambles that paid ridiculous rewards, mystical visions, and unlikely saviors.

Every few weeks reports turn up from religious enthusiasts somewhere in the world who have identified the face of God in a stale croissant in a truck stop café, or in a stain on a restroom window, or in a dent in a badly damaged automobile. Occasionally, curious crowds will even travel some distance in ad hoc pilgrimages to see such wonders, creating a sensation for a few weeks at a time. While these visions may inspire awe in a small handful of fervent believers, the public at large understandably sees them as preposterous and somewhat pathetic—combining imagination, wishful thinking, and a desperate hunger for evidence of the sacred in the mundane world of the everyday.

Looking for indications of fate or providence in the broad sweep of history bears scant connection to a search for the divine countenance in misshapen baked goods. First, there is no effort here to discern or describe God's face, but rather an attempt to recognize a well-established national pattern over the course of many generations—a pattern for which the influence of some higher power remains the most rational explanation. To acknowledge the marvelous, even miraculous aspects of the Republic's past is a matter not of imagining amazements where they don't exist but of refusing to stay blind to them where they do. Despite the contempt of those who believe that American exceptionalism means a sense of chauvinistic superiority, taking destiny seriously shouldn't lead to swagger, overconfidence, or xenophobia on the part of reflexively patriotic Americans.

In the years ahead, as so often in the past, that attitude should rather encourage a sense of responsibility, humility, and gratitude. Like the colorful collection of scoundrels and heroes who lived through countless past episodes of improbable triumph and inexplicable deliverance, we retain the personal and communal choice of how to respond to haunting, plentiful signs of God's continued collaboration in the American miracle.

THE MAYFLOWER: Coated in ice, and 250 miles north of its original Manhattan destination, the sturdy but wayward ship finally arrives in Plymouth Harbor, Saturday, December 16, 1620.

"What could now sustain them but the Spirit of God and His grace?" —William Bradford, Separatist leader and five-time governor of the Plymouth Colony

2

BLOWN BLESSEDLY OFF COURSE

The Mayflower *Pilgrims Find Their Place*

In the age of exploration, no one anticipated that a mighty civilization would emerge in the lightly settled wilderness of North America. And of all the significant states of Europe, Britain looked least likely to plant such a civilization in the New World, or anywhere else.

The English came late, and halfheartedly, to the competition in overseas colonization, trailing the Spanish and Portuguese by nearly a hundred years and lagging behind the French and the Dutch by more than a generation. Richard Hakluyt, an Anglican priest and Oxford-trained scholar who propagandized for settlement in the New World, commented in 1582: "I marvel not a little that since the first discovery of America (which is now full fourscore and ten years) after so great conquest by the Spaniards and Portingales there, that we of England could never have the grace to set fast footing in such fertile and temperate places as are left as yet unpossessed by them."

Despite this tardy start, the struggling British settlements that finally took tenuous hold on the eastern edge of the continent ultimately managed to beat the odds, becoming the most successful colonies anywhere on Earth and giving rise in surprisingly short order to a potently powerful nation. This development has always inspired a heady combination of wonder, puzzlement, and profound suspicion, leaving both beneficiaries and frustrated rivals to ponder the basis and meaning of that unexpected ascent.

In September 1893, for instance, a World Parliament of Religions gathered in Chicago as part of the great Columbian Exposition celebrating the four hundredth anniversary of the discovery of the New World. One of the participants in that assembly, a famous and popular Congregationalist pastor named Leonard Woolsey Bacon, was still musing over it three years later when he wrote his profoundly influential book *A History of American Christianity*. He pondered in particular the timing of Columbus and his voyages, entertaining the possibility that the Almighty deliberately concealed the existence of the New World, keeping it free of European settlement and influence, until new ideas and energy had purified the church:

> The grandeur of human enterprise and achievement in the discovery of the western hemisphere has a less claim on our admiration than that divine wisdom and controlling providence which, for reasons now manifested, kept the secret hidden through so many millenniums, in spite of continual chances of disclosure, until the fullness of time. . . . By a prodigy of divine providence, the secret of the ages had been kept from premature disclosure. . . . If the discovery of America had been achieved four centuries or even a single century earlier, the Christianity to be transplanted to the western world would have been that of the church of Europe at its lowest stage of decadence. The period closing with the fifteenth century was that of the dense darkness that goes before the dawn.

What others might view as random connections, Bacon treated as evidence of a purposeful heavenly scheme. This intriguing idea of divine delay to await enhancements in human faith might also apply to the laggard start of permanent British settlement, which took root only after an uncompromising, idealistic, purifying Protestantism had begun to sweep through England at the beginning of the seventeenth century.

Previous attempts at New World colonization yielded a few seasonal fishing villages near the Grand Banks and an ambitious, ultimately disastrous scheme to build a personal New World empire for the royal favorite (and reputed "atheist") Sir Walter Raleigh.

He named his planned province Virginia to honor his patron, Elizabeth I, the Virgin Queen. Three different well-supplied attempts during the 1580s to settle Roanoke Island off the Outer Banks of North Carolina each failed to take root, with one group of starving settlers gratefully accepting an offer from a passing ship to rescue them from their misery and return them to the comfort and security at the other side of the Atlantic. The final bid to establish the Roanoke Colony involved ninety-one men, seventeen women, and nine children, who sent their governor back to Britain in quest of much-needed new supplies. With his mission interrupted by the menace of the Spanish Armada, Governor John White took two years to make the return trip, finding that all the settlers he had left behind, including his daughter and granddaughter, had inexplicably disappeared, leaving their rude dwellings empty but unmolested. The mystery of the "Lost Colony" has never been definitely solved, though the settlers were presumed kidnapped, and perhaps slaughtered, by local Indian tribes.

The next significant attempt to establish a British foothold on the North American continent occurred nearly two decades later, only after Queen Elizabeth had given way to her more fervently religious Scottish cousin, James I. He authorized the founding of Jamestown with a more explicitly Christian purpose than the failed project at Roanoke. The charter for Jamestown asked that "the Providence of Almighty God" might assist the colonists in the "propagating of Christian Religion to such People, as yet live in Darkness and miserable ignorance." After 144 days crossing the Atlantic in 1607, the settlers arrived at Cape Henry, in the northeast corner of today's city of Virginia Beach. There the first order of business involved the construction of a large wooden cross to express gratitude to the Lord of Heaven.

This sort of faith may have helped beleaguered colonists cope with painful challenges, but it hardly protected them from suffering. The residents of the forlorn outpost of Jamestown planted corpses as the most notable crop of their early years. "Of the 10,000 people transported to Virginia after 1607, only a fifth were still alive in 1622," calculated Professor Malcolm Gaskill of the University of East Anglia in 2014. "Many, in remote plantations dotted along the eastern seaboard, simply disappeared. Communications were poor and loneliness endemic. Wolves were a persistent menace, although the colonists learned to kill them with fishhooks wrapped in fat."

Such accounts, as horrible as they might be, couldn't discourage the hearty souls consumed by the Puritan ferment that stirred the kingdom and, ultimately, deposed a king. The Puritans—who never welcomed the derisive designation that mocked their fervent desire to cleanse the Church of England—initiated an aggressive, vigorous form of Christianity that had scarcely existed in the worldly era of Sir Walter Raleigh. That reformist faith changed forever the relationship of crown and Parliament, but it exerted an even more lasting impact by founding the crucial colonies of New England.

GOD'S SECRET PLAN

The first step in that process involved a minor sub-sect of the larger Puritan movement that had abandoned all hope of purifying the corrupt official church and intended instead to separate from it altogether. The community known to us as the Pilgrims originated as an illegal, radical, separatist congregation in the tiny village of Scrooby in the English Midlands. At no time in Britain—or in the New World, for that matter—did these fervent believers number more than a thousand souls, but they never questioned the cosmic importance of their mission. No one can prove that God actually guided and defended their efforts, but no one can deny that they very much believed that he did.

The colony they founded at Plymouth in 1620 never developed into a growing city, as did the nearby outpost of Boston; by 1691, the Pilgrim settlement ceased to exist as an independent entity, subsumed under the vastly more populous and successful Massachusetts Bay Colony that the Puritans had established. Nonetheless, the Pilgrims saw God's hand sustaining all their endeavors, launching the durable belief in the Lord's special protection of America before there was even an America for the Lord to protect.

Contrary to a common misunderstanding that turns up every year at Thanksgiving, the Pilgrims didn't sail to Massachusetts to escape religious persecution; after all, they departed for their venture into "the howling wilderness" not from England but from Holland, the most famously tolerant nation in Europe. Ten years before boarding the *Mayflower*, they had fled to the Netherlands, where the local authorities offered minimal interference with their rigorous, idiosyncratic version of Calvinist Christianity. They worried more over corruption than oppression, with fears that the influence of the bustling, commercial world around them would leave their children more Dutch than English, more materialistic than godly. In response, they prepared their way with prayer and planning, ready to take their chances on a perilous Atlantic crossing.

Nick Bunker, author of an encyclopedic and fascinating history of the Pilgrims (*Making Haste from Babylon*, 2010) captures the essence of the worldview that has influenced Americans ever since. "The Pilgrims believed that everything followed a plan, laid down by God before the beginning of the world, but it was a *secret* plan," he wrote. "Veiled from sinful humanity, the plan was obscure, as hard to decode as a blazing star. By way of the Bible, clues might be found to the will of God, but only after prayer, study, and discussion, and with the aid of faith, itself a gift of God issued only to the elect."

In a letter to the Virginia Company, which hoped to fund profitable ventures in the New World, the group's leaders clearly expressed this strong sense of their own exceptionalism. "The people are, for the body of them, industrious and frugal, we think we may safely say, as any company of people in the world," they wrote. "It is not with us as with other men, whom small things can discourage, or small discontentments cause to wish themselves at home again."

Though the Virginia Company turned down their plea for support, the Pilgrims eventually found the funds they needed with private investors who backed their voyage with hopes of financial gain. As part of the complicated arrangements, the 102 passengers who finally boarded the *Mayflower* included nearly twice as many "strangers" as members of the separatist congregation. Some of the additional settlers held similar if not identical religious views, rejecting compromise with the Church of England and supporting the construction of an ideal Christian society. Others made the trip out of economic necessity or love of adventure.

The *Mayflower* departed in late August, and its voyage across the Atlantic lasted sixty-six days—nearly twice the time they had expected—and proved both painful and perilous. They faced difficult seas, uncooperative winds, and navigational difficulties that frequently kept the passengers belowdecks for days and nights at a time. In that dark, fetid world, they were forced together with the seasick and suffering in a four-foot-high space in which standing was possible only for children. The stench became unendurable, combining sweat, vomit, overripe cheese, dried fish, and buckets of human waste. In the midst of the crowded hold, one of the Pilgrim women, Elizabeth Hopkins, managed to give birth to a baby boy who, amazingly, survived the voyage. Named Oceanus Hopkins in honor of his Atlantic-crossing birth, he experienced his parents' painful first years in the New World but died sometime before his seventh birthday. Two other young men perished of digestive illness and were buried at sea. Meanwhile, the *Mayflower* drifted hopelessly off course.

The Pilgrims had received official permission to establish their new home in the remote northern portion of the official province of Virginia, at the mouth of the Hudson River—the site of today's New York City—and specifically targeted the island known as Manhattan. They knew that the area already contained a light sprinkling of Dutch fur traders, but they had just spent a decade living among the Dutch and felt confident they would be welcomed. When the *Mayflower* finally sighted land, however, it was the edge of Cape Cod, some 250 miles north of their intended destination. In later years the separatists and their descendants saw this failure of navigation as providential, and the course of regional and even national history undoubtedly would have developed very differently had the *Mayflower* dropped anchor in New York rather than Massachusetts. Among other things, their arrival in remote New England, well beyond the boundaries that even Walter Raleigh had claimed for his would-be empire of Virginia, allowed the Pilgrims to build their settlement without interference from either colonial planners back home or rival communities in the vicinity.

"WHAT COULD NOW SUSTAIN THEM?"

As it was, on November 9, 1620, they got their first glimpse of a forbidding shoreline—a long, sandy stretch of coast covered with scrub pine and dune grass. Despite the harshness of the New England weather and landscape, William Bradford, who went on to serve thirty years as governor of the new colony, recalled the moment with gratitude: "Being thus arrived in a good harbor and brought safe to land, they fell upon their knees and blessed the God of heaven, who had brought them over the vast and furious ocean, and delivered them from all the perils and miseries thereof, again to set their feet on the firm and stable earth, their proper element."

At the same time, Bradford acknowledged

> this poor people's present condition . . . no friends to welcome them, nor inns to entertain or refresh their weatherbeaten bodies, no houses, nor much less towns, to repair to, to seek for succor . . . Whichever way they turned their eyes (save upward to the heavens) they could have little solace or content in respect of any outward objects. For summer being done, all things stand upon them with a weatherbeaten face; and the whole country, full of woods and thickets, represented a wild and savage hue. If they had looked behind them, there was the mighty ocean which they had passed, and was now as a main bar and gulf to separate them from all the civil parts of the world . . . What could now sustain them but the Spirit of God and His grace?

The Pilgrims paid tribute to that grace by recording their progress on a nearly day-by-day basis, compiling a permanent record that they hoped would demonstrate divine favor of their aims. Among all the descriptions of unlikely survival during those harrowing early years in New England, two incidents stand out.

One involved the fortuitous selection of an advantageous site for the fledgling Plymouth Colony. The other centered on the sudden, astonishing appearance of the one individual in all of North America who seemed specifically equipped to rescue them at a time of desperate need.

THE MAYFLOWER COMPACT: Before disembarking in the New World, the Pilgrims pledged their faith in self-government, November 11, 1620.

"We whose names are underwritten ... in the Presence of God and one another, Covenant and Combine ourselves together into a Civil Body Politic, for our better Ordering and Preservation."

Soon after their safe arrival on the sand dunes of Cape Cod, their leaders determined to sail southwest to their original destination at the mouth of the Hudson River. The *Mayflower's* captain, Christopher Jones, agreed to transport them there, but the November climate stubbornly and pointedly refused to cooperate. Howling headwinds, treacherous tides, and dangerous shoals and rocks reaching far out from the New England shore threatened the ship and changed the perspective of Bradford, Edward Winslow, and other respected members of the expedition. What should have been a relatively easy four- or five-day journey looked increasingly difficult if not altogether impossible, and the Pilgrims, naturally, perceived a message from on high. Concluding that the Almighty wanted them to stay near the desolate shore where his previous winds had blown them off course, rather than follow their own flawed and mortal plan, the leaders ordered Captain Jones to return to Cape Cod, where they dropped anchor in the sheltered bay near modern Provincetown. From there, the most intrepid members of the group began exploring the territory on foot to find the right location to plant their new and godly commonwealth.

It took three weeks for the sailors and would-be settlers to repair the shallop (a small boat with sails and oars) with which they intended to navigate the shallow waters of the vicinity. By that time, December had arrived with its unmistakable message that winter in New England would bring more ice and punishing cold than anything they had experienced in England or the Netherlands. They camped around a fire in the freezing temperatures, but the midnight howls and whoops of what they assumed to be hungry beasts chilled them even more than the cold. Just before dawn, as some of the weary Englishmen began preparing breakfast, the posted sentry shouted them on guard as the shrieks drew closer. Suddenly arrows began raining in on them from warriors hidden in the woods. The Pilgrims managed to fire their muskets in the general direction of their attackers, scattering most of the natives. The chief casualties were several cloaks that they had hung around their encampment as a makeshift barricade, which now were full of holes. The site of the brief struggle, which claimed no lives on either side, remains known to this day as First Encounter Beach, in Eastham, Massachusetts.

Other days of exploration brought other dangers, such as a broken mast on the shallop, pounding seas that nearly smashed their little craft against shoreline rocks, and, at night, the cries of a determined wolf pack that might have done more bloody damage than the attacking Indians. During a long march, William Bradford injured his leg when he sprang a carefully concealed deer trap designed and set by the Indians.

Another storm arose, and "the seas were grown so great that we much troubled and in great danger and the night grew on," Winslow and Bradford recalled. At a point in the stormy darkness when their small boat seemed to be coming apart, driven inexorably toward a jagged, rocky shore, one huge wave suddenly pushed the flimsy craft straight onto a clear, sandy beach—the only safe landing spot in the immediate vicinity.

They built a fire, weathered the night with temperatures below freezing, and in the frosty morning realized they had been driven to a heavily forested island. The next day, Sunday, December 10, they rested in place as comfortably as they could to observe the Lord's Day. On Monday, with the weather clearing, they sailed into a wide, protected harbor on the mainland, with waters deep enough to accommodate the *Mayflower* and other substantial craft. Contrary to the misleading legend of landing on Plymouth Rock, what appealed to the desperate Pilgrims was the absence of significant rocks and their attendant dangers. According to logic and all surviving recollections, they waded ashore without the aid of stepping-stones and found the ideal location to build their settlement.

"AND SURE IT WAS GOD'S GOOD PROVIDENCE"

Several details about the site made it seem specially prepared for the desperate new arrivals. Aside from the ideal harbor, a gentle slope led up to a substantial hill. The Pilgrims immediately determined that this elevation would provide huge advantages for the fortifications they meant to build—with excellent sight lines in every direction and an untrammeled command of the area for their muskets and the small cannon they planned to install. Sneak attacks would be impossible because the entire area had been cleared of trees, as had more than twenty nearby acres that apparently had been used as cornfields until recently. Most important, the tract came with an abundant water supply. "A very sweet brook," recalled Bradford and Winslow, "runs under the hill side, and many delicate springs of as good water as can be drunk."

The freezing and exhausted Pilgrims quickly identified this promising location as the site of a once thriving Indian village called Patuxet that appeared on a map of the area prepared by the explorer Samuel de Champlain in 1604. The Frenchman carefully described the settlement as home to several hundred members of a close-knit tribe who had cleared the forests, planted productive gardens, and buried abundant caches of dried corn. When the Pilgrims first discovered such desperately needed supplies of food and seed in the vicinity, they solemnly resolved that they would repay the rightful owners as soon as they could find them. Surely they could find a way to compensate the natives who had harvested and stored the corn that now guaranteed their survival. As Edward Winslow wrote: "And sure it was God's good providence that we found this corn for else we know not how we should have done."

"NOW UTTERLY VOID"

The leaders reasoned that the previous inhabitants of the tract they had chosen could be nomadic natives who had sought more favorable seasonal shelter or even permanently relocated. There were, after all, no signs of destruction, massacre, or mass death. Only later, in conversation with local Indian survivors, did they learn the actual fate of those who had so perfectly "prepared" the site. A devastating plague had broken out in the area in 1616 and raged unabated for more than three years. Most historians identify the disease as either smallpox or chicken pox, likely spread to the local residents by British or French fishermen who traveled through the area. Recent research by the Maine Historic Preservation Commission and the Medical College of Virginia suggests viral hepatitis, most likely spread by contaminated food. In any event, its deadly impact subsided just a year before the Pilgrims' arrival, by which time it had killed up to 95 percent of the local Wampanoags. Before the epidemic, the population of the area surrounding Cape Cod, including Nantucket and Martha's Vineyard, may have reached fifteen thousand. By 1619, the survivors numbered less than a thousand.

Captain Thomas Dermer, who explored the coastline the year before the Pilgrims came to the New World, reported: "I passed along the coast where I found some antient Plantations, not long since populous, now utterly void; in other places a remnant remains, but not free of sickness." The merchant and Indian trader Thomas Morton said that the Indians "died in heapes as they lay in their houses . . . left for crows, kites and vermin to pick upon." With no understanding of disease or how to confront it, the uncontaminated ran from the sick and dying, carrying the pestilence with them to nearby tribes and villages. Charles C. Mann, whose book *1491* recaptures the realities of Indian life before European incursions, vividly describes the resulting devastation along the New England coast: "What had once been a line of busy communities was now a mass of tumbledown homes and untended fields overrun by blackberries. Scattered among the houses and fields were skeletons bleached by the sun."

Mann points out that the Pilgrims and other settlers who followed them built "more than fifty of the first colonial villages in New England" on the remains of "Indian communities emptied by disease." In fact, many English observers of the era viewed the dramatic depopulation of New England as a supernatural gift. Thomas Hariot, the brilliant astronomer and mathematician who had once been involved with Walter Raleigh in his Roanoke schemes, saw the later reduction in native numbers as "the speciall worke of God for our sakes." Twenty years later, John Winthrop, the Puritan leader who led the establishment of the Massachusetts Bay Colony, confronted the question "What warrant have we to take that lande which is and hathe been of long tyme possessed by other sonnes of Adam"? His answer emphasized the unpopulated nature of the territory they discovered: "God hath consumed the natives with a miraculous plague where by a great parte of the Country is left voyde of Inhabitantes."

The Pilgrims themselves, arriving just months after the epidemic had completed its appalling work, couldn't avoid marveling at their own good fortune and seeing in it "the good hand of God," in William Bradford's resonant phase. They never associated the epidemic that preceded their arrival with some form of heavenly punishment for the natives who lived in the vicinity, and in fact professed consistent respect and even admiration for the surviving Indians they encountered. They particularly noted their physical health and strength, their ingenious devices for hunting and fishing, and their regal posture and tall stature—making them notably larger than typical Europeans. Thomas Morton, who eventually offended Pilgrim sensibilities by consorting too intimately with the natives, declared them "as proper men and women for features and limbes as can be found, for flesh and blood as active." The charismatic Puritan pastor Roger Williams, ultimate founder of Rhode Island, later spoke for many of the earliest settlers when he declared that "Nature knows no difference between Europe and Americans in blood, birth, bodies and &c God having of one blood made all mankind. . . . Boast not proud English. . . . Thy brother Indian as by birth as Good."

Rather than viewing the natives as victims of divine wrath, they preferred to see themselves as the beneficiaries of special protection. Cold, hungry, and desperate, deposited by winds, waves, and errant navigation some 250 miles from their original destination, they concluded that a higher power had brought them to precisely the right place. Their expressed desire to pay for the stored corn they dug up might show their discomfort at establishing a godly commonwealth on the recently abandoned site of a once bustling Indian village, but how could heaven possibly object when it was never their intention to plant their new homes anywhere in that vicinity?

Their experience indicated that it was the Lord's work, not their own choices, that guided their path to precisely the right place at precisely the right time. Of all the literally thousands of potential sites along the vast stretch of continent bordering the Atlantic, they somehow stumbled upon the ideal location for their purposes and, they ardently believed, for His.

"WELCOME, ENGLISHMEN!"

But those purposes and the Plymouth Colony's very survival depended on the second major miracle: the unlikely encounter with a true native savior. His personal story seems so bizarre, contrived, and melodramatic that any movie dramatization that faithfully followed its outlines would, I am certain, provoke widespread critical contempt.

The events that led to this fateful association began on the unseasonably mild day of March 16, 1621, as the struggling Pilgrims at last began to emerge from the horrific suffering of their first winter in North America. Forty-seven of the 102 original settlers had succumbed to cold, hunger, or disease, particularly scurvy. Of the eighteen wives who had arrived in New England, thirteen had died; only three families in all of Plymouth remained untouched by mourning. The reduction in numbers left them particularly vulnerable to Indian attack, so they took advantage of the fair March morning to gather at the hilltop behind the row of huts they had built and plan for an organized defense. As if to validate the importance of this effort, a single Indian suddenly appeared in the distance walking toward their settlement with long, quick, purposeful strides.

Naturally, his appearance "caused an alarm," especially as he "very boldly came all alone" along the muddy dirt path between the ramshackle homes. The Pilgrim defense force ran down to intercept him but found themselves dumbfounded when the stranger bellowed, in broken but comprehensible English, "Welcome, Englishmen!" He offered florid but friendly gestures, then repeated the phrase, as if he had been rehearsing it. "Welcome, Englishmen!" he declared again, and added an urgent inquiry: "Do you have beer?"

As it happened, the Pilgrims disappointed him, having exhausted their cherished beer supply by then; it had been deemed safer and healthier to consume the brewed beverage than to drink water of dubious purity. In place of the desired refreshment, they offered the visitor, whose name was Samoset, a beverage that Winslow and Bradford described as "strong water"—what historians guess was aqua vitae, or some form of recently distilled brandy. In any event, the visitor, naked except for a deerskin skirt around his waist, enjoyed the beverage, and hungrily devoured "biscuit, and butter, and cheese and pudding, and a piece of mallard, all of which he liked well."

All the while, Samoset talked energetically, if not always understandably. He explained that he had developed a taste for such food and drink, and his limited but proudly displayed knowledge of the English language, when he befriended cod fishermen who regularly worked near his home, far to the north in the present-day state of Maine. He had journeyed toward the Cape Cod region for unexplained reasons by catching a ride on a British ship and for the time being, at least, served Massasoit, the most important sachem, or chief, in the vicinity. He explained that the location his hosts had occupied had once been the important village of Patuxet and, as the Pilgrim leaders recorded his words, "that all the inhabitants died of an extraordinary plague, and there is neither man, woman, nor child remaining, as indeed we have found none, so as there is none to hinder our possession, or to lay claim unto it."

Having fed him lavishly from their limited supplies, the Pilgrims found it nearly impossible to send Samoset on his way. "All the afternoon we spent in communication with him," the wary settlers recalled. "We would gladly have been rid of him at night, but he was not willing to go this night." Finally the next morning the Englishmen presented Samoset with a knife, a bracelet, and a ring to encourage his departure. He happily accepted the gifts, and produced decidedly mixed feelings when he solemnly assured his benefactors he would be sure to return within the next few days.

SOLE SURVIVOR, NATIVE SAVIOR

When he kept that promise and further tested the hospitality of the newcomers, he brought with him another Indian he had described in glowing terms. This second visitor—Tisquantum, or "Squanto," as the Englishmen rendered it—spoke better English than Samoset and appeared to possess a far more sober and reserved personality. That solemn and lonely nature reflected his recent history of endurance

and loss: he described himself as the sole survivor of the once thriving Patuxet band that had originally called Plymouth their home. He
had escaped the ravages of the local epidemic because he had been
kidnapped as a twelve-year-old by a marauding English sea captain in
1605. Brought to London as a captive, along with five other members
of his tribe, he learned the rudiments of English to answer questions
from Ferdinando Gorges, who dreamed of establishing his own colonies in New England. Squanto spoke in glowing terms, naturally, of
the only home he had ever known and begged for a chance to return,
but Gorges kept him in England as a living advertisement for his various colonial schemes.

After nine harsh, unwelcome years in London, the homesick Indian finally arranged passage back to the New World with Captain
John Smith, who had previously led the Jamestown Colony. After
another difficult ocean crossing, while making his way along the
coast toward the sheltered haven of Patuxet, Squanto found himself
tragically kidnapped once again by one of Smith's unscrupulous associates, locked and bound in the dark hold of a small, crowded ship
with twenty other captured natives. After nearly two months at sea,
the English merchant docked at Málaga, on Spain's Mediterranean
coast, where the captain offered his imprisoned Indians as slaves for
£20 each—the rough equivalent of $3,000 in modern terms. But be-
fore he could dispense with all of his human merchandise, a group of
Spanish monks intervened and took the rest of the captives, including
Squanto, for a much reduced payment. The Spanish church strongly
opposed enslavement of Indians at the time, following the teachings
of the sixteenth-century pope Paul III, who decreed that the natives
of the New World should not be "reduced to our service like brute
animals."

The monks healed the wounded bodies of the brutalized youths
while hoping to elevate their souls by teaching them the fundamentals
of Christianity. Squanto must have felt grateful for their kindness and
education, but he remained focused on the only goal that mattered
to him: returning to his home and family on the other side of the Atlantic. For that purpose, the monks helped him find his way back to
England, where he lived with a merchant's family for a few years and

improved his English skills. Finally, he secured return passage—his fourth trip across the ocean—and at last managed to make his way back to his home village. Arriving just six months before the Pilgrims landed, he saw no familiar faces or structures, no signs of life of any kind, and soon learned from neighboring bands about the catastrophic disease that had killed every remaining member of his tribe.

Seeing himself as a lonely ghost or survivor spirit, Squanto lived in the woods for a time before making his way to Massasoit, the most powerful sachem of the region. This Wampanoag leader welcomed the newcomer warily, realizing that his many travels and his knowledge of European languages would make him valuable in dealing with the alien Englishmen who had established their struggling outpost, with just seven homes and a crude fortification, on the site of Patuxet.

In fact, on the day the Pilgrims met Squanto, Massasoit waited nearby with a formidable force of sixty armed men, hoping that his English-speaking ambassador would help in negotiating a formal alliance with the newcomers. With his own tribe significantly diminished by disease, Massasoit wanted the fearsome power of the Europeans' muskets and small cannon on his side to fend off potential attacks from the hostile Narragansett people, whom he deeply feared.

Squanto achieved total success in this effort, helping bring together the Wampanoag "king" (as the English saw him) with the subjects of the great King James across the water. The Pilgrims wisely greeted Massasoit and his warriors with signs of honor, even reverence, inviting the sachem into one of their homes and sharing some of the same "strong water" that had previously pleased Samoset. The result of the friendly meeting was a formal treaty, preserved in writing by the Pilgrims, pledging the two groups to defend each other from any and all dangers.

"A SPECIAL INSTRUMENT SENT OF GOD FOR THEIR GOOD"

Amazingly, this agreement lasted for more than fifty years and ensured that the Pilgrims would maintain friendly relations with the

Indian tribe closest to them—relations famously celebrated at the first Thanksgiving, some seven months after this initial negotiation. Without Squanto deploying his utterly unique linguistic skills to act as intermediary, this understanding would have been impossible to achieve. His role in helping the Englishmen cope with local natives represents one of the two ways in which he proved indispensable to Plymouth's survival.

The other crucial service unfolded over the months that followed, as Squanto chose to stay with the Pilgrims on the site of his boyhood home and to cast his lot with the struggling settlers. After Massasoit and his followers had departed, the long-suffering, world-traveling Indian remained behind to help the newcomers adapt to the New England environment, and in the process he became an esteemed member of their community. They were amazed to discover that he had been schooled in biblical beliefs during his years in England and Spain. But it's unclear whether he considered himself a Christian in terms his new friends would fully accept. The differences between the Catholicism of the kindly Spanish monks who rescued Squanto and the rigorous Calvinism of the *Mayflower* Pilgrims would have seemed vast and perhaps even unbridgeable to ardent believers of the seventeenth century.

Nonetheless, Squanto's devotion to his new neighbors brought benefits to the Englishmen that they viewed as a gift from God. For instance, he immediately introduced them to the eels that flourished on the bottoms of local streams, creatures the Pilgrims described as "fat and sweet," providing lifesaving nourishment. The Pilgrims found them easy to catch by forcing the eels out of the mud with bare feet and then grabbing them with both hands. Similarly, he taught them the secrets of the spring run of the alewives, fast-moving fish that annually crowded all creeks and rivers in the area. Under Squanto's direction, the Englishmen set up weirs, or low dams, at strategic points that trapped the fish and produced an abundant harvest.

He then provided his most important guidance, showing the right way to plant corn—in April, place five kernels in a freshly made mound surrounded by three fish to nourish growth. The Pilgrims soon saw twenty acres under successful cultivation, producing the harvest that made the first Thanksgiving joyous and possible.

The Pilgrims and most subsequent historians believed that the "fish fertilizer" system of planting represented an ancient Indian practice, but Charles Mann in his 2005 book *1491* challenges the idea. "So little evidence has emerged of Indians fertilizing with fish that some archaeologists believe that Tisquantum [Squanto] actually picked up the idea from European farmers," he writes. "The notion is not as ridiculous as it may seem. . . . In his travels, Tisquantum stayed in places where Europeans used fish as fertilizer, a practice on the continent since medieval times."

If Mann is correct, then the good fortune of the Pilgrims in befriending Squanto becomes even more astonishing. They not only found a most unusual Indian who spoke good English, knew the basics of Christianity, and saw the newcomers as replacements for his departed family, but also managed to find perhaps the only Indian on the continent who had mastered the European agricultural technique that rescued the new colony from hunger and privation.

No wonder that William Bradford saw his native friend as "a special instrument sent of God for their good, beyond their expectation." Squanto became such a valued member of the community that when he was captured by a hostile group of Indians passing through the area, the Pilgrims sent a full armed military expedition to get him back, unharmed.

In 1622, after a year with the Pilgrims, Squanto journeyed to the Wampanoags to refresh the alliance with them and to smooth over some recent misunderstandings, but he fell ill on his way home. In reporting on this affliction, William Bradford referred to it simply as "Indian fever," resulting in "bleeding much at the nose, which the Indians take as symptom of death, and within a few days he died. He begged the Governor to pray for him, that he might go the Englishman's God in heaven." According to Bradford's account, Squanto made a deathbed profession of faith in Jesus Christ and proved his loyalty to his friends by leaving his meager possessions to them "as remembrances." Bradford concluded: "His death was a great loss."

The Plymouth Colony survived that loss because Squanto, in the brief months that he lived in the community, had already made his profound contributions to its well-being. He not only negotiated successfully with neighboring Indians and imparted essential information but also strengthened the battered settlement's core belief in heavenly protection for the Pilgrims' endeavor.

In April 1621, while Squanto was still directing the planting of a new crop of corn, the surviving settlers faced a crucial choice that painfully tested their faith. Captain Christopher Jones, who had kept the *Mayflower* anchored just offshore throughout the fall and winter, now determined to sail back to England with the surviving members of his crew. He implored the Pilgrims, all of whom still mourned the recent deaths of cherished friends and family members, to end their misery and return with him to the familiar comforts of civilization.

In direct contrast to the second settlers of the ill-fated Roanoke Colony of 1586, who had abandoned their mission and gratefully accepted an offer to transport them to the safety of the mother country, not one of the Pilgrims elected to leave.

More than 150 years passed before the descendants of New England's founders finally united with other English colonists to challenge an empire and achieve independence. The passage of five generations meant profound changes in wealth, values, occupations, communication, political philosophy, and even theology among the thriving provinces of eighteenth-century English America. But one characteristic consistently connected the Pilgrims of 1620 and the patriots of 1776: an unshakable conviction in their own significance as part of a divinely ordained design for their country.

THANKS TO A NATIVE SAVIOR: An idealized, nineteenth-century view of the First Thanksgiving, which took place on an unspecified date in autumn of 1621.

Without Squanto, there might have been no feast, and no survival. To William Bradford, he was "a special instrument sent of God for their good, beyond their expectation."

THE BATTLE OF BROOKLYN: August 27, 1776.

"The Fate of Unborn Millions will now depend, under God, on the courage and conduct of this army." —General George Washington, address to the Continental Army

3

REVOLUTIONARY REVELATIONS

Timely Rescues from an Unseen Ally

George Washington and his Continental Army experienced so many episodes of danger and disaster during the eight years of the Revolutionary War that it's difficult to select a single darkest moment. Many history buffs would call to mind the suffering of Valley Forge, where an ill-equipped, dispirited, rapidly dwindling army left bloody footprints in the snow. But the overmatched Americans actually came far closer to losing the struggle a year and a half earlier. By all rules of warfare and logic, a smashing British victory in the largest single battle of the war should have led to the capture of the general in chief and the seizure or dissolution of the great bulk of his battered army. But long before they secured the decisive support of the French, the Americans seemed to have enlisted the assistance of an even more potent ally. As contemporaries on both sides of the conflict suggested, the Continental Army benefited from a series of unusual natural phenomena and a pattern of illogical but consistent good luck that in the painful summer of 1776 rescued the troops from all but certain catastrophe.

In the first year of fighting that preceded this unlikely escape, the Americans fared better than anyone had anticipated—and also benefited significantly from one perfectly timed meteorological oddity. After the opening skirmishes at Lexington and Concord, the hastily assembled New England militias (including the celebrated Minutemen) succeeded in stopping a British raid to seize their weapons and managed to drive the retreating redcoats back into the city of Boston. Stalemate ensued for months, with disorganized colonial volunteers from throughout the region sleeping around their campfires on the outskirts of the town and the British forces trapped inside the city.

On July 3, 1775, the tall Virginian George Washington arrived from the capital, Philadelphia, to take command of these courageous but undisciplined New England forces who had come together under the grand title "Continental Army." The new top general worried over their vulnerability to British attack and, in one of his periodic bouts of self-pity, told his military aide Joseph Reed that he never would have accepted his command had he known of the perilous position in which he found himself. His only hope, Washington confided, involved the necessary intervention of a higher power. "If I shall be able to rise superior to these, and many other difficulties which might be enumerated, I shall most religiously believe that the finger of Providence is in it, to blind the eyes of our enemies," he wrote.

"THE LORD FIGHTETH FOR THEM"

Fortunately for the Americans, the foe remained blinded through most of the winter, allowing Washington to deploy some imposing new artillery that had been seized from the British in a daring raid on Fort Ticonderoga in upstate New York. On the night of March 2, he ordered two thousand of his men to use the cover of darkness to occupy and fortify high ground on Dorchester Heights that would put twenty of his big guns within range of the city below. The unseasonably mild weather seemed to respond to patriot prayers; the Reverend William Gordon observed that "a finer [night] for working could not have been taken out of the whole 365. It was hazy below so that our people could not be seen, though it was a bright moonlight night above on the hills."

The next day His Majesty's loyal troops awoke and looked up in horror to see formidable, newly constructed rebel fortifications glaring down at them. As one officer reported to a London newspaper: "This morning at day break we discovered two redoubts on the hills of Dorchester Point, and two smaller works on their flanks. They were all raised during the night, with an expedition equal to that of the genie belonging to Aladdin's wonderful lamp. From these hills they command the whole town, so that we must drive from their post, or desert the place."

It didn't take long for the British commander, General William Howe, to make his decision: he informed his senior officers before noon that he had chosen the course of honor and intended to attack. Thanks to reinforcements continually provided by the Royal Navy, which still crowded the wharves of Boston Harbor, he now commanded some nine thousand seasoned troops, and he meant to use them in an overwhelming nighttime assault against the newly installed American batteries.

John Trumbull, a recent Harvard graduate and nineteen-year-old major in the Continental Army, watched the British preparations with a painter's eye: after the war, he became the most celebrated artist of the Revolutionary struggle. "Our movement was not discovered by the enemy until the following morning," he remembered, "and we had an uninterrupted day to strengthen the works which we had commenced the night preceding. During this day we saw distinctly the preparations which the enemy were making to dislodge us. The entire water front of Boston lay open to our observation and we saw the embarkation of troops from the various wharves, on board of ships, which hauled off in succession, and anchored in a line to our front, a little before sunset, prepared to land the troops in the morning."

Trumbull and his comrades had no idea that Howe intended to launch his assault well before dawn in the hopes that the darkness would give them the advantage of surprise. "We were in high spirits, well-prepared to receive the threatened attack," Trumbull recalled. "In the evening, the Commander in Chief visited us and examined all our points of preparation for defense."

As soon as Washington departed, however, the weather changed dramatically and, in the eyes of many, miraculously. A balmy day had given way to a breezy but clear early evening with a few light showers before a fierce storm arose without warning, suddenly shattering windows in the town and knocking down fences throughout the region. Two of the British transports were blown ashore, unable to deliver the assault force to its assigned destination. In the crowded harbor, the gale howled across the water, rocking the British ships at their moorings and repeatedly splashing their unsteady decks. The blowing became so fierce that it broke the fleet's formation, "driving the ships foul of each other, and from their anchors in utter confusion."

On the high ground above the port, driving sleet made the still frozen earth near the crest of Dorchester Heights so slippery that it became unthinkable for British troops to ascend the slope, especially with the punishing winds and freezing downpour. An American lieutenant named Isaac Bangs, shivering with his men at their stations overlooking Boston, remembered the storm as "the worst that ever I was exposed to." By midnight he reported that the "wind blew almost a hurricane." Howe had no choice but to call off his nighttime attack, allowing the Americans to continue strengthening their positions.

In his official report to the responsible ministry in London, the British commander stressed the untimely and sudden change in climate "and the weather continuing boisterous the next day and night" as the chief basis for canceling his assault at the last moment. "I could promise myself little success by attacking them under all the disadvantages I had to encounter; wherefore I judged it most advisable to prepare for the evacuation of the town." Under a white flag of truce, Howe transmitted an offer to Washington: if the colonials allowed His Majesty's forces to depart from the city without firing upon them or impeding their departure, they would leave Boston without burning the town to the ground.

When the news spread, supporters of the patriot cause marveled at their good fortune and the altogether unexpected turn of events. Abigail Adams wrote to her husband, John: "The more I think of it, the more amazed I am that they should leave such a harbor, such fortifications, such intrenchments, and that we should be in peaceable possession of a town which we expected would cost us a river of blood." Washington attended church services that Sunday morning, where the Reverend Abiel Leonard selected Exodus 14:25 as the theme of his remarks: "And they took off their chariot wheels, that they drove them heavily; so that the Egyptians said, Let us flee from the face of Israel; for the Lord fighteth for them against the Egyptians." Washington freely acknowledged the intervening hand of God in stirring the fierce storm that facilitated his great victory, and told Joseph Reed he would not "lament or repine at any act of Providence."

He hoped for further assistance from the Continental Army's unseen ally as the fighting shifted away from New England to the raw, rude, rising commercial center near the center of the Atlantic coast's colonial settlements.

"A KIND OF KEY TO THE WHOLE CONTINENT"

Far from the sprawling metropolis it later became, the former Dutch village of New Amsterdam remained overshadowed during the war by more cosmopolitan Philadelphia, some ninety miles to the southwest. That Quaker city not only served as the seat of the Continental Congress but also counted as a more important center of commerce and culture. With more than thirty thousand residents, Philadelphia had emerged as the second-largest city in the British Empire after London. New York, by contrast, boasted barely twenty thousand inhabitants crowded into a single square mile at the far southern tip of Manhattan, known at the time as York Island. Today's famous Wall Street got its name from the wooden palisades that long followed the narrow lane and marked the northern boundary of the town, protecting its residents from wild beasts and Indians who roamed the forests, fields, and marshes that still occupied 90 percent of the island.

The British aimed to conquer New York first not because of its importance but because of its vulnerability. Surrounded on three sides by deep water, the town offered a choice target for the Royal Navy, and at that early stage of the Revolution, the Americans possessed no ships capable of challenging British naval domination. What's more, many of New York's wealthiest and most prominent citizens considered themselves loyalists to Parliament and the crown, and if Britain's

General Howe occupied the city, loyalists believed he could connect with the even more numerous "Friends of Government" reputed to live in the nearby Hudson Valley.

Control of that river, in fact, offered His Majesty's forces a chance to cut the united colonies in half, blocking movement of needed soldiers and supplies between New England and the most populous of all the colonies, Virginia. John Adams understood the importance of New York even before the British moved against it, describing it as "a kind of key to the whole continent" in a letter to Washington in January and declaring unequivocally that "no effort to secure it ought to be omitted."

The British also expected that capturing the town at the mouth of the Hudson could end the war. Lord Francis Rawdon, the first Marquess of Hastings and one of Howe's most gallant officers, looked down with aristocratic disdain on the enemy troops he frequently derided as "Yankee psalm-singers." He wrote home to his friend the Earl of Huntingdon that "we shall soon have done with these scoundrels, for one only dirties one's fingers by meddling with them. I do not imagine they can possibly last out beyond this campaign, if you give us the necessary means of carrying on the war with vigor."

Those necessary means converged on Staten Island in the summer of 1776. General Howe arrived from Halifax with nine thousand men he had evacuated from Boston, while General Henry Clinton showed up from South Carolina with the three thousand troops with which he had failed to capture Charleston. Together with reinforcements from home, as well as some eight thousand newly hired Hessian mercenaries, Howe now commanded more than thirty-two thousand soldiers, constituting "the largest British Army that had ever been landed on an alien shore." Their naval assets alarmed the Americans even more: they had assembled 427 vessels and transports, with fifty-two ships of war and ten formidable ships of the line that each offered fifty guns or more. Counting the sailors on board these vessels, the uniformed British facing the colonists were more numerous than the regular populations of New York and Boston *combined*.

"OVERRIDING AND MYSTICAL FEELING"

To counter this armed might, Washington had begun moving troops toward New York even before the fall of Boston. He followed them with the bulk of the army on April 4, but as they awaited the expected British arrival, Washington and his lieutenants remained uncertain about the wisest deployment of their limited resources. Total British command of the waters gave the enemy unlimited alternatives in planning the takeover of the town.

On July 2, the same day the English armada finally docked at Staten Island, events in Philadelphia raised the stakes of the approaching battle. On that day, the Continental Congress voted to "dissolve the political bands" that had connected them to the mother country; two days later they formally approved the Declaration of Independence.

With that decision, a fraternal struggle to secure their "ancient rights" as Englishmen transformed into a world-shaking conflict to create a new nation with an unprecedented republican form of government. Political and military leaders understood from the outset that proclaiming independence and renouncing their status as British subjects exposed them all to execution as traitors. At the conclusion of debate on the Declaration, John Hancock, president of Congress, reportedly insisted: "We must be unanimous. There must be no pulling different ways, we must all hang together."

To which Benjamin Franklin then cheerfully responded, "Yes, we must indeed all hang together, or most assuredly we shall all hang separately."

Without question, a sense of destiny and divine favor, confirmed for many of the congressional delegates by the astonishing events in Boston some four months earlier, encouraged their determination. Historian Benson Bobrick writes of "the overriding and mystical feeling of providential cover to the boldness of their act." He cites a letter to Thomas Jefferson from Virginian John Page sent two weeks after the Declaration. "God preserve the United States," Page wrote. "We know the Race is not to the swift nor the Battle to the Strong. Do you not think an Angel rides in the Whirlwind and directs this Storm?" This phrase provided Bobrick with the title for his excellent 1997 book, *Angel in the Whirlwind*.

Despite the unconventional religious views of Jefferson and other founding fathers, this unifying notion of supernatural support for their noble cause found expression within the text of the very document with which they launched their new nation. Its concluding sentence reads: "And for the support of this Declaration, with a firm reliance on the protection of divine Providence, we mutually pledge to each other our Lives, our Fortunes and our sacred Honor." As Washington proclaimed to his badly outnumbered troops in New York: "The Fate of Unborn Millions will now depend, under God, on the courage and conduct of this army."

On July 9, that army assembled at six in the evening by order of the general in chief to hear the brave words of the Declaration for the first time in a public reading. The troops offered three cheers for "independency" and then cheered again for Washington's orders of the day, which declared that "the general hopes that this important event will serve as a fresh incentive to every officer and soldier to act with fidelity and courage as knowing that now the peace and safety of his country depends (under God) solely on the success of our arms: And that he is now in the service of a state possessed of sufficient power to reward his merit, and advance him to the highest honors of a free country."

Inspired by the prospect of those rewards and honors, and dismissed by their officers at the conclusion of the presentation, most of the men straggled down the wide road called Broadway in search of liquid refreshment. Joined by similarly excited townspeople in the fading light of early evening, they reached the oval park called Bowling Green, at the foot of Broadway. There the British government had erected in 1770 a ludicrously heroic statue of King George III mounted on the back of a huge, rearing steed. The noted sculptor Joseph Wilton had dressed the monarch absurdly in Roman garb, complete with laurel wreaths around his head, and fashioned the massive work of art in four thousand pounds of lead, covered with a gaudy layer of gold leaf.

TOPPLING KING GEORGE: A patriot mob celebrates the just-signed Declaration of Independence by sacking the royal statue at Manhattan's Bowling Green, July 9, 1776.

"If a good bleeding can bring those Bible-faced Yankees to their senses, the fever of independency should soon abate." —British General James Grant

The statue had become a special target for graffiti and dishonor from the king's rebellious subjects, so authorities had surrounded it with a fence of sharpened metal pikes. The energized mob celebrating the Declaration made short work of this barrier, however, and then used some of its remains, together with ropes, other bars, and brute force, to pull down the royal likeness from its pedestal. To express their deepest feelings toward their former sovereign, the participants proceeded to scrape the gilt from both horse and rider and then to chop off the head of the monarch. They finally impaled what remained of the sculpted head on one of their spikes and posted it outside a tavern while they refreshed themselves after their labors. After quenching their thirst, the triumphant band marched out to the sound of fife and drums and picked up the king's decapitated lead body to have it melted down into bullets for the Continental Army. Amazingly, soldiers and civilians accomplished all this destruction with little thought that the mightiest British army yet assembled was still receiving reinforcements at their encampments just five miles across the harbor.

No wonder that Ambrose Serle, the thirty-four-year-old civilian secretary to General Howe, denounced "the villainy and the madness of these deluded people." After the war, Serle became the author of eloquent, popular Christian devotional books and well-known hymns, but his first reading of the Declaration of Independence in New York produced only intemperate outrage. "A more impudent, false, and atrocious proclamation was never fabricated by the hands of man," he wrote. At the same time he predicted quick and easy victory for His Majesty's men-at-arms because of the high quality of their training and discipline compared with the raw, crude nature of the rebels. "The troops hold them very cheap and long for an opportunity of revenging the cause of their countrymen who fell at Bunker Hill," Serle concluded.

"SOME SECRET PURPOSE"

The redcoats ultimately received that opportunity, but only after General Howe meticulously planned and prepared for his strike against the town, while Washington despaired of either discerning or counteracting his adversary's intentions. Some of his military aides and advisors, including the prominent and powerful lawyer Joseph Reed, urged the general in chief to withdraw from New York to avoid exposing his vulnerable army to destruction. Washington acknowledged the dangers of his situation but felt compelled by political considerations to make some attempt, at least, to defend the city; the Continental Congress and the people of New York expected no less, especially after the excitement surrounding the Declaration of Independence.

After long weeks of anxious anticipation, the elements themselves signaled an approaching climax. As the sun set on the night of August 21, the russet sky went suddenly black. A huge cloud arose from nowhere and then expanded to cover the horizon, while lightning flashes skittered wildly through the gathering gloom. Thunder roared and boomed, shaking the walls of every building in the town, while lightning "fell in masses and sheets to the earth, and seemed to strike incessantly and on every side."

A Connecticut major named Abner Benedict watched the spectacle in awe from his post on Brooklyn Heights. As it began to rain, "then followed a crash louder than a thousand cannon. . . . In a few minutes the entire heavens became black as ink, and from horizon to horizon the whole empyrean was ablaze with lightning." Another witness reported that the great cloud "appeared to stand still and swing round and round like a horizontal wheel." The unearthly display continued for more than three terrible hours, described by both American and British sources as "a storm like a hurricane," "the most vehement I ever saw," "a most terrible storm," and "an awful scene."

Lightning strikes set numerous houses in the town ablaze during the long and terrifying night. And people were struck down, too. "A soldier, passing through one of the streets, without receiving apparently any external injury, was struck deaf, dumb and blind," reported a chronicler of the human cost. "A captain and two lieutenants belonging to McDougall's regiment were killed by one thunderbolt; the points of their swords melted off and the coin melted in their pockets. Their bodies appeared as if they had been roasted, so black and crisp was the skin. Ten men encamped outside of the fort near the river, and occupying one tent, were killed by a single flash. . . . They belonged to one of the Connecticut regiments and were buried in one grave. . . . Familiar as we become with death in the midst of war, it somehow affects us very differently when sent, apparently, direct from the hand of God."

Major Abner Benedict tentatively attempted a pseudoscientific explanation, suggesting that "the vast amount of arms collected in and about the city" might have attracted and held the baffling and stationary black cloud "and drew from it such a fearful amount of electricity." But he acknowledged that the brutal display from the heavens remained ultimately inexplicable and disturbing. He wrote that "there seems hidden meaning, some secret purpose, when the bolt is launched by an invisible arm, and from the mysterious depths of space."

People on both sides of the conflict made similar assumptions: that the furious phenomenon they jointly endured on the eve of a great battle must have been meant to convey an important message. But what message, exactly?

If the leaders imputed some specific meaning to those portents, or to the flashes, crashes, and hideous deaths of August 21, they failed to record their conclusions. Looking back with the incalculable advantage of hindsight, one might interpret the monstrous outburst as a direct warning to the assembled Americans, especially since the lightning did its deadly work almost exclusively on Washington's men in the city rather than the British hordes waiting on Staten Island for their orders to march. Could the general in chief have interpreted the storm as a powerful plea to retreat from the area in order to avoid a direct confrontation with a vastly superior force?

Some of Washington's aides and most-respected advisors had argued for precisely that course, urging the commander to keep his army intact to harry, surprise, and taunt the enemy, rather than facing off in a massive showdown in which the enemy enjoyed every advantage. Had the Americans followed such a course, they would have avoided the largest single battle of the entire war (in terms of the number of troops directly engaged) and spared themselves the loss of a significant segment of their struggling army. As events unfolded, only another demonstration of seemingly supernatural intervention preserved the cause of independence from catastrophic collapse.

"EVERYTHING SEEMS TO BE OVER FOR THEM"

The maneuvers that led to the Battle of Long Island began at dawn of the hot, sweaty summer morning immediately following the horrifying storm. Seeking an element of surprise, General Howe and four thousand British troops embarked at 5:10 a.m. from their Staten

Island base of operations. By eight in the morning they had landed unopposed at Gravesend Bay, near current-day Coney Island, and by noon more than fifteen thousand redcoats and forty pieces of artillery had successfully assembled near the shore, only twelve miles from the main American defenses at Brooklyn Heights.

Unsure of Howe's plan of attack, Washington had dangerously divided his army, deploying some six thousand men on the Brooklyn side of the East River and a similar number either at fortifications on lower Manhattan or scattered among a series of forts the Americans had constructed on both sides of the Hudson River. Only after the English veterans and their Hessian allies had marched through rich farming country and paused at the Dutch settlement of Flatbush did the American commander realize that the village of Brooklyn, with its well-prepared Yankee trenches, represented their first target. Washington quickly redeployed all available resources across the East River to block the British advance, bringing his troop strength to nearly ten thousand.

The fight that followed proved a painfully one-sided affair, despite the reckless courage of a few crack American regiments. Some 270 Marylanders made a gallant stand against a vastly larger British force, attacking five different times to try to break through the enemy's line before giving up the attempt. Their determination invited comparison to the ancient story of Leonidas and his three hundred Spartans at the "hot gates" of Thermopylae, and like those ancient heroes, few of the Americans escaped the field of slaughter.

In the end, such moments of valor counted for little, since a cleverly conceived and perfectly executed plan enabled the British to surround the bulk of the American troops. Only four roads led over the steep, heavily forested Heights of Guan, but Washington and his generals had left one of the routes utterly unprotected. Around midnight, a substantial body of English troops marched through the unguarded pass, completing a flanking movement that brought them to the rear of the already pressed Americans at the very height of the next day's struggle. A Pennsylvania private named Michael Graham recalled the misery of the resulting rout. "It is impossible for me to describe the confusion and horror of the scene," he wrote, "the artillery flying with the chains over the horses' backs, our men running in almost every direction, and run which way they would, they were almost sure to meet the British or Hessians. And the enemy huzzahing when they took prisoners made it truly a day of distress to the Americans. I escaped . . . and entered a swamp or marsh through which a great many of our men were retreating. Some of them were mired and crying to the fellows for God's sake to help them out; but every man was intent on his own safety and no assistance was rendered."

In his official report on the battle, General Howe gloated over his own success and extolled the courage of his men, claiming to have destroyed a third of Washington's army, with more than three thousand killed, captured, or wounded. Modern estimates insist that he probably exaggerated his enemy's losses, but even with half the casualties he claimed, the Americans would have suffered a shattering setback. Historians conclude that Howe's reports of his own light losses were probably accurate: fewer than four hundred killed, wounded, or missing. The British also captured three prominent American generals, one of whom died of his wounds two weeks after the battle.

Writing home to his father, Lord Hugh Percy, a highborn brigadier in Howe's army and later the second Duke of Northumberland, concluded that the Battle of Long Island had broken the rebels' will to resist. "They feel severely the blow of the 27th," he exulted, "and I think I may venture to assert that they will never again stand before us in the field. Everything seems to be over for them, and I flatter myself now that this campaign will put a total end to the war." General James Grant, who capably commanded the British center in the thick of the battle, enthusiastically agreed. He wrote to General Harvey that "if a good bleeding can bring those Bible-faced Yankees to their senses, the fever of independency should soon abate."

MORE METEOROLOGICAL MIRACLES

By nightfall, the remnants of the Continental Army crowded into the trenches on Brooklyn Heights, expecting British pursuit at any moment. To give them better odds of resisting the inevitable assault, Washington brought over most of his remaining troops from New York, so his strength stood again at nearly nine thousand. But even the most inexperienced private understood the desperate nature of their situation. The Americans were trapped at the far western corner of Long Island, a huge English force in front of them and the mile-wide estuary of the East River behind them. The nearby presence of four fearsome enemy men-of-war with their formidable complement of cannon made escape across the water unlikely if not unthinkable. To make matters worse, the next morning the weather changed, the skies darkening and the temperature dropping at least ten degrees. In the afternoon, the Americans faced a cold, soaking downpour, which added to their gloom. Water accumulated in the trenches, so deep that some of the weary and drenched troops stood in it up to their waists. Under the circumstances, the Continentals had been rendered almost defenseless, their powder, muskets, and cartridges soaked by the insistent rain.

But the same thunderstorm that caused them so much discomfort also worked toward their deliverance: with the winds howling from the northeast, the British ships couldn't sail against their force to come up from the lower harbor to surround and shell the cornered Americans. Under the overall command of Lord Admiral Richard "Black Dick" Howe, the chief general's brother, two of the more maneuverable vessels attempted to sail against the wind but found themselves blown back. Benjamin Tallmadge, a recent graduate of Yale and a twenty-two-year-old major in the Continental Army, found it "most wonderful" and "providential" that the weather discouraged General Howe from storming the exhausted Americans: "After sustaining incessant fatigue and constant watchfulness for two days and nights, attended by heavy rain, exposed every moment to an attack by a vastly superior force in front, and to be cut off from the possibility of retreat to New York by the fleet which might enter the East River, on the night of the twenty-ninth . . . Washington commenced re-crossing his troops from Brooklyn to New York." That crossing represented the only hope for escaping death or capture by the confident, triumphant British.

Any chance of success in this desperate effort required two

unlikely conditions: more meteorological miracles and unlikely British inattentiveness. If the wind stopped blowing from the northeast, British men-of-war would immediately sail upriver to cut off any chance of escape. And if Howe's watchful troops detected Washington's effort to withdraw American forces together with horses, cannon, and other military equipment, they could strike at the retreating Yankees at precisely the moment in which they were most exposed and disorganized.

The high-risk effort began with Washington's order to all detachments in the New York–New Jersey area to requisition—or confiscate, if necessary—every available small boat with oars or modest sails to transport his army to a bold surprise attack. This communication amounted to a deliberate deception: the American commander resolved to keep his plan of withdrawal a complete secret from his officers and men in order to minimize any chance of alerting the enemy. The complicated process of emptying the trenches and marching down to the Brooklyn ferry dock could begin only after full dark on a damp and cloudy night. The soldiers closest to the enemy had been instructed to maintain numerous campfires and to make enough noise all along the lines throughout the night to convey the impression that no one had left. Meanwhile, those making their way to the boats were required to muffle the wagon wheels and refrain from conversation of any kind. Private Joseph Plumb Martin of Massachusetts, who had recently joined the army at age fifteen, remembered: "We were strictly enjoined not to speak, or even cough . . . All orders were given from officer to officer and communicated to the men in whispers."

In the course of the long night, a few mishaps nearly brought disaster. As the drenched soldiers staggered through the dark toward the scores of small craft that awaited them, they did make enough racket to awaken the most notorious loyalist in the sleeping village of Brooklyn, an elderly woman who had been outspoken in her support for "King and Country." Understanding that Washington was about to give the redcoats the slip, she dispatched her trusted black servant to cross American lines and to alert General Howe. He made it safely into British-held territory, but as he rushed toward Howe's headquarters a Hessian officer intercepted him. The messenger made an earnest attempt to explain his mission, but the German understood not a word of English and assumed that anyone with a dark face would be aligned with the rebels, since black soldiers played a prominent role in Washington's army. Instead of warning British commanders about the American escape, the servant spent crucial hours under Hessian detention until it was too late.

At two in the morning, a garbled order from one of Washington's adjutants nearly ruined the entire operation. Fresh Pennsylvania units only recently arrived in Brooklyn had been given the crucial task of holding the most forward position on the American lines, where they would maintain the campfires and screen the rest of the American army's departure from the British. Initial instructions clearly indicated that only after the rest of the troops had successfully crossed the river would the Pennsylvanians depart on the very last boats. But in the midst of the post-midnight movement of men and matériel, with the soldiers communicating solely in whispers or not at all, an officer at the front lines gave the impression that Washington wanted them to march to the waiting boats immediately. On the muddy road to the dock they encountered the commander in chief himself, inspecting the progress on horseback. When he recognized these particular units, after identifying the capable veteran, Colonel Edward Hand, he expressed shock and outrage. "Good God!" Washington declared. "I am afraid you have ruined us by so unseasonably withdrawing the troops from the lines." Trying to come to terms with this "dreadful mistake," the general told Hand that "matters were in much confusion at the ferry, and that unless we could resume our posts before the enemy discovered we had left them, in all probability the most disagreeable consequences would follow." The Pennsylvanians trudged dutifully and silently back to their soggy trenches; to their enormous relief, the British had never noticed their absence.

A Connecticut soldier joined the spirited unit of fishermen from Marblehead, Massachusetts, who manned the boats all through the night, and he remembered making eleven trips across the river before their work was done. Steady winds had succeeded in preventing what the Americans feared most: British warships sailing up the East River to disrupt their passage and no doubt achieve a significant slaughter. Nevertheless, as dawn approached, a substantial portion of the retreating army still huddled at the Brooklyn docks. In the clear light of early morning, without the cover of night and rain, they would become easy targets for the enemy.

Contemporaries marveled at the next development, as does historian David McCullough: "Incredibly, yet again, circumstances—fate, luck, Providence, the hand of God, as would be said so often—intervened. Just at daybreak a heavy fog settled in over the whole of Brooklyn, concealing everything no less than had the night. . . . Even with the sun up, the fog remained as dense as ever, while over on the New York side of the river there was no fog at all."

Most remarkably, New Yorkers could think of no other example of such conditions ever before developing in the summer season. Major Tallmadge, who had grown up on Long Island, remembered this experience in almost biblical terms: "As the dawn of the next day approached, those of us who remained in the trenches became very anxious for our own safety, and when the dawn appeared there were several regiments still on duty. At this time a very dense fog began to rise and it seemed to settle in a peculiar manner on both encampments. I recollect this particular providential occurrence perfectly well, and so very dense was the atmosphere that I could scarcely discern a man at six yards distance." These conditions clearly favored the determined New England troops, who had worked all their lives on the water, as they tirelessly rowed their comrades to safety. Still, they marveled that "the atmosphere was clear on the New York side of the river. The wind, too, died away, and the river became so smooth that the row-boats could be laden almost to the gunwale, and a favoring breeze sprang up for the sailboats too."

Despite these indications of supernatural protection, Tallmadge felt enormous relief when he and his men received their final order to "retire" and "we very joyfully bid those trenches a long adieu. When we reached Brooklyn ferry, the boats had not returned from their last trip, but they very soon appeared and took the whole regiment over to New York; and I think I saw Gen. Washington on the ferry stairs when I stepped into one of the last boats that received the troops."

Captain Alexander Graydon, the twenty-four-year-old son of Irish immigrants, estimated it was after seven in the morning when he and his men finally landed in Manhattan. "And in less than an hour after, the fog having dispersed, the enemy was visible on the shore we had left." As Tallmadge recalled, "As soon as they reached the ferry we were saluted merrily from their musketry, and finally by their field pieces; but we returned in safety. In the history of warfare I do not recollect a more fortunate retreat. After all, the providential appearance of the fog saved a part of our army from being captured, and certainly myself, among others who formed the rear guard."

Later, as the astonished and enraged British finally swarmed over the empty American redoubts, "they could not find so much as a biscuit or a glass of rum wherewith to console themselves."

"EITHER OUR FRIEND, OR NO GENERAL"

To the amazement of observers on all sides, Washington had successfully evacuated more than nine thousand men and considerable equipment in the course of a single night. Despite the tense hours of chaos and danger, not one member of his beaten army had been killed or seriously injured in the course of the risky retreat.

Enemy combatants readily acknowledged the scope of this achievement. Charles Stedman, a former student at Virginia's College of William and Mary who served as an aide to Lord Percy in the British army, sketched the nature of Washington's challenge in his well-regarded history of the Revolutionary War: "Driven to the corner of an island, hemmed in within a narrow space of two square miles, in their front . . . near twenty thousand men, in their rear an arm of the sea a mile wide . . . they secured a retreat without the loss of a man." It was, Stedman acknowledged, a close-run business: had the winds died or shifted, allowing the *Rose* and the *Phoenix*, with seventy-two guns between them, to make their way into the East River as they had previously sailed up the Hudson, they could have cut off the Americans "most completely." The capture of the rebel army, along with its already world-famous commander, could have brought the inevitable collapse of the cause of independence just seven weeks after it had been declared.

Despite Howe's failure to finish the war with a single decisive stroke, the British public celebrated with ringing bells and lighted candles when news of his "glorious victory" traveled across the Atlantic. King George III, in far better personal shape than the gilded likeness that had formerly ridden high in New York's Bowling Green, declared his "great satisfaction" with the performance of his commander in North America and honored him with the Order of the Bath.

Nevertheless, questions persisted about why Howe had delayed for days in front of the American lines on Brooklyn Heights, giving Washington and his beaten and battered Continentals the chance to break away to fight another day—another seven years, in fact. The Americans acknowledged that he easily could have overwhelmed their defenses, though they meant to exact a high cost for any such attack. Rumors suggested that the chief British general felt privately sympathetic to the rebel cause, in part due to the married warrior's ongoing romance with the wife of an American loyalist, the "flashing blonde" Elizabeth Lloyd Loring. The tough, grizzled American general Israel "Old Put" Putnam could perceive only two possible explanations for the British failure to finish the job. "General Howe," he commented, "is either our friend, or no general."

Actually, the historical record suggests that Howe's reluctance to press his case on Brooklyn Heights stemmed from the same source as his failure to strike the Americans at Dorchester Heights outside Boston. The worst experience of his life, personally leading hundreds of loyal soldiers to death or mutilation as they tramped up the blood-soaked slopes at the Battle of Bunker Hill, left him with a permanent fear of attacking prepared Americans in entrenched positions. That dread only intensified when the enemy held high ground, necessitating an uphill assault.

While Britons rejoiced in Howe's Long Island victory, Americans hailed Washington's daring and extraordinary escape. The *Virginia Gazette* wrote that "the manner in which our retreat was performed reflects the highest credit upon our commander-in-chief, and the officers in general," while the *New England Chronicle* designated the maneuver "a masterpiece" and a sign that "Providence favored us."

Inevitably, the deeply religious people whom Lord Rawdon dismissed as "Psalm-singing Yankees" and General James Grant insulted as "Bible-faced Yankees" sought some spiritual meaning in the events around New York. A writer in the *Massachusetts Spy* passed over the extraordinary circumstances of the American retreat and instead found signs of divine *dis*favor in the battlefield disasters on Long Island. "We have thought God was for us," he recalled, "and had given many and signal instances of his power and mercy in our favor, and had greatly frowned upon and disappointed our enemies; and verily it was so. But have we repented and given him the glory? Verily no. His hand seems to be turned and stretched out against us—and strong is his hand."

"THE INVISIBLE HAND"

The Americans found consistent evidence of that strength in the difficult years of struggle that followed, but in the end saw providential power deployed more conspicuously in support of their success rather than as reprimand for their failings. The triumphant conclusion of a long, horribly bloody war meant that even the extended list of patriot defeats and disappointments could be seen as part of some grand, eternal plan leading inexorably to independence. The perception that an inscrutable "angel in the whirlwind" directed these great events wasn't limited to zealots or mystics but animated most participants in the cause, from the tireless and fearless politicos in the Continental Congress to the ordinary recruits who served in Washington's often ill-equipped army.

A stirring song that marched these farmers and artisans into battle movingly evokes the faith that fired them. Yes, the jaunty strains of "Yankee Doodle" became popular in the course of the Revolution (and have remained popular ever since), but the Continental Army actually preferred a more somber tune with a more inspiring message.

In 1770, the prominent Boston musician William Billings published *The New England Psalm Singer*, which included a hymn called "Chester," its title presumably honoring the Massachusetts town of that name. Eight years later, in the midst of the struggle for independence, Billings provided new lyrics that turned his church hymn into a patriotic anthem. He specifically invoked some of the astonishing American successes in the opening months of the conflict:

> *Let tyrants shake their iron rod,*
> *And Slav'ry clank her galling chains*
> *We fear them not, we trust in God,*
> *New England's God forever reigns.*

> *The Foe comes on with haughty Stride;*
> *Our troops advance with martial noise*
> *Their Vet'rans flee before our Youth*
> *And Gen'rals yield to beardless boys.*

> *What grateful Off'ring shall we bring?*
> *What shall we render to the Lord?*
> *Loud Halleluiahs let us Sing,*
> *And praise his Name on ev'ry Chord.*

This brief song unforgettably captures the unique combination of warlike determination and unshakable faith that characterized most of the American fighters and inspired twentieth-century composer William Schuman to craft his 1956 concert piece *New England Triptych*. The last section of the work, based on "Chester," brilliantly portrays the transition from church-like reverence to inexorable march with "martial noise" and then to explosive amazement, overwhelming gratitude, and sheer delight at victory. The music lasts only sixteen minutes and is worth sampling by anyone who wants a richer insight into the emotional arc of the American Revolution.

Like most of the men under his command, Washington never doubted providential participation in the cause he served, either during the war or long afterward. In the first-ever inaugural address by an

American president, delivered to a joint session of Congress in New York City on April 30, 1789, the great hero noted his reluctance to assume the presidency and acknowledged genuine fears of his own inadequacy. He then turned immediately to the Almighty's role in guiding the nation to its looming greatness. "In tendering this homage to the Great Author of every public and private good," he declaimed, "I assure myself that it expresses your sentiments not less than my own, nor those of my fellow-citizens at large less than either. No people can be bound to acknowledge and adore the Invisible Hand which conducts the affairs of men more than those of the United States. Every step by which they have advanced to the character of an independent nation seems to have been distinguished by some token of providential agency."

To Washington, that "providential agency" meant more than favor for a worthy cause; it also meant long-standing and bewildering personal protection of an intimate and individual nature that had preceded his prominent role in the Revolutionary conflict by more than twenty years.

THE FIRST PORTRAIT OF WASHINGTON: Painted by Charles Willson Peale in 1772, seventeen years after the unlikely survival of the then twenty-three-year-old officer at the Battle of Monongahela.

"The miraculous care of Providence protected me beyond all human expectation." —George Washington

4

INDISPENSABLE, INDESTRUCTIBLE

The Illogical Survival of George Washington

Long before they recognized him as indispensable, George Washington's contemporaries hailed him as indestructible. As an impetuous youth of twenty-three, the towering Virginian first won the admiration of his countrymen not for his wisdom, dignity, or astute leadership but for a strange, inexplicable ability to cheat death and escape bodily harm. Widely viewed as a sign of divine protection, that remarkable gift remained with him throughout his supremely eventful life.

Born into a "middling rank" of the Virginia gentry, George was the first child of his father's second marriage. In a pattern all too common for the era, death surrounded his childhood and youth. His half sister, Jane, perished when he was two, his full sister Mildred before he was eight, and his father, Augustine Washington, at age forty-eight, when George was still eleven. His much-admired half brother Lawrence became his role model and inspiration, playing the part of substitute parent before he contracted virulent tuberculosis at age thirty-four.

In the belief that a tropical climate might relieve his racking cough, Lawrence traveled with nineteen-year-old George to Barbados—the younger Washington's only trip in his life beyond the borders of the future United States. While his beloved brother suffered and struggled for breath, George contracted smallpox and remained confined to his bed for more than three weeks. Despite the usually fatal nature of the disease, Washington's vigor enabled him to recover. The skin of his face scarred permanently, showing clusters of shallow pockmarks for the rest of his life; more important, though, he achieved immunity from the most feared disease of his era. The great smallpox epidemic of 1775–82 afflicted both American and British troops during the Revolution, as well as devastating Native American tribes. The general in chief remained personally untouched and ordered sensible precautions, including pioneering quarantines and inoculations, to protect his men.

When well enough to travel, twenty-year-old Washington returned to Virginia with his rapidly declining brother, who breathed his last tortured breath in July 1752. From Lawrence, the future president ultimately inherited his beloved estate on the Potomac River, Mount Vernon, along with significant responsibilities in the Virginia militia.

Taking Lawrence's place as a district adjutant, the newly minted militia major received a difficult and dangerous assignment from Virginia's lieutenant governor. Entrepreneurs in Pennsylvania and Virginia (including the lieutenant governor himself) had taken an interest in developing farms and trading posts in the rich, not yet settled land of the Ohio Valley. They had become concerned over credible reports of fort-building incursions by the French to establish control over vast territory simultaneously claimed by Britain and France. Washington's job required a rugged round trip of five hundred miles through heavily forested wilderness to find one of the French outposts and to deliver a written ultimatum demanding its removal.

With the aid of Indians he met and befriended on the way, the young militia officer managed to arrive in Fort Le Boeuf, in present-day northwestern Pennsylvania, near the French base of operations around the Great Lakes. The local commander received the message from the British authorities with great courtesy but sent a firm, unbending response of his own.

Determined to get this letter as quickly as possible back to the capital at Williamsburg, Washington ignored warnings about the impassable winter conditions and began his return trip nine days before

Christmas. After less than a week, the deep snow, ice, and "excessive cold" (in Washington's own words) made it impossible to continue with the struggling horses and the four "servitors" (hired helpers) who had begun the expedition. Washington therefore determined to traverse the remaining two hundred miles on foot, accompanied only by a veteran frontiersman named Christopher Gist.

Staggering forward, they picked up the services of a new Indian guide, who offered to show them the best paths through the forest and over the mountains. Gist distrusted the man from the beginning, and his fears proved justified when they broke into a broad meadow illuminated by dazzling winter sunlight. The Indian, who had offered to assist the weary Gist by carrying his heavy musket, suddenly ran ahead by fifteen paces, then turned and fired directly at Washington. In any cinematic version of this journey, the course of that musket ball would be rendered in slow motion. As biographer James Thomas Flexner eloquently and appropriately reports: "The bullet moved through utter emptiness without changing the history of the world."

The two Americans then rushed their traitorous guide as he attempted to reload. They took back the gun and sent him on his way back into the forest, but worse dangers lay ahead. Worried about follow-up Indian attacks, they didn't even light campfires when they stopped for the night. After two days of painful progress, they reached the banks of the Monongahela River and discovered an all-but-impossible obstacle. They had expected that at this point in the winter the water would be frozen solid, allowing them to cross in safety. Instead, they found black, treacherous rapids, transporting huge and dangerous chunks of ice—conditions similar to those Washington would find more than twenty years later when he led his troops across the Delaware River before the Battle of Trenton.

This time, with no boats available, Gist and George resolved to build their own raft, using the "small hatchet" they carried with them to fell trees and then binding them together. The process took all day, and in the fading light of dusk, with makeshift poles they had fashioned to cope with rushing water nearly ten feet deep, they started across. Almost immediately, a huge block of ice struck their log platform and nearly capsized it. Washington tried to steady their progress with his pole but leaned on it too heavily and pitched headlong into the freezing water. Gasping for air, he reached out his long arm to grab the raft as the current pushed it past him; he held on for some distance before his own strength and Gist's assistance got him out of the water. They tried in vain to steer their logs to one bank or the other of the ice-clogged river but made no progress, finally coming to rest on a desolate, tiny island in the middle of the stream. There they spent the night, Gist enduring excruciating pain in his frostbitten fingers and toes, Washington unable to do anything about the soaking clothes that soon froze solid and covered most of his body in a thick coat of icy "armor."

They endured a miserable night in the bitter cold—so cold, in fact, that when the frosty dawn broke over the treetops they saw that the turbulent river surrounding them had been covered overnight by a sheet of gleaming ice. Unsure whether the new ice could support their weight, they gingerly picked their way toward the other side of the Monongahela. Finally they reached solid ground and continued on their way to Williamsburg.

"WITH HIS BLESSING YOU CAN BE A USEFUL MAN"

Washington's arrival caused a sensation, not only because of the important message he brought back from the much-feared French but also because of the stirring adventures he narrated in his diary of the trip. Lieutenant Governor Robert Dinwiddie insisted that this first-person account be published and distributed widely for the purpose of rousing public support for military missions against the French beyond the mountains. The publication also brought Washington his first taste of renown beyond his immediate circle of family, friends, and associates.

That surging fame led to his designation as commander of a second mission into the contested wilderness west of the Alleghenies. This time he led 159 men of the Virginia militia in another effort to frighten the determined French away from their claims on all of central North America, from Canada to Louisiana. Two brisk skirmishes ensued, bringing Washington mixed success but winning him further admiration for his boyish courage. (Facing the first real battle of his military career, he famously observed: "I heard the bullets whistle and, believe me, there is something charming in the sound.")

These indecisive exchanges marked the opening shots of a global conflict for empire known as the Seven Years' War. That epic struggle between Britain and France and their respective allies featured major battles on the European continent and in South America, India, the Philippines, and West Africa. In the crucial theater of North America, the conflict became known as the French and Indian War because of the heavy reliance of the French on their formidable Algonquin allies. It concluded in 1759 with a glorious British victory on the Plains of Abraham outside Quebec City, but the first important contest, in which young Washington played an outsized role, marked one of the darkest days in the history of the British military.

Taken prisoner by the French after a much stronger contingent had killed or captured his little army, Washington was promptly released and sent back to Virginia to convey the message that the officers of Louis XV could mobilize formidable fighting forces on behalf of their king and would not easily be dislodged. Rather than accept this proposition or leave the defense of colonial interests to the raw and relatively unorganized members of local militias, King George II and his ministers in London dispatched well-trained British regulars to take charge of the situation in the New World.

They arrived under the command of sixty-year-old Edward Braddock, a crusty, well-regarded veteran of forty-five years of military service who arrived with a plan for mopping up the French forts one by one. He would begin with Fort Duquesne, the most substantial of these facilities, at the strategic site of present-day Pittsburgh, where the Allegheny and Monongahela Rivers meet to form the Ohio. As he planned his decisive thrust into the interior he naturally connected with Washington, who had risen to the rank of colonel and knew more than any other prominent Virginian about the Indian-infested territory around Fort Duquesne. Because of military regulations, Braddock couldn't offer the twenty-three-year-old militia officer a suitably lofty rank in the regular army, but Washington agreed to join the expedition as an unranked volunteer aide and advisor to Braddock.

Before he could depart on the march west, Washington had to overcome opposition that he took far more seriously than he did the French or their Indian allies. His widowed mother, Mary Ball Washington, rode two days in her carriage from her Fredericksburg home to plead with her son to avoid danger and remain at Mount Vernon. His response reflected his already solid faith in his own supernatural protection: "The God to whom you commended me, madam, when I set out upon a more perilous errand, defended me from all harm, and I trust he will do so now. Do not you?"

Tearfully she relented. "With his blessing you can be a useful man in war as in peace, and without it you can expect nothing," she declared, promising him her prayers before setting off on her long journey home.

"THE GLOOM AND HORROR"

For George, however, the journey west with General Braddock seemed ill-fated from the first. Progress proved painfully slow, dependent on engineers and sweating troops carving a twelve-foot-wide road through the wilderness to accommodate the train of guns and supply wagons that the English commander considered essential. Many of those wagons had been procured only with great difficulty, making use of personal monetary guarantees provided by the celebrated Benjamin Franklin of Philadelphia.

For Washington, the pace became even slower at the beginning of June when he came down with a punishing fever that left him weak and immobilized; historians suggest he most likely suffered from dysentery (known at the time as the "bloody flux") or from typhoid fever. Under orders from General Braddock, who had taken a special interest in the strapping youth with the grave demeanor, he remained behind for a while. Then, since he continued to feel too dizzy and feeble to travel on horseback, he rejoined the column in a wagon bed provided specially by the general. Even after the fever broke and Washington began to recover, he could only ride with several pillows tied to the saddle to reduce the discomfort remaining from his illness.

As the British column forded the Monongahela successfully and came within ten miles of Fort Duquesne, Washington rode along, still resting on cushions. He insisted on taking part in the seizure of the French fortification, assumed to be an easy task due to the small size of the defending force. The British army included more than thirteen hundred disciplined and well-equipped regulars, with another two hundred members of colonial militias. The fort contained fewer than 100 French regulars, another 150 militiamen from Canada, and some 650 Indian warriors who were dismissed by Braddock as inconsequential and irrelevant.

Washington rode alongside his confident commander at the center of the main column when the sound of gunfire and Indian war whoops indicated that the advance guard had engaged the enemy. Galloping toward the front as quickly as they could, Washington and Braddock collided with their own desperate troops, who were running in panic to the rear. The chaos that ensued left the British vulnerable, resulted in significant losses from friendly fire, and ultimately led to their defeat.

For generations, the legend persisted that the French and Indians prevailed at the Battle of Monongahela because they laid a carefully planned ambush, hiding in the woods on either side of the newly built road until they could fire on the British lines from both directions. More accurate accounts suggest that, hearing the English approach, the French forces left the fort and rushed to confront them, and only after the first exchange of fire did the Indians and the Canadian militia melt into the ravines and gullies alongside the road, crouching behind trees and taking expert aim at their red-coated targets.

They shot the mounted officers first, killing or wounding nearly all of them, while the triumphant whooping of the Indians—never heard before by His Majesty's seasoned troops—combined with the mounting piles of bodies to terrify the English. In response to their unseen attackers, the British fired wildly into the woods, exhausting their ammunition and then running toward the wagons and cannon of the rear guard. Officers attempted to rally the men, trying to lead them to seize higher ground to make a defense or to take cover behind one gigantic fallen log. But before they could reorganize any part of the disintegrating army, the commanders themselves fell to the enemy's unceasing fire. At the end of the day, only twenty-three officers of more than a hundred on the field survived the carnage, and most of those had been badly wounded. Official reports later listed 977 killed or wounded, in an army numbered at 1,459. There were no British prisoners noted, since the Indians eagerly scalped their captives or, in one notorious instance, brought them back in a large group to Fort Duquesne, where they gleefully burned them alive at the banks of the Allegheny River.

General Braddock, wounded in the midst of the fight with a bullet that pierced his arm and lodged in his lung, now relied on Washington to transmit his commands to the troops. Dashing on horseback through the tide of fleeing humanity, the young American made an especially promising target: with his height usually estimated at six foot two at a time when the average for men was half a foot less, he towered over the other officers and men. In the midst of battle, his horse was shot out from under him. Washington secured another mount and this time managed to ride without the aid of his pillowed saddle. The second animal lasted only minutes before it, too, took a bullet and fell, so Washington found a third mount. During the course of the battle, five other bullets penetrated his clothing, one knocking his hat off his head and four leaving holes in the flowing coat he wore despite the July heat. Amazingly, none of the shots grazed his body even slightly, and his biggest problem seemed to be the sickness rising again in his digestive tract, making it difficult for him to stay in the saddle.

Nevertheless, he loaded his wounded commander into a small cart and tried to lead to safety any men who would follow him. With the sun setting behind the forested hills to the west, Braddock, who had remained conscious but silent, began to speak. "Who would have thought it?" he declared, and then ordered the exhausted and weakened Washington to ride forty miles through the night to summon reinforcements. George somehow called upon his remaining strength to accept the mission, though he later recalled that fatigue and illness left him "wholly unfit for the execution of the duty." Along the way, he noted shocking scenes: "The dead, the dying, the groans, lamentations, and cries along the road of the wounded for help ... were enough to pierce a heart of adamant, the gloom and horror of which was not a little increased by the imperious darkness occasioned by the close shade of thick woods." When he finally connected with the officer in command of the potential reinforcements, Colonel Dunbar, that indecisive commander felt too alarmed at the events of the day to move his troops.

The next day Washington rode back to the main body of survivors to find General Braddock still conscious but suffering greatly from his wounds. His reported last words promised that "we shall know better how to deal with them another time." He died minutes later, and his Virginian aide officiated at a torchlight funeral, reading from Scripture and offering brief prayers. He then ordered wagons to pass repeatedly over the fresh grave, to disguise its location and to avoid desecration by the Indians.

Fortunately for Washington's men, the French could not persuade their native warriors to pursue and destroy the surviving elements of the decimated British army. The natives were too busy celebrating their rich harvest of scalps and other trophies of war. Eyewitnesses later saw them dressed in the boots, hats, decorations, and rich uniforms they had stripped from the British dead; they also prized the swords, muskets, and canteens they had collected.

"PRESERVED FOR SOME GREAT SERVICE"

Washington returned to Mount Vernon without prizes of war but with a greatly enhanced reputation. Despite the disaster for the British cause, Virginians hailed their twenty-three-year-old neighbor as the "Hero of Monongahela," one of the few survivors and a man who had performed with composed gallantry at every phase of the catastrophic combat. The story of the two horses shot out from under him, the hat shot from his head, and the bullets that rent his garments but left his body untouched added to his legendary status. According to most accounts, of the seventy mounted officers who rode into battle,

Washington alone escaped unscathed. A survivor baldly declared: "I expected every moment to see him fall. Nothing but the superintending care of Providence could have saved him." Washington himself reached much the same conclusion. "The miraculous care of Providence," he later wrote, "protected me beyond all human expectation."

Remarkably, one of the leading clergymen of the English-speaking world saw the young Virginian's astonishing survival as a hopeful sign of Washington's selection by the Almighty as a future deliverer of his people. Presbyterian minister Samuel Davies eventually became the fourth president of the College of New Jersey (later Princeton), and his five volumes of published sermons enjoyed great popularity on both sides of the Atlantic. In 1755, just weeks after Braddock's shattering defeat, he spoke in his church in Hanover County, Virginia, about the undiminished "martial fire" of the younger generation, adding an uncanny parenthetical remark: "I beg leave to point the attention of the public to that heroic youth, Col. George Washington, whom I cannot but hope Providence has preserved for some great service to his country." The idea that any twenty-three-year-old would strike older contemporaries as anointed for greatness, two decades before his selection for national leadership by the Continental Congress, gives some idea of the spiritual impression Washington left on those who encountered him.

True to the expectations of Reverend Davies and others, Washington's successful defiance of danger became a notable feature of his leadership during his eight years of service in the Revolutionary War. The general in chief frequently and fearlessly exposed himself to enemy fire, rallying his troops on many occasions by his own incomparable example. At the Battle of Princeton in January 1777, he rode at the head of his troops on a huge white horse as they marched directly on a well-formed British line. When the Americans came within range, both sides fired, and smoke from their rifles temporarily obscured Washington, who rode forward halfway between them. His aide, Richard Fitzgerald, covered his face with his hat in order to avoid watching the inevitable death of his beloved commander. But as the air cleared and he lowered his hat, he saw men on both sides who were dead and dying while Washington, unscathed, rose in his stirrups and urged his men forward against the shattered British line. "It's a fine fox chase, my boys!" he shouted.

A year and half later, in June 1778, the Marquis de Lafayette, the aristocratic Frenchman who became an esteemed general in the Continental Army, recalled the great man at the Battle of Monmouth, where "General Washington seemed to arrest fortune with one glance. . . . His presence stopped the retreat. . . . His graceful bearing on horseback, his calm and deportment which still retained a trace of displeasure . . . were all calculated to inspire the highest degree of enthusiasm. . . . I thought then as now that I had never beheld so superb a man."

Finally, one of the strangest episodes of the war again suggested a level of protection "beyond all human expectation."

On September 8, 1779, before the Battle of Brandywine, outside Philadelphia, General Washington and a fellow officer rode alone to reconnoiter the area between a key ford on Brandywine Creek and the British encampment of General Howe. They emerged into a clearing to get an unobstructed view, but came within range of four British sharpshooters who had concealed themselves in the trees. Major Patrick Ferguson, a Scotsman who had established himself as the most celebrated marksman of his day, commanded the snipers, equipped with the newly fashioned, deadly accurate, breech-loading rifles that he had recently invented and which had become known as "Ferguson rifles." Ferguson had amazed King George himself with a demonstration of his skill and took pride in hitting the most difficult of targets.

But on this September afternoon in Pennsylvania there was nothing difficult about the prime target he acquired: a tall American officer on a huge white horse, wearing a buff-and-blue uniform with a "remarkably large cocked hat." As his three associates awaited the command to fire, he decided instead that he preferred to capture the two men. He shouted out a command for Washington's companion to dismount, but instead the other American warned the general to gallop away to safety. Washington wheeled around calmly and apparently fixed Ferguson with his cold gray eyes, then turned away and rode out of range. A few days later, while recuperating from a wound sustained in the battle, Major Ferguson learned the identity of the large officer he had decided to spare. "I could have lodged half a dozen balls in him before he was out of my reach," the marksman observed, "but it was not pleasant to fire at the back of an unoffending individual who was acquitting himself very coolly of his duty—so I let him live." Later he lamented, "I am sorry that I did not know at the time who it was."

Ferguson himself died in combat a year later, leading local loyalists against the rebels at the Battle of Kings Mountain, near the border between North and South Carolina. The victorious forces then desecrated the body of the enemy commander, not knowing that they thereby dishonored the man whose sudden, unaccountable inclination almost surely saved their revolution.

"THE GREAT SPIRIT PROTECTS
THAT MAN"

This history of narrow escapes and battlefield invulnerability led one member of Washington's family to cite a haunting prophecy outside the Christian tradition as at least a partial explanation. The great man died on December 14, 1799, just days before the conclusion of the old century whose turbulent final decades he had dominated.

Ironically, the "Father of His Country" never had children of his own, thereby allowing all Americans of every generation an equal claim on George Washington as their personal forefather. Washington did, however, adopt two children relatively late in life: they were the grandchildren of his wife, Martha, whom George had married as a young widow. After the death of her son Jacky Custis at age twenty-six during the final months of the Revolutionary War, George agreed to adopt Jacky's two youngest children and to raise them as his own at Mount Vernon.

One of these adopted children and stepgrandchildren, George Washington Parke Custis, went on to win some notoriety of his own as a patriotic orator and playwright, and as father-in-law of Robert E. Lee. One of his most popular plays, *The Indian Prophecy, or Visions of Glory*, drew enthusiastic audiences when it was performed across the country beginning in 1827. Custis based his drama on a family story confirmed, he said, by Dr. James Craik, George Washington's lifelong friend and devoted physician, who accompanied him on his first treks into the Pennsylvania wilderness, served alongside the general throughout the Revolution, and applied the leading medical ideas of the era in an effort to overcome his final illness.

The "Indian prophecy" of the title alluded to a strange episode from 1770. Washington and Craik, along with a handful of friends, had ventured west of the mountains to explore wilderness lands in the modern-day state of West Virginia that they had acquired as an investment. Camped along the Kanawha River, they had begun preparing dinner in the late afternoon when a "party of Indians led by a trader" approached their fire. The trader, fluent in English and the native language, introduced the oldest member of his party as a "grand sachem" who had made a special journey when he learned that Colonel Washington was in the vicinity. According to Craik's story, as related by Custis, this aging chief "preserved toward Colonel Washington the most reverential deference. It was in vain that the colonel extended his hand, the Indian drew back, with the most impressive marks of awe and respect."

Eventually, as the visiting Indians joined the Virginians for their evening meal, Washington and Craik offered the "ardent spirits" that normally represented "the delight of the savages," but this time the great chief "bowed his head in submission but wetted not his lips." Finally, as the "council fire" roared, he addressed "our Washington":

> I am a chief, and the ruler over many tribes. . . . I have travelled a
> long and weary path, that I might see the young warrior of the great
> battle. It was on the day, when the white man's blood, mixed with
> the streams of our forest, that I first beheld this chief: I called to my
> young men and said, mark yon tall and daring warrior? He is not of
> the red-coat tribe—he hath an Indian's wisdom, and his warriors
> fight as we do—himself is alone exposed. Quick, let your aim be
> certain, and he dies. Our rifles were leveled, rifles which, but for
> him, knew not how to miss—'twas all in vain, a power mightier
> far than we, shielded him from harm. He can not die in battle. I
> am old, and soon shall be gathered to the great council-fire of my

fathers, in the land of shades, but ere I go, there is a something bids me speak, in the voice of prophecy. Listen! *The Great Spirit protects that man, and guides his destinies—he will become the chief of nations, and a people yet unborn, will hail him as the founder of a mighty empire!*

Custis went on to describe how the encounter in the western Virginia woods left "a most deep and lasting impression" on Dr. Craik, with whom he was personally well acquainted. During the Revolution, with his patient and friend repeatedly cheating death, Dr. Craik reportedly told officers, "Gentlemen, recollect what I have often told you, of the old Indian's prophecy. Yes, I do believe, a Great Spirit protects that man—and that one day or other, honored and beloved, he will be the chief of our nation, as he is now our general, our father, and our friend. Never mind the enemy, they can not kill him, and while he lives, our cause will never die."

Unlike the pretty fables about cherry trees and tossed silver dollars invented from whole cloth by the fanciful Parson Weems, this romantic tale originates with two individuals, Craik and Custis, who knew Washington well. The most intriguing question about the melodramatic "Indian prophecy," if anything like it did occur, would have involved its impact on Washington.

What would it mean to a man to hear again and again from his early twenties that he had been chosen by a higher power for a glorious and important destiny? We may never know if some "great sachem" actually perceived the workings of a "Great Spirit" in Washington's life, but we do know that leading pastors and politicians and even opposing generals most certainly did.

For his part, Washington himself often marveled at the supernatural safeguards that seemed to sustain his endeavors, but he always associated signs of heavenly favor with the cause he served rather than his personal standing. Though he never flinched from the notion that God had prepared a plan for his people, he remained too heavily engaged with the challenges the young nation faced to dwell too long on mystical speculation about his own role. In a typical reflection after the Battle of Monmouth, he wrote that "the hand of Providence has been so conspicuous in all this that he must be worse than an infidel that lacks faith, and more than wicked that has not gratitude enough to acknowledge his obligations—but it will be time enough for me to turn preacher when my present appointment ceases, and therefore I shall add no more on the Doctrine of Providence."

But his colleagues did add more, and joined with Washington in achieving a different sort of miracle, in order to rescue their revolution long after the fighting had ceased.

SIGNING THE CONSTITUTION: Independence Hall,
Philadelphia, September 17, 1787.

"I have no doubt that all their other measures will be good and wise. It is really an assembly of demigods." —Thomas Jefferson to John Adams, writing on August 30, 1787, from his post as minister to France

"AN ASSEMBLY OF DEMIGODS"

Confrontation, Compromise, and a Miraculous Convention

Those who deride the notion of American exceptionalism must confront an inconvenient truth about the struggle that launched the United States: among all such upheavals in some three thousand years of recorded human history, the American Revolution stands as the only one to achieve unequivocal, long-lasting success. In every other instance, revolutionary victories proved fleeting or destructive, leading in short order to disaster or tyranny.

In the first century B.C. the gladiator Spartacus led a sweeping slave revolt against the Roman Republic that achieved stunning triumphs on the battlefield before its complete collapse—and the crucifixion of some six thousand of its surviving participants along the Appian Way.

Nineteen centuries later, French insurrectionists overthrew the ancien régime, just six years after the Americans won independence. They sent the king to the guillotine and proclaimed a visionary republic that lasted barely a decade before yielding to Napoleon's dictatorship and unceasing warfare that brought four million casualties across Europe.

The many revolutions in Latin America against Spanish rule each generated chronic instability and intractable poverty, while twentieth-century upheavals in Russia and China produced tyranny and genocide that have lasted for centuries. The Russian Revolution led, in just seven years, to the genocidal Stalin. The Chinese Revolution brought Mao to power with the resulting slaughter of at least forty million civilians.

By contrast, the American Revolution not only achieved permanent and unequivocal independence for thirteen thriving British colonies but also, and more important, succeeded in establishing a wholly unprecedented, self-governing federal republic that has endured and prospered under the same remarkable blueprint, with periodic adjustments, for more than two hundred years.

The leaders who directed the military victories of the War for Independence viewed heavenly intervention as the key element in their success. But the political turmoil that inevitably followed their battlefield struggles produced benevolent results that contemporaries hailed as equally dependent on providential assistance.

From the Constitutional Convention in Philadelphia, James Madison, anointed by subsequent generations as the "Father of the Constitution," wrote to his friend Thomas Jefferson in Paris that he found it "impossible" to "consider the degree of concord which ultimately prevailed as less than a miracle." George Washington emphatically agreed. "It seems to me, then, little short of a miracle," he wrote to the Marquis de Lafayette on February 7, 1788, "that delegates from so many different States (which States you know are also different from each other in their manners, circumstances, and prejudices), should unite in forming a system of national Government, so little liable to well-found objections."

"A HEROIC AND LAWLESS ACT"

This achievement seemed unexpected and wondrous in part because the grand conclave in Philadelphia over which Washington personally presided had never once called itself a constitutional convention. The Congress that authorized the gathering, operating under the Articles of Confederation, which had linked the states in a flimsy "league of friendship with each other" since February 1781, never anticipated a wholly new charter for a powerful national government. The resolution sanctioning the Federal Convention declared that it would meet for the "sole and express purpose of revising the Articles of Confederation"—not for junking those articles entirely and replacing them with a wholly new constitution. No wonder that Martin Van Buren, president of the United States from 1837 to 1841 and one of the leading lawyers of his age, would look back on the work of the Philadelphia convention as a "heroic and lawless act."

That bold initiative became necessary due to the notorious ineffectiveness of the Confederation Congress during the war and for some six years after—an ineffectiveness that stemmed mostly from governmental design flaws in the Articles of Confederation themselves. The document allotted each of the states a single congressional vote, so mighty Virginia carried no more weight than remote and sparsely settled Georgia, despite Virginia having twenty times the population and perhaps fifty times the wealth. Each state legislature selected two delegates to Congress, and if those two representatives split over any issue, their state registered no vote at all. The often frustrated delegates served only one-year terms, and Congress itself could do nothing to provide a stipend or cover the heavy travel expenses for many of its members; payment came, if it came at all, from the often balky states. As a result, the only empowered body of the national government frequently lacked a quorum (which required both delegates of at least seven states) and could barely function at all when military matters, foreign policy, and financial appropriations required the formal assent of nine states or more.

Even when the Confederation Congress managed to gather a quorum, the government lacked a reliable seat for its functions or any semblance of a national capital. In 1783, a dangerous mutiny in the Philadelphia barracks chased the delegates from the continent's largest city: veterans of the Revolutionary struggle threatened a military coup because the feckless legislature was unable to pay their promised wages and pensions. Congress then wandered from Princeton, New Jersey, to Annapolis, Maryland, next to Trenton, New Jersey, and then to New York, convening endless debates about the difficulty of finding any town that might actually welcome its permanent presence. "It will soon be of very little consequence where Congress go," wrote Oliver Ellsworth, who represented Connecticut in this less-than-august body, "if they are not made respectable as well as responsible, which can never be done without giving them a power to perform engagements as well as make them." Washington and the other leaders who had guided the struggle for independence remained painfully aware that the "eyes of all the world" watched their unprecedented experiment in self-government, and they felt acute embarrassment at its frequent follies and failures.

Worst of all, the lack of any executive authority to represent the loose federation of states exposed the new nation to numerous threats from foreign powers. With Florida and the vast territory of Louisiana recently coming under Spanish control, the colonial authorities in Madrid schemed openly to seize the land that later became the American states of Tennessee and Kentucky, paying generous bribes to a retired American general named James Wilkinson in return for his oath to lead his Tennessee neighbors in repudiation of the United States. Meanwhile, the British plotted shamelessly to divide New York from New England by taking over the rugged region of the Green Mountains and adding it to their Canadian colonies.

Most worrisome of all, the lack of economic organization on a national scale led to widespread hardship that threatened every region with anarchy and even insurrection. The Articles of Confederation allowed the states to issue their own currency, often resulting in paper money that fluctuated wildly in value or proved utterly worthless. Congress also lacked authority to compel its constituent states to help pay the national debts incurred during the fight for independence, and showed itself powerless in resolving bitter commercial and trade disputes that frequently poisoned interstate relationships.

By 1786, leaders of the Confederation Congress and several state legislatures became concerned enough about the deteriorating situation to summon representatives of all states to a meeting in Annapolis to try to reach agreement on a broader plan for regulation of commerce. As soon as representatives of five states arrived in Maryland, they produced a proposal for another convention at Philadelphia the following year with the more ambitious aim of overall reform.

"DISORDERLY, RIOTOUS AND SEDITIOUS PERSONS"

This development coincided with alarming news from embattled villages in western Massachusetts, where frustrated subsistence farmers and war veterans had begun shutting down local courts to stop foreclosure proceedings and other attempts to collect debts and taxes. When the Supreme Judicial Court indicted the leaders of these protests as "disorderly, riotous and seditious persons," the antigovernment activism blossomed into full-scale rebellion. Daniel Shays, the son of Irish immigrants and a wounded but fearless militia captain who fought five years in the Revolutionary War, organized a new rebel army that eventually numbered more than fifteen hundred armed men determined to bring down "the tyrannical government of Massachusetts." Three major bands of rebels converged on the Springfield armory in order to seize more guns. Despite the fact that this was a federal facility, no federal troops appeared in its defense, since Congress lacked the funds to pay them. Instead, local militias rallied to confront the Shaysites (as the insurrectionists became known) and caught a lucky, or providential, break on the snowy eve of their climactic confrontation when they intercepted a message from one of the rebel leaders to the others.

In the fighting that followed, four died and twenty were wounded. Eventually, more than four thousand participants in Shays' Rebellion signed confessions in exchange for amnesty; some of the more prominent figures, including Captain Daniel Shays, were pardoned after their indictment. He lived another thirty-seven years, drinking heavily and surviving on the army pension he belatedly received for his military service in the Revolution, before dying in squalor on a small homestead in upstate New York.

The bloody turmoil in New England generated real terror throughout the country and certainly stirred the delegates to the new Federal Convention, who began gathering in Philadelphia just four months after the rebellion's collapse. "The eyes of the United States are turned upon this assembly and the expectations raised to a very anxious degree," declared George Mason of Virginia. "May God grant that we may be able to gratify them by establishing a wise and just government."

"THE GREATEST MAN IN THE WORLD"

Most important, Shays' Rebellion helped to motivate George Washington to leave comfortable retirement at his beloved Mount Vernon to join the assembling delegates and preside over their deliberations in Philadelphia. "Good God!" he wrote to his friend Henry Lee before departing to the burgeoning metropolis on the Delaware. "I am mortified beyond expression, when I view the clouds that have spread over the brightest morn that ever dawned in any country. . . . What a triumph for our enemies, to verify their predictions! What a triumph for the advocates of despotism, to find that we are incapable of governing ourselves, and that systems founded on the basis of equal liberty, are merely ideal and fallacious."

Four years earlier, he had astonished observers around the globe when he resigned his position as commander in chief of a victorious army and returned to private pursuits in northern Virginia. In England, the famous American expatriate painter Benjamin West spoke with King George III during a garden stroll and predicted that Washington would leave public life at the conclusion of hostilities. "If he does that, he will be the greatest man in the world," replied the doubtful monarch.

The retired general felt naturally reluctant to undermine his claims to greatness by returning to the public fray, whatever his concerns about the feeble status of a failing confederation. Nevertheless, he privately expressed rising confidence in the prospects for the upcoming convention. "These disorders are evident marks of a defective government," he wrote to Lafayette. "Indeed, the thinking part of the people of this Country are now so well satisfied of this fact that most of the Legislatures have appointed, & the rest it is said will appoint, delegates to meet at Philadelphia the second Monday in May next in general Convention of the States to revise, and correct the defects of the federal system."

Eventually all the states save one did eventually select delegates for that purpose, and those representatives slowly made their way toward Pennsylvania. Rhode Island refused to cooperate because its legislature recently had been captured by a radical agrarian faction that stubbornly resisted the idea of providing any expanded powers to a national government. For some three years, "Little Rhody" refused to even consider the Constitution that the other twelve states had approved, richly earning the popular nickname "Rogue Island."

Washington finally made up his mind barely a month before the convention's scheduled start. "I declare to you that my assent is given contrary to my judgment," he wrote to Virginia's recently elected thirty-three-year-old governor, Edmund Randolph. "I have yielded however to what appeared to be the earnest wishes of my friends, and I will hope for the best." As historian Edward J. Larson notes in his spellbinding book *The Return of George Washington* (2014), extensive correspondence with the scholarly, visionary James Madison played a major role in the general's ultimate decision. In laying out his plans for a radical restructuring of the federal government, Madison assured the national hero that some of the driving younger spirits of the convention would fight for the sweeping changes Washington himself considered absolutely necessary, rather than merely readjusting details of the Articles of Confederation.

The general made the 150-mile journey from his home to Philadelphia in five jolting days, riding in an elegant carriage manned by three of his slaves. These attendants included the highly valued William Lee, who had ridden and fought alongside Washington during all the dangerous years of the war. In his will, the general provided for the eventual freedom of all the slaves he owned but singled out Lee for immediate manumission. He also granted his faithful servant a yearly pension in hard currency, along with authorization to live out his life in Mount Vernon if he so chose. Lee is buried there, having outlived his master by twenty-nine years.

SETTING THE AGENDA

In Philadelphia, Washington took up residence as a house guest of the Pennsylvania delegate Robert Morris, the nation's most successful banker and financier and without doubt one of North America's wealthiest individuals. The Morris mansion counted as one of the most gracious homes on the continent, said to rival anything in London. It also provided the advantage of close proximity to the convention's meeting place, the Pennsylvania State House, today known as Independence Hall because the Great Declaration had been approved there some eleven years earlier.

Also within easy walking distance was the home of eighty-one-year-old Benjamin Franklin, the other world-famous figure to grace the Federal Convention with his presence. While waiting for the arrival of other delegates to constitute the quorum, Dr. Franklin invited all those who had already showed up in Philadelphia to a festive dinner at his home. These delegates, almost entirely from Pennsylvania or Virginia, felt surprised when their host replaced the sweet wine customary on such occasions with porter—a strong, dark, hearty English beer. Later, Franklin happily reported to the brewer in London that "when the cask was broached, the company agreed unanimously that it was the best porter they had ever tasted." During the humid, oppressive heat of a Philadelphia summer, delegates followed eighteenth-century practice and sought regular relief in the consumption of prodigious quantities of alcohol—with one account book showing that twelve honored guests at another delegate dinner managed the extraordinary feat of draining sixty bottles of Madeira.

No doubt fueled by the generous libations, delegates from Virginia and Pennsylvania made use of the time before the convention's formal opening to reach agreement on a comprehensive new scheme of government devised by the scholarly, frail, diminutive James Madison. The result was the Virginia Plan, consisting of fifteen detailed "resolves" officially proposed by the Old Dominion's dashing young governor, Edmund Randolph, in one of the gathering's opening sessions on May 29. The plan would establish three distinct branches of government meant to check and balance one another, replacing the ineffectual, unicameral Confederation Congress. A powerful executive, selected by the legislative branch, could work in concert with members of the judiciary in a special council to overrule decisions of the new Congress. That Congress would consist of two chambers, not one, with both based on proportional representation instead of the one-state, one vote provision of the Articles of Confederation. Members of the larger, "popular" House would face election every three years, and would in turn elect the members of the upper chamber to longer, seven-year terms, basing those selections on formal nominations submitted by the state legislatures. Most important, the new national government would exercise "supreme" power even over those decisions made at the state level. To reduce conflict between often quarrelsome states, Congress, by a vote of both houses, could overrule any state law of which it disapproved.

Only portions of the Virginia Plan made their way into the final draft of the Constitution, but Madison and Randolph succeeded in setting the agenda for the convention. From the beginning, the delegates began debating an entirely fresh vision for a powerful national government rather than meeting for "the sole and express purpose of revising the Articles of Confederation," as the Confederation Congress had instructed them to do.

For more than four months, the fifteen elements of the Virginia Plan provided the blueprint for their daily deliberations and bitter disagreements as they struggled to put together a system of government altogether unprecedented in human history. A dozen delegates gave up in disgust during the maddening and seemingly endless process, going home to tend to personal business or local politics. Of the fifty-five delegates who participated at some point in the convention's sessions, only forty-three remained for the conclusion of its work, and three of those expressed such strong disappointment with the final product that they refused to sign the document. At several points in the summer, the participants faced the real prospect that a majority would abandon the entire project due to intractable differences among the states and even within state delegations.

"AN INEVITABLE CHAIN OF CAUSES AND EFFECTS"

Two early but crucial decisions allowed the work to continue and enabled the contentious conclave to complete its daunting task.

First, all delegates pledged total secrecy regarding the nature or substance of their debates; even during the hottest days of summer they covered all windows with shutters and curtains to avoid prying eyes. Philadelphia at the time boasted twelve daily or weekly newspapers, an astonishingly vigorous press for a city of less than fifty thousand. These publications ranged from enthusiastic support for the Federal Convention (expressed by most of them) to a few cynics who sneered at the gathering from the beginning as a conspiratorial power grab. Amazingly, even disgruntled participants who left the convention long before its conclusion maintained their vows of secrecy, confirming their reputations as men of honor. The public knew nothing of the early consensus to scrap the creaky institutions of the Confederation and replace them with a sweeping new scheme, and only learned of the often angry nature of the constitutional debates with publication of the detailed daily notes (and often word-for-word transcriptions) obsessively scribbled by the industrious James Madison during every session. In the spirit of confidentiality that prevailed throughout the summer, he promised to withhold these records from the press and from history until all the delegates had died. In one of those strange coincidences that sounds as if it must have been arranged, Madison himself, who died at age eighty-five in 1836, turned out to be that last survivor.

The second decision that enabled the convention to hold together involved Washington's determination, as unanimously elected president of the body, to allow debate on each issue separately, rather than forcing early decisions on the overall architecture for a new governmental structure. This meant that the fifteen points of the Virginia Plan came up for discussion individually, rather than demanding early resolution of the one explosive, unavoidable dispute that at several points came close to shattering the entire assembly.

That issue wasn't slavery, though delegates debated the existence of that cruel, ancient institution with considerable fervor. Surprisingly, the most passionate voice calling for an immediate end to the "infernal traffic" in captive Africans came from the Virginia delegation. George Mason, a wealthy plantation owner and brilliant lawyer who personally owned more than two hundred slaves, had come to see slavery as "a slow Poison ... daily contaminating the Minds and Morals of our People." He argued that holding slaves would "bring the judgment of heaven on a Country ... As nations cannot be rewarded or punished in the next world they must be in this. By an inevitable chain of causes & effects providence punishes national sins, by national calamities."

Mason's insistence led to a compromise clause (Article I, Section 9) that blocked Congress from ending the "importation" of slaves only until 1808, thereby implicitly authorizing that action thereafter. A previous compromise resulted in the notorious "three-fifths clause" for counting slaves in the apportionment of seats in the House of Representatives. Elbridge Gerry, a Massachusetts delegate and future vice president of the United States, argued that since southern states treated their slaves "as property," enslaved people had no more right to representation in Congress than the horses or dogs their masters also purported to own. As a concession to restive southerners, already worried about more rapid population growth in the northern states, each of their slaves would count as three-fifths of a free citizen for purposes of representation and taxation. None of the delegates expressed pride in this strange arrangement, and all of them seemed to feel embarrassment and discomfort over every question regarding the "peculiar institution." The word "slave" or "slavery" never appears in the Constitution; the framers substituted evasive euphemisms to convey their meaning.

Other issues sparked similarly vigorous disagreement, including the shape of the new executive branch of government. Many delegates feared the concentration of power in the hands of a single chief executive, preferring two or even three "co-executives" who might balance each other's ambitions, on the model of the two consuls who once led the Roman Republic. The constitutional framers also split on whether to authorize financial compensation for members of the new Congress. Franklin and others felt strongly that representatives of the people should serve without payment from the public purse, in order to discourage officeholders from viewing politics as a long-term career that could distance them from the people they were meant to represent.

Despite the significance of these disputes, the delegates managed to reach rough consensus after spirited debate. On every question a majority prevailed, with each state delegation entitled to a single vote. The convention strongly preferred a government with one chief executive to a system of two or three competing authorities. Everyone assumed that Washington would become the first executive under the new Constitution, and he had never displayed a frightening appetite for power that required structural checks. The delegates also decided to allow Congress to pay its members, in part to allow participation by leaders of modest means who otherwise couldn't afford the time and money required to travel great distances to do the people's business.

"IS IT FOR *MEN*, OR FOR THE IMAGINARY BEINGS CALLED *STATES*?"

Only one argument paralyzed the convention and threatened to send its squabbling participants home in frustration: the core question of proportional representation. That issue deeply divided the large states—Virginia, Pennsylvania, and Massachusetts—from their less populous and less powerful counterparts. The Virginia Plan called for proportional representation in both houses of a new bicameral legislature, giving the big states the dominant role to which their wealth and population arguably entitled them. To this, the smaller states countered with the New Jersey Plan, in which a single legislative chamber would resemble the Confederation Congress (or the Federal Convention itself), with each state, no matter how small or how large, receiving the same level of representation.

William Paterson of New Jersey, a small man standing barely five feet two inches, seemed an appropriate advocate for the viewpoint of the small states. He argued that a scheme of government such as the one envisioned by the Virginia Plan would never pass muster with the Confederation Congress, which hadn't authorized such sweeping changes, nor would it win ratification by the smaller states, fearful of their potentially powerless status in the new arrangements. James Wilson of Pennsylvania proved ready with a telling riposte. "Why should a national government be unpopular?" he demanded. "Will a citizen of *Delaware* be degraded by becoming a citizen of the *United States?*"

Wilson, widely recognized as one of the finest legal minds in the country, had been born in Scotland and educated at the venerable universities of St. Andrews (established in 1411) and Edinburgh (established in 1583). A signer of the Declaration of Independence, he became an early advocate for an overriding national identity, above any local or regional loyalties. This position made him intensely controversial with more parochial agitators during the Revolution, some of whom in October 1779 consumed too much alcohol, stormed his house, and tried to lynch him; it took the intervention of scores of soldiers from the Continental Army to rescue him at the last moment. Wilson spoke with a pronounced Scottish burr, and his critics derided him as "Caledonia James." But no one—not Madison, Hamilton, Franklin, or Randolph—played a larger role in the debates at the Constitutional Convention, where Wilson addressed the delegates 168 times, displaying consistent brilliance and persuasive force. Benjamin Rush, who watched Wilson's remarkable performance in that forum, described his mind as "one blaze of light."

In that spirit, he tried to illuminate the logic of the small-state representatives. "Can we forget for whom we are forming a government?" asked Wilson. "Is it for *men,* or for the imaginary beings called *states?*" Later he thundered against the inequity of the one-state/one-vote scheme. "Are not the citizens of Pennsylvania equal to those of New Jersey?" asked Wilson. "Does it require 150 of the former to balance 50 of the latter?" He passionately argued for proportional representation, allowing citizens—but not states—comparable representation in the legislature. "If the small states will not confederate on this plan, Pennsylvania and I presume some other states will not confederate on any other."

For Paterson and his allies, this ultimatum seemed to threaten the cherished principle of state sovereignty. "We are met here as the deputies of thirteen independent, sovereign states, for federal purposes," he pleaded. "Can we consolidate their sovereignty and form one nation and annihilate the sovereignties of our states who have sent us here for other purposes?" If they made that attempt, Paterson warned, the public would reject the product of their labors. "The people of America are sharpsighted and not to be deceived. The idea of a national government as contradistinguished from a federal one never entered into the mind of any of them."

"ON THE VERGE OF DISSOLUTION"

The argument raged for nearly three weeks, with the heat of the rhetoric rising steadily along with the temperature of the summer. The convention allowed occasional interruptions to discuss less contentious topics but returned, inevitably, to the logjam over representation in the new Congress. In an attempt to break the deadlock, Roger Sherman of Connecticut tried to offer a workable compromise. He endorsed the bicameral legislature of the Virginia Plan and accepted the idea that its lower house would rely on proportional representation. But why not offer protection for the smaller states by giving each state an equal vote in the upper house, the Senate? Sherman, rough-hewn and plainspoken, enjoyed considerable respect as one of the "grand old men" of the convention—he had helped to write the Declaration of Independence as well as the Articles of Confederation. But true believers on both sides of the great divide weren't ready for his split-the-difference approach and pushed aside the Connecticut Plan.

Instead, delegates voted to apply proportional representation to the lower house of Congress, ensuring big-state domination of the House of Representatives. Virginia, Pennsylvania, and Massachusetts brought along enough support from smaller-state allies to carry the day. This meant that those who wanted the same representation for each state would make their last stand in fighting to impose that scheme on the Senate; if they lost that battle, several delegates planned to abandon the convention and go home. This sense of desperation came out in two intemperate speeches that drove the gathering to the point of collapse.

First, Luther Martin of Maryland seized the floor and held it for a three-hour harangue that his colleagues unanimously described as an ordeal. A brilliant and pugnacious Baltimore lawyer famous for his angry, confrontational style and his heavy drinking, Martin gave evidence of early morning inebriation to many of those who witnessed his performance. He vehemently attacked even decisions that had been broadly accepted after previous votes by his fellow delegates. He particularly scorned the very notion of a two-chamber legislature. "I have never heard of a confederacy having two legislative branches," he shouted. "What are called human feelings in this instance are only the feelings of ambition and the lust for power."

The following morning brought Martin back to his feet again with, according to Madison, "much diffuseness and considerable vehemence." One message came across unmistakably, however rhetorically impaired the messenger: he dared Virginia, Pennsylvania, and Massachusetts to form their own confederation, while the smaller ten states would form a rival association on a more worthy basis. After the convention, Connecticut delegate Oliver Ellsworth recalled that Luther Martin had disgraced himself in "a speech which held during two days and might have continued two months, but for those marks of fatigue and disgust you saw strongly expressed on whichever side of the house you turned your mortified eyes."

An even more incendiary performance came a few days later from one of the convention's more obscure participants, Gunning Bedford of Delaware. A onetime College of New Jersey classmate of James Madison's, Bedford had become a wealthy, corpulent Wilmington lawyer who seemed to savor every moment of his own fiery oratory. On a steamy Saturday in July, he explicitly accused the big states of bad faith. "They insist ... they never will hurt or injure the lesser states. I do not, gentlemen, trust you," he sneered.

What followed was even worse. "Where is your plighted faith?" he asked. "Will you crush the smaller states?" According to Bedford, if those threatened states formed their own confederation, "the fault will be yours and all the nations of the earth will justify us. . . . The large states dare not dissolve the confederation. If they do, the small ones will find some foreign ally of more honor and good faith to take them by the hand and do them justice."

The mention of "some foreign ally" taking small states "by the hand," with its hints of seeking European aid to damage other Americans, produced shouts of outrage from Bedford's listeners. The ominous words of the delegate from Delaware and the continuing impasse on the substantive issues left all participants in a gloomy mood. During this low point in the proceedings, Washington received a visit from one of his former French officers, DeMaussion. The young man wrote to his mother that the great general wore a solemn, suffering countenance each day when he left the State House: "The expression on his face reminded me of its expression during the terrible months we were in Valley Forge Camp." Washington himself wrote to Hamilton, temporarily back in New York to attend to local business, that "I almost despair of seeing a favorable issue to the proceedings of the Convention and do therefore repent having had any agency in the business." Even bibulous, truculent Luther Martin, who had made his own significant contributions to the crisis, recalled that "we were on the verge of dissolution, scarce held together by the strength of an hair."

"IS IT PROBABLE THAT AN EMPIRE CAN RISE WITHOUT HIS AID?"

Neither historians nor the participants themselves have ever reached full agreement on the factors that enabled the dejected delegates to somehow continue with their great work. But the contemporary accounts of eyewitnesses and the later reflections of the primary participants suggest that some powerful combination of God, the Fourth of July, and providential perspective managed to rescue the Constitutional Convention from looming catastrophe.

The intrusion of the Almighty appeared to occur at a crucial moment between the coruscating speeches by Luther Martin and Gunning Bedford.

After a particularly frustrating morning of declamation and denunciation, Benjamin Franklin took advantage of a lull in the argument to make one of his rare speeches of the convention. At age eighty-one, Franklin attended the proceedings nearly every day, making the brief journey from his nearby home in an elegant sedan chair, carried by four prisoners from a local penal institution he had helped to organize. This prison, like most endeavors to which the old man lent his hand, exemplified the most enlightened ideas of the age: promoting rehabilitation for its errant inmates by assigning them to useful chores outside its walls. The prisoners duly transported their world-famous cargo every morning, and then waited outside the closed doors and shuttered windows of the State House until he was ready to return home. Inside, his fellow delegates viewed the scientist and statesman with awe and reverence, despite his age and infirmities. William Pierce of Georgia wrote home from the convention that "Dr. Franklin is well known to be the greatest philosopher of the present age. The very heavens obey him, and the Clouds yield up the Lightning to be imprisoned in his rod."

The old man watched and listened attentively but seldom participated personally in the ebb and flow of debate. When he did, his unsteady legs made it uncomfortable to stand for more than moments at a time, and his voice generally lacked the firmness and force to allow him to address the gathering directly. On most occasions he handed prepared texts to James Wilson, his fellow member of the Pennsylvania delegation, who in turn read out the carefully chosen words in his ringing Scots burr. But at the critical juncture of June 28, Dr. Franklin appears to have spoken for himself, rising at his table and demanding attention in late afternoon just before the end of the session. The delegates would have observed absolute silence and focused their full attention in order to hear the words of their assembly's most venerable figure.

He began by noting "the small progress we have made" and lamenting the

> melancholy proof of the imperfection of the Human Understanding . . . In this situation of this Assembly, groping as it were in the

dark to find political truth, and scarce able to distinguish it when presented to us, how has it happened, Sir, that we have not hitherto once thought of humbly applying to the Father of lights to illuminate our understandings? In the beginning of the Contest with Great Britain, when we were sensible of danger we had daily prayer in this room for the divine protection. Our prayers, Sir, were heard, and they were graciously answered. All of us who were engaged in the struggle must have observed frequent instances of a Superintending providence in our favor. To that kind providence we owe this happy opportunity of consulting in peace on the means of establishing our future national felicity. And have we now forgotten that powerful friend?

I have lived, Sir, a long time, and the longer I live, the more convincing proofs I see of this truth—that God governs in the affairs of men. And if a sparrow cannot fall to the ground without his notice, is it probable that an empire can rise without his aid? We have been assured, Sir, in the sacred writings, that "except the Lord build the House they labour in vain that build it." I firmly believe this; and I also believe that without his concurring aid we shall succeed in this political building no better than the Builders of Babel: We shall be divided by our little partial local interests; our projects will be confounded, and we ourselves shall become a reproach and a bye word down to future ages. And what is worse, mankind may hereafter from this unfortunate instance, despair of establishing Governments by Human Wisdom and leave it to chance, war and conquest.

I therefore beg leave to move, that henceforth prayers imploring the assistance of Heaven, and its blessings on our deliberations, be held in this Assembly every morning before we proceed to business, and that one or more of the Clergy of the City be requested to officiate in that service.

This remarkable statement, copied by Madison from Franklin's own handwritten text, surely made a profound impact on the delegates. According to one of them, General Jonathan Dayton of New

Jersey, speaking years later to William Steele: "The doctor sat down, and never did I behold a countenance at once so dignified and delighted as was that of Washington, at the close of the address! Nor were the members of the Convention, generally less affected. . . . A silent admiration superseded, for a moment, the expression of that assent and approbation which was strongly marked on almost every countenance."

Still, the delegates declined to approve Franklin's motion. Several leaders of the body, including Edmund Randolph, offered their enthusiastic agreement with the old man's sentiments, but Alexander Hamilton made the sensible argument that suddenly employing local ministers to lead prayers at the previously secret proceedings would surely alert the prying press to the convention's precarious state. The well-intentioned resort to worship would thereby "lead the public to believe that the embarrassments and dissensions within the Convention had suggested this measure."

Madison's notes make clear, however, that the main reason the gathering never voted on Franklin's motion came from Hugh Williamson of North Carolina, who "observed that the true cause of the omission could not be mistaken. The Convention had no funds." In other words, the assembled founding fathers lacked the resources to pay pastors to preside over formal prayers, according to the custom of the time.

Franklin drily summarized the response to his eloquent plea in a handwritten note at the bottom of the original draft of his speech: "The convention, except three or four persons, thought prayer unnecessary." Nevertheless, many of those who listened to the old man's plea remember the occasion as a turning point. William Few of Georgia described the morning session of that steamy day at the end of June as "an awful and critical moment. If the Convention had then adjourned, the dissolution of the union of the states seemed inevitable." Franklin's words altered the atmosphere, reminding his bickering colleagues of the eternal significance of their endeavors and of the divine supervision that they all perceived as essential to the success of their revolution. He called their attention to the fateful coincidence that they toiled every day in precisely the same chamber in which an earlier group of squabbling delegates had declared independence eleven years earlier, almost to the day.

With commemoration of that sacred occasion just six days away, Governor Randolph closed the proceedings with a widely praised suggestion: "that a sermon be preached at the request of the convention on the 4th of July, the anniversary of Independence." As the weary delegates spilled out onto the sultry streets and made their way to taverns, rooming houses, or private clubs to take their dinner and refresh their spirits, they surely looked forward to the upcoming celebration—with the convention in recess for the day—and thought of the improvised union of disparate states that had made independence possible.

After the break for church and rest on Sunday, July 1, the delegates reassembled on Monday morning for the most fateful single vote of the convention. The small states still insisted on imposing the one-state/one-vote plan on the upper house of the new legislature, and they had never withdrawn their strongly implied threat to bolt both the convention and the union of states if they proved unable to get their way. Madison, Wilson, and the big-state bloc felt confident that they had the votes to prevail with their demand for proportional representation, and expressed the determination to move ahead with their plans for union even if some small states petulantly excluded themselves.

AN INEXPLICABLE STROLL

As it happened, the final decision depended on the one most obscure and mysterious participant in the writing of the Constitution. Two riddles about Daniel of St. Thomas Jenifer have never been solved: the origins of his odd and aristocratic middle name and the burial site of the wealthy scion of a prominent Maryland family. A lifelong bachelor consumed by politics, he left his famous and extensive library to his close friend James Madison and his eight-hundred-acre plantation to a distant relative. In his will, he also arranged to free his remaining twenty-two slaves within six years of his death.

At Philadelphia, Daniel Jenifer cut an elegant but mostly silent figure with his expensive imported clothes and ruffled sleeves, at age sixty-four enjoying his status as one of the convention's "wise old men" along with Ben Franklin and Roger Sherman. Though representing Maryland, which was numbered among the small states, Jenifer voted reliably with Madison and the Virginia-Pennsylvania axis on the issue of proportional representation. He believed strongly in a powerful central government deriving its power directly from the people, rather than supporting a loose confederation of coequal states. In this he disagreed, respectfully, with his fellow Marylander, the obstreperous Luther Martin.

Throughout the summer, with two of Maryland's other delegates frequently absent from the proceedings, Martin and Jenifer canceled each other and thereby nullified their state's vote in every final tally. The big-state coalition depended on this Maryland deadlock to protect its majority at the convention and counted on the genial, reliable Jenifer to show up for every important vote; his attendance record in Philadelphia registered as second to none. But on the decisive Monday morning on which the state delegations finally faced the single most contentious issue of the convention, Jenifer inexplicably got up from his chair, ambled out of the State House, and wandered off onto the city streets. No one ever learned exactly where he went, but the gentleman returned to the proceedings as soon as the tally had concluded. He had absented himself from history just long enough for Luther Martin alone to control Maryland's vote on equal representation for every state.

Jenifer left behind no explanation for his baffling behavior before he died three years later, but historians have no doubt as to his motivations: he knew that small-state representatives weren't bluffing when they spoke of leaving the convention over this issue. Given the fact that representation in the House of Representatives had already been arranged in the way the big states desired, Jenifer's broad, nationalist viewpoint led him to allow their triumph over equal votes in the Senate and to save the convention. In other words, he deliberately threw the result and ensured the defeat of his faction in order to deliver a larger victory for his country. Without the foresight of this forgotten founder, it's likely that several states would have left the convention and ruined any chance that the Constitution could have been ratified by the nine states needed. It's not too much to conclude that a brief midmorning stroll by the little-known Daniel of St. Thomas Jenifer changed the course of the history of the world.

One other unexpected factor helped the small-state faction in its final vote total and made a contribution to the convention's survival. On the Sunday night before the deciding vote, two Georgia delegates boarded a carriage for New York that took them away from the convention at its most important moment. These two delegates, William Pierce and William Few, were both members of the Confederation Congress and hurried off to its sessions to help settle a dispute on western lands in which they probably had a personal financial interest. Both men also counted as strong supporters of the Virginia Plan and its scheme of proportional representation because they believed a stronger national government would help in the development of the West. With Pierce and Few riding through the night to the temporary capital in Manhattan, the Georgia delegation was left with just two members. One of them, Abraham Baldwin, had lived most of his life in Connecticut before moving to the Deep South and maintained friendships with Roger Sherman, Oliver Ellsworth, and other small-state die-hards from the Nutmeg State.

Since voting proceeded geographically, from north to south, in convention roll calls, Georgia enjoyed the privilege of voting last. Before its decision the tally showed a precise tie: five states (including Jenifer's Maryland) in favor of equal representation in the Senate, and five states firmly against. The Madison-Wilson faction confidently awaited the final vote; on all previous occasions, Georgia had sided with proportional representation and against equal votes in the Senate. This time, however, with two delegates suddenly missing, Abraham Baldwin cast his lot with his Connecticut friends, dividing his delegation and canceling Georgia's vote. This left the tally evenly divided and caused relief and jubilation among the small-state champions; their hopes had survived a vote they expected to lose.

While Madison, Wilson, and most of their allies sat in stunned consternation, General Charles Cotesworth Pinckney of South Carolina shot to his feet with a motion. While he declared his personal reluctance to abandon the principle of proportional representation, which he had always supported, he insisted that a saving compromise must now be reached. To achieve that purpose he proposed a committee, with one representative from every state, to work out the necessary details. Crusty old Roger Sherman rose to announce his support. "We are now at full stop," he drawled, "and nobody I suppose meant that we should break up without doing something." Other delegates from every faction took the floor and quickly, adamantly declared their support. The convention's choice of members for this committee made clear the emerging consensus for a viable compromise that would satisfy the nervous small states. The designated committee members included Benjamin Franklin, Roger Sherman, Luther Martin, William Paterson, and Abraham Baldwin, whose last-minute switch paved the way for the new spirit of accommodation that seemed suddenly to sweep the gathering.

THE STALE AIR ITSELF SEEMED TO CHANGE

That same cooperative attitude gathered further momentum with the great patriotic holiday celebrated across the country just two days later. In Philadelphia, festivities began before dawn with the mustering of the city's militia, firing its first celebratory blasts into the air at 6:00 a.m. and waking any laggards who remained in bed. The artillery followed, using all available field pieces to deliver three-times-thirteen rounds of booming cannon fire—a "triple huzzah" to honor all thirteen states of the Union. Throughout the morning, bells rang out from every steeple, and the city vibrated with joyful noise.

At eleven, George Washington led many of the delegates through the crowded streets to hear a special Independence Day sermon delivered in their honor at the Reformed Calvinist Church, as promised by Edmund Randolph to Dr. Franklin. The remarks by James Campbell expressed soaring hopes for the work of the visiting statesmen, who, he assumed, were busy with the great work of "binding our states together by mutual interests and obligations." The orator expressed total confidence in their ultimate triumph, as if it had been preordained. "Methinks I already see the stately fabric of a free and vigorous government rising out of the wisdom of the Federal Convention," he concluded. Some of his listeners must have felt grateful for their vows of secrecy, which kept such admirers from knowing how close their proceedings had recently come to exploding in acrimony.

After midday, young troops joined with grizzled veterans of the Revolutionary War in parading to the stirring music of fife and drum. As the balmy evening descended, a prodigious display of fireworks produced gasps of amazement and attracted a huge crowd, while similar throngs made their way to the city's many taverns. There the libations flowed freely, with frequent toasts to honor the delegates gathered in William Penn's city. One typical example: "To the Federal Convention—may the result of their meeting be as glorious as its members are illustrious." Across the river in New Jersey, they toasted "the Grand Convention, may they form a constitution for an eternal republic."

With such exhortations in mind, those illustrious members returned to their familiar places in the State House the next morning, filled with renewed dedication and confidence about the mission at hand. After just three days of quick deliberations, fueled by another well-lubricated dinner at Franklin's house, the compromise committee presented its report providing a permanent outline for the American system of government. Representation in the lower house of Congress would be based on the population of each state, while every state would receive the same number of senators in the upper chamber, to be chosen by state legislatures. As a concession to big-state advocates, money-related bills could originate only in the populist House of Representatives. In essence, the committee's scheme mirrored the structure of Roger Sherman's Connecticut Plan, which had been discussed and dismissed on three occasions. This time the desire for amicable resolution swept aside all resistance.

By the time the delegates cast their final votes on the Great Compromise, the weather had cooled along with the tempers in the State

House. To that point, conditions had been miserable; old-timers described it as the hottest, most humid summer since 1750. The sudden thunderstorms that normally refreshed the city provided scant relief in June and July of 1787. A French visitor complained of wilting in the punishing heat. "At each inhaling of air," he wrote, "one worries about the next one. The slightest movement is painful." Insects offered additional torment to the visiting delegates. "A veritable torture during the Philadelphia hot season is the innumerable flies which constantly light on the face and hands, stinging everywhere and turning everything black because of the filth they leave wherever they light." Sleep seemed impossible because one either kept the windows closed and choked in the stifling air or else opened them to the winged intruders whose brazen attacks defeated every attempt at rest.

On Friday, July 13, the stale air itself seemed to change when the Lord of Winds displayed his mercy with a brisk, cleansing breeze from the northwest. After more than a month of sweaty misery, the temperature dropped dramatically, allowing sleep for the weary and a surprisingly pleasant Sunday when the entire town seemed to enjoy the out-of-doors. The next day, Monday, July 16, the delegates voted final approval to the committee's solution to their most intractable dilemma. In her vivid account of the high drama of the convention, Catherine Drinker Bowen speculates: "Perhaps the delegates would never have reached agreement, had not the heat broken." For the rest of the convention, the delegates' letters and diaries provide far fewer complaints about the weather, and about each other.

They polished and perfected their work over the next month, never again threatened by dangerous division. Once the Great Compromise had settled the dispute that Madison characterized years later as "the most serious and threatening excitement" of the summer, an aura of fellowship and cooperation prevailed. The new constructive attitude survived emphatic arguments over dozens of maddening details because the participants had come to see their labors in their historical and even eternal context. "We should consider," urged James Wilson, "that we are providing a Constitution for future generations and not just for the circumstances of the moment," while Madison reminded his colleagues that they were "framing a system which we wish to last for ages" and would "decide forever the fate of republican government." South Carolina's John Rutledge emphatically agreed that "as we are laying the foundation for a great empire, we ought to take a permanent view of the subject and not look at the present moment only."

"A RISING AND NOT A SETTING SUN"

That "permanent view" came into sharper focus as they approached the conclusion of their work. Celebrations began even before the final debates and the signing of the finished document. On Friday, September 14, most of the delegates accompanied Washington to a crowded dinner party given in his honor at City Tavern, the town's most celebrated gathering place. The event was sponsored by Philadelphia's elite cavalry unit, the Light Horse Troop, famous everywhere for their gaudy, gold-braided uniforms and high-crested helmets. The revelers indulged themselves with prodigious quantities of claret, beer, porter, Madeira, rum punch, and other beverages. Though no record remains of the full nature of their festivities, the cavalry unit received a crushing bill for breakage by their boisterous guests.

Those celebrants gathered in a far more sober mood on Monday morning, September 17, for their closing session and the formal signing of the Constitution. The weekend had been turbulent with clouds and drenching rain, but the new week dawned clear and cool with the unmistakable edge of Pennsylvania autumn in the air. As the delegates made their way to the State House, which had been their center of operations for nearly four months, many realized they would see its familiar walls for the last time. As always, shutters and drapes remained tightly closed to protect the secrecy of the proceedings. Dramatic and popular paintings later altered the scene to show golden sunlight pouring through opened windows, but such romantic liberties conflict with the recollections of all participants.

Washington called the meeting to order and immediately recognized Franklin, who unsteadily rose from his chair and handed a paper he had prepared to his colleague James Wilson, who then read its contents aloud. The arresting opening immediately seized the delegates' attention:

> I confess that there are several parts of this constitution that I do not at present approve. . . . But I am not sure that I shall *never* approve them. For having lived long, I have experienced many instances of being obliged by better information or fuller consideration to change opinions even on important subjects, which I once thought right, but found to be otherwise. . . . In these sentiments, Sir, I agree to this Constitution with all its faults, if they are such. . . . I consent, Sir, to this Constitution because I expect no better and because I am not sure that it is not the best. . . . I cannot help expressing a wish that every member of this Convention who may still have objections to it, would with me, on this occasion doubt a little of his own infallibility—and to make manifest our unanimity, put his name to this instrument.

Most of the delegates gathered for the occasion honored Dr. Franklin's plea, but three prominent leaders pointedly refused to sign: Elbridge Gerry of Massachusetts, together with George Mason and Governor Edmund Randolph of Virginia. Randolph's last-minute defection particularly rankled with his colleagues: after all, he had been the young champion who initially introduced the Virginia Plan that provided the basis for much in the final document, and he had fought alongside Madison and his nationalist allies in nearly all of the convention's significant disputes. He explained himself by predicting a wretched future: he felt certain that at least nine of the thirteen states would refuse to ratify the Constitution as it stood, and if that occurred, then "confusion must ensue." Randolph's Virginia colleague George Mason, legal scholar and fervent foe of the slave trade, agreed that the new plan would face overwhelming opposition and warned that any government formed under its scheme would eventually be "vibrating between a monarchy and a corrupt, oppressive aristocracy." The outspoken opponents of the Constitution knew they spoke for four other participants (including Luther Martin) who had already left the convention in indignation over its results and would never have affixed their names to the final document.

Nevertheless, shortly after three in the afternoon, the remaining delegates rose from the tables they had occupied over the sweltering days of a difficult summer and lined up to sign their names to the "engrossed" copy of their nation's new charter, handsomely copied by a professional scribe onto a large piece of fine parchment. As president of the convention, Washington began the process, writing his name in large, bold letters that recalled John Hancock's oversized signature on the Declaration. After him, the others stepped up to the president's table, slightly elevated on a low platform, and picked up the quill. They arranged themselves by state, ordered geographically from north to south, as always.

In the middle of the process, Franklin received help from his fellow delegates, who recalled afterward that he wept openly as he signed. After he resumed his seat, as the last members attached their names, he looked toward the president's chair at the front of the room and focused on the half sun that decorated its high back. James Madison, continuing his role as faithful reporter to the very last, recorded the old man's words to those delegates closest to him. He criticized the painters "who had found it difficult to distinguish in their art a rising from a setting sun. I have often and often, in the course of the session, and the vicissitudes of my hopes and fears as to its issue, looked at that sun behind the President without being able to tell whether it was rising or setting: But now at length I have the happiness to know that it is a rising and not a setting sun."

But before that sun could rise in the firmament of nations to illuminate the darkness that still engirdled most of the globe, the authors of the new Constitution had to win the difficult fight for its ratification.

"YOU HAD ALL BETTER GO HOME"

Critics of the proposed new government lost no time in expressing their occasionally intemperate opposition. Elbridge Gerry hurried back to Massachusetts to organize opponents, while George Mason published his long list of objections in the *Pennsylvania Packet*. The Virginian feared potential tyranny from the federal courts and particularly disliked the office of vice president, which he considered unnecessary and dangerous. John Lansing of New York, having fled the convention in horror when it took the strong nationalist direction he most feared, went much further. He denounced the Constitution as a "triple-headed monster, as deep and wicked a conspiracy as ever was invented in the darkest ages against the liberties of a free people." In North Carolina, a Baptist preacher fixated on the provision for a new federal city that would become the national capital, fearing it would be "walled and fortified. Here an army of 50,000 or perhaps 100,000 men will be finally embodied and will sally forth and enslave the people, who will be gradually disarmed."

In response to such charges, and to lay out the reasons for ratification in a persuasive and philosophical style, a series of articles began appearing in New York newspapers in October under the pen name Publius. Primarily written by Alexander Hamilton, with significant contributions from Madison and also from John Jay (who never attended the convention), these arguments later became *The Federalist*, the most celebrated example of political journalism in American history. While arming constitutionalists with the intellectual ammunition they needed for upcoming battles, *The Federalist* exerted limited influence on the general public, which remained uncertain, at best, regarding the radical changes proposed in Philadelphia.

The first challenge in a long process involved winning the approval of the Confederation Congress in New York, which would promptly dissolve as soon as the Constitution succeeded. According to the new charter, it would take effect immediately upon ratification by nine states, providing a direct conflict with the Articles of Confederation, which required approval by all thirteen state legislatures for any amendment of its terms. Virginian Richard Henry Lee urged his fellow congressmen to send the Constitution to the states with a firm expression of disapproval, while James Madison argued for an alternative resolution that declared congressional approval of the Constitution and requested that states "speedily" convene ratification conventions.

Congress predictably disregarded both proposals and declined to take a position either for or against the new plan for government, merely relaying the Constitution to each legislature for consideration by "a convention of Delegates chosen in each state by the people."

The resulting battles proved consistently fierce and occasionally violent. In Pennsylvania, the legislature approved the plan for a ratification convention only after a rowdy mob dragged two recalcitrant assemblymen from their Philadelphia rooming house and forcibly held them prisoner at their State House desks to ensure the presence of a quorum. Later, drunken thugs on the other side attacked James Wilson as he addressed a bonfire rally in the town of Carlisle, nearly beating him to death for his advocacy of the new federal charter.

In the all-important states of Massachusetts and Virginia, the final votes to approve the Constitution proved uncomfortably close—187 to 168 in the Bay State, and 89 to 79 in the Old Dominion. In both ratification conventions, the outcome depended on unexpected last-moment support from popular sitting governors—the mercurial and vain John Hancock in Boston, and the passionate but perplexing Edmund Randolph in Richmond. Having shocked his allies at the Constitutional Convention with his rejection of the document he had done so much to shape, Randolph startled everyone else by reversing himself nine months later and endorsing the proposed plan as long as the new Congress moved quickly to attach a Bill of Rights that would place explicit limits on federal power.

Such assurances failed to soothe the fears of the most implacable "Anti-Feds," who continued to rage against the dangers of centralized authority and called for a mass meeting in Richmond the night after Virginia voted for ratification. The restive, angry crowd talked of organizing resistance to the new regime until their leader, the fiery ex-governor and esteemed Revolutionary orator Patrick Henry, told them the time had come to give up the fight. "As true and faithful republicans, you had all better go home," he pleaded.

"MADNESS TO TRUST TO FUTURE MIRACLES"

By the time the first Congress convened in April 1789 and began its work on the first ten amendments to the Constitution, remaining opposition had already melted away. North Carolina belatedly joined the Union at the end of the year, leaving stubborn little "Rogue Island" as the only state still resisting the federation. After considerable economic and political pressure, the legislature in Providence finally gave in and made Rhode Island the thirteenth state on May 29, 1790.

Congress and the states made significant constitutional alterations over the years—adjusting the method of selecting the president and vice president after the chaotic election of 1800, and then putting an end to slavery and guaranteeing "equal protection" with three amendments after the Civil War. For the most part, however, the great charter organizing the Republic has changed remarkably little since the four months of bickering and brilliance in the summer of 1787.

Americans rightly embrace the Constitution as a cornerstone of the country, a fortunate foundation both inevitable and (mostly) immutable. In recent years, Tea Party populists and many others have seemed to suggest that the words of the national charter were inscribed by the Almighty on tablets of stone; they urge a return to those sacred precepts with the same fervor that religious believers demand renewed adherence to the Ten Commandments. Even among those who most revere the Constitution, few recognize how close the founders came to failure in drafting it, and then again in fighting for its ratification. To the fifty-five flawed and colorful individuals who framed the founding charter in Philadelphia, there was nothing inevitable about their success. The what-ifs haunted them, as they should amaze us: What if Washington had declined to participate, or if eighty-one-year-old Franklin had proven too infirm to ride in his sedan chair to the red-brick State House? What if Madison had failed to lay out a detailed blueprint in advance of the convention, or if the amiable Daniel of St. Thomas Jenifer had neglected to take his bewildering little stroll on the day of a crucial vote, or if Few and Pierce of Georgia hadn't boarded a stagecoach for New York before the same decisive moment because they considered the business of the Confederation Congress more important than the work of the Constitutional Convention?

The hopes of the framers could have collapsed at any number of intersections along the way. They wanted their work to last for generations, even centuries, but they remained uncertain as to its long-term prospects. From faraway Paris, where he represented his country at the court of the French king, Thomas Jefferson hailed the Philadelphia convention as "an assembly of demigods" and, in a letter to Adams, expressed "no doubt that all its measures will be good and wise." But he had no knowledge of the bruising battles and occasional blunders that the demigods endured in their top-secret proceedings. He could only marvel at the final result as a charter that was "unquestionably the wisest ever yet presented to men."

Whether or not divine providence actually guided their efforts, a providential perspective unmistakably fostered the vision and determination that enabled them to persevere. Eight of the convention delegates had previously signed the Declaration of Independence with its concluding phrase announcing a "firm reliance on the protection of divine Providence." Washington, who calmly presided over the convention's sometimes doubtful deliberations, later began his First Inaugural Address by telling "the people of the United States" that "every step, by which they have advanced to the character of an independent nation, seems to have been distinguished by some token of providential agency." Washington and Madison, two of the guiding spirits of a perplexing process, both described the result as a "miracle," as did other participants.

Charles Pinckney wrote from Charleston in 1788 that "when the general convention met, no citizen of the United States could expect less from it than I did, so many jarring interests and prejudices to reconcile! . . . But when the great work was done and published . . . I was struck with amazement. Nothing less than that superintending hand of Providence, that miraculously carried us through the war (in my humble opinion), could have brought it about so complete, upon the whole."

In *Federalist No. 37* Madison expressed similar sentiments about what he and his colleagues had achieved in Philadelphia. "It is impossible for any man of candor to reflect on this circumstance, without partaking of the astonishment," he wrote. "It is impossible for the man of pious reflection not to perceive in it a finger of that Almighty hand which has so frequently and signally extended to our relief in the critical stages of the revolution."

Even Alexander Hamilton, one of the most pragmatic and hardheaded of all the founders, saw the gathering at Philadelphia as a marvel, with overtones of supernatural assistance. On the floor of the convention, he reflected on the ability of the delegates to make fateful adjustments to the badly flawed Articles of Confederation. "It is a miracle that we are now here to exercise our tranquil and free deliberations on the subject," he declared, but added an important note of caution concerning new challenges: "It would be madness to trust to future miracles. A thousand causes must obstruct a reproduction of them."

Americans of that generation may not have expected more miracles, but they did experience them, again and again. Within Hamilton's own lifetime, one utterly unexpected stroke doubled the size of the nation and all but sealed its future greatness.

THE YOUNG CONQUEROR MAKES AN IMPULSIVE DECISION.

"Irresolution and deliberation are no longer in season. I renounce Louisiana."
—Napoleon Bonaparte, April 11, 1803

6

PROVIDENTIAL PURCHASE

Disconnected Developments Double America's Size

Napoleon Bonaparte earned the adulation of his people by conquering territory for France, not by giving it up. But for reasons that still seem mysterious after two hundred years, the great conqueror awoke after a brief sleep one bright spring morning in 1803 with a sudden determination to present the United States with an incomparable gift the new nation neither demanded nor expected.

Defying his closest advisors and ignoring normal rules of national self-interest, the impetuous thirty-two-year-old dictator insisted on transferring to the Americans a vast tract of land four times larger than France itself—a tract of land, moreover, that Napoleon had acquired for his country after arduous, top-secret negotiations that had concluded just two and a half years before. The puzzling change of course resulted in an astonished America receiving immediate title to all of present-day Missouri, Iowa, Oklahoma, Kansas, Nebraska, and Arkansas, with large parts of Minnesota, the Dakotas, Montana, Wyoming, Colorado, New Mexico, Texas, and Louisiana—fifteen future states plus, initially, portions of two Canadian provinces.

No wonder that the people of the United States saw this shocking stroke of fortune as one more sign of the Almighty's continued favor to their young Republic. Alexander Hamilton, despite bitter political divisions with President Jefferson, hailed the Louisiana Purchase as "being essential to the peace and prosperity of our Western country, and as opening a free and valuable market to our commercial states." In an unsigned editorial he wrote for the *New York Post* in July, the former treasury secretary tartly insisted that he credited a power far more formidable and far-seeing than the president of the United States: "Let us then, with all due humility, acknowledge this as another of those signal instances of the kind interpositions of an overruling Providence, which we more especially experienced during our revolutionary war, & by which we have more than once, been saved from the consequences of our errors and perverseness."

Whatever the "errors and perverseness" of leaders on either side of the Atlantic, Americans perceived something magical about a deal that doubled the size of their nation and thrust it squarely into the ranks of recognized world powers. "It must ... strike the mind of every true friend to freedom in the United States as the greatest and most beneficial event that has taken place since the Declaration of Independence," wrote General Horatio Gates, the hero of the Battle of Saratoga in the Revolutionary War. "I am astonished when I see so great a business finished, which but a few months since we whispered to one another about; it has the air of enchantment!"

That enchantment resulted from a series of events both brutal and bizarre, ranging from impassable ice in a crucial Dutch harbor to unspeakable slaughter on the richest island in the Caribbean. Without these seemingly disconnected developments, the inhabitants of the Mississippi Basin might still be speaking French, and the growth of the United States blocked by disparate and hostile powers on both sides of the great river.

DECISIONS AND DISASTERS

The sequence of decisions and disasters that gave Thomas Jefferson his chance to take control of the broad, unsettled center of North America began with a complicated, multinational peace agreement in 1763. The Treaty of Paris, which ended the Seven Years' War (known in North America as the French and Indian War), reflected Britain's comprehensive victory in a worldwide struggle against France and Spain. The agreement put an end to French claims to territory any-where on the mainland of the continent, with the British taking per-manent possession of the Canadian colony of New France, which they had already conquered militarily. They also gained title to the strug-gling French forts and trading posts in the wild lands between the Appalachian Mountains and the Mississippi River. King Louis XV accepted these huge territorial losses since the treaty allowed him to keep France's prosperous sugar colonies in the Caribbean, which gen-erated far more income for the royal treasury than did any returns or, it seemed, potential returns from the wilderness of North America. The philosopher Voltaire famously dismissed his nation's loss of Can-ada as an insignificant sacrifice of "some acres of snow," and its claims to the south looked even less significant.

This territory stretched as far west as the modern-day state of Idaho and as far north as the current Canadian border, pushing into wild lands so remote that its boundaries remained uncertain. This entire tract became known as the Colony of Louisiana, in honor of the great "Sun King," Louis XIV. It contained only a single settle-ment of any note—the riverside trading outpost of New Orleans, with its multiracial and polyglot (but mostly French-speaking) population of slightly more than five thousand. Before the Treaty of Paris, the defeated French had deeded all of Louisiana to their Spanish allies, instead of waiting for their hated British rivals to seize the territory as a prize of war. The English government agreed to leave this empty and seemingly worthless province in the hands of the rapidly declining Spanish Empire, knowing that the government in Madrid remained far too feeble and preoccupied to promote new settlement in the re-gion or to mount any sort of military challenge to their thriving Brit-ish colonies on the eastern seaboard.

When those colonies stunned the world and won their indepen-dence some twenty years later, the leaders of the new United States strongly preferred continued Spanish rule and worried over specula-tion that the French might someday attempt to reclaim Louisiana. Despite the fact that the Bourbon monarchy had provided indis-pensable assistance that enabled the embattled Americans to prevail in their struggle with the mother country, the relationship between the new nation and its first ally deteriorated rapidly after revolutionary violence installed a series of turbulent, unstable governments in Paris. Impassioned disagreements about the appropriate response to the radical changes on the other side of the Atlantic bitterly divided George Washington's administration. Secretary of State Thomas Jefferson, who had served as minister to France in the years preceding the Constitution, counted himself a proud Francophile and felt generally sympathetic to the French revolutionaries.

When the U.S. government under President John Adams stopped paying its debts to France on the grounds that the money had been borrowed from the previous regime, a crisis ensued that led to French seizure of American shipping and a series of bloody battles at sea that tested the mettle of the newly constructed U.S. Navy. In the midst of this undeclared Quasi War, Alexander Hamilton, former secretary of the treasury, wanted to recruit a new American army of ten thousand that he would lead personally in seizing New Orleans from the inept and vulnerable Spanish. Hamilton, who had been a bold and successful officer in the Revolutionary War, pleaded with the Adams administration to strike first, before the French grabbed Louisiana and threatened the United States from the west. Yankee pioneers had already begun pouring over the Appalachians by the tens of thousands and settling the territory east of the Mississippi that Britain had ceded to the Americans after the Revolution. The only practical way for these frontier farmers to get their crops to market involved transporting them by boat on the river system that fed the Mississippi, winding up at the remote but crucial port of New Orleans. Many feared that renewed French control of that shabby, exotic town would choke off trade or result in the imposition of crippling fees before Americans could take their goods to market. A return of the bellicose French also menaced the grand hopes of American visionaries who saw the young nation's destiny as spreading, inevitably, into the limitless spaces to the west that the Spanish colonial authorities did nothing to develop or explore.

Thomas Jefferson counted himself as one of those dreamers. Yes, he loved the culture of France, but the wild, uncharted American West stirred his soul even more. In 1793 he persuaded the American Philosophical Society to organize an expedition of exploration under the leadership of French botanist André Michaux. While Jefferson hoped that the intrepid band of scientists and adventurers might eventually reach the Rockies, Michaux never got farther west than Kentucky, disappointing his ambitious sponsors at the Philosophical Society. Jefferson's eighteen-year-old aide and protégé, Meriwether Lewis, had ardently pleaded to accompany the Michaux expedition, but the fatherly, protective secretary of state wouldn't permit it. A decade later, with Jefferson as president, Lewis made it all the way to the Pacific in the far more famous trek he led in partnership with William Clark.

CHAOS, CRUELTY, AND SECRET ORDERS

Fortunately for lovers of peace and sanity, neither Alexander Hamilton nor the revolutionary government in Paris actually launched an armed assault on New Orleans, which continued under the sleepy control of the cheerfully incompetent Spaniards. Meanwhile, the two erstwhile allies, America and France, managed to settle their undeclared naval war with an 1800 agreement, brokered by the new First Consul of France, Napoleon Bonaparte. With his nation engaged in a long-term struggle for supremacy with Great Britain, the young, dynamic, recently installed dictator had no interest in trifling with the Americans. When it came to the New World, Napoleon focused his attention on the wealth-producing islands of the French Caribbean, which had always obsessed his countrymen far more than the undeveloped wilderness of the North American mainland. By the 1790s, just one of those islands—Saint-Domingue (today known as Haiti)— was producing more wealth than all of Europe's other American and Caribbean settlements *combined*. The eight thousand plantations of Saint-Domingue used half a million horribly oppressed slaves to provide 60 percent of Europe's coffee and 40 percent of its sugar, while accounting for more than 40 percent of all of France's foreign trade.

According to legend-shrouded accounts still honored as part of the heritage of modern Haiti, this economic powerhouse exploded in violence that began on the rainy, steamy night of August 14, 1791. A crowd of escaped slaves convened a secret ceremony in the heavily forested mountains in which a high priest of the African Vodoun tradition co-officiated with a languidly dancing priestess. They butchered a sacred black pig and then led all participants in drinking its blood in a solemn vow of vengeance on their white oppressors. Within a month, more than eight hundred plantations were sacked and burned, and more than a thousand members of slaveholding families were grotesquely slaughtered. Many of them had been hacked to death by machetes, in some cases after their eyeballs had been pulled out with corkscrews.

In the midst of the chaos and cruelty, a charismatic figure emerged to unify the revolutionary forces and to seek recognition from the French government in the name of its professed ideals of liberty, equality, and fraternity. A self-educated former slave and reputed son of a powerful African king, Toussaint Louverture played a singular and decisive role in securing the future greatness of the United States, even though he never traveled to America or knew much about the young republic to the north. Louverture rose to power at nearly the same moment as Bonaparte, earning the popular nickname "Napoleon Noir" (Black Napoleon), and in true Napoleonic style he proclaimed himself "governor for life" and lavished plum appointments on members of his family.

From Paris, the original Napoleon watched these developments with more alarm than admiration. He wanted above all to rebuild the shattered plantation economy on Saint-Domingue and became increasingly convinced that this restoration would be impossible without the reimposition of slavery. To accomplish that goal, he organized a lavishly equipped army that eventually included some forty thousand troops and an armada of seventy-four ships—the largest overseas expeditionary force in French history to that time. Bonaparte assigned command to his twenty-nine-year-old brother-in-law, General Charles Emmanuel Leclerc. He traveled to the New World with secret orders: once he had conquered the black rebels and restored them to slavery, he was instructed to sail to New Orleans with most of his enormous force to reestablish French control of the entire Mississippi Basin—realizing the ultimate American nightmare.

MAKING PURCHASE POSSIBLE: Haitian revolutionary and "governor for life" Toussaint Louverture (1743–1803), whose leadership of the only successful slave rebellion in history blocked a French army from reoccupying the Mississippi Valley and seizing the center of the North American continent.

Before Leclerc left on this fateful errand, Napoleon had already concluded a confidential treaty with his Spanish allies, under which they returned all of Louisiana to France some thirty-seven years after the French monarchy had given it up. When Leclerc arrived on the Mississippi, the Spaniards were supposed to welcome him without resistance and to replace their royal flag with the French tricolor. In return, Napoleon promised to set up a tidy little kingdom in the conquered Italian province of Tuscany as a consolation prize for the Spanish royal family. The canny Corsican always treated diplomacy like a complex board game, seizing nations, trading far-flung provinces, or setting up new alliances with scant regard for anything beyond his own advancement toward global domination.

"THERE IS ON THE GLOBE
ONE SINGLE SPOT"

Thomas Jefferson in faraway Washington got wind of the disturbing developments shortly after he moved into the newly completed President's House (known later as the White House) in the spring of 1801. He saw the prospect of a French return to Louisiana as a dire threat that "works most sorely on the U.S." In an insightful letter instructing his newly appointed minister to France, he forcefully declared: "There is on the globe one single spot, the possessor of which is our natural and habitual enemy. It is New Orleans, through which the produce of three eighths of our territory must pass to market, and from its fertility it will ere long yield more than half of our whole produce and contain more than half our inhabitants."

The new president hoped that the reports of Napoleon's plans proved groundless, but he feared the worst: "France placing herself in that door assumes to us the attitude of defiance. . . . The impetuosity of her temper, the energy and restlessness of her character, placed in a point of eternal friction with us . . . render it impossible that France and the U.S. can continue long friends when they meet in so irritable a position."

The minister who received those instructions, Robert Livingston, had already achieved a distinguished judicial career in his home state of New York, and twenty-seven years earlier had served with Jefferson on the committee of five tasked with writing the Declaration of Independence. He had supervised foreign affairs for the Continental Congress under the Articles of Confederation, but he had no experience representing his nation abroad and seemed a peculiar choice to deal with the wily French at such a critical moment. Tall and dignified, the product of a distinguished family of Hudson Valley aristocrats, and the owner of some two hundred thousand acres in rustic Dutchess County, Livingston was also plainspoken, unassuming, and notoriously hard of hearing. In the gilded salons and drawing rooms of Paris, he would be ill-equipped to follow the oblique hints and whispered intimations of Napoleon's crafty foreign minister, Charles Maurice de Talleyrand.

Nevertheless, Livingston traveled to France with a clear and attainable mission: to purchase the town of New Orleans from the French by offering at least $2 million to their cash-strapped treasury. Jefferson and his secretary of state, James Madison, informed their representative that they would go even higher to secure control of the crucial port, even while resigning themselves to the idea that Napoleon would retain the rest of the vast province of Louisiana. It seemed impossible to divert Napoleon from his apparent determination to restore the lost glory of France's once promising American empire because no one expected the intensity of the resistance that would be encountered by the huge French expeditionary force on Haiti.

HOUNDS OF HELL

Only subsequent generations fully understood the ultimate importance of the slave struggle in the Caribbean to the future of the United States. "Before Bonaparte could reach Louisiana, he was obliged to crush the power of Toussaint," wrote Henry Adams, grandson of John Quincy Adams, in 1889. "If he and his blacks should succumb easily to their fate, the wave of French empire would roll on to Louisiana and sweep far up the Mississippi; if St. Domingo should resist, and succeed in resistance . . . America would be left to pursue her democratic destiny in peace."

The successful resistance of the Haitian armies began with Toussaint's cunning strategy: withdrawing most of his forces to the mountains to avoid direct confrontation and engage in guerilla warfare, while counting on his strongest ally—yellow fever—to devastate the newly arrived European troops. This dread disease quickly claimed nearly half of the first wave of French forces, with its hideous symptoms deeply terrifying the survivors. According to contemporary accounts, the victims initially felt "sharp pains in the eye sockets, feet, loins and stomach" before the skin turned "a deep yellow or leaden color." Blood oozed from eyes and nose of the patient, who was "already a corpse, putrid and horrible."

At the height of combat, the French commanders lured Toussaint to join them in negotiating terms of disengagement, but as soon as the governor-for-life arrived, they seized him, loaded him onto a fetid prison ship, and sent him to France, separated forever from his armies and his people. Locked into a dank cell high in the Jura Mountains, he died of malnutrition and exposure within a year.

Rather than breaking the morale of Toussaint's troops, his martyrdom inspired even more courageous resistance and brought together some of his onetime rivals in the cause of the rebellion. By that time, the French expeditionary force had largely collapsed, with its small surviving remnant scuttling back to Europe. In desperation, General Leclerc proposed genocidal war as the only solution. "We must destroy all the mountain negroes, men and women, only keep the children under twelve years old," he wrote to Napoleon on October 7, 1802.

In November, the First Consul wrote back to Leclerc regarding reports of the ill health of his flirtatious, beautiful younger sister, the general's wife, who had accompanied Leclerc to the Caribbean. Napoleon declared himself "highly satisfied with the conduct of Paulette. She ought not to fear death, as she would die with glory in dying with the army and being useful to her husband." As it happened, she survived her illness, but Leclerc himself perished before he received this letter, dying of yellow fever like so many of his troops.

The new commander, Donatien-Marie-Joseph de Rochambeau, was the son of a French general who had fought alongside Washington in the last years of the American Revolution. The younger officer, however, may have been best known for the desperate tactic he adopted in a last-ditch attempt to save his broken army in Saint-Domingue from total destruction. In May 1803, his agent purchased three hundred vicious and specially trained bloodhounds for the purpose of chasing and eating the rebels. As Rochambeau wrote to an adjutant, "I don't need to tell you that no rations or expenses are authorized for the dogs' food; you must only give them negroes to eat." To inaugurate this new weapon, the French army set up an amphitheater in the courtyard of a former Jesuit monastery. They tied a boy to a post in the center and turned some of the prized hounds loose on him. An eyewitness reported that as the child screamed and spectators applauded, the hungry beasts "devoured his entrails and didn't abandon their prey until they had gorged themselves on the twitching flesh. Nothing was left on the post but bloody bones."

Despite all the horrors they perpetrated in the last days of the war, not even the hounds of hell could turn the tide of battle. Napoleon finally allowed the eight thousand sick and terrified survivors of his once formidable force to board waiting ships and sail for home. More than thirty thousand French soldiers died in the course of the war, as did an estimated 350,000 residents of Saint-Domingue, most of them former slaves.

CHANCE OR DESTINY?

The outcome of this hideous conflict played an important role in shaping America's destiny. First, reports from Haiti terrified the world at the time, and particularly the Americans, who couldn't decide whether the brutality of an invading French army or the savagery of a vengeful slave insurrection represented the more fearsome threat to the nation. Napoleon later admitted that "the Saint-Domingue business was a great piece of folly on my part. It was the greatest error that in all my government I ever committed. I ought to have treated with

the black leaders, as I would have done the authorities in a province."
Still, even after giving up hope for success in the Caribbean, he clung
to the dream of reestablishing a profitable new colony in Louisiana.

In the summer of 1802, Napoleon began organizing another
grand expedition that would establish his new base of operations in
New Orleans. With no prospect for a quick end to the Haitian war,
and with no troops to spare from the desperate fighting, Napoleon
devoted two million francs to raising a new fleet on the river Scheldt,
in the Dutch town of Helvoet Sluys. These ships would travel directly
to Louisiana under the command of General Claude Victor-Perrin,
who had preemptively been designated the new governor. Cooperat-
ing with their Continental allies, the French worked furiously to ready
nearly a hundred ships, with close to ten thousand soldiers and the
most sophisticated equipment, preparing to complete their assignment regardless of the miseries in Saint-Domingue.

Why didn't this Louisiana expedition make it across the ocean
and foreclose any chance for American acquisition? In *Chance or Destiny*, a brief, fascinating, and all but forgotten volume from 1954, Harvard historian Oscar Handlin classifies the endless delays afflicting
the Victor-Perrin fleet as one of the key "turning points in American
history." As Handlin writes, "Materials were difficult to come by and
were assembled slowly. Then, it seemed, no definite sailing date could
be set, because the Spanish court continued its intolerable evasive tactics and had not yet actually issued the order to cede the territory to
the French." These annoyances frittered away weeks of the summer
and fall seasons, which offered the best time to cross the Atlantic.
Nevertheless, General Victor-Perrin "hastened his final preparations.
One morning, as he was almost in readiness, he woke to find an advancing edge of frost moving across the harbor at Helvoet Sluys. Before he could act, the whole expedition was icebound."

The ice closed the Dutch harbor through the end of February,
and during this time the hungry troops consumed most of the supplies
that had been intended to feed them en route to Louisiana. Waiting
idly in their quarters, the general and his staff prepared meticulously
detailed plans for the occupation of the new territory and the firm but

enlightened government they would bring to it. The arrival of spring began to deliver the harbor from the imprisoning ice, but even as the fleet at last prepared to break anchor and head toward open sea, a violent storm made their departure impossible.

Two more weeks passed. Finally, in April, the weather cleared, new supplies were secured, and the troops eagerly embarked. As Handlin writes, "The pilots boarded the ships and were on the point of taking the fleet through the estuary to the open waters when a halt was called. Word had come that a courier bore dispatches from Paris. General Victor now learned to his amazement that the whole expedition had been recalled. Louisiana had been sold to the Americans. The delay had altered the plans of his government."

THE TEMPER OF A YOUNG CONQUEROR

Of course, that sort of alteration reflected the fact that government plans in France followed the whims of a single individual—and that individual could change his mind with startling speed. François Barbé-Marbois, the worldly-wise finance minister under Bonaparte, tried to explain his chief to the bewildered Americans who had come to negotiate with him. "You know the temper of a young conqueror," he sighed. "Everything he does is rapid as lightning."

Napoleon never fully explained his sudden determination to hand Louisiana to the United States; it's also probable that he never fully understood it. As much as any major ruler in history, the "young conqueror" trusted his own instincts and impulses. After all, those split-second decisions had resulted in many brilliant military victories, and as a result, he had developed an unshakable sense of himself as fortune's favorite. On his wedding day in 1796, the twenty-six-year-old general presented his bride, Josephine de Beauharnais, with a gold medallion inscribed "To Destiny." By April 1803, the people of France certainly embraced their dashing dictator as destiny's darling and accepted his decisions as if they were mandates from heaven.

But even for a ruler so supremely sure of his own abilities, the disastrous news from Haiti forced a change of plan. Napoleon had visualized Louisiana and Saint-Domingue as the twin foundations of a New World empire, supporting each other militarily and economically, trading profitably in raw materials and slaves, and guaranteeing French dominance of the Caribbean. With Haiti lost in the world's first (and only) successful slave rebellion, the dream became unattainable and Louisiana became indefensible. Without a solid base of operations nearby to anchor a French fleet, New Orleans would be painfully vulnerable to attacks from the sea by the British navy or overland invasion by American militias.

Secretary of State James Madison had given the First Consul another reason to give up his dreams of grandeur regarding Louisiana. In a private dinner with the French minister to Washington, Louis-André Pichon, Madison warned his guest that Napoleon could never retain long-term control of such vast territory in North America. Even with a prodigious investment of money and manpower to make the remote territory into a self-sustaining colony, the benefits to France would be short-term: the distance from New Orleans to Paris—a thousand miles greater than New England's distance from Britain—made independence inevitable. A growing, prospering Louisiana colony would ultimately separate from the mother country, just as the thirteen colonies had successfully split from England. By the first week in April, Napoleon had received a copy of the *New York Chronicle* describing debates in Congress over preparations for war in case the French used New Orleans to interfere with American commerce.

To address his growing doubts about the increasingly tricky situation, Napoleon consulted with senior aides, beginning with the foreign minister. One of the most durable survivors in the history of politics, Talleyrand had begun his strange career as a priest of the Catholic Church, rising to bishop of a country diocese. His love of gambling, fine wines, and sex with both married and unmarried ladies of fashion left him imperfectly suited for a clerical life of celibacy and self-denial. He first played a diplomatic role under the old monarchy before shifting his allegiance to the new revolutionary government and then to the Napoleonic rule that followed. As foreign minister for various regimes, he developed special expertise in collecting bribes (though he preferred the more polite terminology of "gratuities" or "commissions") from nations eager to find favor in France. Over the years, these gratuities helped him amass a fortune estimated at more than ten million francs. After military defeats badly dented the emperor's power and popularity, Talleyrand switched sides once again and helped to engineer Napoleon's exile, taking his customary role as foreign minister in the renewed monarchy that replaced Bonaparte. Though a congenital clubfoot left him with a pronounced, lifelong limp and earned him the nickname "Le Diable Boiteux" (the lame devil), this suave operator managed to glide gracefully from one regime to another.

When Napoleon told his foreign minister about his doubts regarding Louisiana, Talleyrand tried to persuade him to hold firm to his plans to develop and exploit the faraway American colony. During a particularly turbulent period of the French Revolution, Talleyrand dodged the guillotine by spending two years in the United States, traveling in the highest circles of politics and business and becoming deeply involved in land speculation in the American West. He spent months traveling to the frontier and inspecting wide-open territory of enormous promise and possibility. He warned his chief that passing up the chance to exploit similar opportunities in Louisiana would amount to sacrificing potential wealth on a far grander scale than what France had already lost in Saint-Domingue. The First Consul heard similar messages when he discussed the matter with his chief of staff and war minister, Alexandre Berthier, as well as with his two brothers, Joseph and Lucien Bonaparte. All of these advisors expressed strong opposition to any sale or cession of the huge colony of Louisiana to the United States.

"IRRESOLUTION AND DELIBERATION
ARE NO LONGER IN SEASON"

With these forceful opinions to consider, the First Consul arose early on Easter Sunday, April 10, and attended mass. Perhaps something in the service stirred him, or at least the time in church and the pageantry of the occasion gave him a chance for reflection. After church, he wanted more discussion of the overwhelming decision that seemed to temporarily obsess him. Returning to his palace at Saint-Cloud, just west of Paris, he summoned two more counselors: the crusty, no-nonsense minister of the navy, Admiral Denis Decrès, and his brilliant finance minister, Barbé-Marbois. Like Talleyrand, Barbé-Marbois had spent time in America, where he served as secretary to the French legation during the Revolutionary War. During his years in Philadelphia, he developed a readily acknowledged love for the nation and its people, marrying the daughter of a governor of Pennsylvania. On the afternoon of Easter Sunday, Napoleon strolled with these two worthies through his formal gardens and drew out their opinions on the issue of the day.

According to Barbé-Marbois's recollection of their conversation, Napoleon insisted, "I have not a moment to lose." He cited his immediate concern that the British might soon move to seize Louisiana for themselves. "I wish, if there is still time, to take from them any idea that they may have of ever possessing that colony. I think of ceding it to the United States. . . . They ask of me one town in Louisiana, but I already consider the colony as entirely lost, and it appears to me that in the hands of this growing power, it will be more useful to the policy and even to the commerce of France, than if I should attempt to keep it."

Barbé-Marbois listened respectfully and then offered his tentative agreement. "We should not hesitate to make a sacrifice of that which is . . . slipping from us," he observed. Admiral Decrès gruffly disagreed, declaring that a failure to take full possession of a province only recently reacquired from Spain would be "contrary to the honor of France."

Still undecided as to the proper course his destiny demanded, Napoleon asked Barbé-Marbois to stay over at the palace in Saint-Cloud to await a final decision the next morning. When that day arrived, Napoleon had returned to his customary certainty and forcefulness. "Irresolution and deliberation are no longer in season," he crisply announced. "I renounce Louisiana. It is not only New Orleans that I cede; it is the whole colony, without reserve; I know the price of what I abandon. . . . I renounce it with the greatest regret: to attempt obstinately to retain it would be folly."

The ruler then asked his finance minister to handle the final negotiations with the Americans; he didn't trust Talleyrand for the job because his personal opposition to the policy—and his perpetual hunger for personal enrichment through "commissions"—might alienate or offend the straitlaced representatives of the United States. Napoleon wanted to reach quick agreement, especially with a new envoy due to arrive in Paris at any time. James Monroe had been dispatched across the Atlantic not to replace Ambassador Livingston but rather to add new political force to the stalled negotiations. A Revolutionary War hero, two-term governor of Virginia, former U.S. senator, and onetime ambassador to France, Monroe would go on to become the fifth president of the United States. Jefferson believed that Monroe's impressive résumé and personal prestige would impress Napoleon, as would the explicit threat that if the negotiations failed, Monroe would proceed directly to London to try to strike some sort of deal with the British.

With this complicating factor in mind, and with the lingering hope that it might not be too late to reinsert himself into the process and collect one of his cherished "commissions," Talleyrand summoned Livingston to his huge and lavish office on the afternoon of the same day Napoleon had declared his intentions. The officious Livingston had already expressed American interest in purchasing New Orleans on so many occasions, and so frequently insisted that the United States would pay fairly for the rights to the town, that the foreign minister and other officials had come to view him as a tiresome bore. On that Monday afternoon following Easter, the American once more offered his familiar recitation while Talleyrand listened with a distracted and restless demeanor, offering no sign of interest or open-mindedness. Livingston described the conversation in a letter to Secretary of State Madison, reporting faithfully on the Frenchman's studied indifference and casual air as he unexpectedly inquired "whether we wished to have the whole of Louisiana."

This thunderbolt forced the American representative to hide his amazement when Talleyrand tartly noted that the rest of Louisiana was of little use or interest to France without New Orleans. Since the United States had made it abundantly clear that the sale of New Orleans would be the price for continued friendship, the only remaining question was what price America would pay for all of Louisiana's territory. Livingston refused to give a definitive response before the arrival of James Monroe, who might come bearing new instructions, and the crafty foreign minister then backed out of the negotiations from which Napoleon had wanted him excluded from the beginning.

With the earnest Barbé-Marbois taking over the business of bargaining with the Americans, the negotiations proceeded quickly and smoothly. By the time Monroe showed up, the outlines of a deal had emerged: the Americans would pay a total of $15 million, which included assuming the $4 million that France had previously agreed to pay for damages to American shipping during the recent undeclared naval war. In total, the United States would come up with a bit more than double the amount the Americans had previously offered for a parcel of land less than one-hundredth the size, covering only New Orleans and its environs. The final acquisition amounted to 828,000 square miles—529,920,000 acres—at a fire-sale price of 3 cents an acre. In twenty-first-century terms, the price comes to about 41 cents an acre for the largest single-stroke transfer of land in all of human history.

To frame the elements of the agreement, Livingston and Barbé-Marbois continued their give-and-take well past midnight, and the American promised to share the results with his recently arrived colleague, Monroe. In parting, the French finance minister reminded Livingston of the significance of their nearly concluded transaction: "Consider the extent of the country, the exclusive navigation of the

HARD OF HEARING, CLEAR OF VISION: Robert Livingston (1746–1813) served on the Committee of Five that drafted the Declaration of Independence, spent twenty-five years as the senior judicial officer of the State of New York, and negotiated the Louisiana Purchase.

"From this day the United States take their place among powers of the first rank." —Robert Livingston, April 1803

river, and the importance of having no neighbor to dispute with you, no war to dread." He also stressed the urgency of finalizing their understanding before Napoleon made another of his "rapid as lightning" reverses and decided to cancel the deal. In the small hours of the morning, Livingston wrote to Madison that "the field open to us is infinitely larger than our instructions contemplated" but that this perhaps fleeting opening "must not be missed."

Some of those closest to Napoleon viewed the looming agreement as a grotesque giveaway and tried to persuade him to shut the door decisively to the Americans. His older brother, Joseph, and younger brother, Lucien, played key roles in Napoleon's inner circle; in future years, both would occupy prestigious royal thrones in Spain and Italy, respectively, for which their sole qualification involved their good fortune in sharing parentage with the most powerful man on earth. Concerning Louisiana, the two brothers felt so passionately opposed to surrendering dreams of North American grandeur that they interrupted Napoleon in his bath, as he lounged sensuously in steaming water scented with rare cologne. They not only protested his decision but threatened to speak openly against it and to mobilize public opinion to block the sale of Louisiana. The indignant ruler then rose from his bath, confronted his brothers, and dressed them both down. "You will have no need to lead the opposition," he growled, "for I repeat there will be no debate, for the reason that the project . . . conceived by me, negotiated by me, shall be ratified and executed by me, alone. Do you comprehend me?" With that, he hurled himself back into his tub with a splash that soaked Joseph. In his anger, the conqueror also smashed a valuable snuffbox decorated with his wife's portrait.

"THE NOBLEST WORK OF OUR WHOLE LIVES"

In the United States, official acceptance of the deal would prove considerably more complicated, as the Constitution kept any one man, even the president, from wielding such uncontested power. Jefferson got the news with a packet of letters from Livingston that arrived in

Washington on the sultry Sunday evening of July 3, 1803. As principal author of the Declaration of Independence, President Jefferson always prized and revered Independence Day, but this stunning, altogether unexpected development gave profound new meaning to the next day's celebrations. Pondering the wondrous details late that night at the President's House, he slightly underestimated the size of the acquisition but clearly understood its importance. "It is something larger than the whole U.S.," he wrote, "probably containing 500 millions of acres, the U.S. containing 434 millions . . . This removes from us the greatest source of danger to our peace."

But the greatest source of danger to concluding this spectacularly favorable transaction came from Jefferson's own doubts as to its constitutionality. He remained pointedly aware of legal limitations to federal power and persisted in viewing the national government as a confederation of sovereign states. Nowhere did the Constitution authorize either the president or Congress to purchase new territory never claimed by any state—let alone to double the size of the Republic without the participation or explicit approval of those existing states. Secretary of State Madison, who had played such a prominent role in the Philadelphia convention that drafted the national charter, answered Jefferson's reservations with the salient point that the Constitution also said nothing to *prohibit* acquisition of new lands in the national interest.

Dissatisfied with such a flimsy basis for so fateful a change in the nation's very nature, the president applied his subtle legal mind to the drafting of two versions of a constitutional amendment specifically approving the Louisiana Purchase. Neither draft would have provided for a permanent expansion of presidential power; both would have applied only to the unique and unprecedented situation that Napoleon's unexpected offer made possible.

Although introducing either of these amendments and securing its ratification would have solved any of the worrisome constitutional problems regarding the pending treaty with France, the political and practical difficulties associated with such a course argued powerfully against it. Even if Jefferson succeeded in getting two-thirds majorities in both houses of Congress to back an amendment, he would still need approval by legislatures in three-fourths of the states. That meant prevailing in at least thirteen of the seventeen states of the time. The New England states—all five of them—looked askance at a change that would shift power and, ultimately, population from the eastern seaboard, with its Atlantic mercantile focus, to the remote interior of the continent and new agrarian interests. In the House of Representatives, the witty Fisher Ames of Massachusetts had already criticized the deal with France in a memorable epigram: "We are to give money of which we have too little for land of which we have too much." He also viewed with contempt the proposed enlargement of the nation, characterizing the multicultural town of New Orleans as a "Gallo-Hispano-Indian omnium gatherum of savages and adventurers." If Ames's Massachusetts persuaded just three of its four New England sisters to join in opposition to the prospective amendment, they would be able to block it—definitively killing the bargain with Napoleon.

In August came an alarming letter from Livingston in Paris indicating that Napoleon himself might try to kill the deal even without New England's cooperation. Just weeks away from crowning himself as emperor, he reportedly began to think in more grandiose imperial terms, dropping broad hints that his sale to the Americans of such a huge piece of the planet might not be final. Treaty terms included an official deadline of October for final approval by the U.S. Senate; if that august body proved balky, recalcitrant, or slow, the ruler of France might well tear up the one-sided agreement that Americans had already begun celebrating.

This ticking clock led Jefferson to put aside his legalistic scruples and get down to the rough business of persuasion: winning treaty approval from two-thirds of the Senate and financial authorization from the House for money to pay Paris. One early vote had been disturbingly close: John Randolph of Virginia, a radical advocate of states' rights, introduced a ringing resolution to deny the money for Louisiana, and it failed by only two votes in the House, 57 to 59.

As the autumn advanced, however, momentum shifted, and on October 20 the Senate voted 24 to 7 in favor of the deal. Fortunately, James Monroe had already taken the bold (and possibly illegal) step of arranging with two banking houses, one in Britain and one in Holland, to get a $2 million down payment into Napoleon's hand to prevent any outbreak of seller's remorse.

As for Jefferson, he apparently never regretted the compromise of his principles that made the deal possible. In 1810, a year after leaving the White House, he justified his course of action in a memorable letter. "A strict observance of the written laws is doubtless one of the duties of a good citizen, but it is not the *highest*," he wrote. "The laws of necessity, of self-preservation, of saving our country when in danger, are of a higher necessity. To lose our country by a scrupulous adherence to written law, would be to lose the law itself, with life, liberty, property and all those who are enjoying them with us; thus absurdly sacrificing the end to the means."

Napoleon also felt proud of his performance after the deal had been done, with the tricolor replacing the Spanish flag in New Orleans at the end of November, but then lowered permanently three weeks later and giving way to the Stars and Stripes. He took comfort in the idea that the transmission of such an epic piece of real estate to the Americans would ultimately harm his British archenemies. "This accession of territory strengthens forever the power of the United States," he told Barbé-Marbois, "and I have just given to England a maritime rival that will sooner or later humble their pride." Napoleon's biographer Andrew Roberts notes the prophetic nature of this boast: within ten years, the United States challenged Britain in the War of 1812 and continued the bloody struggle until February 1815, engaging valuable British forces that otherwise could have been used at Waterloo.

Another distinguished English historian, Paul Johnson, takes a far less charitable view of the First Consul's decision to hand Louisiana to the Americans. He writes that "if Bonaparte had used France's legitimate rights to its American territory to explore and create an enormous dominion across the Atlantic, instead of trying to carve out an illegitimate empire in Europe, he would have enriched France instead of impoverishing her, provided scope for countless adventurous young Frenchmen instead of killing them in futile battles, and incidentally inflicted more damage on his British opponents than all his efforts in Europe." Johnson calls this blunder "Bonaparte's greatest single failure of imagination," which stemmed from the fact that "he knew nothing of America and desired to know nothing until it was too late."

Considering the odd and tortuous path to the triumph of the purchase, historian Charles Cerami in his 2004 book *Jefferson's Great Gamble* observes that "to have been given such an imperial gift as the Louisiana Territory must have convinced many of the seriously faithful that nature's design for the planet included a special role for America."

Aside from the whims of the mercurial emperor, the instantaneous enlargement of the United States required a complicated series of interconnected, unforeseen developments; in the absence of any one link, the whole chain could have been broken. Had Napoleon allowed Spain to continue its sleepy administration of the territory, had the Spanish monarchy refused to cooperate with his aggressive land grab, had the former slaves in Haiti not rebelled against their masters and liquidated a mighty French army, had Napoleon not changed his mind with sudden vehemence and declined to take possession of the colony, had Jefferson sent less able representatives to France or maintained his scruples and insisted on amending the Constitution in order to double the size of the country—had any of these disparate issues played out in a different way, it could have prevented or at least delayed America's emergence as a true continental power. As Cerami put it, "One must credit the success of the negotiation to a long list of events that somehow all fell into place as if by design."

Oscar Handlin also discerned design in the territory the United States gained so surprisingly in 1803, and specially credited the unusually early winter on the Scheldt River in the Netherlands. "Perhaps it was the destiny of this land to be American—to await the conglomerate hosts from New England and the South and from all the ends of Europe who were to make its potentialities real," he wrote. "But without . . . the miscalculations of an emperor, and a trick of the climate, Louisiana might long have remained foreign soil. . . . Thanks to the ice that had formed across the waters of a remote Dutch harbor, the advancing host of American settlers moving westward towards the Pacific at a turning point in our history now found the way open before them."

Even at the time, the participants in the process understood the significance of their achievement. After the negotiations successfully concluded in France, Robert Livingston wrote with justifiable pride: "We have lived long, but this is the noblest work of our whole lives. The treaty which we have just signed has not been obtained by art or dictated by force; equally advantageous to the two contracting parties, it will change vast solitudes into flourishing districts. From this day the United States take their place among powers of the first rank."

"DIRTY SHIRTS" VS. "WELLINGTON'S HEROES": At "Line Jackson," a nearly mile-long, seven-foot-high, improvised rampart built of mud, straw, sugar barrels, and cypress logs; New Orleans, January 8, 1815.

"It appears that the unerring hand of Providence shielded my men from the powers of balls, bombs, and rockets." —General Andrew Jackson

7

AMERICAN AGINCOURT

Astonishing Victory, Answered Prayers

It's easier to discern the influence of destiny or divine direction on grand, sweeping, instantly significant events, but providence can play an equally obvious role in intimate, obscure, even squalid encounters. Victory in the greatest battle of America's most difficult war, for instance, required a fortunate outcome in a nasty, bloody, little brawl outside a frontier tavern in Tennessee.

The chief victim and principal instigator of that ugly, nearly fatal scrap was Andrew Jackson, who almost bled to death just months before leading his outclassed, greatly outnumbered troops to astounding triumph at the Battle of New Orleans. Without Jackson that victory would have been impossible, and without that victory the badly battered forces of the United States never could have claimed success in what historians have called the "Second War for American Independence." In other words, the fate of the young nation depended on dumb luck—or providential protection—in a dumb fight at the City Hotel in Nashville on the morning of September 4, 1813.

Jackson should have known better than to involve himself in an utterly unnecessary confrontation: at age forty-six, he was already Tennessee's most celebrated citizen, having previously served in both the House of Representatives and the U.S. Senate. In the midst of the

War of 1812, he'd won appointment as major general of the militia in order to defend the region from Indian uprising and possible British invasion.

He had also racked up painful prior experience on the field of honor, fighting several duels with political rivals or fellow lawyers who dared to disrespect him in court. On one occasion he tried earnestly to kill the sitting governor of Tennessee, whose determined efforts to follow anti-dueling laws and escape death frustrated Jackson's desire for "satisfaction." In a later instance, he succeeded in arranging a duel at dawn with a business associate who had quarreled with him over a horse race, and who may have obliquely insulted Jackson's wife. Allowing his opponent to fire the first shot, Jackson took a bullet an inch above his heart, which he carried with him for the rest of his life. Nevertheless, he managed to stay on his feet, laboriously aimed and cocked his pistol, and then squeezed off a shot that killed his adversary with a bullet to the abdomen.

It was another duel that exploded into the wild, brutal 1813 melee that almost changed the course of history. This time, General Jackson served as second for one of his brigade majors in the militia who meant to settle a complicated quarrel with pistols at sunrise. The solemn encounter produced a scratch on the hand for Jackson's man but a far more embarrassing injury for his opponent. Jesse Benton took a nonfatal bullet in his buttocks—widely interpreted as a sign that he had tried to dodge the shot and thereby violated the code of honor demanding that the duelists must face each other directly without moving.

As the story circulated in military and political circles throughout Tennessee, Benton nursed his bloodied backside and blamed his humiliation on Jackson, alleging that the general had improperly counted off the paces between adversaries and allowed his friend to violate protocol by "wheeling" while taking his shot. These charges enraged the wounded man's brother, Thomas Hart Benton, who held the rank of lieutenant colonel and functioned as principal aide on the general's military staff. When the Benton brothers publicized their complaints, Jackson felt betrayed as well as insulted: he told friends that he might not kill his colleague Colonel Benton, but he had every intention of horsewhipping him if he ever got the chance.

With that purpose very possibly in mind, he rode the twelve miles from his plantation home, the Hermitage, into the center of Nashville on a Saturday morning when he heard that the Benton brothers had checked into the City Hotel. Jackson and two friends armed themselves with pistols, and the general also carried a riding whip. They went to the town post office to pick up their mail, and on their return they spotted the Benton brothers refreshing themselves in the hotel's tavern. Thomas Hart Benton came to the doorway as Jackson approached, with the general ostentatiously brandishing his whip and bellowing, "Now, you damned rascal, I am going to punish you. Defend yourself!"

Accounts differ on which man drew first, but within moments they held pistols at each other's chests. Jackson pushed forward as Benton tried to back away, heading down a hallway toward wooden steps that led to the river. Meanwhile, Benton's brother, Jesse, still suffering from the wounds to his rear end and to his pride, came up behind the general and fired. Jackson fell forward, shooting as he did; his bullet grazed the sleeve of Tom Benton's coat, who then fired twice at Jackson's falling figure. Jesse Benton ran toward them to finish the job, aiming his gun at Jackson, who lay facedown in a spreading pool of blood, but a bystander shielded the general. At that point, Jackson's friends came onto the scene, firing at Tom Benton, who pitched backward down the stairs, and attacking Jesse Benton with a dagger and a sword cane.

When horrified observers finally managed to separate the combatants, it became obvious that only General Jackson had been seriously wounded; he was bleeding profusely and falling in and out of consciousness. His friends carried Jackson to a room at another hotel across the street, while most of the doctors in town rushed to the scene to try to save the state's most famous citizen. One bullet had shattered his left shoulder, and another was wedged deeply into the upper bone of that arm. His blood soaked through two mattresses, and the physicians determined that he would die if they didn't amputate his arm. As they prepared the limb for surgery, the unconscious general suddenly opened his burning, blue-gray eyes and issued a growled command: "I'll keep the arm." Even in his desperate state, none of the physicians dared defy his wishes. Instead, they applied Indian remedies such as slippery elm until the bleeding finally stopped. Jackson remained immobilized for weeks.

Meanwhile, the Benton brothers, who shouted their defiance after Jackson supporters had taken the general's broken body away, found themselves threatened and despised by Jackson loyalists in the state. "I am literally in hell here," Tom Benton wrote immediately following the fight, and with his brother he quickly escaped to Missouri. There he rose quickly in frontier politics and won election to the U.S. Senate in 1821. He served there for thirty years and, as Senator Thomas Hart Benton, became one of President Andrew Jackson's most important allies without ever apologizing for the gunfight that almost claimed the future president's life.

Another eerie connection added to the air of destiny surrounding the brawl at City Hotel. One of the guests at the establishment who had been frightened by the screams and gunfire that shattered the Saturday morning calm was Charles Frémon, who occupied a room with his wife and his infant son. That baby, who later amended the spelling of his last name, became the "Great Pathfinder," John Charles Frémont, the first presidential nominee of the new Republican Party and a Union general in the Civil War. He also became the doting husband of one of the famous beauties of the age, Jessie Benton—daughter of the same Tom Benton who had survived the Nashville encounter by falling conveniently down a flight of stairs.

"THEY MUST NOT ASK IN VAIN"

A month after the fateful, nearly fatal fight, Andrew Jackson defied his wife and his doctors to rise from his sickbed and lead his men into battle. His recovery remained perilously incomplete: still weak and pale from loss of blood, he suffered from almost constant pain and had difficulty riding with his damaged left arm in a sling. The Tennessee militia he commanded affectionately called him "Old Hickory" because hickory wood provided the toughest, most stubborn, least malleable material for any frontier workman. When he returned from his much-discussed ordeal, they noted that their indomitable general looked even more gaunt and cadaverous than usual: though he was nearly six foot one, his estimated weight had fallen below 130 pounds.

Whatever his physical infirmities, Jackson felt unshakably determined to heed the pleas from governors of several states and to rush to the eastern portion of the Mississippi Territory (today's Alabama), where newly mobilized and highly motivated Indian warriors, encouraged by the British enemy, had perpetrated a massacre that claimed five hundred lives. "Those distressed citizens of that frontier . . . implored the brave Tennesseans for aid," he told his troops. "They must not ask in vain."

The crisis arose from a civil war within the Creek tribe. Young Creek radicals known as "Red Sticks" had been inspired by the Shawnee visionary Tecumseh to ally themselves with the English side in the War of 1812 in order to resist the unending American encroachment on their land. "Let the white race perish!" the warrior chief declared. "War now! War always! War on the living! War on the dead!"

As the first targets for that perpetual warfare the Red Sticks chose members of their own tribe who traded profitably with the settlers and built towns and farms on the American model. The young warriors yearned for a return to the old ways, uncorrupted by the alien influence of the white man. The Americanized Indians retreated to Fort Mims, about thirty-five miles north of Mobile, where they crowded together with 250 white civilians who had fled their farms to escape the violence. When the Red Sticks captured the fort, they butchered nearly everyone, with thirty survivors who managed to escape and reported the ritual scalping of women and the deaths of children who had been picked up by their ankles to bash their heads against the stockade.

Motivated by these horrific reports, Jackson's Tennesseans vowed revenge. Driven by their determined general, they moved at remarkable speed, marching an average of thirty-six miles a day through mostly wild and difficult country. Along the way, the two thousand

American fighters were joined by more than six hundred native allies, including Cherokee, Choctaws, and loyal Creeks, before attacking the heavily fortified enemy stronghold at Horseshoe Bend. The five-hour battle that followed claimed the lives of 857 Creek warriors, while Jackson held his losses to just forty-seven of his American troops and twenty-three Indian allies. During the struggle, a young third lieutenant named Sam Houston played an especially courageous role, leading the way over the barricades and into the Creek compound despite an arrow that pierced his thigh and remained there for the duration of the battle. His colleagues took note of the miraculous nature of Houston's success and survival, rightly predicting a fateful future.

"LITTLE BETTER THAN PRISONERS IN THEIR OWN COUNTRY"

After Horseshoe Bend, Jackson returned to Tennessee for a quick visit home, but his main concern remained the possibility of a British invasion. Had the English been able to synchronize their own massive assault with the Creek uprising, the preoccupied Americans could hardly have defended the Crescent City and the lower Mississippi Valley. But as it was, the British cabinet considered their American war a secondary priority until they had secured the decisive defeat of Napoleon with the Battle of Leipzig in October 1813.

At that point, they began executing elaborate schemes for the decisive defeat and potential dismemberment of the United States. American forces had failed miserably in two major attempts to strike against the British in Canada and offered only intermittent challenges to the dominance of the Royal Navy. With battle-hardened armies and unlimited sea power now available to humble the upstart Americans, the English devised a three-pronged invasion that, in the words of the foreign secretary, Lord Castlereagh, would leave "the Americans little better than prisoners in their own country."

The eastern element of the coordinated attack involved an amphibious force in a successful drive to seize the new nation's capital and nearby Baltimore, while driving out the desperate government and burning its public buildings. The assault from the north sent an army of ten thousand from Montreal to cross Lake Champlain by boat and march into New York State, but the attack stalled because of the unexpectedly spirited defense by a newly constructed American fleet on the lake. The most important thrust of the British war-ending plans would come from the Gulf of Mexico with an even larger force (up to fourteen thousand) to seize the crucial port city of New Orleans and separate the Mississippi Valley from the rest of the country. Napoleon had given up on Louisiana in fear that he could never defend the territory against a determined British invasion. Now, just eleven years after Bonaparte sold the colony to the United States, and weeks after his decisive defeat on the European continent, the English felt ready to make his Mississippi nightmares a reality.

In facing the crisis, General Jackson made a series of crucial decisions entirely on his own. Normally he would have corresponded with the Department of War and won authorization for his major maneuvers, but the burning and occupation of the nation's capital left no functioning government with which to communicate. For more than a month he operated as an independent, instinctive force of nature. On his own responsibility, he demanded more troops from Mississippi, Tennessee, and Kentucky, though Kentucky was clearly outside his sphere of responsibility.

On the East Coast, the flight from Washington left President James Madison in a reputed state of "nervous prostration" (the equivalent of a nervous breakdown). He turned to his steady, unflappable secretary of state, James Monroe, for help, asking him to take over as secretary of war from the discredited Pennsylvanian John Armstrong, who had staked his position on assurances that the British would never attack Washington. Monroe suddenly found himself in charge of the two most important departments of government simultaneously; the revolutionary hero who had helped negotiate the purchase of Louisiana in the first place now took responsibility for defending the new territory from invaders. As Jackson wrote to his wife, Rachel, "The burning of the Capitol may be a disgrace . . . but it will give impulse and energy to our cause, the change too, in Secretaries of war will add much." Monroe, for his part, placed full faith in General Jackson, scraping together $100,000 from the government's depleted treasury to cover his army's expenses and adding Georgia as an area from which to draw recruits. Despite this confidence, a dispatch from the War Department warned Jackson: "A war of seven years may be expected."

Jackson refused to accept the idea of such a prolonged campaign, acting boldly to block enemy progress. Though he understood the British aim to occupy New Orleans, he first moved his own troops in the opposite direction, heading east toward the town of Pensacola in Spanish Florida to capture the area's major fort and deny the English a convenient place to land their troops. In the process of his Pensacola raid, the rogue American general violated the official Spanish status of neutrality, while dashing off a letter to the War Department declaring that he had acted entirely on his own initiative.

At the end of November 1814, Old Hickory changed direction and rode as quickly as possible to take personal command of the increasingly frightened defenders of New Orleans. By this time his militia army had dwindled dramatically, as many of its members headed home for the winter. Jackson determined to defend the city with the one thousand men who followed him to Louisiana, supplemented by local volunteer companies with their gaudy, French-style uniforms, a few veterans of the regular army, some Indian allies, and a well-disciplined, spit-and-polish regiment of freed blacks who had escaped to America from the bloody rebellion in Saint-Domingue. He also demanded the return of major contingents of militia from Tennessee and Kentucky; more than two thousand of them arrived just in time to take part in the most significant military engagements at the end of the year.

"UNSPEAKABLE THE RICHES AND SPLENDOR"

The booming, bustling New Orleans that welcomed General Jackson as its designated defender impressed its contemporaries as the most exotic and polyglot metropolis in the United States. The population had more than doubled since the American takeover in 1803, with 24,552 residents counted in the 1810 census, of whom only 3,200 identified themselves as English-speaking Americans. The rest were French, Spanish, Portuguese, Italian, German, or Irish, along with a substantial population of mixed-race "free people of color," many of whom owned slaves. While a sprinkling of recently arrived Yankee merchants and traders played prominent roles in the city's business establishment, the social elite spoke French and looked down on American manners as crude, raw, and uncivilized. The haughty Creoles who defined the distinctive culture of the town felt proud of their descent from the original French, Spanish, or even African settlers of Louisiana and accepted American rule in part because they hated the British even more—especially after Britain prevailed in twenty years of global warfare against revolutionary and Napoleonic France. American visitors to the Crescent City felt shocked at its languid, semitropical, carefully cultivated licentiousness. When Rachel Jackson, the general's pious wife, visited New Orleans after the battle that determined its fate, she found it difficult to adjust to local mores. "Great Babylon is come up before me," she declared in horror. "Oh, the wickedness, the idolatry of the place! Unspeakable the riches and splendor."

The sophisticated Creoles in turn viewed General Jackson with considerable condescension, not at all sure what to make of the frontier fighter who had taken control of their city. One of the leading ladies of society described Jackson when he first came to town as "a tall, gaunt man, very erect . . . with a countenance furrowed by care and anxiety. His dress was simple and nearly threadbare. A small leather cap protected his head, and a short blue Spanish cloak his body, whilst his high dragoon boots [were] long innocent of polish or blacking. . . . His complexion was sallow and unhealthy; his hair iron grey, and his body thin and emaciated like that of one who had just recovered from a lingering sickness. . . . But a fierce glare . . . [lighted] his bright and hawk-like eye."

In dealing with the local gentry, the real problem involved not Jackson's looks but his language: he spoke no French at all and required a translator for even mundane conversations. Fortunately, he found an old friend in New Orleans who became an indispensable aide. Edward Livingston had served alongside Jackson in the House of Representatives some fifteen years earlier, and the two Jeffersonians had formed both personal and political bonds. By one of the odd quirks of fate, Edward Livingston was the younger brother of Robert Livingston, who, as minister to France, had negotiated the Louisiana Purchase together with James Monroe. After three terms in Congress and a single term as mayor of New York City, Edward Livingston's finances collapsed due to mismanagement by an unscrupulous clerk. In desperate need of a fresh start, the middle-aged widower fled to the remote Territory of Orleans, which his older brother had helped to add to the United States, and there he played a role in qualifying Louisiana for statehood in 1812. He also met and married a French-speaking nineteen-year-old widow famous for her extraordinary beauty. With her olive skin, piercing dark eyes, and elegant, long neck, Louise d'Avezac had fled to New Orleans with her wealthy family after the bloody slave rebellion on the island colony of Saint-Domingue. This marital connection to the local gentry not only boosted Edward Livingston's status but also proved invaluable to Jackson in his efforts to unify and motivate the city for its own defense.

The general's first order of business involved rousing the port town to the impending English assault through a series of ringing proclamations that Livingston duly translated into French. One of them centered on a reported British attempt to recruit a notorious and powerful band of local pirates to their cause, with the general condemning the very idea that "men of honor" could possibly ally themselves with "pirates and robbers ... this hellish Banditti." Instead, Jackson appealed to national pride of every sort to stir the emotions of the decent residents of the state.

"Louisianans!" his announcement declared. "The proud British, the national and sworn Enemy of all Frenchmen, of all Americans, and of all freemen, has called upon you by proclamation; to aid her in her tyranny, and to prostrate the Holy Temple of our liberty.... I know that every ... Louisianian, either by birth or adoption, will promptly obey the voice of his Country ... rescue it from impending danger, or nobly die, in the last ditch in its defense."

"THIS HELLISH BANDITTI"

Much to Jackson's consternation, the "hellish Banditti" he so roundly denounced also wanted to "obey the voice" of their country and to join the motley forces defending the city. The pirates, numbering an estimated eight hundred fighters, had established their own illicit empire on two islands in Barataria Bay, a bay of the Gulf of Mexico. They were led by two enterprising and energetic brothers, Jean and Pierre Lafitte, and by a diminutive "bantam cock" of a fearless fighter known as Dominique You, who may or may not have been an older Lafitte brother. The origins of these three enterprising buccaneers remain an item of historical dispute, but best evidence suggests that, like so many new residents of Louisiana after the purchase, they were refugees from the bloodshed in Saint-Domingue. There are also strong indications that the Lafittes were descended from Sephardic Jews who had cruelly been expelled from Spain in 1492, so hatred of all things Spanish came naturally to them as an organizing principle of their piratical operations. With their own fleet of ships, manned by some of the best sailors and gunners in the Caribbean, the Lafittes happily harvested any Spanish craft unlucky enough to encounter them, then smuggled the cargoes (including slaves) into New Orleans for sale to the grateful populace.

The British naturally hoped to contact these illicit entrepreneurs and to solicit their support in conquering Louisiana, but Jean Lafitte wrote to the American governor suggesting that he and his men harbored very different inclinations. "This point of Louisiana that I occupy is of Great Importance in the present situation. I offer to defend it," he wrote. "I am the Lost Sheep who desires to return to the flock . . . for you to see through my faults such as they are."

Governor William Claiborne, a protégé of Thomas Jefferson's who had been dispatched to New Orleans to supervise its initial transfer to the United States, found himself deeply impressed by Lafitte's letter and prepared to put aside his personal history with the pirate. Two years before, Claiborne had offered a bounty of $500 for anyone who brought him Jean Lafitte's head; the next day a handbill appeared throughout the city in which Lafitte offered $1,000 for the head of the governor. Both men managed to escape decapitation long enough to agree to the idea of cooperation in defense of the threatened city.

General Jackson, on the other hand, refused to go along, maintaining his stubborn anti-pirate prejudice in defiance of all pleas to reconsider from the Creole grandees who valued the fighting spirit of Lafitte and his irregulars. The impasse continued until early December, when Lafitte and the diminutive Dominique, who customarily wore oversized hats decorated with huge plumes, "accidentally" stumbled upon Jackson at the corner of St. Philip and Royal Streets, near the general's headquarters. According to Lafitte's own recollections many years after the fact, he took a confrontational tone with the American commander. "I challenged the general to a duel, in reply to the unfounded and punishable insults directed upon us," he recalled. Though Jackson's past demonstrated his vigorous appetite for such encounters, his responsibilities in New Orleans left him too busy dueling with the British Empire to consider a risky break to duel with a saucy pirate. Instead, he found himself impressed enough by the man's bravado to agree to a private meeting to continue conversation over Lafitte's proffered service.

That late-night session at Old Hickory's candlelit headquarters provided a fitting cinematic climax to the pirate's campaign for military participation. In fact, the dramatic confrontation received the Hollywood treatment in Cecil B. DeMille's 1938 movie *The Buccaneer*, with Frederic March as Lafitte and Hugh Sothern as Jackson; twenty years later, DeMille remade the film (this time with his son-in-law Anthony Quinn directing), casting Yul Brynner as the pirate and the formidable Charlton Heston as the future president. The only summary of the actual encounter comes from Jackson's chief of engineers, who reported that "Mr. Lafitte" solicited on behalf of his men "the honor of serving under our banners, that they might have an opportunity of proving that if they had infringed the revenue laws, yet none were more ready than they to defend the country." Jackson at last accepted their offer, while welcoming specific pledges to provide much-needed cannon, powder, shot, and flints to the American defenders. Most important, the artillery expertise of the pirate gunners and their deep familiarity with the bays and bayous of the region could prove indispensable to defense of the city.

"WE MUST FIGHT THEM TONIGHT"

By all rules of logic, the outcome never should have been in doubt: the English invaders enjoyed an enormous edge over the Americans not just in the quantity of their troops but in their quality as well. These veterans, including some of the most storied regiments of the British Empire, had fought with the Duke of Wellington in the Peninsular Campaign in Spain, defeating Napoleonic armies reputed to be the best in the world. In their expedition to America, the soldiers reveled in their well-earned designation as "Wellington's Heroes" and took special pride in their daring, battle-scarred thirty-six-year-old commander, Sir Edward Michael Pakenham, who happened to be Wellington's brother-in-law and one of the more celebrated soldiers of the realm. "Pakenham might not be the brightest genius," Wellington said of his wife's younger brother, "but my partiality for him does not lead me astray when I tell you he is one of the best we have."

If this much-admired officer possessed a characteristic flaw as a commander, it would have been his impetuosity, which stemmed from a reckless confidence in his own inevitable success. During the expedition to occupy the Mississippi Valley, his superiors at the War Office encouraged the smug certainty that magnificent victory had been preordained: they sent him to America with a secret royal commission naming him the new governor of Louisiana as soon as he captured New Orleans, and promising an earldom to accompany the appointment. To enjoy this prestigious new status, Sir Edward's aristocratic young fiancée accompanied him to the New World, planning to wait with the British ships in the Gulf of Mexico until the fighting finished and the celebrations began.

From their base of operations on the island colony of Jamaica, nearly fifteen thousand military personnel (including seamen of the Royal Navy) assembled for the capture of the Crescent City, more than three times the number of oddly assorted troops Jackson could muster to oppose them. Admiral Cochrane, in overall charge of the invasion force, attempted to undermine morale in New Orleans by circulating the boast that he planned to enjoy Christmas dinner in the town. "Perhaps so," Jackson reportedly replied. "But I shall have the honor of presiding at that dinner."

For all its advantages, the British fleet, with its fearsome complement of cannon, depended on sail, like all other warships of the era. Fortunately for the defenders of Louisiana, that meant the Royal Navy couldn't easily cruise upriver against the powerful current of the mighty Mississippi to simply shell New Orleans into submission. Instead, they deposited the invading force well to the east and the south of the city, where they loaded their heavy equipment onto barges to cross marshy Lake Borgne, then pushed and poled their way along the alligator-infested Bayou Bienvenue in the hopes of surprising the defenders of the town.

Two days before Christmas at eleven in the morning, the British advance guard seized Villeré Plantation, some eight miles from the city, and captured its owner, Major Gabriel Villeré. Colonel William Thornton wanted to continue immediately to march into the lightly defended town and to capture or kill the unprepared Americans, but his superior officer, General John Keane, inexplicably halted the eager, advancing redcoats. He insisted on waiting for hours, or for days if necessary, until the rest of the army joined them and regrouped. His ill-advised hesitation cost the British their best chance at victory: for most of the afternoon on that cold, clear December day, no organized opposition stood between crack British troops and the vulnerable city just a few hours' march away.

At his elegantly furnished headquarters at 106 Royal Street, General Jackson extended his long, thin legs under his writing desk and busied himself with a series of letters. One of them, to his brother-in-law back home in Tennessee, expressed surprise that "the British had made no movement of importance" and concluded with the confident summary "All well."

Even as Old Hickory penned these words, Gabriel Villeré risked everything to warn the general of the two thousand lavishly equipped British regulars who had already occupied his plantation. Waiting for a moment of inattention, Villeré suddenly bolted from his captors, jumped out of a window of his own home, pushed aside several soldiers who blocked his path, and ran for the cypress swamps at the edge of his property. Redcoats fired at him as he leaped over a high picket fence, and Colonel Thornton screamed, "Catch him or kill him!" As British troops fanned out to find him, he hid in the foliage of a huge oak tree, where he tearfully killed a favorite dog who had loyally followed him in his race for safety but now threatened to expose his hiding place. Finally running to the home of a neighbor, he galloped into town together with a member of the New Orleans Committee of Public Safety.

Admitted to see Jackson, they spoke excitedly in French while a translator conveyed their message about the concentration of British forces just eight miles away, with more troops arriving by the hour. According to an eyewitness, the general immediately sprang up from his sofa. "With an eye of fire and an emphatic blow upon the table," he furiously shouted, "By the Eternal, they shall not sleep on our soil!" As his temper subsided, Jackson called for his chief aides and invited his excited visitors to share a glass of wine with him. "Gentlemen, the British are below," he announced in a tone of firm determination. "We must fight them tonight. . . . I will smash them, so help me God!"

To fulfill this pledge, Jackson hastily organized a surprise attack on the newly established English encampment. He ordered one of the two U.S. Navy gunboats anchored at New Orleans to make its way downriver after dark and to prepare to shell the enemy position. Meanwhile, he assembled most of the men available to him—a mix of army regulars, militia forces, local volunteers, a crack regiment of free men of color, and eighteen Choctaw warriors—instructed them on the importance of silence and stealth, and then led them on horseback toward the enemy. The December sun set at five o'clock, and the American columns paused behind trees and fields of sugar cane stubble, waiting for full dark. They remained so well concealed that British sentries just five hundred yards away never sensed their presence. The rising moon remained shrouded in a dense, protective mist, while Jackson noted that the enemy's campfires, "burning very bright . . . [,] gave a good view of his situation." At precisely seven-thirty, by prearrangement with Old Hickory, the *Carolina* opened fire from the other side of the dark river. The young British lieutenant George Robert Gleig felt the same sense of shock and dread as his more experienced colleagues. "Flash, flash, flash, came from the river," he remembered, "the roar of cannon followed, and the light of her own broadside displayed to us an enemy's vessel at anchor near the opposite bank, and pouring a perfect shower of grape and round shot, into the camp."

The skirmish that followed lasted for two hours and illustrated the famous poetic lines written fifty years later by Matthew Arnold, who described the human condition as "swept with confused alarms of struggle and flight / Where ignorant armies clash by night." The hand-to-hand combat matched British swords and bayonets against American hunting knives and tomahawks. In a square mile of wintry plantation fields, 24 Americans fell, with 115 wounded. The British losses proved heavier, but they managed to hold their ground until the Americans withdrew and returned to the town. Nevertheless, military analyst Robert Quimby, author of a 1997 operational and command study of the War of 1812, maintains that Jackson's bold night attack left the British "disabused of their expectation of an easy conquest. The unexpected and severe attack made Keane even more cautious."

"BLOW THEM UP"

That caution gave Jackson two full weeks to build formidable earthwork fortifications along the Rodriguez Canal, south of the city; now that he knew the location of the enemy, he could prepare properly for the inevitable attack. The canal, a ditch four feet deep and ten feet wide, ran nearly three-quarters of a mile from the Mississippi River up to the edge of a swamp with cypress trees and undergrowth so thick it would surely deter advancing troops. On Christmas Eve, the Americans concentrated on deepening the canal and using the mud to form thick walls behind this moat. To prevent the soil from sliding back into the ditch, they felled cypress logs and installed them as part of the rampart, placing artillery pieces at regular intervals along what they called "Line Jackson." Throughout the length of this defensive fortification, the walls rose seven or eight feet above the bottom of the broad, muddy trough that the British would have to cross before they could get at the Americans.

Despite these intensive preparations, the civilians of New Orleans felt increasingly fearful. After all, the British recently had burned the national capital in Washington, so they would feel no compunction over torching the Crescent City. Dread of this wretched fate left the fashionable ladies of the community in an especially hysterical state. They had heard lurid stories of mass rape and pillage by the redcoats during their brief occupation of Maryland, and some of those accounts may even have been true. Without doubt, the English commanders in Louisiana encouraged the aggressive instincts of their soldiers by promising each of them a fair share of "booty and beauty" if they succeeded in seizing the wealthy, cosmopolitan port that dominated the Mississippi Valley.

Though he had already imposed martial law, Jackson couldn't stop the hysteria that increasingly afflicted the beleaguered town. When the general heard rumors that the Louisiana legislature wanted to offer the British terms of surrender if they guaranteed to spare the city from serious damage, he ordered Governor Claiborne to arrest the legislators if necessary and to "blow them up" if they resisted. Claiborne dutifully responded by closing the legislative chamber with a heavy lock and posting guards to prevent the representatives from assembling during the crisis. In a later exchange with the state's chief executive, Jackson threatened Claiborne in the midst of an artillery duel. "By the almighty God," Jackson bellowed at the governor as his gunners began to run out of ammunition, "if you do not send me balls and powder instantly, I shall chop off your head, and have it rammed into one of those field pieces."

CHEATING DEATH ONCE AGAIN

The fierce, three-hour exchange of cannonades on New Year's Day frustrated British hopes of bombarding the Americans into surrender or withdrawal. It began with the early morning targeting of Jackson's headquarters at 106 Royal Street in an audacious effort to remove the American commander as a factor in the fight. Jackson's French-born chief engineer, Major Latour, recalled that the redcoat artillerymen showed menacing skill, interrupting a festive New Year's breakfast for the general and his aides. "In less than ten minutes, upwards of one hundred balls, rockets and shells struck the house and rendered it impossible to remain there. The general-in-chief and all his staff were in the apartments when the firing began, but though bricks, splinters of wood and furniture, rockets and balls were flying in all directions, not a single person was wounded." Old Hickory had cheated death once again.

At Line Jackson, the improvised walls of mud, straw, sugar barrels, and cypress logs also managed to survive and for the most part did their job of protecting precious artillery, while the American gunners fired back at the enemy with uncanny accuracy. The general took particular pleasure at the performance of a battery manned by the well-practiced pirates, led by the plumed, preening Dominique You. "I wish I had fifty such guns on this line, with five hundred such devils as those fellows behind them," Jackson declared as he rode along the rampart to encourage his troops. When Captain You sustained a wound to his forearm, he only redoubled his efforts, cursing the hated English and promising that he would "make them pay for that." Jackson reportedly told an aide: "If I were ordered to storm the gates of hell with Captain Dominique as my lieutenant, I would have no misgivings of the result!"

With the British batteries running out of ammunition, the volleys finally came to an end. Immediately a group of fiddlers and French horn players ran down to the ramparts of Line Jackson and began playing merry tunes for the entertainment of the delighted troops; after all, this was New Orleans and it was New Year's Day. The hoots and clapping of the noisy American celebration only increased the sense of humiliation on the part of the frustrated redcoats, who heard the music from the enemy fortifications as they sweated and strained to pull back their own guns out of range. Old Hickory, meanwhile, increased the joy of his weary soldiers with a general order dictated to an aide: "The Major General tenders to the troops he has the honor to command his good wishes for a happy new year, and especially to those officers & men at the pieces of Artillery. . . . Watch Word Fight on—the Contractor will issue half a gill of whiskey around."

The experience of the night attack and the artillery duel should have been enough to convince General Pakenham and his lieutenants that the forces they faced were unexpectedly fierce and formidable, but Sir Edward refused to accept the idea that the ragtag band opposing them could fight on anything like equal terms with Wellington's Heroes. During the night battle of December 23, the English took a few prisoners from the Kentucky militia and laughed out loud at their filthy, homespun hunting shirts of "a dark and dingy color" and their loose-fitting headgear made from the skins of raccoons and foxes. The British celebrated the name "redcoats" and took pride in their crisp, bright uniforms, while they began applying the designation "Dirty Shirts" to their bedraggled backwoods opponents.

"WE HAVE SLEPT ENOUGH"

Weary of all the delays and disappointments, General Pakenham prepared a bold plan to surprise the Americans with a well-coordinated, decisive attack, marching after midnight toward the sleeping city and then storming the American ramparts just before dawn. He would send columns to either side of Line Jackson to outflank the enemy, while elite troops rushed to the center with scaling ladders to place against the mud walls. With the aid of this equipment, the well-prepared detachment could climb eight feet out of the broad, deep ditch in front of the Yankee battlements and use their deadly bayonets as they poured over the top. Meanwhile, the trusted and aggressive Colonel Thornton would quietly cross the river at midnight and then seize the lightly defended artillery batteries, turning their guns on whatever defenders remained on Line Jackson or, if necessary, on the city itself.

The plan may have made some sense in tactical terms, but it depended heavily on the element of surprise. Pakenham also seemed unaware or at least unconcerned that Jackson had recently followed Jean

Lafitte's advice and extended his defense line and its mud barricades all the way into the overgrown cypress swamp on the American left. That meant that advancing columns could never get around that flank without floundering in murky, alligator-infested waters. Fortunately for the defenders, their sharp-eyed frontier scouts and omnipresent local spies did a much better job monitoring the enemy and discovered the British intentions at least twelve hours before the scheduled pre-dawn strike on Sunday morning, January 8.

Jackson deposited himself on a couch at his damaged headquarters, hoping to catch some sleep before the climactic confrontation, with his fully uniformed aides resting on the floor around him. At 1:00 a.m. a courier pounded on the door with dramatic news. Sentries had heard and seen Thornton's men hauling unwieldy flat-bottom boats toward the river, so it was obvious that the long-anticipated attack could commence at any moment. "Gentlemen," Jackson announced to his bleary-eyed lieutenants, "we have slept enough. Rise. The enemy will be upon us in a few minutes."

They silently made their way through the damp and freezing darkness to Line Jackson for final words of encouragement to the troops. Orders were passed to keep all voices down and avoid unnecessary noise in order to avoid tipping off the enemy that the Americans expected them. Jackson made a brief stop at Dominique You's battery, where a circle of pirates surrounded the glowing embers of a coal fire, patiently dripping pots of strong coffee in the traditional Creole manner. Taken with the powerful aroma, Jackson addressed Captain You. "That smells like better coffee than we can get," Old Hickory observed. "Smuggle it?"

"Mebbe so, Général," the elegant buccaneer observed, and cheerfully filled a steaming cup for his commander.

At four in the morning, after tense hours of watchful waiting, the militia general John Adair received an unexpected order to march forward with his reserve force of one thousand Kentuckians to reinforce the Tennessee commander William Carroll at the very center of Line Jackson. As battle historian Robert Remini notes, this predawn decision by the general in chief was "a stroke of pure luck, for this was the very part of the line where the British would concentrate their assault." Pakenham had selected this target because a deserter had told him it constituted the most vulnerable spot in the American defenses, not knowing that the reserves would strengthen the center at the last moment by nearly doubling the available manpower.

Back in the sleeping town, a community of Ursuline nuns kept an all-night vigil of a different sort. Dedicated to the spiritual education of young ladies and to performing acts of mercy for the sick and the poor, the holy sisters built the first convent in the United States and also opened the first girls' school in the country. Their gracious headquarters, dating from 1751, still stands in the heart of the French Quarter, the oldest surviving structure in the Mississippi Valley. In 1812, an apparent miracle served to protect that building from a raging conflagration that was sweeping through the town. As the flames approached, the sisters carried a recently arrived statue of the Blessed Virgin to a front window and placed it in the path of the fire; the wind shifted immediately and the convent remained untouched.

On the eve of the great battle in 1815, the Ursulines sensed the imminence of the English attack and feared for the total destruction of the city and an end to their godly works. They placed this same wonder-working figure, now known as Our Lady of Prompt Succor, on top of their chief altar and made it the focus of a long, sleepless night of tears and prayer, begging for divine intercession to rescue the seemingly hopeless, outnumbered American defenders. Before dawn on Sunday, the prioress, Mother Ste. Marie Olivier de Vezin, made a public vow to ordain a solemn mass of thanksgiving to be sung every year, for eternity, should Jackson's forces secure an improbable victory. Reviewing the calendar of saints shortly before dawn, the sisters found to their delight that January 8 was the feast day of Saint Victoria. They took this to be an auspicious sign, but as light broke, they still shuddered on hearing the roar of distant cannon that punctuated their earnest prayers.

"I WILL WAIT MY PLANS NO LONGER"

Perhaps those prayers brought immediate results, as British forces faced a series of paralyzing mishaps as they prepared for their massive attack. Thornton's fourteen hundred troops, sent to overwhelm the American detachment on the other side of the river, arrived at their point of embarkation just after dark to find no boats available to transport them across the water. Instead of crossing the Mississippi and falling on the sleeping Yankees without warning, they spent the next eight hours dragging heavy barges two hundred yards over the murk and mud separating them from the shore. With the imperative of managing the crossing before first light, they never gathered enough boats to accommodate the entire strike force, transporting barely a third of the intended soldiers and marines. As if this weren't bad enough, Pakenham hadn't reckoned on the powerful currents of the Mississippi: as Thornton's men rowed with desperate intensity, the dark river carried them far downstream, depositing them on the opposite shore several miles away from their intended destination, and making a coordinated attack all but impossible.

Meanwhile, an even more costly blunder afflicted the decisive attack force aimed at the American center. As Sir Edward Pakenham rode up to see if his elite forces were ready to unleash their planned lightning strike, he found Major General Samuel Gibbs fretful and frustrated. The 44th Regiment, a well-regarded Irish outfit, had not yet arrived to play its crucial part at the head of the column: they had been assigned to carry the bundles of sticks that would cover the mud of the Rodriguez Canal, allowing the redcoats to rush forward without sinking, as well as bearing the ladders that would give them a chance to climb over the American walls. Gibbs had already sent out messengers to try to find the missing Irishmen, ladders, and fascines; now Pakenham dispatched his own courier for the same purpose.

In the confusion, precious minutes ticked away as the approaching dawn made it patently impossible for the British to attack under cover of darkness. With any hope of pinpoint coordination altogether dissipated, a more cautious commander might have suspended the attack, but Pakenham continued to believe in the invincibility of Wellington's Heroes and in his own greatness as an inspirational leader of men. He assumed that Jackson's embarrassingly undisciplined forces would turn and run as soon as they saw a wave of glinting steel bayonets advancing implacably in their direction. Without waiting to see if Gibbs had successfully located the needed ladders and sticks, or learning much about the tardy progress of Thornton's diminished force on the other side of the river, Sir Edward impatiently declaimed, "I will wait my plans no longer."

He gave the order to advance, though the rising sun now denied him the advantage of darkness. The British commander nonetheless felt reassured by a thick fog that hung over the battlefield and could possibly work as well as night to conceal his marching regiments. Between the redcoats and the waiting Americans, open fields extended for nearly a half a mile with a crust of glistening frost covering the sugar cane stalks that had been cut back to stubble for the winter.

Behind Line Jackson, the general in chief called to the commanders at his center, Carroll and Adair, to make sure that their men aimed carefully and made every shot count. Their rifles could do little damage to targets until they came within four hundred yards. A "fire step" had been installed inside the mud walls, allowing the men to climb up to take aim over the ramparts. After each shot, they were supposed to step down and reload, giving their places immediately to the next line of riflemen, and then the next, so there would be no interruption in the sheet of heavy fire directed toward the relentlessly advancing enemy.

"THAT LEADEN TORRENT"

Jackson was standing atop the parapet, squinting toward the moving red line, when a stiff breeze arose from nowhere and promptly blew the thick fog into rapidly dissolving patches. For the first time, the British troops with their bright uniforms and glinting bayonets were clearly exposed as they moved relentlessly forward. The sudden gust of wind that revealed the enemy at precisely the right moment counted as one of those fortunate occurrences on the battlefield that struck participants as supernatural and wondrous.

One of the Dirty Shirts on the line, facing the British ranks for the first time, remembered that "the men were tense, but very cold. The enemy was now within five hundred yards.... Then—boom! Went our first guns . . . Then all the guns opened. The British batteries . . . concealed from us by the fog replied, directing their fire by the sound of our guns . . . their flashes lighting up the fog into all the hues of the rainbow."

The drums and bugles of the oncoming British regiments could faintly be heard beneath the thunder of the cannon, and the proud banners of these fabled units could be glimpsed above the smoke of the artillery. In fact, General Adair complained that the smoke interfered even more than the dissipating fog with the attempts of his sharpshooters to take aim. Jackson immediately ordered batteries seven and eight to cease firing. The air began to clear, revealing the line of redcoats within three hundred yards and now running rather than marching toward the defenders.

Among them, General Pakenham on horseback cut a striking figure, urging the troops forward despite the lead that thickened the air around them and the comrades who fell at every side. Sir Edward remained preoccupied with the scaling ladders and bundles of sticks that his men would need if they ever reached the soggy ditch in front of the ramparts of Line Jackson; without them, they would be easy targets for the Americans, mired in mud beneath the enemy's walls. He had called repeatedly for Lieutenant Colonel Mullens to lead his 44th Regiment to the front of the line with the needed equipment, but Mullens had disappeared. In an act of insane courage and reckless heroism, Pakenham decided to take personal command of the confused and frightened 44th, urging them forward with their heavy burdens.

"For shame!" he yelled in reaction to their hesitation. "Recollect that you are British soldiers. This is the road you ought to take!" He pointed directly toward the American ramparts, where the rifles continued exploding in innumerable flashes of flame. As Sir Edward continued shouting and gesturing, trying to rally the men, a blast of grapeshot from American artillery shattered his left knee and killed his horse. The general struggled to get up, helped to his feet by his loyal aide-de-camp, Major Duncan MacDougall. Before he could mount MacDougall's horse, another bullet whizzed into his right arm, but he still managed to struggle onto the saddle. As they wheeled around and began to ride to safety, an additional volley of grapeshot tore into his spine. Carried from the field on a stretcher, the doomed, fearless thirty-six-year-old hero died two hours later even as his adoring fiancée anxiously awaited news of triumph.

As the casualties mounted all around them, some of the veteran British troops turned and fled to the rear in panic. Others began falling to the ground, lying down beside their dead or wounded colleagues in hopes of avoiding the lethal, ceaseless waves of American fire. A lieutenant who had fought for king and country around the world remembered: "Never before had British veterans quailed. But it would be silly to deny that they did so now. . . . That leaden torrent no man on earth could face. I had seen battlefields in Spain and in the East . . . but nowhere such a scene as this."

"PROVIDENCE SHIELDED MY MEN"

By eight o'clock in the morning, after less than an hour of fighting, it was over. The British forces had abandoned the field, as Americans rushed out of their lines to capture stragglers. One lightly wounded officer heard an unkempt frontiersman addressing him as he tried to walk away. "Halt, Mr. Red Coat," the Dirty Shirt ordered. "One more step and I'll drill a hole through your leather." The officer paused for a moment and then resigned himself to his fate. "What a disgrace for a British officer to have to surrender to a chimney-sweep!" he declared.

The bizarre nature of the outcome, the sense of unreality and wonder, struck observers on both sides. The British captain Henry Cooke noted that the spectacle seemed "more like a dream, or some scene of enchantment, than reality."

The Americans who wandered out over the fields of slaughter described an unending "sea of red," not because of the blood that had been shed but because of the scarlet coats of the fallen enemy, who lay so thick upon the ground, often piled two or three deep, that for hundreds of yards there was not a glimpse of earth to be seen between them. General Jackson surveyed the scene and reported: "I never had so grand and awful an idea of the resurrection as . . . when I saw more than five hundred Britons emerging from the heaps of their dead comrades, all over the plain rising up, and . . . coming forward as prisoners."

After Jackson agreed to a cease-fire with General John Lambert, the highest-ranking British officer to escape death or wounding, Lieutenant Gleig made his own review of the scene. "Prompted by curiosity, I rode to the front. . . . Of all the sights I ever witnessed, that which met me there was beyond comparison the most shocking and the most humiliating. Within the narrow compass of a few hundred yards were gathered together nearly a thousand bodies, all of them arrayed in British uniforms. Not a single American was among them; all were English, and they were thrown by dozens into shallow holes, scarcely deep enough to furnish them with a slight covering of earth. An American officer stood by smoking a cigar, and apparently counting the slain with a look of savage exultation, and repeating over and over to each individual that approached him, that their loss amounted to eight men killed and fourteen men wounded."

Actually, the official tally of American dead reported by General Jackson to War Secretary James Monroe proved even more miraculous: "only seven killed and six wounded" in the battle itself. Jackson allowed, however, that "afterwards a skirmishing was kept up in which more of our men was lost." With those losses included, modern historians typically conclude that thirteen Americans died and thirty-nine were wounded—a shockingly low total of fifty-two casualties.

The British, meanwhile, reported 2,037 official losses, including 291 killed, 1,262 wounded, and 484 taken prisoner—with additional hundreds possibly missing and uncounted. Among the acknowledged casualties were three generals, seven colonels, and seventy-five other officers. As Secretary of War James Monroe wrote in jubilation to his triumphant general: "History records no example, of so glorious a victory, obtained, with so little bloodshed, on the part of the victorious."

Jackson himself recognized that the shocking casualty figures seemed illogical, even preposterous, acknowledging that such "a disproportion in loss, when we consider the number and kind of troops engaged must, I know, excite astonishment, and may not, everywhere be fully credited; Yet I am perfectly satisfied that the amount is not exaggerated on the one part, nor underrated on the other."

To contemporaries of a literary cast of mind, the lopsided results at New Orleans called to mind Shakespeare's description of the Battle of Agincourt in *Henry V*. In that epic encounter of 1415, the Bard cited "ten thousand French / That in the field lie slain," while the badly outnumbered English lost "but five-and-twenty." Marveling at these numbers, King Henry declaims:

Was ever known so great and little loss
On one part and on th' other? Take it, God,
For it is none but thine!

Andrew Jackson never spoke in poetic or Shakespearean terms, but he reacted to his improbable triumph in the same terms as royal Henry in the play. Looking back with amazement on what he had witnessed in the single most eventful hour of his life, the general concluded: "It appears that the unerring hand of Providence shielded my men from the powers of balls, bombs and rockets, when every ball and bomb from our guns carried with them a mission of death." General John Adair, commander of the Kentucky militia at the center of Line Jackson, emphatically agreed. "History will scarcely furnish us an account of such a battle," he wrote to his state's governor. "May we not rationally conclude that our men were shielded as well as strengthened by that power that rules in war as well as peace."

"THE GOD OF BATTLES AND OF RIGHTEOUSNESS TOOK PART"

In New Orleans in the days after the battle, Jackson continued to emphasize the miraculous and providential aspects of his victory. On January 19, he sent a message to Abbé Guillaume Dubourg, the apostolic administrator of the diocese of Louisiana and in effect the bishop of the region. The general requested a "service of public thanksgiving to be performed in the Cathedral in token of the great assistance we have received from the Ruler of all events and of our humble sense of it for the signal interposition of Heaven in giving success to our arms."

At that grand celebration, for which nearly all of the troops and most of the population of the town turned out, Abbé Dubourg welcomed Jackson on the porch of the cathedral and congratulated him for "proving yourself the worthy instrument of Heaven's merciful designs." As the crowd cheered and applauded, Dubourg went on to denounce the very idea that good luck or mere coincidence could account for the incredible victory. "Let the infatuated votary of blind chance deride our credulous simplicity: let the cold-hearted atheist look up for the explanation of such important events to the mere concatenation of human causes; to us the whole universe is loud in proclaiming a supreme Ruler, who as he holds the hearts of man in his hands, holds also the thread of all contingent occurrences. . . . Immortal thanks be to His supreme majesty, for sending us such a gift of his bountiful designs!"

The cleric then handed Old Hickory a laurel wreath that he blessed "as a prize of victory, the symbol of immortality." In his response, Jackson said, "I receive with gratitude and pleasure the symbolic crown which piety has prepared. . . . For myself, to have been instrumental in the deliverance of such a country is the greatest blessing that heaven could confer."

The general also made a point of visiting the Ursuline convent where the nuns had prayed so fervently for his success the night before the battle. He also heard from them an account of their mass on that fog-shrouded Sunday morning, where at the very moment of holy communion a courier suddenly burst into the chapel to announce to the frightened congregation the news of glorious American success.

In a 1915 account for the Louisiana Historical Society commemorating the one hundredth anniversary of the battle, Stanley Clisby Arthur described the visit of the "tall grizzled victor" to the convent that had prayed for him. "Staunch Presbyterian that he was, 'the Savior of New Orleans' came to the nunnery to pay his respects to the members of that pious sisterhood. He thanked the Mother Superior for the prayers the sisters offered while his ragged handful were at death-grapples with the invading army; he thanked them for their unceasing vigil at the bedsides of the wounded defenders of the city; he thanked them for the care and attention they gave the wounded and captured of the enemy. And he did not fail to visit them when he returned to New Orleans in after years."

Nor have the nuns failed to keep their promise to celebrate a solemn mass of thanksgiving every year on the January 8 anniversary of the battle. In 1851, Pope Pius IX specifically authorized the Ursuline order to observe that date as the Feast of Our Lady of Prompt Succor in honor of the statue of the Blessed Virgin to which they prayed in 1815.

Beyond New Orleans, it took weeks for the public to get word of Jackson's stunning success, and Americans everywhere reacted with emotional expressions of amazement, gratitude, and joy. Federal judge Wilson McCandless later recalled that the news "came upon the country like a clap of thunder in the clear azure vault of the firmament, and traveled with electromagnetic velocity through the confines of the land." Headlines in leading newspapers gave the best indication of the national reaction:

ALMOST INCREDIBLE VICTORY!! GLORIOUS NEWS

GLORIOUS!!! UNPARALLELED VICTORY

SPLENDID VICTORY: RISING GLORY OF THE AMERICAN REPUBLIC

On the floor of the House of Representatives, a young Georgia congressman and future governor named George Troupe spoke on behalf of a resolution congratulating Jackson and his army "on the glorious termination of the most glorious war ever waged by any people . . . The God of Battles and of Righteousness took part with the defenders of their country and the foe was scattered as chaff before the wind."

"A SMOKING GUN"

The outcome seemed no less incredible or meaningful when, more than a month after the battle, Americans finally discovered that the war had actually concluded even before they won their epic victory in New Orleans. On Christmas Eve 1814, American and British negotiators in the Belgian city of Ghent reached agreement on a treaty of peace that granted no gains to either side, restoring the borders between the United States and British possessions in North America to the lines that had existed before the war began. In other words, the late General Pakenham had led his doomed troops against the lethal fire from Line Jackson on a foggy morning two weeks *after* his government had made peace with its adversary.

This information reached the New World on February 11, when a Royal Navy sloop sailed into New York Harbor with the relevant dispatches and a copy of the treaty for submission to Congress and the president. It took another three days for word to reach Washington, with a messenger bursting into a late-afternoon cabinet meeting to give President Madison the exhilarating news. The Senate ratified the Treaty of Ghent unanimously on February 16, and the celebrations of peace blended almost seamlessly with the celebrations of the New Orleans victory that had already been going on for nine days across the country. Jackson's success allowed the nation to view the whole conflict as successful and significant, despite the fact that it had been characterized for the most part by American disappointments and disasters. To the exultant public, it seemed as if the British had surrendered outright rather than sign an inconclusive treaty, because word of that agreement arrived only after the glad tidings about the war's most one-sided battle.

As historian Robert V. Remini observes: "To the modern world it is virtually impossible to convey what this victory meant to contemporary Americans. Never again—ever—did they feel compelled to prove to themselves or anyone else the worth of their unique experiment in liberty and constitutional government."

But aside from its impact on American morale, did the battle possess any practical significance, given that its outcome did nothing to alter the official terms of peace? And if not, how could Jackson's contemporaries, let alone subsequent generations, perceive providential direction in a meaningless fight that took place only after the signing of a treaty that put a formal end to the conflict?

Newly published research in 2015 surrounding the two hundredth anniversary of Jackson's victory demonstrates an overwhelming geopolitical importance of the battle that goes well beyond its emotional meaning. Military historian Ronald Drez of the University of New Orleans, a former captain in the Marine Corps, made a major discovery among British war records: a set of secret orders issued in October 1814, instructing Pakenham to continue with the invasion and occupation of New Orleans regardless of any peace agreement with the Americans. Drez found the papers among military records in the National Archives at Kew in London. "It truly is the smoking gun," Drez told the Associated Press. "They say to Pakenham: 'If you hear of a peace treaty, pay no attention, continue to fight.'" To realize their long-term goals, Britain secretly inserted government officials and experienced bureaucrats within military units in order to immediately establish administrative control once General Pakenham, the designated governor, had completed his conquest.

Though they had negotiated an agreement in which both sides would return to the boundaries they had accepted before the war, the British had never accepted America's purchase of Louisiana. They challenged Napoleon's seizure of the territory from Spain and his right to sell it to the Americans. In his book *The War of 1812, Conflict and Deception: The British Attempt to Seize New Orleans and Nullify the Louisiana Purchase*, Drez makes clear the English plan to conquer and colonize the entire Mississippi Valley as a key addition to their territory in Canada and as a means of limiting the growth and power of the United States. In spite of the ironic timing that saw the Treaty of Ghent signed before the Battle of the Bayous, Jackson's miraculous victory played an absolutely essential role in allowing the United States to build a continental nation "from sea to shining sea."

"A STROKE OF MILITARY GOOD FORTUNE"?

Without contesting these conclusions, other historians reflecting on the battle's two hundredth anniversary portrayed the victory as the result of dumb luck, not the product of military genius or heavenly intervention. Professor James McWilliams of Texas State University, San Marcos, wrote a piece in the *New Yorker* emphasizing that Jackson won the day "in large part because of a logistical snafu by the 44th Regiment, which was supposed to haul over the ladders." Because of this seemingly minor mishap, the ill-prepared Americans "unexpectedly found themselves, eyes wide and guns drawn, hovering over hundreds of British soldiers who had scuttled into the ditch below, awaiting the arrival of ladders that would enable them to climb out and fight." After the battle, McWilliams claimed, "with help from a partisan media that was openly sympathetic to Western interests, Jackson and his acolytes essentially transformed a stroke of military good fortune into an idealization of American exceptionalism."

But to see the breathtaking victory as nothing more than "a stroke of military good fortune" is to ignore the configuration of good fortune that delivered to the Americans one lucky break after another: Jackson's escape from death or amputation in the tavern brawl in Nashville, his beneficial alliance with the Barataria Bay pirates, General Keane's inexplicable halt when he could have marched directly into New Orleans, the timely flight by Major Gabriel Villeré from his British captors in order to warn Jackson, another escape from a hundred cannonballs that wrecked Jackson's headquarters, the last-minute assignment of Adair's Kentuckians to reinforce the defense lines at precisely the point where they needed it most, and the suddenly clearing fog that exposed the advancing redcoats to devastating fire.

Yes, the British suffered from an abundance of logistical blunders, including the famously lost ladders, the boats that had to be dragged two hundred yards over mud to reach the bank of the river, and the failure to allow for the powerful Mississippi current, which would carry them extra miles from their goal just hours before the scheduled attack. Such problems definitely contributed to Pakenham's defeat, but who would have expected that all of the significant problems with equipment and preparation would afflict the well-trained and battle-hardened veterans who styled themselves "Wellington's Heroes" rather than the improvised, badly outnumbered army of "Dirty Shirts" who faced them? A pattern of consistent good fortune, or ceaseless bad luck, nonetheless indicates a discernible design.

"AN ALLY CONSTANTLY CONCERNED IN HIS MATERIAL WELL-BEING"

In the thirty years of Jackson's life that followed, his ardent admirers perceived a similarly supernatural scheme at work in promoting his success and protecting his very survival. As with his hero George Washington, some otherworldly force seemed to shield Old Hickory from death despite constant exposure to deadly dangers. Unlike Washington, however, who never endured a serious wound in his long military career, Jackson regularly absorbed bullets and sword wounds in brutal confrontations that began in his childhood.

His father, a poor farmer who had recently emigrated from Northern Ireland, died from overwork and exhaustion shortly before Andrew's birth in 1767. At age thirteen, the fatherless boy volunteered to serve the patriot cause in the Revolutionary War, taking part in bitter battles against local Tories and ruthless British dragoons that raged across the frontier district along the border between North and South Carolina. Taken prisoner after a bloody skirmish, Andy and his sixteen-year-old brother Robert came under control of an arrogant British officer who intended to humiliate the captives by ordering the younger boy to polish his muddy boots. Jackson refused, insisting on the proper treatment due to a prisoner of war, and the enraged redcoat drew his sword and brought it down on the boy's head. Andrew raised his left arm at the last moment, but sustained a severe gash on his hand and another on his head, leaving visible scars he carried with him for the rest of his life. With blood pouring down his face, the boy challenged the dragoon to strike him again. Instead, the indignant officer forced the still-bleeding teenager to help him find other rebels in the vicinity, then dragged both captured brothers on a forty-mile forced march, without food and water, to a makeshift prison camp in Camden, North Carolina. They subsisted there on a diet of moldy bread for two weeks before their widowed mother managed to negotiate their release in a prisoner exchange. By that time, both Jackson brothers had contracted smallpox, and Robert died from the sickness the day after they returned home. Though suffering and incapacitated for weeks, Andrew somehow survived, bearing the same pockmarks from the dread disease that marked Washington from his own teenaged brush with smallpox.

In the course of his long life, Jackson also suffered from dysentery, chronic diarrhea, malaria, almost constant abdominal pain, and hacking, presumably tubercular coughs that frequently brought up blood—all conditions that generally led to death in the early nineteenth century. He also suffered great pain from the two bullets lodged permanently in his body from his long history of duels and brawls, finally having one of them removed in painful surgery while he occupied the White House. By that time, he had already taken to heart an abiding belief in his own indestructibility as an indispensable servant of the Almighty. Arda Walker, who wrote a 1945 analysis of Jackson's religious views for the East Tennessee Historical Society, concluded that "Providence . . . must have appeared to him as a sort of an ally that constantly was concerned in his material well-being."

"A DEEP IMPRESSION UPON THE PUBLIC FEELING"

Of course, most modern historians scoff at such ideas, and in his influential book *Andrew Jackson: Symbol for an Age*, Princeton professor John William Ward devotes considerable energy to debunking the "imaginative projections" that portrayed Jackson as divinely designated for leadership. Yet even Ward acknowledges that one incident provided "objective support" for the popular notion that destiny specially sheltered Andrew Jackson.

That troubling occurrence involved the first assassination attempt on any American president. In January 1835, nearing the end of his second term, the sixty-seven-year-old Jackson attended a memorial service at the Capitol for a recently deceased congressman from South Carolina. On Jackson's way out of the building, a flamboyantly dressed dandy emerged from the crowd of onlookers and aimed his pistol at the president's heart from a distance of eight feet. The percussion cap fired as normal but for undetermined reasons failed to light the powder in the barrel. "The explosion of the cap was so loud that many persons thought the pistol had fired," reported Senator Thomas Hart Benton, who had engaged in his own nearly fatal gunfight with Jackson some twenty-one years earlier. "I heard it at the foot of the steps, far from the place, and a great crowd between."

Despite his multiple infirmities, President Jackson instinctively sprang into action and began beating his assailant with his cane. The foppish figure then raised his second pistol and, from point-blank range, squeezed the trigger for a second shot at the president's heart. Again the cap loudly exploded but failed to ignite the powder. By this time, members of the crowd (including Congressman Davy Crockett of Tennessee) fell upon the would-be assassin and after some notably rough handling carried him off to police custody.

The visibly deranged gunman turned out to be an unemployed house painter and English immigrant, fitting perfectly into Jackson's lifelong pattern of implacable enmity with the sons of Albion. Richard Lawrence believed himself to be the rightful heir to the British throne and concluded that President Jackson's opposition to the Bank of the United States had kept him from receiving the titles and wealth due to him. The authorities who examined Lawrence deemed him too insane to stand trial, and he remained confined to asylums for the remaining twenty-six years of his life.

In the course of their investigation, police officials repeatedly tested the weapons Lawrence had fired at the president. Each time they operated perfectly. A consulting expert on small arms calculated the odds of two successive misfires under these circumstances as approximately 125,000 to 1. These revelations profoundly moved Senator Benton, who wonderingly observed: "The circumstances made a deep impression upon the public feeling and irresistibly carried many minds to the belief in a superintending Providence, manifested in the extraordinary case of two pistols in succession—so well loaded, so coolly handled, and which afterwards fired with such readiness, force and precision—missing fire, each in its turn, when leveled from eight feet at the President's heart."

ANDREW JACKSON (1767–1845), seventh president of the United States.

"Providence ... must have appeared to him as a sort of an ally that constantly was concerned in his material well-being." —Arda Walker

That fierce heart continued beating for another decade, allowing Jackson to see two of his protégés installed in the White House— Martin Van Buren in 1837 and in 1844 James K. Polk, a youthful governor of Tennessee widely known as "Young Hickory."

Another follower, Sam Houston, made heroic efforts to rush to Jackson's deathbed with his family as soon as he got word of his idol's rapidly deteriorating condition. Houston had played a conspicuous role fighting with Old Hickory in defeating the Red Sticks at the Battle of Horseshoe Bend. More recently, as president of the Republic of Texas, he had led efforts to incorporate his independent nation into the United States as the twenty-eighth state of the Union, helping Jackson to achieve the most cherished goal of his retirement.

The seventy-eight-year-old former president, racked by tuberculosis, dropsy, diarrhea, and cataracts, had begun to fail in the spring of 1845. After an operation to drain fluid from his abdomen, he fell unconscious and appeared to have died, but a quick shot of brandy revived him.

Meanwhile, Houston left Texas with his twenty-five-year-old wife and their year-old son in order to see for the last time the national hero who had become his second father. They boarded a steamboat in New Orleans to take them upriver to Nashville, and the towering Texan tried to force the captain to push his boat faster against the Mississippi's current. Disembarking on the evening of June 8, they secured a carriage and raced their horses at top speed through the thickening twilight to reach the Hermitage in time. Unfortunately, they arrived too late; Jackson's doctor informed them that the old man had expired peacefully at six o'clock.

Houston nonetheless brought his little family upstairs to pay tribute to the greatest man he had ever known. Looking at Jackson's lifeless form, the founding father of Texas bent his huge frame toward the bed and then fell to his knees, weeping openly. Moments later, he took Sam junior in his arms and raised the one-year-old child over the old general's high bed. "My son, try to remember that you have looked on the face of Andrew Jackson," he declared.

As it happened, that tiny boy and the generations that followed would look on the triumphs and torments of the elder Sam Houston as further evidence of godly favor for the young Republic.

"THE RAVEN": Sam Houston (1793–1863), adopted Cherokee, militia general, governor of Tennessee, president of Texas. To him, the astonishing ups and downs of his career could be no accident.

"Let those who laugh at a Divine Providence, which watches over its chosen instruments, sneer as they read this."

8

"BIG DRUNK" AND
LONE STAR LUCK

A Broken Marriage, an Indian Exile, and a Scrap
That Changed History

Texas might still be part of Mexico today if a rising young Tennessee politician hadn't proven profoundly unlucky in love.

Had Governor Sam Houston's infamous wedding night proceeded as planned, had his fairy-tale marriage not exploded into searing, well-publicized humiliation, he easily could have continued on the carefully prepared path to which his mentor assigned him, succeeding Andrew Jackson as president of the United States.

As it was, Houston's life fell apart and he passed through dark years of depression and drunkenness, featuring a desperate scrap with a sitting congressman that surely would have killed him if a loaded pistol pressed against his chest hadn't inexplicably misfired. Instead, the sad figure anointed "Big Drunk" by his Indian friends lived to endure more misery before seconding the sentiments of his friend Davy Crockett, who declared, "You may all go to hell; I will go to Texas." There the exiled alcoholic played a central, indispensable role in destroying a mighty Mexican army, capturing a wily dictator, and, after exertions as president of the independent Republic of Texas, bringing the Lone Star State at long last into the Union.

Houston himself had no doubt as to the role of a higher power in sustaining him through these exhausting adventures. He viewed himself as a man of destiny and maintained a distinctive, providential perspective that blended his stern Presbyterian upbringing, the traditional Cherokee spirituality he adopted as a teenager, and the evangelical fervor of the born-again Baptist faith he adopted in the last stage of his life.

Sam's path to glory began in Virginia's Shenandoah Valley, where his father, the grandson of Scots-Irish immigrants who had first settled in Pennsylvania in the 1730s, played a prominent role in local political and military affairs. He served as captain and paymaster for Morgan's Rifles, a storied unit of the Continental Army, then came home after the Revolution and fathered nine children.

Sam arrived in 1793, fifth in line of this impressive brood. In the best middle-child tradition, he stood out as the family's misfit and troublemaker. His towering stature guaranteed he would always attract special attention: he was identified as a "giant" even as a boy, and contemporary sources report his adult height as somewhere between six foot two and six foot six, with a broad-shouldered, fleshy, and rugged frame. Young Sam derided his devout and hardworking older brothers as the "Holy Apostles" and resented their leadership of the Houston clan after the death of their father in 1807. Now a widow, the strong-willed Elizabeth Paxton Houston loaded the children into two wagons and completed her late husband's planned migration to the new state of Tennessee, in part to escape the inconvenient accumulation of debts back in Virginia.

Under the direction of their indomitable mother, the responsible older boys quickly set up a 419-acre farm in the foothills of the Great Smoky Mountains and established a flourishing country store in nearby Maryville. All family members were expected to toil at these efforts, but strapping fourteen-year-old Sam had no appetite for farming and even less tolerance for working for the sanctimonious Holy Apostles behind the counter of their commercial establishment. One worried uncle reportedly commented, "I have no hope for Sam. He is so wild."

"MAKING LOVE AND READING
HOMER'S *ILIAD*"

At age sixteen, the young giant acted on that wild streak and ran away
to join a band of some three hundred Cherokee Indians who had established their headquarters on lush, thickly forested Hiwassee Island
near the confluence of the Hiwassee and Tennessee Rivers, not far
from present-day Chattanooga. He brought with him few possessions
from the family home other than a favorite volume from his late father's leather-bound library: Alexander Pope's stirring 1720 translation of *The Iliad*. Houston loved the poetic descriptions of ancient,
epic battles and superhuman heroes manipulated for impenetrable
purposes by the all-powerful Olympian gods. He committed choice
passages to memory and for the rest of his life occasionally startled
friends and colleagues by reciting verses from Homer and relating
them incongruously to the passionate political warfare of his own era.

On Hiwassee Island, Sam absorbed another form of mythology:
immersing himself in the rich Cherokee culture of his hosts. He found
himself powerfully attracted to their personal dignity and elemental
connection to nature. He learned the rudiments of their complex, delicate language and tried to speak only Cherokee after he left home,
dressing, hunting, and eating like an Indian. The venerable local chief
Oolooteka, an important leader with wide-ranging influence through
the region, took an immediate liking to the respectful American lad
and adopted him as his son. This meant a new name, Colonneh, or
"the Raven"—a prominent symbol of good luck and purposeful wandering in many Native American traditions.

Houston spent three years with his replacement father,
Oolooteka, and looked back on the interlude as "the molding period of life, when the heart, just charmed into the feverish hopes and
dreams of youth, looks wistfully around on all things for light and
beauty." He found particular light and beauty among the young ladies of the community, who seemed eager to keep company with the
tribe's adopted son. In later years he reminisced about happy hours

spent "wandering along the banks of streams, side by side with some Indian maiden, sheltered by the deep woods ... making love and reading Homer's *Iliad*." In the nineteenth century, the term "making love" designated the exchange of tender sentiments rather than physical sexuality; Cherokee elders remained nearly as concerned as their Presbyterian counterparts with protecting the virtue of their young women. Such restrictions hardly prevented Houston from concluding that "there's nothing half so sweet to remember as this sojourn ... among the untutored children of the forest."

DISTINGUISHED—AND NEARLY DEAD

The idyll ended abruptly—and, Sam hoped, temporarily—when the year 1812 brought the United States to the cusp of conflict with Great Britain. As war fever swept through the mountains and valleys of Tennessee, the Raven flew abruptly back to the family home near Maryville. There, despite his own lack of formal education, he taught school for several months to get closer to the legal enlistment age of twenty-one. At least part of his motivation for joining the military stemmed from his unfortunate replication of his late father's pattern of running up unpaid debts: he had spent heavily to buy expensive gifts for his friends, family, and would-be sweethearts among the Cherokee. The army offered an enlistment bonus of a shiny silver dollar along with promises of future payment, not to mention its natural appeal to an ambitious young man with dreams of Homeric glory. Because of his commanding size and his father's reputation as a hero in the Revolutionary War, Houston won quick commission as an ensign, and then nearly instantaneous promotion to third lieutenant.

He also won the blessing of his mother, who needed to grant permission for his underage enlistment. She reportedly told him, "I had rather that all my sons should fill one grave than that one of them should turn his back to save his life," and she presented him with a simple, thin gold ring with the single word HONOR inscribed on its curve. He cherished that band, which remained on his hand until the day he died.

Fortunately for the Raven, his Cherokee friends split from other tribes in the area by allying themselves with the Americans in the coming struggle, and they even sent warriors to fight alongside General Andrew Jackson in his campaign against the British-aligned Creek Red Sticks. In the climactic showdown at Horseshoe Bend, young Lieutenant Houston distinguished himself—and nearly died.

After softening up the enemy with artillery, Jackson ordered the 39th Infantry to assault the center of the well-prepared fortifications, where the best fighters among the fanatically dedicated Creeks awaited them. Major Lemuel Montgomery led the way over the battlements but was killed instantly; the future capital of Alabama would be named in his honor. Next over the top was platoon leader Houston, waving his sword in the air for his men to follow. Fending off the Red Sticks with his saber in one hand and a pistol in the other, the towering figure fought alone for several moments before his soldiers joined him in hand-to-hand combat. In the midst of the struggle, an arrow pierced Houston's thigh and wedged painfully into his groin as the young lieutenant watched two other officers from his regiment overwhelmed and killed beside him. Despite gushing blood and the agony of his wound, the Raven continued to lead the fight until the Creeks pulled back from the breastwork and retreated to a covered log fortification at the bottom of a nearby gully.

As Jackson's surging forces paused to regroup, Houston found another officer and asked for help with the arrow in his thigh. After a sharp pull failed to dislodge the barbed shaft, the injured lieutenant raised his sword and ordered the other man to pull it loose at all costs. The removal that followed brought forth a mass of blood and sinew, forcing Houston to limp off the field in search of medical assistance to bandage his wound. He rested just behind the front lines as Andrew Jackson rode past; noting the blood-soaked third lieutenant who had just celebrated his twenty-first birthday, Jackson directed him to stay out of combat the rest of the day.

After another artillery bombardment against the new Indian defenses, word passed at twilight through the American ranks that the general wanted volunteers for a final attempt to storm the enemy position. Houston received the message, staggered to his feet, grabbed a musket, and, waving away the protests of his comrades, hobbled down the ravine toward the waiting enemy. Five yards from their battlements, two balls shattered his right arm and crashed into his shoulder simultaneously, but he held his ground and gallantly ordered his men to charge. Glancing back over his shoulder, he saw no one to follow his command—he stood on the field alone, in the gathering dusk, bellowing in vain for support.

Somehow he managed to drag himself back up the slope toward the American camp before collapsing. Jackson ultimately obliterated the last pockets of Indian resistance with more cannonades, as well as flaming arrows that ignited the log fortifications, while a field surgeon operated on the unconscious Houston. Bandaging the badly injured groin, stanching the flow from the wounded shoulder, and removing the ball from the upper right arm, he worked by firelight until a second doctor told him to waste no further time. The patient had lost so much blood he couldn't possibly survive till morning, they concluded, and so they deposited him untended on the damp, cold ground while they concentrated on lesser wounds that offered better chances of survival.

But the chilly March dawn found Sam still alive, though barely. The medical staff made a decision to place him on a litter and drag him sixty excruciating miles to Fort Williams, where he could receive better treatment or, far more likely, die in relative comfort. With the Creek War successfully concluded and General Jackson soon turning his attention to the threatened British invasion of New Orleans, another litter transported Lieutenant Houston toward his mother's home in Tennessee. Swigs of whiskey and frequent blackouts provided only intermittent relief from the overwhelming pain; by the time he reached the family farm in May 1814, two full months had passed since the Battle of Horseshoe Bend.

His mother barely recognized his delirious, emaciated form at the time of their reunion and dispatched him as soon as possible to the town of Knoxville to receive medical treatment from a celebrated physician renowned for his healing powers. After an initial examination, the doctor, a Scotsman, concluded that Sam couldn't live for more than a few days and saw no point in running up a bill. Houston refused to accept his conclusions and took a room in the city to rest and gain strength. He returned to the reluctant physician two weeks later, showing sufficient progress to merit further treatment. After half a year of convalescence, he felt strong enough to rejoin his regiment. For the Raven and for those closest to him, his defiance of all logical predictions of his imminent demise proved that a higher power—God, or the Great Spirit, or an ancient Greek decree of destiny—had marked him for great achievements and heroic tasks.

"UNBOUNDED POPULARITY"

Those tasks began with a return to his adoptive Cherokee father, Oolooteka, on Hiwassee Island. This time he arrived as a representative of Major General Andrew Jackson, who, having driven the British from Louisiana with his celebrated victory in New Orleans, now focused his attention on removing the Cherokee from the path of booming American settlement in Tennessee. As an official Indian agent of the War Department, the Raven arrived in full Indian garb and found himself welcomed as a returning prodigal and conquering hero. The Cherokee had heard tales of his battlefield exploits and counted the young warrior as one of their own, according him a level of trust they could give to no other government representative. Fortunately, Houston came with authorization for an acceptable bargain: if the band agreed to relocate to the wilderness of Arkansas Territory, they would secure abundant land on which the white man could never intrude, as well as generous compensation from the government in Washington. Each of the warriors would also receive a good new rifle—a sign of trust and friendship that helped Houston close the deal. Boarding a fleet of flatboats laden with supplies, and proudly brandishing their new firearms overhead, Oolooteka's community made the journey west from Tennessee with little of the cruel suffering that characterized the Trail of Tears imposed on their fellow Cherokee some twenty years later. Nevertheless, the Raven shared their inevitable melancholy at abandonment of the river-island home that once had represented his adolescent Eden.

Indian agent Houston then accepted a new challenge. A far more significant Cherokee community under the leadership of Oolooteka's powerful older brother asked the Raven to help resolve their dangerous disagreements with the War Department. Escorting a delegation of prominent chiefs to Washington, Houston conducted another successful negotiation but also gave birth to a lifelong feud with one of the most powerful political figures of the age. After a ceremonial session with Secretary of War John C. Calhoun, the influential cabinet member ushered the Cherokee dignitaries to their scheduled meeting with President Monroe but detained Houston, their representative, for an indignant tongue-lashing. How could an officer of the army who was also an appointed official of the U.S. government appear in the nation's capital wearing the "savage" garb of buckskin, beads, feathers, and moccasins? Houston tried to explain the advantages of relating to the natives as an ally rather than as an adversary, but Calhoun never surrendered his potent, persistent antagonism to the tall Tennessean.

Jackson's favor more than made up for the disfavor of any rivals, and under the sponsorship of his former commander, Houston entered politics in the home state they shared. After resigning from the army, he studied law for several months in Nashville before earning the post of local prosecutor. He also received appointment as commander of the state militia, with the rank of general, and won election to the House of Representatives in 1822. During two terms in Washington, he gained respect as a loyal Jacksonian and a vigorous representative of his mentor's interests during Old Hickory's first (unsuccessful) race for the presidency.

In 1827, Houston returned home for a campaign to replace the popular governor, William Carroll, who was forced by term limits to give up his chair. Storming Tennessee with zest and confidence, campaigning in his distinctive outfit of Cherokee hunting shirt decorated with extensive beadwork and a bright red sash, crowned with a tall beaver hat that made his height seem even more impressive, he handily defeated two older, well-established rivals. The victorious thirty-five-year-old candidate then assumed office as chief executive of one of the Union's most dynamic states and seemed ready to make the leap to a larger arena. A local judge named Jo C. Guild preemptively boosted

Tennessee's new governor as an all-but-inevitable president, noting Houston's "commanding and gallant bearing" and his "fine features" together with a "magnetism approaching that of General Andrew Jackson." Judge Guild concluded that the state's new chief executive "enjoyed unbounded popularity among men and was a great favorite with the ladies."

"WHAT THE DEVIL IS THE MATTER WITH THE GALS"

That appeal to the fairer sex resulted over the years in a half dozen halting approaches to potential brides, but the fearless commander had not yet succeeded in storming the battlements of love. In a letter after one of these blighted romances, Houston wrote to a friend: "I have as usual had a 'small blow up.' What the devil is the matter with the gals I can't say."

Jackson himself, awaiting his elevation to the presidency, took a lively interest in this matrimonial quest and gruffly urged Houston to find a wife. Fortunately, the ideal candidate seemed ready to hand: the lovely blond Eliza Allen, the eighteen-year-old daughter of a prominent, politically connected plantation-owning family in the Cumberland River Valley north of Nashville. Her uncle Robert had served with Houston in the House of Representatives, and the Raven had been a frequent guest at Allen family gatherings, first meeting Eliza and capturing her childish fascination when she was only thirteen. Five years later, her beauty, breeding, and dark blue eyes attracted widespread admiration and several serious suitors. One of them, a local lawyer of poetic temperament and notoriously frail health, had apparently inspired reciprocal feelings from Eliza, but when it came to potential sons-in-law her parents naturally preferred the ferocious force of nature who had just taken over as governor. Perhaps the teenage girl's initial indifference helped to fire Sam Houston's ardor, leading to frequent interruptions in affairs of state as he rode at top speed the thirty miles from the capital to the Allen home to spend even a few fleeting moments with the object of his adoration.

Like many others who encountered him on military or political battlefields, Eliza soon understood that resistance to Houston would prove futile. Under heavy pressure from her parents, she agreed to become his bride in an elegant candlelit ceremony at the family's Allenwood plantation, witnessed by many if not most of the leading citizens of the state.

The obviously infatuated Houston galloped to the occasion in giddy high spirits, but recalled years later that he experienced a momentary chill when a raven suddenly plunged from the winter sky and fell dead on the road in front of him. Despite this grim omen, which alarmed his Cherokee sensibilities, and despite the talk at Allenwood that Eliza wept openly when her attendants cinched her into her wedding gown, the solemn Presbyterian ceremony went off without incident and the guests happily toasted the state's new first couple.

The next afternoon they planned to ride together on horseback toward Nashville, but an unexpected snowstorm interrupted their honeymoon journey just as the sun began to set. The newlyweds sought shelter at gracious Locust Grove, home of their mutual friends Robert and Martha Martin, who felt honored to receive them. In the morning, the governor arose early and went outside with the family's two young daughters to frolic in the fresh snow. He had engaged the girls in a fierce snowball fight when Eliza came down the stairs and glanced out the window at her boyish husband. In an unpublished memoir, Martha Martin remembered offering the new bride a friendly greeting. "I said to her: it looks like General Houston is getting the worst of the snowballing; you had better go out and help him. Looking seriously at me, Mrs. Houston said: 'I wish they would kill him.' I looked astonished to hear such a remark from a bride of not yet forty-eight hours, when she repeated in the same voice, 'yes, I wish from the bottom of my heart that they would kill him.'"

Eliza remained subdued for the rest of the visit, but when they arrived at Nashville and settled for a few nights into the home of Houston's cousin Robert McEwen, any problem between them seemed to have been resolved. Mrs. McEwen noted their desire to spend all their time alone together, a healthy sign for newlyweds, and commented that she had never seen a more affectionate couple. It was the desire for privacy, she assumed, that led them to relocate to a comfortable suite of rooms at the Nashville Inn. There the governor plunged into the whirlwind of political affairs, facing a spirited fight for reelection, while Eliza kept mostly to herself and avoided social occasions as much as possible.

"UNITED TO A WOMAN THAT DID NOT LOVE ME"

In the upcoming campaign, Houston faced Billy Carroll, the same beloved governor he had replaced. Freed from his term limits by his two-year absence from office, Carroll meant to reclaim the post he considered his rightful possession. Houston refused to clear a path for this triumphal return, and the battle began on April 11 with a Saturday afternoon open-air debate at Cockrell's Spring, ten miles from Nashville. Eliza naturally elected to avoid the boisterous all-male political crowds and remained behind in their rooms while the governor rode off with friends to enjoy the rhetorical combat. He planned to spend the night away from home, but when most observers proclaimed him the clear winner of the exchange with Governor Carroll, he felt so exhilarated that he decided to ride back to the capital to share the excitement with his beautiful young wife. But when he arrived at the Nashville Inn, Eliza had gone. She left no explanation other than a terse indication that she had returned to her father's home. The glamorous new couple had separated after less than eleven weeks of marriage.

For the Raven, the timing couldn't have been worse, especially since his horrified in-laws were known to be longtime friends and supporters of his powerful opponent. At the moment of crisis, however, Houston resolved to put politics aside and began campaigning fulltime for the return of his wife. He dashed off a desolate letter to her father, addressing him as "Mr. Allen" and reporting that "the most unpleasant & unhappy circumstance has just taken place in the family & one that was entirely unnecessary at this time." He went on to declare undiminished affection for his departed bride:

That I have & do love Eliza none can doubt and that I have ever
treated her with affection she will admit; that she is the only earthly
object dear to me God will bear witness . . .

Eliza stands acquitted by me. I have received her as a virtuous,
chaste wife and as such I pray God I may ever regard her, and I
trust I ever shall. She was cold to me, & I thought did not love
me. She owns that such was the cause of my unhappiness. You can
judge how unhappy I was to think I was united to a woman that did
not love me. . . . You may rest assured that nothing on my part shall
be wanting to restore it. Let me know what is to be done.

This letter represents the only occasion on which Houston hinted
at his version of the breakup; as part of his personal code of honor, he
refused for the rest of his life to speak of the issues that destroyed his
marriage for fear that such discussion might impugn Eliza's "virtue."

Every biographer of Houston has attempted to solve the mystery, and some of the nineteenth-century writers had the benefit of
interviews with friends and relatives who knew the two principals. According to a story that circulated through the Allen family for several
generations, the eighteen-year-old Eliza reacted in unavoidable horror
to Houston's war wounds when she saw them for the first time, perhaps on their wedding night at the Allen home, or perhaps the next
evening at the home of Martha Martin. Shortly before her death from
stomach cancer at age fifty-one, Eliza reputedly confessed to her physician son-in-law that she felt particularly disgusted by the "running
sore" on the Raven's groin, "a festering wound that never healed." If
Eliza felt repelled by his wound in such a sensitive area, it would make
sense that Houston could tell her father "she was cold to me" without
revealing the humiliating fact that she found him physically repellant.

The other common explanation for what went wrong for the
state's first couple involves the assumption that the teenage Eliza had
already "given her heart" to a younger, gentler man but felt pushed by
her ambitious family to accept the rowdy, cyclonic, domineering war
hero who had become one of the most powerful men in the country.
This explanation would account for her tears while stepping into her

wedding gown and her trembling hands as the new couple exchanged vows. Several sources who claimed to have heard accounts directly from Eliza say that Houston sensed her distance and dread on one of the first nights of their marriage and demanded to know if she loved someone else. When she confirmed that she did—with her adored admirer assumed to be a consumptive village lawyer named Will Tyree—the wounded Raven lost his temper and condemned her as unfaithful, even though she had done nothing to violate his trust after her family pressed her into engagement with the governor.

Whatever the particulars of their separation, the governor most ardently desired his wife's return, and one of Eliza's aunts even recalled the lumbering giant falling to his knees and tearfully begging the startled girl for forgiveness and reconciliation. During the five days following her abrupt departure she persistently turned down his pleas, and he pushed aside all the demands of his friends and supporters to provide some explanation to the press and public. The news of the separation created a sensation in the capital, with agitated, occasionally angry crowds milling day and night in the square across from the Nashville Inn, where Governor Houston mostly kept to his rooms. Because the delicate matter involved the honor of a lady, the Raven repeatedly refused to "breathe any word of it" that might question his wife's behavior or to defend his own. "Remember," he declared, "that whatever may be said by the lady or her friends, it is no part of the conduct of a gallant or a generous man to take up arms against a woman."

On April 16, Willoughby Williams, sheriff of Davidson County, managed to push through the mobs of detractors and supporters and go upstairs for a private meeting with the governor. They had grown up together and enlisted in the army at the same time; Williams had helped to nurse Houston back to health after he returned home from his purportedly fatal injuries at Horseshoe Bend. In the midst of his marital crisis, the big man looked as wounded, weakened, and doomed as he had in those dark days. Williams pleaded for a public account of "this sad occurrence . . . else you will sacrifice your friends and yourself."

"I can make no explanation," the governor replied. "I exonerate this lady freely and I do not justify myself. I am a ruined man; will exile myself, and now ask you to take my resignation to the Secretary of State."

Sheriff Williams tried to dissuade him, but the governor had apparently already composed most of his letter of resignation. In flowery language, he expressed appreciation for the honor of serving the people, and thanked them for their frequent signs of support. But he then alluded to feeling "overwhelmed by sudden calamities" and concluded that it is "more respectful to the world that I should retire from a position which, in the public judgment, I might seem to occupy by questionable authority."

Ten days later, with newspapers across the country reporting breathlessly on the shocking events in Tennessee, Houston tried to disguise his identity with a dark cloak and tall hat and slink down to a wharf on the river, boarding a steamboat called *The Red Rover* to carry him away from the tumult and humiliation. His rival Billy Carroll wrote to the newly inaugurated president of the United States, Andrew Jackson, that the "fate of Houston must have surprised you . . . His conduct, to say the least, was very strange and charity requires us to place it to the account of insanity. I have always looked upon him as a man of weak and unsettled mind."

Meanwhile, the Raven himself had begun to question his mental state. Years later, he recalled of his mournful river journey toward a reunion with his Cherokee friends: "I was in an agony of despair and strongly tempted to leap overboard and end my worthless life. At that moment, however, an eagle swooped down near my head, and then, soaring aloft, with wildest screams, was lost in the setting sun. I knew then that a great destiny waited for me in the west."

"IT WAS DONE BY THE GREAT SPIRIT"

That great destiny began to unfold only after five more years of darkness, drunkenness, and confusion.

On board *The Red Rover*, Houston tried as much as possible to conceal his identity, growing a bushy beard to hide his recognizable features. He traveled in the company of a wandering Irishman he had met at the bar of the Nashville Inn; in Cairo, Illinois, they disembarked and bought a flatboat to take them up the Arkansas River to Little Rock, the rustic capital of Arkansas Territory. Pushing farther into the West, the Raven switched traveling companions and covered 120 miles with a onetime Virginia lawyer who had drifted to the frontier after a term in a penitentiary. They camped near the squalid, struggling settlement of Fort Smith and spent several days celebrating the onset of summer and their escape from the constraints of civilization. As a "sacrifice to Bacchus," Roman god of wine, they shed their clothing and burned it all in a roaring bonfire before hoisting toasts to each other and passing out.

The Raven meant to wear exclusively Indian garb in any event, and he headed toward the wilderness reserve to which he had helped to move the more than three hundred Western Cherokee. At a trading post near Webber's Falls, an assemblage of Indian dignitaries who had heard numerous reports of Houston's approach came out to greet the traveler. Their revered chief led the party, though he'd grown notably older, heavier, and slower in his movements in the eleven years since the Raven had seen him last.

"My son," Oolooteka told him in Cherokee, "I have heard you were a great chief among your people. . . . I have heard that a dark cloud has fallen on the white path you were walking. . . . I am glad of it—it was done by the Great Spirit. . . . We are in trouble and the Great Spirit has sent you to us to give us counsel." They prepared an elaborate feast to celebrate Houston's return, slaughtering several of the cows they raised in abundance in their woodland settlement. Writing about himself in the third person, as he often did, Houston remembered that "when he laid himself down to sleep that night, he felt like a weary wanderer returned at last to his father's house."

The Raven expressed gratitude for the loving reception he received by working feverishly to provide the counsel and service that the Cherokee desired. Having removed Oolooteka and his followers from Tennessee to Arkansas, some governmental authorities wanted to remove them once again to facilitate white settlement, this time pushing them along with other Cherokee populations all the way to the desolate plains of Oklahoma. Meanwhile, the warlike Osage tribe threatened renewed war with the Cherokee, the American settlers, or both, as federal Indian agents, traders. and army officials attempted to pit the various factions against one another for their own advantage. Houston plunged energetically into this dangerous maelstrom, traveling throughout the region and deploying his political and lawyerly skills to preserve the peace and prevent the government from breaking its promises.

He also forged a close connection with a tall, slender, and handsome thirty-year-old widow he had known when she was still a girl, and their practical relationship required none of the formalities or complications that had poisoned his experience with Eliza. Historians refer to Tiana as his "wife," though it's likely no formal marriage accompanied their intimacy; in Cherokee tradition, if a woman had been previously married, her subsequent associations merited scant communal concern. Described by white visitors as "graceful as a bounding deer," Tiana also counted Oolooteka as her uncle, so her companionship bound Houston even closer to the first family of the tribe. They established a home together that he called Wigwam Neosho at the edge of Indian territory, about thirty miles from the tribal center and the old chief's commodious lodge. According to Marquis James, author of the 1929 Pulitzer Prize–winning biography *The Raven*: "Houston bought or built a large log house and set out an apple orchard. There he lived in style, transacting his affairs and entertaining his friends. There was no concealment. Tiana was his wife, her barbaric beauty a part of the solace he had found, as he said, amid 'the lights and shadows of forest life.'"

"THE FATAL ENCHANTRESS"

But that solace didn't prevent him from drinking to excess and plunging deep into the shadows of the worst years of his existence. His frequent letters, even to his revered mentor, President Jackson, took on a self-pitying, increasingly incoherent tone. The Raven rightly pointed to the government's cynical use of alcohol as a means of influencing Indian tribes and undermining their progress, but he had no basis for blaming hostile agents for his own painful problems with the bottle. "The fruit of this world turns to ashes and the charm of life is broken," he wrote. In the third person again, he described the pathos of a once respected figure who "gave himself up to the fatal enchantress" and "buried his sorrows in the flowing bowl."

The Cherokee wouldn't give up on Houston, but in recognition of his degeneration they did give him a new name. Instead of calling him Colonneh (the Raven), they began referring to him as Oo-tse-tee Ardee-tah-skee (Big Drunk). This insult stung with special force because it employed the crude language of the tribe's traditional enemies, the Osage. Nevertheless, Oolooteka made sure that on the frequent occasions when his adopted son consumed too much whiskey, a group of young men stayed close to his side to prevent disastrous consequences.

At one point, Houston flew into a rage at a young white clerk who worked for him at a little trading post he operated at Wigwam Neosho and absurdly challenged the boy to a duel with pistols. Big Drunk's Cherokee attendants reasonably insisted that it made no sense to force the innocent lad into the confrontation, but Houston refused to heed their objections. The confrontation took place in the traditional style, with each combatant firing his weapon at his opponent at close range; fortunately, both shots missed, so Houston and his assistant could each walk away feeling satisfied and vindicated. Only later did Big Drunk discover that his friends had loaded both pistols with plenty of gunpowder to make a resounding pop, but no balls to strike the other party and do damage.

In another instance, Houston interrupted an angry binge and made his way to Oolooteka's lodge, insulting the old man and eventually striking him. Loyal warriors watched the scene with horror before they grabbed the wildly flailing Big Drunk and beat him into unconsciousness. He later awoke with only dim memories of what had happened, as the sorrowful chief bathed his self-destructive son and lovingly tended to his bruises. Later, the humiliated Houston made a formal and emotional apology to the tribal council.

"MOST DARING OUTRAGE
AND ASSAULT"

Reports of the former governor's sad decline spread throughout the country but circulated with particular intensity in Tennessee, where they even reached Sam's stoic mother before her death in September 1831. After rushing to her bedside in time for tearful goodbyes, he resolved to restore his damaged dignity, and he departed for Washington to plead the case of various Indian tribes in their tormented dealings with the federal government. On his way east he stopped at Nashville and sought further inspiration with a pilgrimage to the Hermitage, home of Andrew Jackson. While strolling through the grounds of Jackson's gracious estate, Houston used a newly purchased knife to cut a hickory sapling that he shaped into a walking stick to take with him to the national capital.

Once in Washington, he confronted disturbing reports concerning Congressman William Stanbery of Ohio, a hulking, grossly overweight, and combative figure who had won election as one of Andrew Jackson's staunch supporters but then turned with a vengeance against the administration and its prominent allies. On the floor of the House, Stanbery made a wild accusation that Houston had conspired with the secretary of war to steal money on a fraudulent government contract meant to provide lifesaving rations to often desperately hungry Indian tribes. The charge had no basis: funds had never been allocated to the secretary, and Houston's role in the whole affair stemmed from a sincere effort to help his native friends.

Deeply offended at the nasty personal attack, Houston sent a note to Stanbery demanding an apology and a retraction, hinting that if the congressman did not apologize, they should settle the matter with a duel. The corpulent Stanbery refused even to open the sealed letter, but he knew enough about Houston's bellicose reputation that he became concerned for his personal safety. He armed himself with two loaded pistols and a concealed dagger for all of his subsequent trips to the House floor.

On the evening of April 13, 1832, just three years after his separation from Eliza, Houston chatted with two friendly senators and a congressman from Tennessee in offices near the Capitol; given the well-established habits of the various participants, it's likely that libations lifted their spirits. Striding out into the gentle spring air, the friends walked together down Pennsylvania Avenue toward Houston's rooms at Brown's Indian Queen Hotel. By chance, in the light of the flickering street lamps, the congressman recognized the lumbering figure of his colleague Stanbery crossing the street in front of them. Houston approached the object of his scorn and asked directly, "Are you Mr. Stanbery?"

When the congressman confirmed that he was, the Raven shouted, "Then you are a damned rascal!" With that, Houston proceeded to whack him over the head with the hickory cane he had recently fashioned for other purposes. Despite his size, Stanbery could hardly match his opponent's strength, and Houston continued the blows against his adversary's head, face, and shoulders. When Stanbery tried to run out of range, yelling for help, Houston jumped onto his back and brought the congressman's enormous girth crashing down onto the pavement. As they wrestled on the ground, Stanbery reached into his belt, withdrew one of the pistols, and in front of horrified witnesses pressed it directly against Houston's heart and pulled the trigger.

Senator Alexander Buckner of Missouri, who had been walking with Houston, saw the flint strike fire, but the powder in the gun's chamber failed to explode. An astonished Houston checked to see that he remained uninjured, then ripped the gun out of Stanbery's hand and jumped up to finish his foe's humiliation. Lifting the beaten man's legs into the air, Houston aimed one final, climactic blow at his broad backside before dusting himself off and strolling back to his hotel.

Neither man had been seriously injured, except for the obvious wound to Stanbery's pride, but that affront caused enough embarrassment that he couldn't possibly let the matter drop. The next day he sent a note to the Speaker of the House, demanding that Houston should be punished for the humiliating encounter. The next edition of the *United States Telegraph* featured a lurid headline ("MOST DARING OUTRAGE AND ASSAULT") that portrayed Sam Houston as a bullying boozer whose hickory cane represented a menace to all decent elements of society. In that same spirit, the House voted 45 to 25 to order Houston's arrest: as a former representative himself, he had violated congressional privilege by attacking a current member for words spoken on the House floor.

The resulting trial consumed the House of Representatives for the next four weeks, with the galleries filled every morning and saturation coverage in the nation's newspapers crowding out reports of any other business by either chamber of Congress. To be his legal representative, Houston retained the well-known Baltimore lawyer Francis Scott Key, author of the already popular patriotic hymn "The Star-Spangled Banner," which, almost precisely a hundred years later, became the official national anthem of the United States. During the long trial, Key looked tired and disoriented most of the time and said almost nothing, allowing the irrepressible Houston to conduct nearly all his own defense.

Despite Sam's obvious enjoyment of the process of the trial, and the unmistakable support he received every day from the packed, partisan House galleries, the president worried intensely over the outcome and summoned his erstwhile protégé to the White House to urge a change of strategy. For one thing, Jackson snarled at the fact that Houston came to the House floor every day dressed in his beaded buckskin jacket, Cherokee blankets, or both and asked if the former governor owned a decent suit of clothes. Without explaining that much of his formal wardrobe had disappeared years ago as a "sacrifice to Bacchus," Houston admitted that he lacked proper garb. Ready for that answer, Old Hickory tossed a silk purse of coins across the presidential desk and ordered his beleaguered follower to upgrade his appearance as quickly as possible.

From that point forward, Big Drunk appeared before the House in a well-tailored black coat and white satin vest but failed to alter the unconventional means with which he and Key prepared their case. The night before his scheduled summation speech, Houston convened a merry gathering in his hotel room that included the presiding officer of the trial, Speaker of the House Andrew Stevenson. This distinguished gentleman consumed so much liquor that he passed out on the couch, while another congressman, future president James Knox Polk, who generally shunned heavy drinking, left early. Houston himself showed no such restraint: awakening with a thunderous headache, he "took a cup of coffee but it refused to stick." The next cup also failed to wake him up, and "after something like an hour had passed I took another cup and it stuck and I said, 'I am all right' and proceeded to array myself in my splendid apparel."

"A NATIONAL TRIBUNAL FOR A THEATRE"

The speech that followed created a national sensation, though reading its flowery, melodramatic text from the distance of more than 180 years suggests that it must have been one of those "you had to be there" moments that seasoned orators can create. The accused assailant began with a ringing declaration: "I disclaim, utterly, every motive unworthy of an honorable man." Though he pityingly described himself as "a man of broken fortune and blasted reputation," he made clear that "all I demand is that my actions may be pursued to the motive which gave them birth."

The galleries, even more jammed than usual, exploded in wild applause, and an unidentified admirer threw down a bouquet of flowers that dropped at the defendant's feet. A woman's voice heard above the din exclaimed: "I had rather be Sam Houston in a dungeon than Stanbery on a throne!"

After a half hour more of emotional outpourings, Houston suggested, in effect, a personal right to beat another citizen who had insulted him, arguing that restraining that right would "have destroyed the pride of American character . . . But Sir, so long as that flag shall bear aloft its glittering stars . . . so long I trust, shall the rights of American citizens be preserved safe and unimpaired—till discord shall wreck the spheres—the grand march of time shall cease—and not one fragment of all creation be left to chafe the bosom of eternity's waves."

This was star-spangled nonsense, of course, but contemporaries hailed it as a masterpiece, and the tearful crowd in the House galleries stood and cheered. Pushing through the congratulatory mob that pumped Houston's hand on the House floor, the celebrated English-born actor Junius Brutus Booth (father of a future presidential assassin) warmly embraced the triumphant orator. "Houston, take my laurels!" he declaimed.

Despite unmistakable sympathy for the accused, the facts of the case showed him unmistakably guilty of assault. Amazingly, the House still managed to debate the matter for four full days before voting 101 to 90 to convict Sam Houston, sentencing him to a reprimand by the Speaker. The climactic scolding arrived May 14, with Houston solemnly approaching the raised dais and the chair of Speaker Stevenson—the same worthy who had collapsed during the Raven's pre-speech drinking festival. After praising the convicted culprit for his "character and intelligence," Stevenson concluded that in view of the judgment of the House "that you be reprimanded at this bar by the Speaker . . . I do reprimand you accordingly."

The breathless publicity associated with this melodramatic affair worked magic in restoring Houston's badly bruised reputation and making him a center of national attention as never before. As he recalled several decades later: "I was dying out and had they taken me before a justice of the peace and fined me ten dollars it would have killed me; but they gave me a national tribunal for a theatre, and that set me up again." As a commanding figure in Washington for several months, he effectively ended his self-imposed exile and returned to the good graces of President Jackson, who made him such a frequent White House guest that the opposition press claimed that Houston "practically lived in the executive mansion."

From this center of power and possibility, Houston felt no compulsion to return to the operation of a shabby trading post in far-away Cherokee country. Allowing his sense of the "great destiny" that awaited him to guide his next steps, he turned away without hesitation from his Indian life and the destructive drunkenness that he associated with it. In his recollections of this period he makes no mention of a decision to stop drinking, but in the great projects that soon absorbed him he gave evidence of single-minded sobriety. Like many other adventurers and empire builders of the era, he focused his attention on a vast stretch of mostly uninhabited real estate that seemed to invite an audacious conqueror: the Mexican state of Coahuila y Tejas.

After returning to Wigwam Neosho, he invited his companion, Tiana, to accompany him to a new and potentially glorious life south of the border. She declined, preferring to remain with her Cherokee family, so Houston left her behind, "barbaric beauty" and all. Tiana went on to partner with a man named John McGrady, then died of pneumonia at age forty-two, after her onetime partner had earned one of the more astonishing victories in the history of warfare and established himself as first president of the independent Republic of Texas.

AN EAGLE FLYING JUST AHEAD

His determination to win the Texas territory for Americans and, ultimately, for the U.S. government began with the vision of his mentor and sponsor, Andrew Jackson. In the first years of his presidency, Old Hickory made serious efforts to purchase Texas from the Mexican government, but they turned away his overtures. American authorities beginning with Jefferson had long insisted that the ill-defined boundaries of the Louisiana Purchase included all of Texas, but the same 1819 treaty that secured Florida from Spain ceded the territory west of the Sabine River to the Spanish colonial authorities. Just two years later, the Mexican War of Independence drove out the Spaniards and opened the region for the first time to immigrants from the United States.

Eager to build the economy of the sparsely populated territory and to block constant, bloody raids by Comanche warriors, the new Mexican government granted generous tracts of land to Yankee *emprasarios* who agreed to plant crops and bring in new settlers. In nine years of steady immigration, the population of Texas swelled from 3,500 in 1825 to 37,800 in 1834, with nearly all of the boisterous newcomers arriving from the United States. Inevitably, the members of the American majority felt closer to their country of origin than they did to the struggling regime in Mexico City, especially after battling warlords engaged in a series of coups and countercoups that destroyed any semblance of democratic rule. After 1830, the central government became increasingly concerned that the ever-growing American population would attempt to detach the state of Coahuila y Tejas from the Mexican Republic and join the United States, especially in light of Jackson's persistent efforts to purchase the territory. By prohibiting any further U.S. immigration and imposing customs duties that had previously exempted the Americans living in the state, the ruling cadre in Mexico City produced an angry response from the restive American colony. The Convention of 1832 brought American settlers together to demand the autonomy promised by the Mexican constitution of 1824, rolling back attempts to rein in the prosperous, freewheeling, unassimilated enclave.

This was the unsettled situation that welcomed Sam Houston as he splashed across the muddy Red River as a lone horseman in December 1832. Naturally, he spotted an eagle flying just ahead of him to erase any doubts as to the new course he had taken in his life. He also felt encouraged by the $500 that President Jackson had loaned him to make the trip. Settling in the village of Nacogdoches, he opened a law practice and converted to Catholicism, a statutory requirement for any newcomer who wanted to own land. Though he treated the process respectfully, there's no indication of a meaningful spiritual shift from the Indian mysticism that had shaped him since his teenage years. He had been charged by the War Department and the Jackson administration to try to use his deep identification with Indian culture to make peace with some of the warlike tribes on the border of Mexican Texas and the United States, but he concentrated instead on the political ferment that had brought the American community to the point of open revolt.

His new neighbors selected Houston as a delegate to the Convention of 1833, where he identified with the more radical faction that sought independence, not just greater rights and local control under the Mexican constitution. These firebrands consciously identified with the rebel patriots of the American Revolution who had stood up against efforts by a distant, unresponsive, domineering establishment to impose new taxes that interfered with existing traditions of self-government.

But key differences with the revolutionaries of 1776 made the situation even more difficult for the bold insurgents of 1833. For one thing, the brewing rebellion against Mexico seemed to lack the population base for a successful mass movement. The numbers in Texas included some thirty thousand "Texians" (as the American settlers styled themselves), joined by perhaps three thousand "Tejanos" (Spanish Mexican residents who ultimately supported the independence cause). The colonies that had stood up against the British crown boasted nearly a hundred times those numbers, with a population of some three million from which to draw troops and political leadership. Moreover, the patriots of American independence had benefited from deep roots in the New World, with most of the thirteen colonies well established for a hundred years or more. By contrast, none of the Texians boasted more than a quarter century in their new homes, and they had established few durable political institutions—certainly nothing like the proudly independent colonial legislatures that shaped the resistance to British authority.

"THE NAPOLEON OF THE WEST"

Nonetheless, the Texians' determination to protect their "rights"—including the right to own slaves in defiance of the anti-slavery policies of the Mexican government—led to an outbreak of violence in October 1835 when Mexican troops made an unsuccessful attempt to seize a tiny cannon from the American settlement in Gonzales.

A few weeks later, Sam Houston attended the "Consultation" in which delegates from throughout Texas came together to form a provisional government but failed to make a stable, definitive decision on a new governor for the rebellious province. Nevertheless, the delegates to the Consultation did manage to select Houston as commander in chief of the so-called Provisional Army. This meant placing him in charge of any new forces he could raise from the Texas countryside or by luring adventurers from the United States. In addition to recruiting a new army, Houston tried to coordinate efforts by several bands of volunteers who had elected their own officers and refused to recognize his authority.

Some of these units wanted to broaden the fight by striking directly at the Mexican heartland, while Houston preferred concentrating all available resources to defend Texas itself. Protective preparations became especially urgent with the change of leadership in Mexico City: the dashing, ruthless General Antonio López de Santa Anna took undisputed control after a long series of coups and countercoups, promising to crush resistance of every kind. Since winning an 1829 victory against a feeble attempt by the Spanish to recapture their lost colony, Santa Anna modestly styled himself the "Savior of the Motherland" and the "Napoleon of the West." If he lacked the military genius of his French-Corsican role model, he fully replicated Bonaparte's grandiose self-infatuation and irresistible allure to all available (and unavailable) females. With his tight, tailored, gilt-heavy uniforms and carefully pomaded black hair arranged with one curled, romantic forelock plastered to the right side of his "noble" forehead, the strutting little general most certainly constituted a legend in his own mind.

To display the serious intentions of his freshly minted dictatorship, the Napoleon of the West led his fiercely loyal and well-trained Army of Operations into the restive state of Zacatecas, halfway between Mexico City and San Antonio, the traditional Spanish capital of Texas. Like the Texians, the Zacatecans had resisted the new emphasis on centralized power, until Santa Anna punished them in May 1835 by murdering two thousand civilians, including women and children, during two days of unrestrained looting by his men. With their bloodlust only temporarily sated, this arrogant army with its amorous commander turned north for a devastating three-pronged attack on Texas.

Intercepted dispatches gave Houston three months' warning that *el presidente* intended to lead a reported ten thousand well-equipped, battle-hardened veterans against the Texians. The Raven never fielded more than one thousand raw, contentious, independent-minded volunteers in the course of the whole campaign, initially describing them as "busy, noisy, second-rate men." He complained that he was "a General without an army, serving under . . . a pretended government, that had no head, and no loyal subjects to obey its commands." Through sheer force of will and the power of personal example, he resolved to shape his ad hoc troops into something like a functioning fighting force. In that effort, he faced not only frequent desertions from bored volunteers who tired of long, hungry marches to evade the onrushing enemy but also mutinies organized by prominent officers who felt that another commander could do a better job than the imperious Houston, for all his fame.

"THE ENEMY ARE LAUGHING YOU TO SCORN"

This defiant attitude proved profoundly costly to the rebel cause. Houston never wanted to make a stand at the vulnerable provincial capital of San Antonio, which was dangerously close to Mexico and far away from the most populous American settlements, where he knew the war would be decided. Nevertheless, a group of outnumbered volunteers acted on their own initiative to fight a determined six-week campaign against San Antonio's Mexican garrison, forcing its surrender and taking possession of the thick-walled, eighty-year-old mission-turned-fortress known as the Alamo.

Despite this encouraging success, in January 1836 the commander in chief ordered these two hundred victorious, high-spirited scrappers to get out of the way of Santa Anna's approaching hordes. The San Antonio cadre—including Houston's old friend from Tennessee, former congressman Davy Crockett—rejected these orders as unmanly and defeatist. Instead, they held out for thirteen days against the Mexican siege before Santa Anna overwhelmed them and butchered at least 182 fighters in the old fort, including those survivors who attempted to surrender. All the American bodies were immediately stacked and burned.

Only three noncombatants lived to describe the slaughter: the young widow of A. M. Dickinson, her fifteen-month-old baby, and the black "body servant" of the dead Texian commander, Colonel William Barret Travis. President Santa Anna received them graciously in his headquarters and placed a horse and an attendant at their service so they could transmit a message to the remaining rebels. He asked Mrs. Dickinson to "convey the compliments of General Santa Anna to Señor Houston, and to assure him that the story of the Alamo would be repeated for all who raised arms against the Mexican government." The fighters in this "unworthy" cause would escape with their lives only if they immediately abandoned their resistance.

Two weeks later, a major force of 420 Texas militiamen near Goliad ignored Houston's repeated orders to withdraw in the face of a Mexican strike force pushing toward the Gulf Coast. The Mexicans surrounded them and forced their surrender, holding them for a week in Goliad jail. On Palm Sunday, General Santa Anna marched the prisoners in military columns back out to the countryside. There the Mexicans shot more than four hundred prisoners at point-blank range, clubbing or knifing those who initially survived the bullets. As they had done at the Alamo, they stacked the bodies and burned them, leaving the remains in the open for vultures and coyotes.

As word of these grisly atrocities spread through the American enclaves of East Texas, the news had the intended effect: civilian populations, including the interim government, fled in desperate panic, loading wagons with any property they could move and clogging the rutted, muddy roads. Scores of Houston's ad hoc troops suddenly lost interest in the conflict and joined the refugees, causing his numbers to dwindle at one point down to four hundred, though irregular arrivals from the United States and returning Texians ultimately doubled that number. Houston knew his only hope involved rapid retreat, forcing Santa Anna to split his vastly superior forces to catch them. He consciously imitated George Washington, who had miraculously kept his outclassed army intact through frequent withdrawals in the face of the enemy, taking opportunistic advantage of every chance for some surprise strike.

Critics among the civilian leadership saw Houston's strategy as evidence of derangement, drunkenness, or both. They circulated stories that the general in chief's reluctance to stand his ground and fight stemmed from his chronic alcoholism or from his deep immersion in pagan Indian mysticism. In fact, abundant evidence indicates that the former Big Drunk remained sober and fiercely focused during the entire period of the "Runaway Scrape," making tireless personal efforts to encourage his men and keep them involved in the struggle.

Nevertheless, the frustrated, frightened, and deeply ineffectual interim president of the Republic of Texas, David Burnet, demanded some immediate military miracle. This feckless official, best known for the fact that his father had served in the Continental Congress during the American Revolution, wrote to his general in chief: "Sir: the enemy are laughing you to scorn. You must fight them. You must retreat no farther. The country expects you to fight. The salvation of the country depends on you doing so."

Houston wrote back with scarcely concealed irritation that "I have kept the army together under the most discouraging circumstances and I hope a just and wise God, in whom I have always believed, will yet save Texas."

President Burnet, famous for traveling everywhere with a Bible in one pocket and a pistol in another, seemed notably less confident in his faith and fled with his cabinet to the undefended village of Harrisburg. Santa Anna learned of the whereabouts of the rebel government from reliable spies and decided on a chancy move to capture the traitors and end the revolution with a single blow. After all, the Savior of the Motherland had lost fortunes in pursuing his passion for gambling, and he always proved ready to take bold risks for the sake of personal glory. He separated his forces, just as Houston had hoped, detaching elite elements of his army under his personal command for the anticipated strike.

"RELY UPON HIS PROVIDENCE"

Fortunately for their survival, Burnet and his associates fled from Harrisburg just ahead of Santa Anna's arrival and boarded a steamboat for the relative safety of Galveston Island. The approach of the Mexicans had been seriously slowed by torrential spring rains, viewed by the Texians as "providential." Although Houston couldn't maneuver his little army into position in time to protect a government that did a better job fleeing than functioning, he did manage to march his soggy, constantly complaining, frequently deserting troops some fifty-five miles in two and a half days to place them in position for a confrontation with Santa Anna. Both officers and men loudly expressed their desire for some showdown, despite the unmistakable superiority of the Mexican force arrayed against them.

By the time of the final confrontation, the Mexican president's personal strike force, manned by his army's best, hand-picked troops, had been supplemented by five hundred quick-marching reinforcements from the main body of his men, so he now outnumbered the bedraggled Texians two to one.

But Houston had received reinforcements of another kind that encouraged him to take risks of his own. Five months earlier, a rebel representative had journeyed to Cincinnati to rally support from local patriots for the Texas Revolution. A few volunteers immediately headed southwest, while many other concerned citizens contributed funds to support the cause. With this money, the Ohioans commissioned two small cannon from a local foundry, discreetly describing their purchase as "hollow ware" so as not to run afoul of the official U.S. policy of strict neutrality on the bloody war south of the border. The well-concealed six-pounders traveled down the Mississippi by steamboat to New Orleans and from there boarded a schooner to Galveston Island. Christened the "Twin Sisters" to honor twin daughters of another passenger on that ship, the precious guns finally found Houston's army on April 11, just ten days before the climactic fight with Santa Anna.

The Mexicans relied on a much bigger gun, a twelve-pounder, but it proved less mobile and effective than the newly arrived sisters from Cincinnati. Houston deployed his forces behind some trees less than a half mile away from the enemy and awaited an inevitable attack, but the commander of his sixty-man cavalry insisted on riding off on a daring raid to capture or at least disable the single piece of Mexican artillery. The raiders failed miserably in their mission, and they came close to annihilation by Mexican regulars who surrounded them; even worse, they ran the risk of provoking a general engagement in an open prairie on terms distinctly unfavorable to the Texians.

When cavalry colonel Sidney Sherman shamefacedly returned to the camp, Houston delivered a public dressing-down and removed him from command, handing leadership of the cavalry to a just-arrived private from Georgia who had managed to rescue two wounded, imperiled comrades from the ill-fated skirmish. The resonantly named Mirabeau Buonaparte Lamar (his famous banker cousin boasted the even more memorable moniker Gazaway Bugg Lamar) was a prolific poet, newspaperman, and former state senator with big dreams; promoted from private to colonel on the spot, he later became one of Houston's principal rivals in Texas politics.

That night, though greatly relieved that Santa Anna had not yet attacked, the general in chief found it difficult to sleep when battle looked certain the following day. He knew that elements of his army murmured openly of mutiny and only intermittently accepted his authority. He finally went to bed on bare ground, having surrendered his saddle blanket to be cut up for powder cartridges for the Twin Sisters. In his exhaustion, he enjoyed his first sleep of more than three hours in the last six weeks. When he opened his eyes, it was already full daylight; he lay back and stared into the cloudless April sky to see an eagle—his "medicine animal," a promising omen, to be sure—floating and tilting just above him, as if to offer supernatural reassurance.

His officers needed reassurance of their own, and demanded a council of war. For two full hours he listened to their arguments before they voted five to two to fight a defensive battle rather than launch a risky attack against an enemy more numerous and better equipped. Houston kept his own counsel about his ultimate decision but privately described his thinking in a hastily scribbled letter to his friend

Henry Raguet, revealing that "we will only have about seven hundred to march with, besides the camp guard. We go to conquer. It is wisdom growing out of necessity to meet the enemy now; every consideration enforces it. No previous occasion would justify it. The troops are in fine spirits, and now is the time for action. I leave the result in the hands of a wise God, and rely upon his providence."

"LIBERTY OR DEATH"

As Houston began deploying his men for the attack that he had planned, a trusted scout named Erastus "Deaf" Smith volunteered for an audacious mission to prevent Santa Anna from benefiting from the further reinforcements he awaited and expected. With six men, the farseeing but hard-of-hearing stalwart rode off to destroy Vince's Bridge, preventing any newly arrived Mexicans from crossing over Buffalo Bayou and joining the scene of battle. The dismantling of this span would have the additional effect of preventing either party from executing a safe retreat. As Deaf Smith rushed away for his crucial errand, Houston commanded him to "come back like eagles, or you will be too late for the day."

The general, meanwhile, deployed his men in a thin line two deep and nearly a thousand yards across, intending to sweep down on the Mexicans less than five hundred yards away. At four o'clock he gave the orders to a drummer to begin beating time, and the army's sole fifer played the only tune he knew: an off-color drinking song about seduction, "Will You Come to the Bower." A company from Kentucky displayed the Texians' only battle flag: a white silk banner donated by local ladies that depicted a crudely stitched, bare-breasted figure of a Roman goddess lifting high a sword with a ribbon proclaiming LIBERTY OR DEATH.

Houston unsheathed his own sword, lifted it overhead, and roared his order: "Trail arms, forward!" He rode on a huge white stallion well ahead of his advancing men with the Twin Sisters wheeled along on either side of him. "Hold your fire, men. Hold your fire!" the commander ordered. Following his instructions, the troops advanced as quietly as possible, hoping for an element of surprise.

That surprise was possible because the Napoleon of the West felt certain that the Americans would never attack and so neglected to post sentries who could give advance warning of enemy movements. Houston had spent more than a month avoiding conflict, pushing his men in constant retreat, so Santa Anna concluded that his opponent had no appetite for a fight. In the late afternoon, his men sought relief from the heat of the day in the traditional siesta, leaving their arms stacked. The Savior of the Motherland retreated to the privacy of his spacious tent, reportedly engaging in his favorite hobby with a beautiful but unidentified señorita.

The dictator's indulgent afternoon came to an abrupt end with the first blasts from the Twin Sisters: broken horseshoes and musket balls rained down directly on the loosely constructed Mexican barricades of pack saddles, trunks, baggage, and boxes. An alarm bugle sounded and the startled troops began rushing for their boots and their weapons. Colonel Pedro Delgado recalled his general-president emerging from his tent, with "His Excellency running about in the most excited manner, wringing his hands and unable to give an order."

In front of the American line, artillery commander Ben McCulloch rolled forward with the Twin Sisters after each shot, but at one point he almost obliterated his own commanding officer. Houston rode his handsome white horse about thirty yards ahead of his line; McCulloch "had aimed the gun, but was delayed in firing it for a moment by General Houston who passed across." The artilleryman snatched the burning brand at the last moment from the touch hole, narrowly avoiding a disaster. "After this, I saw him advancing upon the enemy, at least one-third of the distance between the two armies, in front of Colonel Burleson's regiment, when it was not more than seventy or eighty yards from the enemy's breast works. About this time, the enemy gave way, and the rout became general."

Still far ahead of his troops, Houston offered a prime target: his big horse was shot out from under him, and some of the troops helped him mount a second pony. He recalled one musket ball that whizzed toward him, then pinged against a metal stud on his leather bridle, keeping him from harm. One more shot did shatter his left ankle (he later had twenty-two fragments of bone removed by a surgeon) and his boot filled with blood, but he continued waving his broad hat with its ornamental plume and urging his men forward.

Seeing the panic and confusion of the Mexican troops, Houston's army broke into a run and ignored his orders to stop and reload. The men had no bayonets, but they used their rifles like clubs and took out their hunting knives. Yelling "Remember the Alamo!" and "Remember Goliad!," they vaulted over the Mexican barricades and fell on the enemy forces before they could even attempt to surrender. The entire battle lasted for only eighteen minutes before its outcome became unmistakably clear.

According to all accounts, the enraged Texians continued to massacre the enemy after that point, offering the same quarter and mercy the Mexicans had provided to their prisoners at the Alamo and Goliad. The wounded Houston finally succeeded in restoring order and putting a stop to the killing, as hundreds of Santa Anna's elite troops surrendered in orderly groups. Any chance of flight or retreat had been blocked by Deaf Smith, who rode back on his lathered steed just in time to take part in the battle. At one point, Houston spotted long lines of Mexican regulars marching in parade-ground columns at the rear of his own vulnerable forces. Assuming that the reinforcements he feared had arrived at precisely the wrong time, he shouted, "All is lost; my God, all is lost!" But the men he saw were actually prisoners, under custody, on their way to the American camp.

"BORN TO NO COMMON DESTINY"

By the time darkness fell, the Texians had taken a total of 730 prisoners, with 630 killed and estimates of the Mexican wounded running as high as 208. Their own casualties counted as remarkably low. Of 910 engaged in some way in the battle, only three died on the field, six more died later of their wounds, and another twenty-one (including Houston) had been injured seriously enough to be incapacitated.

In addition to the disproportionate casualties, the Americans also captured more than six hundred muskets, three hundred sabers, two hundred pistols, and several hundred mules and horses—invaluable supplies that gave new life to the struggling cause. They also took possession of more than $12,000 in gold contained in handsomely decorated chests; the Savior of the Motherland never traveled, even into battle, without some of the treasure that he cherished.

The victorious troops spent the night in raucous celebration, while keeping a watchful eye on their hundreds of prisoners, but Houston rested only fitfully. He suffered intense pain from his badly damaged leg and worried that Santa Anna, who had somehow escaped the scene, would soon reunite with the chief portion of his army and then return to surround and annihilate the temporarily triumphant rebels.

Toward evening, a five-man patrol rode up to General Houston where he rested on a blanket under an oak tree. They brought a bedraggled Mexican prisoner with them, "a well-mannered little fellow" in a loose-fitting blue smock with red felt slippers. They had found him near the ruined bridge of Buffalo Bayou, sitting dejected and alone on a stump at the edge of the water. They were going to throw him into the general herd of captured Mexicans when a number of the troops recognized his face, if not his civilian outfit, and began calling out, "El Presidente! El Presidente!"

As the Raven listened to this compelling narrative, the oddly dressed prisoner stepped forward and bowed low toward the Texian conqueror. "I am General Antonio López de Santa Anna, president of Mexico, commander in chief of the Army of Operations. I place myself at the disposal of the brave General Houston."

Despite his pain, the Raven managed to raise himself on one elbow and find the words to overcome his astonishment. "General Santa Anna—Ah, indeed—Take a seat, General, I am glad to see you, take a seat."

Houston gestured toward a black box and summoned an interpreter. That meant that he could fully savor the prisoner's next declaration. "That man may consider himself born to no common destiny who has conquered the Napoleon of the West," El Presidente declared. "And it now remains for him to be generous to the vanquished."

"You should have remembered that at the Alamo," Houston sharply responded.

Though many of his troops craved an even sharper response—the summary execution of Santa Anna—Houston understood that the little dictator was worth far more alive than dead. He eventually negotiated the terms of a cease-fire that kept his little army safe from the much larger Mexican forces in the vicinity. Ultimately the civilian authorities who took possession of the high-value prisoner agreed

"SAVIOR OF THE MOTHERLAND" AND "NAPOLEON OF THE WEST": Antonio López de Santa Anna (1794–1876), who served eleven nonconsecutive terms as president of Mexico.

"Convey the compliments of General Santa Anna to Señor Houston, and ... assure him that the story of the Alamo would be repeated for all who raised arms against the Mexican government."
—Santa Anna's message to General Sam Houston, March 1836

to his release only after he had officially signed a treaty recognizing Texas independence. At the Battle of San Jacinto (named for the lazy river that ran alongside the scene of the fight), Sam Houston had not only destroyed an enemy army but won (and ended) the entire war.

"NEVER IN THE ANNALS OF WAR"

As that reality began to sink in during the days following the fight, participants in the unexpectedly consequential confrontation couldn't keep from seeing the hand of God behind their victory. Thomas Jefferson Rusk, the thirty-two-year-old "secretary of war" of the fledgling Texas Republic, had fought alongside General Houston at San Jacinto and rejoiced in their "unparalleled triumph." But in his formal report to President Burnet he took care to give the credit to heavenly assistance. "Never in the annals of war was the interposition of Divine Providence [more] signally displayed," he wrote. "These brave men achieved a victory as glorious as any on the records of history, and the happy consequences will be felt in Texas by forty generations to come." Rusk understood that the eighteen minutes of battle by the Buffalo Bayou had ensured that Texas would remain forever American, in culture and language, if not yet as a formal state in the Union.

Houston himself, with little time for religious ruminations, still acknowledged the miraculous nature of the great events as they unfolded. It wasn't surprising that San Jacinto had ended the war, but it was shocking that it concluded that conflict with an American victory. The general and his men fully understood that a far more likely outcome would have seen them losing the battle, then losing their lives in a mass slaughter that followed the examples of the Alamo or Goliad. Such a conclusion would have wiped out the last resistance forces in Texas. By contrast, the American destruction of Santa Anna's strike force still left the bulk of the Mexican Army of Operations in the field, well equipped and with high morale and a deep hunger for revenge. If it hadn't been for the phenomenally fortunate—some would say blessed—capture of Santa Anna himself, those remaining forces easily could have continued the conflict, and likely annihilated the Texas Revolution.

The newly independent Republic of Texas quickly recovered from the invader's devastation and held its first presidential election less than five months after the fateful fight at San Jacinto. Naturally, the conquering hero, though still recovering from his badly wounded leg, won in a landslide, drawing 79 percent of the vote against two well-known opponents. As president, he hoped to bring Texas into the federal Union, but fears of a new war with Mexico and the complicated sectional politics of the era made it impossible to win congressional approval for the admission of a gigantic new slave state.

Since the constitution of the Texas Republic prohibited presidents from serving consecutive terms, Houston had to relinquish control in 1838 to Mirabeau Buonaparte Lamar, the poetic private he had instantly elevated to cavalry colonel on the eve of the Battle of San Jacinto. As a representative in the Texas Congress, the old warrior fiercely resisted President Lamar's more grandiose policies, especially his plans to "exterminate" the Indians who remained within the Republic's borders. After three years in opposition, Houston won election to a second term as president of the Lone Star Republic—again by a landslide. The month before he left office, his old friend from Tennessee, James Knox Polk, won election as president of the United States on an expansionist platform that strongly favored Texas annexation, and Congress finally approved Texas as the twenty-eighth state of the Union on December 29, 1845.

"HE WILL NOT LIVE WITH HER SIX MONTHS"

During his years between presidential terms, Houston also made a determined effort to terminate his status as an aging bachelor. While promoting Texas land sales to wealthy planters in Alabama, he met a tall, self-possessed, "violet eyed" twenty-year-old belle named Margaret Moffette Lea and found himself instantly smitten. She wrote poetry, played both piano and guitar with consummate grace, loved to read romantic novels, and deeply admired Sam Houston, despite an age difference of more than twenty-six years. Her family looked skeptically on the match: the girl's mother had emerged as one of the most devout and influential Baptist leaders in Alabama, and Margaret herself had studied the Bible at Judson Female Institute and remained a knowledgeable, outspoken, passionately committed Christian throughout her life. The battle-scarred Houston, on the other hand, still bore a reputation for heavy drinking and hard living, with persistent rumors about his brief marriage in Tennessee and the Cherokee companion he had left behind in Arkansas. Moreover, he continued

LATE-IN-LIFE-LOVE: With an age gap of twenty-six years and profound differences in religious outlook, friends looked on skeptically at forty-seven-year-old Sam Houston's newfound passion for Margaret Moffette Lea Houston (1819–1867). "Resort to any expedient rather than marry," they told him, and predicted "he will not live with her six months."

to invoke the spirituality he had learned from the Indians, had gone through a pro forma conversion to Catholicism to qualify to buy land in Mexican Texas, and hardly seemed ready to share Margaret's fervent, evangelical Baptist faith.

Houston's friends also scoffed at the prospective nuptials and urged him "to resort to any expedient rather than marry." He ignored them, but as guests began arriving at the Alabama wedding one of Margaret's close relatives took him aside and said that unless the bridegroom provided some satisfactory explanation for his shattered marriage with Eliza Allen eleven years earlier, the family meant to cancel the wedding. Houston politely explained that he had never spoken to anyone of the reasons for the separation and he had no intention of breaking his silence now, inviting the objecting family member to "call his fiddlers off."

The fiddlers stayed and played, and Houston's friends openly mourned the development. The Texas secretary of state, Barnard Bee Sr., wrote to a mutual friend: "I see with great pain the marriage of Genl Houston to Miss Lea! In all my acquaintance with life I have never met with an Individual more disqualified for domestic happiness—he will not live with her six months."

Actually, they lived together with romantic intensity the remaining twenty-three years of the Raven's life and produced eight children, the last one born when Houston was sixty-seven. Defying the norms of that time and place, all of these offspring lived into healthy adulthood. Consumed with her family responsibilities, Margaret never moved to Washington during the thirteen years that Sam served as one of his state's first representatives in the U.S. Senate. But their letters remained ardent and affectionate, and even during his frequent absences she conducted a long-distance campaign for her husband's religious conversion and ultimate redemption.

Under her influence, the onetime Big Drunk gave up alcohol altogether and even wrote earnest, pleading letters to his sons, insisting that they avoid the perils of strong drink. When a group of pastors approached Senator Houston in 1853 asking for his support for a ban on liquor sales on Sunday, he turned them down because he considered the idea a pointless expansion of governmental power. But in his written response he alluded to his own alcoholism and ultimate reformation. "I do not object to total abstinence," he explained. "I believe that total abstinence is the only way by which some intemperate drinkers can be saved. I know it from my personal experience. When a person's appetite for stimulating beverages becomes uncontrollable, he should 'touch not, handle not.'"

Houston's newfound sobriety and steadily intensifying religiosity delighted his wife and impressed his colleagues. A Texas congressman who occupied the quarters below him in a Washington rooming house said he could hear the senator falling to his knees in fervent prayer every morning upon rising and every night before retiring. He attended church regularly, especially when home with his family, but refused to take communion with the rest of the congregants. He discussed these conflicted sentiments during a difficult period in his Senate career, as he defied his constituents and his fellow southerners by opposing the Kansas-Nebraska Act, which allowed the spread of slavery north of the Missouri Compromise line.

During a visit home, he traveled for ten miles through the countryside with Dr. George Washington Baines, a scholarly pastor who later served as president of Baylor University and became the great-grandfather of President Lyndon Baines Johnson. As they walked their horses, Houston confessed that "my wife and other friends seem anxious for me to join the church and I would do so if I could. But with my present convictions, which I reached when a boy, it is impossible."

He then described a fiery Presbyterian sermon he had heard from a celebrated visiting pastor that cited the Book of Corinthians to the effect that unbelievers who took communion would suffer sure damnation. Since he maintained persistent doubts about biblical claims, he worried that partaking of the Lord's Supper would guarantee an eternity of torment. Dr. Baines readily explained that Paul's reference concerned only those who intentionally mocked communion by using it to satisfy physical hunger. Houston seemed gratified and relieved, declaring: "I see it clearly. Your view is news to me. I will return home and read that chapter carefully."

When he did, he agreed to full-immersion baptism and a new life as part of the Body of Christ. His wife's excitement over this development helped to spread the word, and hundreds of friends, admirers, and curious onlookers came to witness the event on November 19, 1854. The hero of San Jacinto plunged into the cold, bracing water of Rocky Creek at the "Baptizing Hole"—a large pool just downstream from a picturesque waterfall. Margaret shouted in ecstasy, and after the ceremony a friend commented, "Well, General, I hear your sins were washed away."

"I hope so," Houston responded, keeping a realistic perspective on his long, complicated life, "but if they were all washed away, the Lord help the fish down below."

"IN THE NAME OF MY OWN CONSCIENCE AND MANHOOD"

This new religious perspective helped lend a prophetic tone to the last fight of his perpetually embattled career, as he worked tirelessly to prevent his beloved Texas from joining other states of the South in seceding from the Union and provoking civil war. He began warning of the consequences as early as 1854, telling a pastor close to the family that in the election of 1860 "the Free Soil Party, uniting with the Abolitionists, will elect the president of the United States. Then will come the tocsin of war and the clamor for secession. . . . What fields of blood, what scenes of horror, what mighty cities in smoke and ruins—it is brother murdering brother . . . I see my beloved South go down in the unequal contest, in a sea of blood and smoking ruin."

He left the Senate to come home and make a race for governor to stop the headlong rush toward disunion. Running independent of any party affiliation, he lost in 1857 but then won two years later with the slogan "Constitution and Union." This placed him in direct opposition to the secessionist legislature during the crisis following Lincoln's election. The legislators authorized a secession convention over his vehement objections, and that assembly ultimately demanded that all state officials take an oath of loyalty to the new Confederacy of slaveholding states. Governor Houston replied: "Fellow-Citizens, in the name of your rights and liberties, which I believe have been trampled upon, I refuse to take this oath. . . . In the name of my own conscience and manhood, which this Convention would degrade by dragging me before it, to pander to the malice of my enemies, I refuse to take this oath. I deny the power of this Convention to speak for Texas."

The secession convention then removed Houston from office as numerous firebrands called for his assassination or execution for treason. After leaving the capital, the Houston family traveled toward Galveston and the little home the family maintained near the bay, experiencing threats, jeers, and condemnation at every stop. On April 19, one week after the first shots of the Civil War at Fort Sumter, he addressed an angry and obstreperous crowd from a hotel balcony and once again played the role of prophet and seer. "Some of you may laugh to scorn the idea of bloodshed as the result of secession," he began,

> but let me tell you what is coming. Your fathers and husbands, your sons and brothers, will be herded at the point of the bayonet. You may, after the sacrifice of countless millions of treasure and hundreds of thousands of lives, as a bare possibility, win Southern independence, if God be not against you, but I doubt it. I tell you that, while I believe with you in the doctrine of state rights, the North is determined to preserve this Union. They are not a fiery, impulsive people as you are, for they live in colder climates. But when they begin to move in a given direction, they move with the steady momentum and perseverance of a mighty avalanche; and what I fear is, they will overwhelm the South.

He would die before his predictions had been entirely fulfilled, expiring from pneumonia in July 1863, just three weeks after the Battle of Gettysburg.

"ONE OF THE DECISIVE BATTLES
OF THE WORLD"

After his Baptist conversion, Houston began thinking more deeply about the workings of destiny and divinity in guiding his strange and often tortured path, and saw himself more clearly as an instrument of God's will. He maintained his long-standing belief in the "augury of birds" and other Indian traditions, arguing occasionally with Christian friends about the meaning he discerned in the flight of eagles and ravens. Nearing the end of his life, he unequivocally acknowledged that the suffering and humiliation he had endured played a necessary role in achieving great and consequential ends.

The Raven surely would have agreed with the sentiments inscribed on the base of the soaring, 567-foot San Jacinto Monument, constructed to mark the one hundredth anniversary of the battle in 1936. "Measured by its results, San Jacinto was one of the decisive battles of the world," it reads. "The freedom of Texas from Mexico won here led to annexation and to the Mexican War, resulting in the acquisition by the United States of the states of Texas, New Mexico, Arizona, Nevada, California, Utah, and parts of Colorado, Wyoming, Kansas and Oklahoma. Almost one third of the present area of the American nation, nearly a million square miles of territory, changed sovereignty."

In 1855, at a time when ardent supporters urged Houston as a nominee for president of the United States, the general published his memoir, *The Life of Sam Houston*. Writing of himself in the third person, he recalled with considerable emotion his exile from Tennessee after the mysterious breakup of his marriage:

> His separation from his friends at the steamboat, was a touching scene. He was a young man, for he had not passed his thirty-fifth year. And it was a strange sight to see one so young, around whose brow the myrtle wreath of fame was twining, cast aside his robes of office and give up a bright future for a home in the wilderness. . . . It was no flight of a criminal. . . . It was a voluntary exile from scenes

which only harrowed his feelings while he stayed, and the Almighty Providence, which had shaped out his future life was leading him in a mysterious way through the forests to found a new empire.

Houston knew that skeptics in his own day, and in all future generations, would scoff at his mystical notions of divinely directed destiny, but he brusquely dismissed their objections. He wrote: "Let those who laugh at a Divine Providence, which watches over its chosen instruments, sneer as they read this; they may sneer on—they are welcome to their creed."

THE CRUCIAL COG: Nicholas Trist (1800–1874), aide to Jefferson and Jackson; State Department clerk assigned to negotiate peace with Mexico.

"If there was any legal provision for his punishment, he ought to be severely handled. He has acted worse than any man in the public employ whom I have ever known." —President James K. Polk, January 15, 1848

9

GOLDEN TIMING

Defying a President, Detaching California,
and Discovering Gold

On a crisp January morning in the forested foothills of the Sierra Nevada, a frontier carpenter spotted a few shiny pebbles in a drainage ditch running from the sawmill he had been hired to build. Four days later he rode thirty-six miles to show the glittering flecks to his boss, who soon confirmed the fact that they contained gold. Despite their uncertainty on how to exploit the discovery and their joint determination to keep the find a secret, news got out within weeks, provoking the fastest mass migration in American history and the nearly instantaneous development of California, destined to become the most powerful and prosperous state in the federal Union.

It's easy enough to write off that fortuitous find, and the wave of humanity that followed, as one of those happy accidents that turn up so frequently in the history of the United States. But the confirmation of the discovery of gold near present-day Sacramento occurred in the same week, and possibly on the same day, that a rogue bureaucrat on the outskirts of Mexico City, more than nineteen hundred miles away, risked arrest and imprisonment by defying the president he had been assigned to serve, signing final documents that ended the Mexican War and awarded California to the United States of America.

The synchronized schedule of these epochal events suggests conspiratorial planning, or at least conscious coordination, but the disconnected human beings directly involved couldn't possibly have worked together. Instead, the fateful occurrences of January and February 1848 offered new evidence of what recently had been described as America's "Manifest Destiny."

THE CRUCIAL COG

The crucial cog in this elaborate machinery of fate was an obscure, eccentric federal officeholder who remains largely unknown, even to scholars. Nicholas Philip Trist enjoyed important, even intimate relationships with five American presidents and served for a time as a principal aide to three of them. At the most decisive moment of his life, however, he disregarded law and protocol and acted entirely on his own authority; following some deep, inexplicable instinct, he unwittingly and singlehandedly ensured that the future Golden State became an American possession at the precise moment news of gold's discovery caused a sensation around the globe.

Nicholas Trist's trajectory toward the very center of early America's power elite began with his grandmother, who ran an elegant redbrick rooming house in Philadelphia. There Thomas Jefferson liked to stay when attending crucial sessions of the Continental Congress, and there James Madison lived for four months during the Constitutional Convention. As a teenager Trist's mother, Eliza, prepared meals and provided sparkling conversation for the distinguished guests, developing lifelong friendships with both Jefferson and Madison. Later, she married a footloose British adventurer who died of yellow fever while seeking his fortune on the Mississippi frontier, but the young widow received correspondence and consolation from the third and fourth presidents of the United States. The two great men took a protective interest in her orphaned sons, ages four and two, and the boys came to revere Jefferson in particular as a dominant figure in their upbringing.

Nicholas, the older child, seized on every opportunity to visit the former president and Revolutionary sage, joining a lively group of young followers who gravitated toward Jefferson's hilltop home at Monticello. Inevitably, young Trist fell deeply, hopelessly in love with the tall, willowy Virginia Jefferson Randolph, adored granddaughter of Thomas Jefferson himself. In a remarkable letter to the girl's mother, Jefferson's daughter Martha, Trist solemnly declared: "You may possibly have perceived that an attachment has existed for some time in my bosom, to your daughter Virginia; that the attachment is strong, and *must* be lasting, I am fully convinced. Hoping that my sentiments may be agreeable to yourself and Mr. Randolph, I address you these lines to request the permission of making them known to Miss Virginia."

The Randolphs and the Jeffersons liked young Trist and admired his fine mind, sharply chiseled features, and aristocratic bearing, but in view of the tender years of both principals they bundled the ardent suitor off to West Point to study military science for three years. Before graduating and earning his commission with the army, Nicholas left the academy in order to study law and to follow the example of his idol, Jefferson. He took up legal training in Louisiana with Edward Livingston, a friend of the family, and Andrew Jackson's aide-de-camp at the Battle of New Orleans.

By the time he reached his twenty-third birthday, Trist had achieved sufficient progress in his law studies that Jefferson accepted him as a personal student, inviting him to return to Monticello and, of course, renewed proximity to the adored Virginia. The young couple married in 1824, living up to Trist's confident, teenage prediction of a "lasting" attachment through forty-nine years of an unusually affectionate union. That union began with husband and wife sharing Thomas Jefferson's home and Trist serving as the former president's principal aide during the final two years of the statesman's life. From that point, the story of Trist's strange career calls to mind some improbable, early-nineteenth-century version of Woody Allen's fictional character Zelig, who somehow turns up at crucial turning points in history, always at the elbow of one or another of his era's most significant figures.

Trist handled the former president's voluminous correspondence (arthritis in his right wrist made it difficult for Jefferson to write) and tried to help in various schemes to deal with the demands of creditors. He generally accompanied the elderly sage on his daily rides around the property, during which Jefferson enjoyed testing the young man by breaking into French or Spanish, languages in which both of them were fluent. On the Glorious Fourth of 1826, when the new nation celebrated the anniversary of the Declaration Jefferson had penned fifty years before, Trist remained at the bedside of the eighty-three-year-old legend, carefully recording the details of his final hours as the great man passed into eternity.

CONVENIENT CONNECTIONS

With Jefferson gone, James Madison took his turn as Trist's prime sponsor and chosen mentor. Madison's intervention enabled the young man to secure a State Department post in the administration of John Quincy Adams, where he earned a meager government salary of $1,400 a year and supervised an army of clerks who wrote out dispatches to ambassadors around the world. He dismissed the tedious work as beneath his formidable abilities but agreed to continue it when General Andrew Jackson, the candidate he most admired, won the presidency on his second try in 1828.

Old Hickory particularly valued Trist because of the younger man's well-advertised connection to Jefferson, and he found occasions to pepper the State Department clerk with personal, probing questions, sometimes posed late at night, about the last days of the Sage of Monticello. The new president's nephew, Andrew Jackson Donelson, had come with him to Washington to serve as secretary to the president; in one of those convenient connections that defined Trist's life, Donelson had been his best friend during his years at West Point. They renewed their friendship in the nation's capital until frustrations with the Jackson administration sent Donelson and his wife temporarily back to Tennessee.

At that point, it made sense for Old Hickory to summon Trist as his nephew's unofficial replacement, installing him as acting secretary to the president, with his own room at the White House and responsibility for accompanying the elderly chief executive whenever he traveled. While still officially on the payroll of the Department of State, Trist spent his time serving the president, for which Jackson rewarded him with confidential payments from his own funds, regularly presenting envelopes containing $300—a significant sum to the struggling Trist family. This generosity recalled Jackson's similarly paternal concern for Sam Houston during low points in the Raven's unpredictable career, and the president made parallel pledges to support Trist's rise in government service.

He delivered on those promises at the beginning of his second term by naming Nicholas as American consul to the Cuban port of Havana. Trist's fluent, unaccented command of Spanish seemed to qualify him for the job, but his prickly, opinionated personality and occasionally haughty demeanor made him ill-suited to diplomatic work in a provincial backwater. Trist's problems in Cuba, where he worried that the tropical climate would threaten his delicate health, led to frequent complaints from American ship captains who found him officious and uncooperative. They also provoked more serious charges by the English government, which denounced him for allegedly protecting slave traders from determined efforts by the British government to suppress the traffic in human beings. Trist penned an indignant, 140-page handwritten letter to his superiors, denying all accusations and denouncing his critics in vehement terms. This elegantly written but nearly interminable document typified one of the consul general's most visible failings: an astonishing ability to generate verbose, exhausting, and erudite testaments on even the most trivial issues.

The wordy defense of his "integrity and honor" enabled Nicholas to retain his diplomatic post under Jackson's successor, Martin Van Buren, who had previously been his boss as secretary of state. But when "Matty Van" lost his reelection bid to the Whig Party's William Henry Harrison—one of the few important figures of the period who didn't know Trist—the embattled consul general found himself out of a job. He meant to stay in Cuba anyway and bought his family a thirty-seven-acre farm outside Havana that provided stunning views of the crystalline bay and promised proceeds that could satisfy their modest needs. Unfortunately, neither the bookish bureaucrat nor his aristocratic wife displayed skill at agriculture. To make ends meet, they sold off possessions and took in boarders, operating the equivalent of a modern bed-and-breakfast.

When Andrew Jackson, eight years out of the White House, heard of his former protégé's predicament, it reportedly moved the old man to "tears of pity." Just months before his death, Jackson contacted another protégé, President-elect James K. "Young Hickory" Polk, and asked him to find a place for Trist in the new administration. Conveniently enough, the new secretary of state, James Buchanan, had been a member of the congressional committee that had cleared Trist of wrongdoing regarding his service in Havana, so "Old Buck" welcomed Nicholas back to his old job of chief clerk. The two men soon became personally close, with the courtly, slightly stuffy Buchanan, a lifelong bachelor, frequently joining Nicholas and Virginia at their home for afternoon tea and becoming a regular guest at their Sunday dinners.

"OUR MANIFEST DESTINY TO OVERSPREAD AND POSSESS"

At work, Trist provided loyal support to the administration's determination to keep its campaign promises by enlarging the boundaries of the American Republic. The resonant term "Manifest Destiny" made its first appearance after the ardently expansionist Young Hickory took over the White House.

With a looming dispute between the United States and Great Britain over control of the future U.S. states of Oregon and Washington, as well as the later Canadian province of British Columbia, the New York *Morning News* published a widely cited editorial that expressed contempt for legalistic English claims: "Away, away with all these cobweb tissues of rights of discovery, exploration, settlement, continuity etc. To state the truth at once in its neglected simplicity, we are free to say . . . our claim to Oregon would still be best and strongest. And that claim is by the right of our manifest destiny to overspread and possess the whole of the continent which Providence has given us for the development of the great experiment of liberty and federated self-government entrusted to us."

To John L. O'Sullivan, the fervent Jacksonian who edited the *Morning News*, unfolding events left little doubt as to the future fate of all of North America. "The God of nature and of nations has marked it for our own; and with His blessing we will firmly maintain the incontestable rights He has given, and fearlessly perform the high duties He has imposed."

While O'Sullivan receives credit for popularizing the notion of "Manifest Destiny," the ideas behind the phrase had flourished for decades. As early as 1811, future president John Quincy Adams wrote to his father, former president John Adams, to share his conclusion that "the whole continent of North America appears to be destined by Divine Providence to be peopled by one *nation*, speaking one language, professing one general system of religious and political principles, and accustomed to one general tenor of social usages and customs."

Thirty years later, Adams himself rejected his previously expansive view of American destiny, opposing the annexation of Texas and the acquisition of other formerly Mexican territory because it meant the inevitable spread of slavery. But other political leaders felt no such compunctions about the seemingly unstoppable emergence of an American empire. In 1845, one member of Congress baldly declared: "This continent was intended by Providence as a vast theater on which to work out the grand experiment of Republican Government, under the auspices of the Anglo-Saxon race." At the Democratic State Convention in New Jersey in 1844, an orator identified as Major Daveznac stirred the delegates with his grand visions for new national boundaries. "Land enough! Land enough! Make way, I say, for the young American Buffalo," he bellowed. "He has not yet got land enough! He wants more land as his cool shelter in summer—he wants more land for his beautiful pasture grounds. I tell you, we will give him Oregon for his summer shade, and the region of Texas as his winter pasture!" This pronouncement produced uproarious applause.

While Polk and Buchanan focused on practical efforts to provide such shade and pasture, the most fervent advocates of continental expansion explicitly relied on supernatural sponsorship in securing the young Republic's glorious mission. After all, citizens who lived through the first four decades of the nineteenth century discerned incontestable evidence of divine intervention in the nation's shockingly rapid growth. In 1803, the Louisiana Purchase offered such a stunningly favorable deal from the dictator of France that it seemed to defy rational explanation. Nine years later, Jackson's improbably one-sided victory at New Orleans confirmed that acquisition, and twenty-one years after that, Sam Houston's equally improbable triumph at San Jacinto delivered the vastness of Texas to the control of a few thousand American settlers.

Who could fail to see in such wonders the suggestion of a master plan?

Six years before his famous "Manifest Destiny" editorial, John L. O'Sullivan rhapsodized over "The Great Nation of Futurity" in *United States Magazine and Democratic Review*:

> The far-reaching, the boundless future will be the era of American greatness. In its magnificent domain of space and time, the nation of many nations is destined to manifest to mankind the excellence of divine principles; to establish on earth the noblest temple ever dedicated to the worship of the Most High—the Sacred and the True. Its floor shall be a hemisphere—its roof the firmament of the star-studded heavens, and its congregation an Union of many Republics, comprising hundreds of happy millions, calling no man master, but governed by God's natural and moral law of equality, the law of brotherhood—of "peace and good will amongst men."

"THE PEACEFUL ACQUISITION"

To the relief and satisfaction of President Polk and his State Department, the administration succeeded in preserving that spirit of "peace and good will" in negotiating the resolution of the Oregon boundary dispute with Britain and permanently establishing the northern border at the 49th parallel.

Settling the question of the nation's southern boundary presented a far more complicated challenge. Mexico suffered through a series of unstable and ineffective governments, none of which fully accepted either Texas's independence or the annexation of the Lone Star Republic by the United States. Most pointedly, the Mexicans rejected the American idea that the Rio Grande represented the proper dividing line between the two republics and insisted that the Nueces River, far to the north, counted as the legal boundary. To reduce the likelihood of conflict, President Polk dispatched representatives to Mexico City to offer up to $50 million to settle the border at the Rio Grande and to purchase the sparsely settled territories of California and New Mexico.

The insulted Mexicans angrily declined to negotiate, and Polk sent troops into the disputed territory to support American claims. Mexican cavalry ambushed a scouting party of sixty soldiers in April 1846, killing ten and capturing the rest. When the president received word of this skirmish several weeks later, he had already begun preparing a war message based on Mexico's refusal to negotiate. He viewed the news of their attack as "providential," knowing it would ensure congressional support for a declaration of war. He spent a hectic Sunday, usually reserved for worship and religious reflection, rewriting his war message, which now announced that "Mexico has passed the boundary of the United States, has invaded our territory and shed American blood upon American soil. . . . The cup of forbearance had been exhausted even before the recent information from the frontier of the Del Norte." Congress voted overwhelmingly for war, by margins of 174 to 14 in the House and 42 to 2 in the Senate.

"THE GREATEST LIVING SOLDIER"

Despite these lopsided margins, the resulting conflict proved difficult, costly, and ultimately unpopular. By any measure, Mexico represented a formidable foe in 1846: in both land area and population, America's southern neighbor counted as the second-largest republic in the world. The Mexicans took special pride in their large professional army, trained along European lines, with crisply uniformed troops outnumbering prewar American regulars by more than two to one. In nearly all decisive battles, the Mexicans enjoyed superiority in numbers; in the decisive showdown at Buena Vista, General Zachary Taylor's 4,700 Americans fought a successful battle against more than 20,000 Mexicans. The enemy also enjoyed a consistent advantage because it was fighting a mostly defensive struggle, helped by familiarity with difficult and often forbidding terrain.

Nonetheless, the Americans prevailed from the beginning, thanks to more sophisticated weaponry and vastly better generals. The most gifted leadership on either side came from General Winfield Scott, a six-foot-five, 260-pound behemoth who rode into battle on an appropriately imposing steed while wearing spotless uniforms with golden epaulets and a helmet with a prominent snow-white plume. Inevitably, his admiring troops gave him the nickname "Old Fuss and Feathers," to contrast his formal elegance with the slovenly, down-to-earth habits of his popular colleague (and sometime rival) Zachary Taylor, who became known as "Old Rough and Ready."

In Scott's case, his personal heroism and tactical brilliance won him national fame in the War of 1812 and in four subsequent Indian conflicts. After writing several well-regarded textbooks on military strategy, he became commanding general of the U.S. Army and by far the nation's most respected officer. The outbreak of war with Mexico finally gave him the chance to take overall command in the field, and he executed a daring, flawlessly conceived campaign. Landing a well-prepared force at Veracruz on the Gulf of Mexico in March 1847, he then marched three hundred miles due west through enemy territory in order to occupy the capital city and end the war. Badly outnumbered at every turn, Old Fuss and Feathers never allowed the enemy to outmaneuver him or to block his advance. The legendary Duke of Wellington, conqueror of Napoleon, praised this masterly display of strategic genius as "unsurpassed in military annals" and respectfully declared that "Scott is the greatest living soldier."

But while the Mexicans never came close to defeating him, the "greatest living soldier" faced a more dangerous enemy in the person of the president of the United States. A passionately partisan Democrat, Polk feared that Scott, a well-known Whig, might use any claims of battlefield glory to make a successful run for the White House, as had a previous Whig general, William Henry Harrison. These political considerations stiffened the president's resolve to keep Winfield Scott from riding into Mexico City on his huge, gleaming white horse to dictate terms of peace as a conquering hero. With dispatches from the south reporting impressive new victories for Old Fuss and Feathers nearly every week, Polk wanted desperately to send his own representative to negotiate with the enemy so that credit for peacemaking would go to the Democrats, not to a towering Whig commander.

"DECIDEDLY THE GREATEST IMBECILE I HAVE EVER MET"

The challenge for the administration was that all previous efforts to reach a settlement had been frustrated by the chronic instability south of the border: as soon as a Mexican government expressed interest in making peace, it would be deposed and disgraced, replaced by a more warlike faction. With this pattern in mind, Polk hit upon the idea of sending a top-level diplomatic representative to travel with the army in its relentless advance and to make some quick, generous deal with the beleaguered Mexicans before Winfield Scott rode into the capital in triumph.

The obvious candidate for this assignment was James Buchanan, but the secretary of state hoped to win the Democratic presidential nomination in the next year's election, so he couldn't absent himself from the nation's capital for an extended period of time. Instead, he proposed to send his close friend and loyal deputy, Nicholas Trist, in his place. After all, Trist spoke fluent Spanish and had served as consul general in Cuba, and his studies at West Point had prepared him for interaction with the leading officers of the military. When Polk called the State Department's chief clerk into the White House, the president told him, "Mr. Trist, if you can but succeed in restoring peace, you will render a great service to your country and acquire great distinction for yourself."

Suitably inflated with a sense of his own importance, Trist left Washington in April and made the arduous journey to New Orleans, where he boarded a revenue cutter to transport him to Veracruz in hopes that he would soon catch up with Scott's steadily advancing army. Unfortunately, General Scott himself had little warning about the White House emissary who was supposed to take the job of peace-making out of his hands, and he reacted with undisguised indignation when he received a brusque letter from Trist announcing his arrival. Scott fired back: "I see that the secretary of war proposes to degrade me by requiring that I, as commander-in-chief of this army, shall defer to you, the Chief Clerk in the Department of State, the question of continuing or discontinuing hostilities." When the two men finally met, their distaste for each other only increased. In letters home to Virginia, Nicholas described Scott as "utterly incompetent" and "de-cidedly the greatest imbecile I have ever met."

To add to Nicholas's misery, he developed a high fever and for more than a week he couldn't eat, talk, read, or write. Informed of Trist's wretched state, Scott felt compassion for the visitor, despite his obnoxious mission. He sent a package with a note: "My Dear Sir— Looking over my stores I find a box of guava marmalade which per-haps the physician may not consider improper to make part of the diet."

The arrival of this offering struck Nicholas as a major miracle and a most unlikely gift of fate: General Scott had no way of knowing that during Trist's service in Cuba, guava marmalade had become a favorite indulgence. He considered this exotic delight a tonic for both body and spirit, and credited the general's present with beginning his pro-cess of recovery. As he continued to recuperate, he wrote to Buchanan: "With General Scott's reply to my letter I received a message from him evincing so much good feeling that it afforded me the sincerest plea-sure." In the days that followed, Scott made several lengthy personal visits to Trist's bedside, where they discussed philosophy, literature, tactics, and mutual friends. In the process, the corrosive contempt and blustery enmity that had characterized their previous interactions turned into a warm and unwavering friendship that flourished for the remaining nineteen years of Winfield Scott's life.

"A GREATER SERVICE THAN ANY LIVING MAN CAN RENDER"

While this unexpected development most certainly pleased Nicholas, it only alarmed the president and the secretary of state: they had sent their unconventional emissary to Mexico to undermine Scott and to preempt his role as peacemaker, not to assist him as a comrade and collaborator. They also began to get the troubling impression that Trist, after four months in Mexico, had assumed the role of an independent operator, guided by his own perceptions of the national interest rather than dutifully executing the partisan schemes of the Polk administration. These suspicions only intensified when General Scott, after a series of brilliantly executed victories, halted his inexorable advance just five miles from the Mexican capital and offered the enemy an armistice without Washington's authorization or approval. He wanted to give his new friend Trist the chance to work out terms of peace without further loss of life and before the complete humiliation of the proud Mexicans made negotiations even more difficult.

These hopes collided with the old problem of finding some plausible partner with whom to parley, especially with the loudest voices in the Mexican Congress coming from the *puros*—the "pure ones"—who refused to consider surrender or compromise of any kind and meant to keep fighting the Yankee invaders, with guerrilla tactics if necessary. The presidency had been taken over once again by the irrepressible General López de Santa Anna, the same "Napoleon of the West" who had been vanquished by Sam Houston at San Jacinto eleven years earlier. Serving one of his eleven nonconsecutive terms as his nation's chief executive, the wily Santa Anna welcomed the armistice but had no intention of negotiating terms with the Americans. He preferred to use the break in the fighting to try to reorganize his defeated, demoralized forces for later counterattacks, while Trist attempted to work with the British legation in Mexico City to press the more responsible elements in the shattered, scattered government to begin talking peace.

On November 16, Trist received two curt dispatches from his onetime friend Secretary of State Buchanan, dated October 4 and 25.

Both ordered him to bring an immediate halt to all efforts at negotiation and return at once to Washington. This abrupt termination of Trist's assignment reflected President Polk's growing anger at his special representative. He declared in his diary: "Mr. Trist has handled the negotiation very bunglingly and with no ability." He also seemed to believe charges from some jealous political officers serving under Scott that the commanding general had conspired with Trist to arrange the unauthorized armistice and to somehow advance the Whig Party cause in the next year's elections.

Nicholas acknowledged the recall order but asked Buchanan to send an immediate replacement so that negotiations could proceed. He also recognized that he couldn't safely return to Veracruz to sail back to the United States without a strong military escort, and with the armistice collapsed and Scott making his final push into Mexico City that force wasn't available. While he continued his contacts with peace-seeking Mexicans, he acknowledged that his diplomatic role had come to an end. He wrote to his wife, Virginia: "I have bid adieu forever to official life. This decision is irrevocable. Say so to Mr. Buchanan, with my kindest regards."

Meanwhile, members of the feebly functioning Mexican government, though informed of Trist's recall, either pretended it had never occurred or expressed the opinion it soon would be revoked, and they insisted on continuing to negotiate. The British legation also urged Trist to maintain his mission, while General Scott expressed the opinion that if he did manage to hammer out a treaty, the reluctant politicians in Washington would feel forced to accept it. A young reporter for a New Orleans newspaper gave the same advice when he met with Nicholas early in December. "Mr. Trist, make the Treaty. Make the Treaty, Sir! It is now in your power to do your country a greater service than any living man can render her. I know your country. I know all classes of people there," James Freaner insisted. "They want peace, Sir. They pant for it. They will be grateful for it. . . . Your country, Sir, is entitled to this service from you. Do it, Sir! She will support you in it, instructions or no instructions."

Stirred by these exhortations, Trist waited just two days before taking pen in hand and releasing an emotional torrent of complaint, denunciation, and self-righteous rhetoric in the form of a typically verbose, sixty-five-page justification for defying the direct orders of his boss, the secretary of state, and the clearly stated commands of the president of the United States: "I place my determination on the ground of my conviction, first, that peace is still the desire of my government; secondly, that if the present opportunity not be seized at once, all chance for making a treaty at all will be lost, probably forever."

Part of his fear stemmed from reports he had received from the reporter Freaner, and very probably from other sources back home, of the alarming spread of the All Mexico movement among congressional leaders and elements of the public, particularly in the South. With the enemy utterly defeated on the battlefield but unwilling or unable to reach agreement on terms for peace, land-hungry Americans began agitating for immediate annexation of all of Mexico. According to their arguments, the administration need not settle for the acquisition of Texas, California, and much of the territory in between; since American forces had conquered all of Mexico, the government in Washington should rule all of Mexico. Many influential southerners rallied to this idea and saw the vast territory of the Mexican Republic as an ideal site for economic exploitation through the spread of slavery. Most northerners opposed the All Mexico movement for similar reasons, fearing that the addition of so much land and population adjacent to Dixie's "Cotton Kingdom" could only result in new slave states, strengthening the southern bid to control the federal government. Despite his role as slavery's most formidable defender in Congress, Senator (and former Vice President) John C. Calhoun passionately opposed annexation. "More than half of the Mexicans are Indians, and the other is composed chiefly of mixed tribes," he snarled to the Senate. "I protest against such a union as that! Ours, sir, is the Government of a white race."

Meanwhile, visionary advocates of Manifest Destiny such as John O'Sullivan and, apparently, Nicholas Trist feared All Mexico for another reason: they had resisted the notion that the authority and laws of the United States should be imposed on a subject people against their will. California and Texas were thinly populated, with a significant proportion of American settlers. The teeming Mexican heartland around the capital city was another matter entirely, as demonstrated by the doomed but determined resistance to the conquering campaign of Old Fuss and Feathers and his victorious army.

"I HAVE NEVER IN MY LIFE FELT SO INDIGNANT"

President Polk himself remained undecided on just how much of Mexico to add to the federal Union but felt no confusion whatever about his angry indignation at the apparent mutiny of Nicholas Trist. He finally received the bulging diatribe from his rogue emissary on January 15, nearly six weeks after Nicholas wrote it, and the president reacted with breathless rage at the State Department clerk's audacity and insubordination. "His dispatch is arrogant, impudent and very insulting to his Government, and even personally insulting to the president," Polk complained in his diary. "I have never in my life felt so indignant. . . . If there was any legal provision for his punishment he ought to be severely handled. He has acted worse than any man in the public employ whom I have ever known. His dispatch proves that he is destitute of honor or principle and that he has proved himself to be a very base man."

To stop this supposed scoundrel from continuing to represent a government that had meant to fire him, Polk took two dramatic steps. First, he cut off all of Trist's compensation, expenses as well as salary, retroactive to the day two months before when he had received his recall order. Second, the president relieved the "greatest soldier in the world" of his Mexican command, replacing Scott with the militarily inexperienced but politically sound General William O. Butler, a partisan Democrat of unquestioned loyalty who would follow White House orders. Polk wanted to arrest Trist and transport him back to Washington—in chains, if necessary—but he didn't trust the defiant envoy's good friend General Scott to carry out any such command. That meant that Polk would have to wait for General Butler's arrival in Mexico City before bringing Trist to heel and removing him definitively as any sort of factor in relations with Mexico.

By the time the president implemented this course of action, and long before his new commanding general arrived on the scene, Nicholas Trist had already deeply involved himself in final negotiations with a handful of Mexican aristocrats who basically took it upon themselves to represent their barely functioning Congress. Paralyzed by disagreements between *puros* who wanted to keep fighting to the death, liberals who sought annexation by the Americans, and *moderatos* who looked to get the best deal possible from the Yankees occupying their country, the Mexican legislators seemed as powerless to halt the ongoing negotiations as the distant and impotent Polk.

Trist's diplomatic efforts would have been altogether unthinkable, in fact, were it not for the painfully slow pace of communication and transportation between Mexico City and Washington. It generally took a month for dispatches to travel between the two capitals. As a result, Nicholas was able to function as a powerful, top-level representative of his government for a full four months after the secretary of state signed an order terminating his assignment, and for nearly three weeks after the president of the United States expressed his conviction that the insubordinate emissary should be "punished" and "severely handled."

The only biography of Nicholas Trist, a fascinating but unheralded book called *Defiant Peacemaker*, gives a detailed account that conveys something of the surreal atmosphere that prevailed in the top-secret negotiations playing out at Villa de Guadalupe Hidalgo. Wallace Ohrt, a retired Boeing executive and amateur historian with obvious admiration for his subject, makes clear that the Mexican swells knew full well that Trist had been fired by the officials who sent him, but in their own desperation they preferred to ignore that inconvenient fact. They liked Nicholas, with his flawless Spanish, courtly manners, and air of European culture and breeding, and they certainly preferred working with him, whatever his standing in Washington, to facing a blustery, newly arrived gringo general with no knowledge of their country and its recent ordeals.

The deal making unfolded like a complex, time-consuming board game in which the engrossed participants remained unsure to the end whether the outcome mattered at all. One major disagreement involved money: Nicholas had been authorized to offer up to $30 million for all the territory Polk sought, and months ago the Mexicans had heard him mention the figure of $20 million. But now, after stubborn Mexican resistance had prolonged the war and swelled its cost, he wanted to cut the compensation to $15 million to pay for all of California and parts of nine other future states extending east to the Sabine River and the border of Louisiana. Trist made the price stick, but he compromised on Polk's express desire to take possession of both Alta California (Upper California) and Baja California (Lower California) for the United States. Trist gave up on the long, narrow peninsula of Lower California, sparsely settled then as it is today, in return for drawing a new boundary between the two territories that placed San Diego, with its valuable harbor, on the American side of the line.

When the Mexican commissioners hesitated at the last moment, Trist threatened to cancel the negotiations unless they quickly agreed to the terms they had painstakingly crafted. On February 2, 1848, they finally staged a formal signing of the Treaty of Peace, Friendship, Limits and Settlement on the altar of the old Basilica of Guadalupe in the leafy, quiet neighborhood. Nicholas Trist, with no official authorization whatever to represent his country, boldly and unhesitatingly committed the United States to its terms. All parties recognized the date and the ceremony as significant, fateful, and historic, despite the uncertain future of their agreement. With the document sealed and signed, Don José Bernardo Couto faced Trist with a sigh: "This must be a proud moment for you; no less proud for you than it is humiliating for us." Trist tried to reassure him. "We are making peace," he said. "Let that be our only thought."

Later, he recalled other thoughts:

> Could those Mexicans have seen into my heart at that moment, they would have known that my feeling of shame as an American was far stronger than theirs could be. . . . My object, through out was, not to obtain all I could, but on the contrary to make the treaty as little exacting as possible from Mexico, as was compatible with its being accepted at home. In this I was governed by two considerations:

one was the iniquity of the war, as an abuse of power on our part; the other was that the more disadvantageous the treaty was made to Mexico, the stronger would be the ground of opposition to it in the Mexican Congress by the party who had boasted of its power to frustrate any peace moves.

His sense of hidden embarrassment and his insistence that the recently concluded war "was a thing for every right-minded American to be ashamed of" carry an unmistakably modern tone that seems incongruous for a stalwart Jacksonian and supporter of Manifest Destiny. But Trist proceeded to pursue that peace agreement with his own mysterious sense of fate and mission, never fully articulating what drove him to enrage a president and to risk both reputation and career in order to finish his work according to some urgent imperative he strongly felt but never consciously understood.

Certainly he had no indication that the completion of his exhausting work and the ceremonial signing he carefully staged occurred at virtually the same time that the builder of a new sawmill on California's American River belatedly identified the ore samples he had collected as containing gold "of the finest quality, of at least 23 karat (96% pure)."

"IT SHOULD NOT BE REJECTED ON ACCOUNT OF HIS BAD CONDUCT"

Hesitation in recognizing the huge significance of this find, combined with the months of rugged travel required to carry word from a location as remote as Northern California to Washington, D.C., meant that Trist's unauthorized treaty reached the Capitol long before any hint of the world-changing discovery. James Freaner, the same newspaperman who had so passionately urged Trist to conclude the treaty, rushed back to the East Coast from Mexico City in the near-record time of seventeen days and presented the signed document to Secretary of State Buchanan at seven in the evening of February 19. Two hours later, Buchanan went to the president and the two men reviewed the treaty by flickering lamp light at the White House. Before sleep that night, Polk acknowledged in his diary that Trist's agreement appeared entirely acceptable in terms of "the important question of boundary and limits," and he resolved to consider the treaty on its own terms without regard to the president's seething, undiminished hostility toward the fired diplomat who negotiated it. "Mr. Trist has acted very badly," he wrote, "but notwithstanding this, if on further examination the Treaty is one that can be accepted, it should not be rejected on account of his bad conduct."

Polk spent most of the next day considering all six thousand words of the Treaty of Guadalupe Hidalgo and "deemed prompt action upon it so indispensable" that he called an emergency cabinet meeting that same night. Secretary of the Treasury Robert Walker and Secretary of State James Buchanan both strongly urged the president to disregard the agreement and begin new negotiations, in part to avoid providing any form of approval to Trist's outrageous behavior. Buchanan, despite his previous close friendship with the Trist family and professed loyalty to the president, had begun undermining the administration and openly flirting with the increasingly popular All Mexico movement as part of his maneuvering in pursuit of the presidential nomination. Polk listened to emotional arguments on both sides and announced his intention to sleep on the matter before reaching a decision.

When he called his cabinet back the next morning the president brusquely announced his intention to send the treaty to the Senate immediately for official approval. To delay the matter further, or to send fresh negotiators on the long journey to Mexico City, meant continuation of the war, with all its cost in blood and money, and risked further division of the country. American indecision also risked the further collapse of the Mexican government, which would make it even more difficult to win approval for an agreement of any kind.

Nevertheless, a bipartisan coalition in the Senate remained powerfully determined to reject Trist's handiwork. Southern Democrats who still hoped to take over all of Mexico joined with northern "Conscience" Whigs who wanted to seize none of Mexico. Both factions denounced Polk and his surprising support for an agreement that had been drafted in an unorthodox, probably illegal process. The Foreign

Relations Committee voted overwhelmingly against approval but heeded White House pleas to send the treaty to the Senate floor without a recommendation. There the heated debate and the battle over proposed amendments served to highlight the dangerous polarization of public opinion. Some wanted the troops to come home immediately and unconditionally; others insisted that the army should remain in Mexico permanently, to ensure that nation's incorporation into the United States. In the end, the weary Senate approved the compact with a barely sufficient margin: the switch of a single senator to the fourteen who voted no or to the four who abstained from voting would have denied Polk the two-thirds majority he needed under the Constitution.

SUTTER'S MILL: Coloma, California, circa 1850. The figure at the front may be James Marshall, the wandering carpenter who reported finding gold in a drainage ditch near the mill he had built.

"It had been so ordered by Providence, that the gold might not be discovered until California should be in the hands of the Americans." —French prospector "Baptiste," 1849

As it was, the president rushed a new commissioner to Mexico City to secure final approval by the Mexican Congress before leaders of either country became aware of the dramatic developments in the faraway province of Upper California, which, under terms of Trist's treaty, officially became part of the United States.

SUTTER'S SECRET

Persistent confusion surrounds historical efforts to establish the precise date that James Marshall first noticed metallic yellow flakes in the millrace of his new construction project in the tiny settlement of Coloma, California. A thirty-seven-year-old native of New Jersey, Marshall had fallen prey to the yearning for exploration and adventure that drove so many Americans of his generation to drift ever farther into the West. He worked his way through Indiana, Illinois, and Missouri, eking out a meager living as a farmer and a carpenter. After contracting malaria, he trekked all the way to Oregon in the hope of improving his health, then moved on to the more promising climate of California. He struck up a partnership with Captain Johann Augustus Sutter, the Swiss immigrant who had built an adobe fort in present-day Sacramento and made grand plans for an expansive agricultural settlement, called New Helvetia to honor his beloved homeland. Marshall agreed to supervise the building and operation of a new sawmill some thirty-six miles upriver from Sutter's Fort; in return he'd receive a portion of the lumber he managed to produce.

In later years, Marshall recalled that he first noticed the gleaming chips of gold on the morning of January 19, 1848, but others remembered the date as several weeks later. A local newspaper in 1855 reported the account of Peter L. Weimer, who said he walked alongside Marshall when he first picked out the golden particles from the murky water in the freshly dug channel for his water wheel. According to Weimer, it was "early in February—the exact date is not remembered—in the morning." Afterward, "the gold was taken to the cabin of Weimer, and Mrs. Weimer, "engaged in making soap, pitched the piece into the soap kettle, where it was boiled all day and all night.

The following morning the strange piece of stuff was fished out of the soap, all the brighter for boiling."

Forty-five years later, in 1893, the pioneering San Francisco historian John Shertzer Hittell corresponded with Henry W. Bigler, who as a young man had worked with Marshall on his sawmill. Bigler produced a weathered diary with a brief but significant entry for the twenty-fourth of January 1848. It reported that "this day some kind of mettle was found in the tail-race that looks like goald—first discovered by James Martial, boss of the mill." Marshall always remembered that he waited four days before he rode down to New Helvetia to show his gleaming pebbles to John Sutter. Sure enough, Sutter's journal for January 28 records: "Mr. Marshall arrived from the mountains on very important business."

The Swiss captain inspected the samples from the mill with avid interest, but he knew no more about gold than did his carpenter. Together they read an encyclopedia entry that enabled them to perform primitive tests, which indicated that Marshall had indeed found slivers and chips of the precious metal. Sutter commanded him to maintain the strictest secrecy and to finish the sawmill as if nothing had happened. He also disclosed his intention to acquire as much land as possible before it became widely known that the property might contain valuable minerals. In mid-February the captain rode up to the mountains for the first time, to inspect his sawmill and to negotiate with local tribes. The Indians happily traded a huge tract of land "for a lot of beads and a few cotton handkerchiefs." Sutter managed to enforce his dubious title to the territory for only a few months before a tidal wave of prospectors and adventurers swept over his property and proceeded to stake claims of their own.

The definitive betrayal of Sutter's secret began with a dozen Mormon workmen who assisted Marshall with his building project in Coloma. They had walked as a group from Iowa to the Pacific Coast as part of the intrepid "Mormon Battalion" that fought alongside American irregulars for control of California during the Mexican War. The Latter-day Saints community amounted to more than two hundred in the area, and represented more than half of the population in the Pueblo of Yerba Buena, which later took the name San Francisco. A leader of the Mormon settlers, Samuel Brannan, ran a general store in the village and traveled up to Coloma in the springtime to collect tithes from the millworkers. They paid him with gold nuggets they had collected in their free time.

Returning to San Francisco, Brannan saw his opportunity. He quietly bought up every shovel, pick axe, and pan he could find and then in May began running through the streets of San Francisco, holding up gold samples in both hands. "Gold! Gold!" he shouted. "Gold on the American River!" The pans he had purchased for 20 cents each promptly sold out at a price of $15. In his first nine weeks, Brannan made $36,000 profit. Nearly everyone in town, and most of the sailors on ships in the harbor, bought Brannan's equipment and headed to the Sierra to search for instant wealth. Brannan opened more stores to sell goods to the miners, and his emporium at Sutter's Fort sold $150,000 worth of goods every month in 1849. Brannan went on to become one of San Francisco's wealthiest and most influential citizens, though he was disfellowshipped from the Mormon Church because of his violent role in the vigilante movement that tried to protect the city from rowdy squatters and miners.

The virulent "gold fever" that afflicted the local population in May and June spread around the Pacific Rim long before it reached the eastern seaboard, since news traveled more rapidly over the ocean than it did across mountains and prairies. In July, eager prospectors departed from the west coast of Mexico and from the Hawaiian Islands. By the end of the summer, two-thirds of the white males in Oregon had left their homes to seek instant fortunes in California. In the late fall and early winter, gold hunters arrived in San Francisco from Peru, Chile, China, and even Australia. With the deterioration of morals and social order associated with what quickly became known as the "gold rush," the leaders of the Mormon Church decided that California had become unsuitable—at least temporarily—for Latter-day Saints. In June 1848, even the loyal workmen who had served James Marshall in Coloma left the teeming gold fields when Brigham Young summoned them to join him in building the new Zion in Utah.

By the time gold seekers began to arrive in massive numbers, everyone knew about the Treaty of Guadeloupe Hidalgo and the formal American takeover of California. That transition mattered to the thousands of new arrivals, since the new U.S. authorities showed little inclination to enforce the sweeping land titles that had been granted by the defeated Mexicans. Legally, gold country fell under the control of the federal government, and Washington could have demanded payment from those who staked a claim and tried to mine gold. Colonel Richard Mason, military commander of the new American territory, quickly rejected that notion and decided that any attempt to impose bureaucratic order on the creative chaos stood no chance of success. In explaining his policy, he wrote: "Upon considering the large extent of the country, the character of the people engaged and the small, scattered force at my command, I resolved not to interfere but to permit all to work freely." The result allowed for the stunning growth of the California population but brought personal ruination to the grand dreams of Sutter, Marshall, and other established residents, as the impatient, unruly new arrivals from around the world showed no regard for decorum or property rights.

Near the end of August, nearly seven months after Marshall's discovery and Trist's treaty, the first news of the gold rush reached New York, Philadelphia, and Washington. An item in the *New York Herald* provided a summary of the situation from an anonymous soldier under the headline "AFFAIRS IN OUR NEW TERRITORY." In the midst of glowing reports on the landscape and the agricultural opportunities, the correspondent provided one intriguing sentence: "I am credibly informed that a quantity of gold, worth in value $30, was picked up lately in the bed of a stream of the Sacramento."

"WAS THERE EVER A MORE MANIFEST SIGN . . . ?"

President Polk, preparing to leave the White House after his single exhausting and eventful term, received similar reports at the same time and decided to feature them in his last annual message to Congress, submitted on December 5—the equivalent, in written form, of the modern State of the Union address. He began by celebrating the incalculable value of California, with its "safe and commodious harbors" that "must command the rich commerce of China, of Asia, of the islands of the Pacific, of western Mexico, of Central America, the South American States, and the Russian possessions bordering on that ocean." Ahead of his contemporaries, Polk understood the profound importance of establishing American ports on both coasts of the continent, giving the United States the unique and unprecedented ability to dominate both of the world's greatest oceans.

After reveling in this prospect, the president then dropped his bombshell, making sure that every American learned of the glittering opportunities in their country's new real estate along the Pacific: "The accounts of the abundance of gold in that territory are of such an extraordinary character as would scarcely command belief were they not corroborated by the authentic reports of officers of the public service who have visited the mineral district and derived the facts which they detail from personal observation. . . . The explorations already made warrant the belief that the supply is very large and that gold is found at various places in an extensive district of the country."

Polk's message eloquently acknowledged the supernatural blessings showered on the United States by "the Sovereign Arbiter of all Human Events" and contrasted "the agitated and disturbed state of other countries with our own tranquil and happy condition." But he never mentioned the extraordinary coincidence by which "the abundance of gold" in California became apparent at almost precisely the same time that negotiations concluded for the acquisition of the territory. He may have been reluctant to give too much credit to a treaty that had been concluded in direct defiance of his presidential will. Nevertheless, he proudly informed Congress that relations with Mexico now displayed "the most friendly character" and that the neighboring republics shared "every motive of sympathy and of interest to bind them together in perpetual amity."

If the president failed to acknowledge the bizarre and fortunate timing of the discovery of gold, other contemporaries most certainly took note of it. A Frenchman named Baptiste arrived in the Sierra Nevada in the latter part of 1848 and wondered at the activity and opportunity that he saw. He had mined for several years in Mexico and now proudly declared that "it had been so ordered by Providence, that the gold might not be discovered until California should be in the hands of the Americans." In our own day, historian Walter R. Borneman notes: "Had this first great gold rush occurred only a few years earlier, California might not have dropped so easily into the American orbit." In *Seizing Destiny* (2007), Richard Kluger writes: "Spain had owned California for three centuries and let it drowse in the sun. Mexico had owned California for three decades and likewise left it fallow. Scarcely a week before California passed formally into the hands of the United States, gold was found there, sparking one of history's most spectacular examples of wealth creation. Was there ever a more manifest sign that Americans enjoyed providential favor and had been destined to possess the best part of the continent from sea to sea?"

The president's reference to the riches of California sparked excitement in every corner of the country and inspired dreamers to choose one of three routes to the gold fields. The safest, most reliable passage from the East Coast required an ocean voyage of fifteen thousand miles, sailing around the tip of South America and then through the southern Pacific all the way to the "Golden Gate" of San Francisco Bay. The voyage required four to eight months in transit and cost a minimum of $300—a fee beyond the reach of most of the young men drawn so powerfully to the West Coast. A faster, less expensive journey involved more risk, especially from the danger of tropical diseases: sailing down to Nicaragua or Panama, traversing the jungle with pack mule and dugout canoe, and then waiting for a second ship for the passage through Pacific waters to San Francisco.

The cheapest, most popular route involved an overland trek, possible only during the late spring and summer, making use of wagons drawn by oxen or mules. Historian John Shertzer Hittell, who joined the hordes who crossed the continent in 1849, remembered the unprecedented magnitude of that famous migration: "Not fewer than one hundred thousand men, representing in their nativity every State in the Union, went to California that year. . . . They formed an army; in daytime their trains filled up the roads for miles, and at night their camp fires glittered in every direction about the places blessed with grass and water." This migration, Hittell declared, "developed

California from rudeness, poverty, obscurity and semi-barbarism, into brilliant, complex and wealthy enlightenment, under our eyes, in the midst of our labors and as part of our personal consciousness."

When the newcomers arrived, they not only populated the mining camps in the mountains but also created the first significant city on the Pacific Coast. As British historian Paul Johnson notes, the new arrivals transformed San Francisco from a village of a few hundred to "a boomtown of 25,000 people, crowded with gamblers, financiers, prostitutes and wild women, actors and reporters, budding politicians and businessmen. It was free-for-all America at its best and worst."

"A WORLD-HISTORICAL EVENT OF SOME IMPORTANCE"

Census numbers told the story: in March 1848, as the United States took official possession of California under Trist's treaty, only 7,500 people of European ancestry lived in the territory, with the great majority of them Spanish-speaking "Californios" and only eight hundred identifying as Americans. Two years later, on the eve of statehood, the non-Indian population of the American Territory had swelled to more than one hundred thousand. By the mid-1850s, some three hundred thousand adventurers from around the world had already settled in the Golden State, producing an incalculable impact on the economy of the rest of the country.

During the first five years after Marshall picked up his glistening pebbles, California provided twelve million ounces of gold, worth $17 billion at today's prices. The value of gold coins in circulation in the United States increased by a factor of twenty, seeming to vindicate the policies of President Polk and other Jacksonian Democrats. In 1846, Polk established the Independent Treasury system, by which government funds were held in the federal treasury instead of in private or state banks or the private Bank of the United States, which Jackson had killed. With an abundance of gold coinage (much of it provided by the new federal mint in San Francisco), there was less need for the varied and confusing banknotes on which the economy had previously relied, despite their many possibilities for fraud. Just months after the president put an end to the old system of paper currency, fate provided more than enough gold to allow specie to take its place. As Paul Johnson writes: "Indeed, the California gold rush as a whole was a world-historical event of some importance. Until its gold came on the market, there had been a chronic shortage of specie, especially gold bullion, from which the United States, in particular, had suffered. Until the 1850s in fact there was no true gold standard simply because there was not enough gold to maintain it. Once the California gold began to circulate, the development of American capital markets accelerated and the huge expansion of the second half of the century became financially possible."

Unfortunately, James K. Polk never lived to see this validation of his fiscal policies or even the immediate impact of the territorial acquisitions of the Mexican War. His last months in the White House had been plagued by ill health and a painful struggle with "chronic diarrhea," in the description of his physicians. On the day he left office he confided in his diary, "I feel exceedingly relieved that I am now free from all public cares." He and his wife, Sarah, had purchased a gracious plantation near Nashville that they renamed Polk Place and where the childless couple planned a comfortable retirement. A month-long journey to New Orleans and then up the Mississippi to Tennessee, with formal events in Polk's honor in every city along his route, exhausted the former president. By the time they arrived at Polk Place and began the arduous task of remodeling it for their purposes, he was complaining of fatigue and a "derangement of the stomach and the bowels." He died on June 15, 1849, just three months after leaving the White House, at the age of fifty-three.

Polk's passing removed any chance of reconciliation with Nicholas Trist, who had finally returned from Mexico in May of the year before. Despite the fact that Senate ratification and the discovery of gold in California had proven the value of Trist's service in hammering out the Treaty of Guadalupe Hidalgo, the president refused to acknowledge the achievement in any way. Though he set aside his previous notions of arrest and imprisonment, Polk decreed that Nicholas should receive no government payment for either his expenses or his

salary during the six months he had toiled in Mexico after his official
recall. Trist's friends saw the injustice in this decision and urged the
fired diplomat to press his case with the president or the secretary of
state, but Nicholas felt too proud to demean himself with such pleas.
Instead, he moved his family to Pennsylvania, where, desperate for
funds, he helped his wife, Virginia, set up a small boarding school for
girls.

The Trists faced acute financial struggles for the next twenty
years, in part because of a string of bad investments. No sooner would
Nicholas accumulate capital than he would risk it on various "promising" schemes, including a cattle ranch in Florida and, ironically, a
California gold mine. He nonetheless managed to stay just ahead of
his creditors through two decades of tedious toil in a clerical position
as paymaster for the Philadelphia, Wilmington, and Baltimore Rail-
road Company. General Winfield Scott felt deeply concerned over the
way that overwork and adversity had weakened his onetime colleague,
and determined to use his influence to help the Trists. Old Fuss and
Feathers had conducted an unsuccessful presidential campaign as the
Whig nominee in 1852, but when he was reinstalled as general in chief
of the army in the nation's capital, he contacted various high-ranking
members of the executive and legislative branches to plead Trist's case.
For more than a decade these efforts produced scant results.

Finally, five years after the Civil War (and four years after Scott's
death), the eloquent and idealistic Charles Sumner of Massachusetts
took up the cause and made one of his florid, dramatic, and well-
researched speeches on the Senate floor to demand belated payment
for Nicholas Trist's uncompensated service to the nation. Coming
from a celebrated abolitionist and "Radical" Republican, Senator
Sumner's arguments carried special weight in making the case for a
lifelong Democrat. Though the process took another year, the Senate finally awarded the seventy-year-old Nicholas Trist, onetime chief
clerk of the State Department, his long overdue salary and expenses,
coming to a grand total of $14,559.90. On that sum, Trist enjoyed
nearly three years of retirement before his death in 1874.

The nation took little note of his passing, but his wife, Virginia,
Thomas Jefferson's granddaughter, had always looked in awe at the

haunting connections and coincidences that linked her husband to the titans of the past and the development and expansion of the United States. On the eve of the Civil War, Virginia wrote of Nicholas to an intimate friend: "I have little doubt myself that he is perhaps the only man now living in our country who has any real knowledge of the Science of politics as it was understood by Jefferson, Madison and other great minds of their day."

After all, Trist had been a protégé of Madison, the "Father of the Constitution." He had served as private secretary and chief aide to Jefferson, who secured the Louisiana Purchase, and he had played the same role with Andrew Jackson, whose miraculous victory at New Orleans defended that territory as a permanent possession of the United States. Finally, Trist's own officially unsanctioned, insubordinate efforts made sure that the beaten Mexicans acknowledged the American annexation of Texas and ceded California at the very moment of the discovery of gold—helping to enlarge his country by nearly a million square miles.

In one of his last significant political judgments, Trist abandoned his lifelong commitment to the Democratic Party to endorse the candidacy of Abraham Lincoln, nominee of the new Republican Party. He thereby linked his own visionary legacy to the God-haunted fatalism of the nation's most unlikely president, whose illogical life and prophetic insight make their own case for divine entanglement in the nation's destiny.

"I AM HUMBLE ABRAHAM LINCOLN": First photograph of Lincoln, taken in 1846, the year he won his single term in Congress.

"In the deepest of his depression he said one day he had done nothing to make any human being remember that he had lived." —Lincoln's close friend, Joshua Speed

10

THE MIRACLE OF LINCOLN

America's Most Unlikely President and
His Supernatural Success

The face and figure of Abraham Lincoln feel so familiar, and his life story sits so comfortably in our consciousness, that we seldom acknowledge just how strange, how downright weird, that story really is.

How did an aging prairie lawyer and frequently frustrated politician, whose only high office involved a single two-year term in the House of Representatives, suddenly claim the presidency of the United States?

How could an ungainly partisan operator with a difficult marriage, a tendency toward clinical depression, and profoundly peculiar habits, with no military experience and less than a year of formal education, best the most celebrated minds of his generation on battlefields both political and military?

These questions offer no easy answers, since nothing in Lincoln's fifty-two years before the presidency seemed to prepare him for handling the most momentous crisis in the nation's history. All other presidents who have (even occasionally) earned designation as "great" achieved great things *before* they won elevation to the nation's highest office. Lincoln did not.

For Washington, Jefferson, Jackson, both Roosevelts, Wilson, Ike, and Reagan, their pre-presidential careers would have received extensive attention in history books even had they never won the White

House. In Lincoln's case, no one today would recognize his name. Lincoln himself worried in his early thirties that he had "done nothing to make any human being remember that he had lived." The little-known Nicholas Trist, just nine years older than Lincoln, assembled a far more noteworthy career and held stronger claims to historical significance than did the improbable presidential candidate Trist supported in 1860.

Like Barack Obama, Lincoln first gained public attention through his speeches, but he did so long before television or radio could carry that oratory to a broad audience. He relied upon the sheer power of his words, captured in written form by newspapers and pamphlets, with carefully crafted, lucid argumentation that employed biblical cadences and occasional biblical references:

> A house divided against itself cannot stand. I believe this government cannot endure, permanently, half slave and half free. I do not expect the Union to be dissolved—I do not expect the house to fall—but I do expect it will cease to be divided. It will become all one thing or all the other. Either the opponents of slavery will arrest the further spread of it, and place it where the public mind shall rest in the belief that it is in the course of ultimate extinction; or its advocates will push it forward, till it shall become lawful in all the States, old as well as new—North as well as South.

He delivered this majestic declaration in June 1858, as the holder of no public office. He had just launched an underdog challenge to a well-established senator in the remote, frontier state of Illinois, yet the prophetic ring of his words caused a nationwide sensation. Even today, it feels ennobling to deliver them aloud and to savor their sonorities. It is easy to imagine Americans of the era reading Lincoln's addresses to one another in taverns, in train cars, or across dinner tables, marveling at the distinctive, arresting voice that few of them would ever actually hear.

But how did a desperately poor and self-educated boy develop such a voice, becoming one of the preeminent prose writers in the history of the English language? To his detractors, Lincoln remained a backwoods bumpkin, "the original gorilla," whose installation as president represented a cruel trick of fate, reflecting the ignorance and folly of the American people or, very possibly, the workings of a malevolent conspiracy.

His admirers, on the other hand, came to view Lincoln's rise to power as the most meaningful miracle in the history of the Republic— especially after the uncanny timing of his death as the first chief executive to fall to an assassin's hand.

On the very morning of his murder, the president took time at a cabinet meeting to discuss a vivid, recurrent dream that he had experienced again the night before, in which he saw himself aboard a mysterious boat hurtling across the water at impossible speed toward a dark and unknown shore. In fact, his entire life possessed a dreamlike, haunted, otherworldly quality that suggested the impact of supernatural forces.

Without recognition of those forces, and an abiding belief in his role as an instrument of a higher power, Lincoln himself couldn't make sense of his position at the center of the catastrophic conflict that consumed his presidency and convinced his countrymen that even in the midst of unspeakable suffering, God's hand still shaped and shielded America.

UNWELCOME INHERITANCE

Lincoln always shared the common conviction that his country had been specially blessed, but he struggled from boyhood with the fear that his family had been uniquely cursed.

He knew enough about the tangled lineage of both parents to worry over a heritage of illegitimacy and madness—dreading the impact on his own life of two of the most painful misfortunes of the nineteenth century. In the 1850s, he traveled with his law partner of seventeen years, Billy Herndon, to an important trial in a nearby county, and on the return trip he spoke of this unwelcome inheritance. The just-concluded legal proceedings turned on questions of property and personal characteristics passed from one generation to another, and as he drove the horse and buggy over primitive country roads, the senior partner took the younger man into his confidence.

Herndon recalled Lincoln's words years later. "Billy, I'll tell you something, but keep it a secret while I live. My mother was a bastard, was the daughter of a nobleman, so called, of Virginia. My mother's mother was poor and credulous and she was shamefully taken advantage of by the man. My mother inherited his qualities and I hers."

Over the years, most historians who have researched the matter have concluded that "Honest Abe" told his friend the truth: his grandmother Lucy Hanks appears to have borne two daughters out of wedlock. Extensive testing in 2015 analyzed the DNA of her numerous descendants and concluded that her two eldest offspring—including the future president's mother—almost certainly counted as illegitimate. At the time, these children constituted not only a scandal but a criminal offense: legal records from November 1789 show the president's grandmother facing charges of "fornication" in Mercer County, Kentucky. Before she stood trial and faced potentially dire consequences, a local farmer of honorable character offered to marry her and the court agreed to drop its indictment. Lucy went on to produce eight more children in her new home and earned local admiration as "a fine Christian woman."

Despite his grandmother's story of forgiveness and redemption, Lincoln felt the mournful burden of intergenerational guilt. In their backroads buggy ride through the thickening twilight on the Illinois frontier, he reportedly told Herndon that the well-born swell who had wronged Lucy Hanks had passed on "his power of analysis, his logic, his mental activity, his ambition, and all the qualities that distinguished him." After a long pause in his early evening ruminations, Lincoln asked Herndon. "Did you ever notice that bastards are generally smarter, shrewder and more intellectual than others? Is it because it is stolen?"

Whatever the genetic advantages Nancy Lincoln may have gained for her progeny, she managed few moments of joy or tranquility for herself in her brief, harsh life. The first child, Sarah, arrived seven months and twenty-nine days after her wedding at age twenty-two; Abraham entered the world almost exactly two years later. A third child, Thomas junior, arrived three years after that but clung to life for only three days, providing little Abe with some of his earliest and most painful memories.

The celebrated cabin in which the future president began his life had been hastily constructed on a small ridge above a spring near Hodgen's Mill, Kentucky, assembled from freshly cut logs with clay used to seal the gaps between them. The one-room structure measured no more than sixteen by eighteen feet, for a total living area of 288 square feet to accommodate husband, wife, and their two surviving children. It also contained a fireplace assembled of sticks and sandy clay, or perhaps built of stones. The little home also likely featured a small opening covered with greased paper to act as a window and, inevitably, a dirt floor—a common attribute that may have helped give rise to the term "dirt poor."

Unlike other notables who arose from such circumstances, Lincoln displayed scant interest in describing or discussing the bleak aspects of his upbringing. When he became a candidate for president at age fifty-one, a friendly journalist named John Locke Scripps asked him for details about his childhood in order to flesh out a campaign biography. "Why, Scripps, it is a great piece of folly to attempt to make anything out of my early life," the candidate replied. "It can all be condensed into a single sentence; and that sentence you will find in Gray's *Elegy*—'The short and simple annals of the poor.'"

In fact, the annals of the president's own father counted as neither simple nor short by the standards of the day: Thomas Lincoln lived till seventy-three, and hardly lacked for ambition or stubborn hopes of grandeur. His hunger for land led him to uproot his little family three times in the first five years of marriage and ultimately to move them from a series of rustic homesteads in Kentucky to the vicinity of new settlements in Indiana and then to several sites in even less developed territory in Illinois. Lincoln's 1952 biographer Benjamin Thomas defends Thomas Lincoln against charges of "shiftlessness" by noting that "from the time he reached manhood he always owned one or more horses; once he paid taxes on four. He had good credit, and no unpaid debts incurred by him have ever been discovered."

He also impressed his neighbors as an enthusiastic churchgoer, firmly committed to the emotional worship of the "Separate Baptists" or "Primitive Baptists," who thrived on the Kentucky frontier. The Lincolns followed several preachers who made it their practice to thunder from the pulpit against the evils of slavery. As a boy, Abraham absorbed the sermons but took them far less seriously than did his parents. He used to entertain other children by mounting tree stumps in open fields and delivering clever imitations of the language and gestures of the local clergy.

"THE LINCOLN HORRORS"

Despite his family's unequivocal commitment to faith, hard work, and self-improvement, Abe could never fully separate himself from the family misfortunes known to relatives as the "Lincoln Horrors." Dr. Nassir Ghaemi, a psychiatrist at Tufts University, reviewed the nineteenth-century records and concluded: "Regarding family history, insanity and melancholy abounded in the Lincoln clan. Lincoln's father was gloomy; a neighbor commented that he 'often got the "blues," and had some strange sort of spells, and wanted to be alone all he could when he had them.'"

Relatives displayed far more serious signs of imbalance and mental illness. In his powerful and groundbreaking study *Lincoln's Melancholy* (2005), Joshua Wolf Shenk writes of one of Abe's great-uncles who admitted in a court of law that he suffered from "a deranged mind." Another first cousin went before a jury to commit his thirty-nine-year-old daughter, Mary Jane Lincoln, to the Illinois State Hospital for the Insane. The Hancock County jurors concluded that "her disease is of thirteen years duration" and that "the disease is with her heredity." An attendant at the hospital later noted that "her father was cousin to Abraham Lincoln, and she has features much like his."

For Thomas and his two older brothers, the most shocking and significant event of their childhood may have fueled the family tendency toward despondency. On a mild May afternoon in 1786, the three boys were helping their father, a Revolutionary War veteran known as Captain Abraham Lincoln, to plant corn on their recently cleared farm near today's Louisville. From the nearby woods, a renegade Native American, most likely a Shawnee, took aim at Captain Lincoln and shot him. As the wounded war hero gasped for air and bled into the freshly plowed soil, the Indian emerged from the forest and tried to seize the wailing Thomas, who clung to his dying father. Only the intervention of fourteen-year-old Mordecai, who raised his own flintlock rifle and killed his father's murderer, saved little Thomas.

Later, this same Mordecai suffered from wild, unpredictable mood swings exacerbated by alcohol. He produced three sons with acute emotional troubles of their own, described by an acquaintance as melancholy men who possessed the two prominent "Lincoln characteristics": "moody spells and great sense of humor."

Thomas understandably determined to raise his own children far away from this constellation of troubles but ironically chose a wife with emotional challenges of her own. Nearly all descriptions by those who knew Nancy Hanks Lincoln cite her sorrowful nature, conceivably related to the scandalous circumstances of her birth. Her cousin John Hanks described her essential qualities as "kindness, mildness, tenderness, sadness." No likeness of her survived, but neighbors recalled her light hair, gray eyes, and lean, tall, big-boned body similar to that of her famous son.

In that boy's eighth year, the family moved to southern Indiana to carve out another farm in rough, sparsely settled country. Twenty-eight years later, when he returned to this childhood home on a political trip to campaign for his hero Henry Clay, Lincoln wrote to a friend that he found "that part of the country is within itself as unpoetical as any spot on earth: but still seeing it and its objects and its inhabitants aroused feelings in me that were certainly poetry." One of the poems that followed described a bear hunt shortly after the family's arrival:

> *When first my father settled here*
> *'Twas then the frontier line*
> *The panther's scream filled night with fear*
> *And bears preyed on the swine.*

The arrival of a few of his mother's relatives helped to relieve the sense of isolation and vulnerability. Abraham quickly grew close to Nancy Lincoln's aunt Elizabeth and uncle Henry and to her first cousin Dennis Hanks, but within a year a dreaded and mysterious illness known as the "milk sick" tore through the settlements. Modern medical research suggests that the affliction originated from cows who consumed poisonous roots in the vicinity and then passed the toxin to humans through milk or meat. The stricken suffered from nausea, twitching, and "the trembles"; then, after "fits of retching," they generally fell into a coma from which they seldom recovered. After Abraham's great-aunt and great-uncle sickened and died, his mother contracted the disease and lay powerless in their cabin for about a week as her nine-year-old son tried to comfort her. She died on October 5, 1818, at an age generally estimated as thirty-five. Her husband laid her to rest in an unmarked grave on their property, after building her coffin from logs left over from the cabin's construction. He asked young Abe to whittle the pegs used to attach the planks to one another.

Having lost a mother, brother, great-aunt, and great-uncle before even entering adolescence, Lincoln developed a permanent sense of death itself as his relentless, personal pursuer. In another poem inspired by his return visit to Indiana he wrote:

> I hear the loved survivors tell
> How nought from death could save
> Till every sound appears a knell
> And every spot a grave.

"A VERY LAZY MAN"

His chief comfort during his youth came from his stepmother, Sarah Bush Johnston Lincoln, a widow with three children of her own. Thomas Lincoln brought her back from Kentucky to his crude wilderness cabin just fourteen months after the death of his first wife, and she found his two children "wild-ragged and dirty" under the haphazard care of their teenage cousin, Dennis Hanks. The new lady of the house remembered that she "dressed Abe and his sister up" so that "they looked more human," and she developed a particularly close relationship with the ten-year-old boy. She indulged his passion for books, in quiet defiance of his father's wishes and the norms of the time and place. The Lincolns couldn't afford the minimal fees to send Abe to frontier schoolhouses for more than a few weeks at a time, so his intermittent formal education never totaled more than a year of instruction. Nevertheless, Dennis Hanks recalled that by the age of twelve his young cousin had become "a Constant and I may Say Stubborn reader, his father having Sometimes to slash him for neglecting his work by reading."

Thomas Lincoln himself could neither read nor write—beyond an ability to painstakingly sign his name—and felt resentful toward a son who seized every chance to shirk the toil of the struggling family farm in favor of seemingly insignificant pursuits. Cousin Hanks obviously shared that attitude. "Lincoln was lazy—a very lazy man," he remembered. "He was always reading—scribbling—writing—ciphering—writing poetry &c. &c." His stepsister Matilda Johnston made similar observations in a more generous light: "Abe was not energetic Except in one thing—he was active & persistent in learning—read Everything he Could." Whenever he returned to the cabin from "farming, grubbing, hoeing, making fences," another cousin remembered, "he would go to the cupboard, snatch a piece of corn bread, take down a book, sit down in a chair, cock his legs up as high as his head, and read."

The life of the mind provided the only meaningful escape from his family's cramped circumstances. Shortly after he turned seventeen, his adored big sister, Sarah, married, left home, and became pregnant almost immediately. She gave birth to a stillborn child and died shortly thereafter. A neighbor who attended the stricken woman vividly recalled Lincoln's reaction: "We went out and told Abe. I never will forget the scene. He sat down at the door of the smoke house and buried his face in his hands. The tears slowly trickled from between his bony fingers and his gaunt frame shook with sobs."

Despite his sorrows, he devoted the great majority of his time to punishing manual labor, especially after the strapping adolescent reached his full height of six feet four inches and his father began sending him on arduous assignments for minimal pay at nearby farms. The few coins earned in such tasks went to pay the family's bills, as the law decreed that any earnings by a child below age twenty-one must go directly to his father. The rule rankled, as did the notion that Abe exercised no personal choice over the terms of his own work and enjoyed no direct benefit from that toil. He sardonically recalled in later years that "I used to be a slave."

Nevertheless, Lincoln functioned as a dutiful son till he reached the official age of maturity, helping the family relocate yet again from Indiana to the banks of the Sangamon River in Illinois. At that point he "lit out" on his own, getting jobs on flatboats that moved produce downriver toward the Mississippi and into the wider world, ultimately carrying him all the way to New Orleans.

Once he left the family behind in their new Illinois homestead, the break with his father became decisive and permanent. Thomas Lincoln never met Abraham's wife, nor, in the years to come, any of the four sons of his only surviving child. When Thomas suffered his final illness at the beginning of 1851, Abraham turned down the pleas of a stepbrother to make a sickbed visit with the declaration that "it is doubtful whether it would not be more painful than pleasant." He also declined to attend the funeral, or to purchase a headstone for his father's grave. As biographer David Herbert Donald concluded: "In all of his published writings and, indeed, even in reports of hundreds of stories and conversations, he had not one favorable word to say about his father."

"I AM HUMBLE ABRAHAM LINCOLN"

At age twenty-two, Abe settled in the newly established village of New Salem, Illinois, and found work as a clerk in the general store in return for sleeping quarters in the back and a salary of $15 a month. He quickly became well known in the two-year-old settlement, which included no more than twenty-five families. Within a year of his arrival, he responded to the governor's call for volunteers to combat a formidable Indian uprising led by Chief Black Hawk, and the new recruit's local popularity led to his election as captain. He served for three months but saw no combat, though he faced reprimands for discharging his weapon in camp and failing to prevent his men from stealing liquor. In later years, he noted that the only blood he lost while fighting for his country was in "a good many bloody struggles with the musquetoes."

After his discharge, the militia captain ran for the state legislature and attracted attention by his decisive action in restoring order at a rowdy public meeting. In Pappsville, a fight broke out just as Lincoln began to speak. The candidate immediately jumped off the platform, shouldered his way through the crowd, lifted one of the assailants by the seat of the pants, and, according to eyewitnesses, threw him twelve feet through the air. When he had finished with this chore, the future author of the Gettysburg Address delivered one of his earliest reported public utterances: "Fellow citizens, I presume you all know who I am. I am humble Abraham Lincoln. I have been solicited by my friends to become a candidate for the Legislature. My politics are short and sweet, like the old woman's dance. I am in favor of a national bank. I am in favor of the internal improvements system and a high protection tariff. These are my sentiments and political principles. If elected I shall be thankful; if not it will be all the same."

Even at age twenty-three, the candidate displayed the same preference for brevity and concision, and the same hint of resignation and fatalism, that characterized his later eloquence. On Election Day, he finished eighth among thirteen candidates, but won 277 votes of the 300 cast in the precinct that included his hometown. With this mixed result, he attempted to capitalize on his local standing by joining a partner in launching another village store, which ran in the red for several months before it "winked out." His insistence on repaying every penny of what he wryly described as his "national debt" may have contributed to the nickname "Honest Abe." He learned surveying to earn extra cash and secured appointment as the local postmaster before another run for the legislature.

This time he won, and served four consecutive two-year terms as a leader of the badly outnumbered Whig Party caucus in the state capitol. He also played a conspicuous role in a group known as the "Long Nine" (because each stood more than six feet tall) in relocating the capital from Vandalia to Springfield, closer to the state's center of population and within Lincoln's home base, Sangamon County. After his first term he also earned admission to the bar after self-study of the law and moved to Springfield himself in order to launch a legal practice. He partnered first with John Todd Stuart, a friend from the Black Hawk War and fellow Whig member of the legislature, and ended up marrying Stuart's Kentucky cousin, the cultured and well-educated Mary Todd. She encouraged him in his first bid for Congress, but he failed to win the Whig nomination. Three years later, at age thirty-seven, he succeeded in securing a place in the U.S. House of Representatives and served a single term in the growing federal capital still widely known as "Washington City."

"HIS MELANCHOLY DRIPPED FROM HIM AS HE WALKED"

Despite these slow, relentless advances in his legal and electoral careers, Lincoln never displayed the glad-handing, cheery self-confidence of more typical politicos. From early adolescence, he wore his aura of long-suffering despondency far more comfortably than he did his ill-fitting clothes. The harsh, impoverished circumstances of his early life hardly counted as extraordinary among nineteenth-century Americans, but his reaction to that misery most certainly did: he struck both comrades and casual acquaintances as bearing the weight of personal tragedies in distinctive, even dangerous ways.

Henry C. Whitney, a fellow lawyer who spent months riding with Lincoln from courtroom to courtroom on the Illinois legal circuit, remembered that "no element of Mr. Lincoln's character was so marked, obvious and ingrained as his mysterious and profound melancholy." His longtime law partner Herndon made strikingly similar observations: "He was a sad-looking man; his melancholy dripped from him as he walked. .... The perpetual look of sadness was his most prominent feature." Francis B. Carpenter, an artist who lived in the White House for several weeks in 1864 in an effort to capture Lincoln on canvas, noted the same feature in his most famous subject. "I have said repeatedly to friends that Mr. Lincoln had the saddest face I ever attempted to paint," he remembered.

Later generations might associate this mournful countenance with the mature Lincoln, connecting his sadness to the grieving father figure who presided over the crushing carnage of the Civil War, but young Abe conveyed an identical impression even as a rising legislator twenty-eight years old. He began his lifelong, intimate friendship with Joshua Speed by walking into his general store in the new state capital, Springfield, and asking to buy a bed. The onetime shopkeeper recalled: "As I looked up at him I thought then, and think now, that I never saw a sadder face."

Speed took pity on the ungainly stranger who couldn't afford the seventeen dollars to purchase a bed of his own and invited him to share the room above the store. In fact, Herndon concluded that Lincoln's aura of patient suffering helped to explain his appeal and facilitated his surprising ability to form lasting bonds with ardent admirers. "His apparent gloom impressed his friends, and created sympathy for him—one means of his great success," he wrote. "I have often and often heard men say: 'That man is a man of sorrow, and I really feel for him, I sympathize with him.' This sadness on the part of Mr. Lincoln and sympathy on the part of the observer were a heart's magnetic tie between the two."

"THE MOST MISERABLE MAN ALIVE"

At times, however, his mood swings threatened his career and even his survival. The first of these disabling disruptions occurred in the summer of 1835, a year after Lincoln's initial election to the legislature. The sudden death of Ann Rutledge, a lively local beauty with large blue eyes and flowing blond hair, appeared to provide the immediate trigger. Historians have debated for nearly 150 years about the true nature of their relationship: Lincoln obviously liked and admired this daughter of the local tavern keeper, though no real evidence exists that they had become sweethearts. Nevertheless, when she died at age twenty-two from typhoid fever, "the effect upon Mr. Lincoln's mind was terrible," recalled Ann's brother, Robert Rutledge. "He became plunged in despair, and many of his friends feared that reason would desert her throne. His extraordinary emotions were regarded as strong evidence of the tenderest relations between himself and the deceased." Another friend remembered that "the thought that the snows and rains fell upon her grave filled him with indescribable grief." This reaction left his neighbors feeling "compelled to keep watch and ward over Mr Lincoln, he being from the sudden shock somewhat temporarily deranged. We watched during storms—fogs—damp gloomy weather . . . for fear of an accident."

Mentor Graham, the village schoolmaster, said more directly that Lincoln "told Me that he felt like Committing Suicide often." One more resident noted that "Lincoln was locked up by his friends . . . to prevent derangement or suicide." Elizabeth Abell recalled, "That was the time the community said he was crazy."

Six years later, in the midst of his final term in the state legislature, a different community expressed similar fears. After a break in his troubled engagement with Mary Todd, he wrote to her cousin and his former law partner, John Todd Stuart, who was then serving in Congress, with apologies for not reporting on the latest political developments back home. "For not giving you a general summary of news, you must pardon me, it is not in my power to do so. I am now the most miserable man living. If what I feel were equally distributed to the whole human family, there would not be one cheerful face on the earth. Whether I shall ever be better I cannot tell; I awfully forebode I shall not. To remain as I am is impossible; I must die or be better, it appears to me."

In order to recover, Lincoln sought urgent medical attention: he missed numerous legislative sessions to spend several hours a day with Dr. Anson Henry, one of central Illinois's most respected physicians.

"All we know for sure of Henry's treatment is that he put Lincoln to bed and kept him isolated," observes Joshua Wolf Shenk. "But if Dr. Henry followed the standard course with Lincoln, he would have bled him, purged and puked him, starved him, dosed him with mercury and pepper, rubbed him with mustard and plunged him in cold water."

Acquaintances took note of his lamentable condition. Jane Bell, a woman who knew Representative Lincoln from the Springfield social whirl, wrote at the time: "Poor fellow, he is in rather a bad way. Just at present he is on the mend now as he was out on Monday for the first time for a month dying with love they say. The Doctors say he came within an inch of being a perfect lunatic for life. He was perfectly crazy for some time, not able to attend to his business at all. They say he don't look like the same person." A local lawyer named James Conkling also commented on Lincoln's wretched condition, noting that "he now appears again . . . reduced and emaciated in appearance and seems scarcely to possess strength enough to speak above a whisper. His case at present is truly deplorable but what prospect there may be for ultimate relief I cannot pretend to say."

For Lincoln, that "ultimate relief" seemed for a time to require his suicide. His friend Joshua Speed, speaking to a biographer following the president's death, remembered that Lincoln had written a long poem about killing himself and even allowed it to be published in the local Springfield newspaper, the *Sangamo Journal*. Because earlier writers made wrong guesses about the date of the publication of the anonymous piece, scholars only discovered it in 1977. Nonetheless, the precise match with Speed's recollection and the unmistakable stylistic similarities to Lincoln's other published poetry make the case for identifying the piece as an authentic product of his tormented imagination.

"The Suicide's Soliloquy" appeared on the front page of the paper on August 25, 1838—as it happens, the third anniversary of the death of the much-mourned Ann Rutledge. Preceding the poem, the editors added a brief note saying that verses had been found in the deep woods along the Sangamon River "near the bones" of an apparent suicide.

The concluding lines convey a sense of mad exultation:

Sweet steel! Come forth from out your sheath,
And glist'ning, speak your powers;
Rip up the organs of my breath,
And draw my blood in showers!

I strike! It quivers in that heart
Which drives me to this end;
I draw and kiss the bloody dart,
My last—my only friend.

Further strengthening the case that Lincoln actually wrote and published these gruesome lines are recollections from friends in both New Salem and Springfield who describe his specific fear of wounding by blades: they say he made it a point never to carry pocketknives to avoid the risk that he would use them to harm himself.

"WITH *ME*, THE RACE OF AMBITION HAS BEEN A FAILURE"

In light of his long history of emotional distress, breakdowns, punishing medical treatment, suicidal fantasies, and all-consuming gloom, Lincoln's startling elevation to the nation's highest office looks not only unlikely but utterly miraculous. Even in the twenty-first century, with our vastly improved understanding of mental illness and its treatment, a provincial politician with Honest Abe's record of psychiatric troubles would find it difficult to qualify as a credible candidate for the presidency. After all, in 1972 a Missouri senator named Thomas Eagleton had to withdraw as the Democratic nominee for *vice* president due to episodes of depression less frequent and debilitating than those reported by multiple associates and neighbors of the sixteenth president.

Of course, Lincoln never had to deal with the scandal-obsessed media of the modern era; in stark contrast, the *Sangamo Journal* managed to obscure the authorship of the anonymous "Suicide's Soliloquy" for well over a century. But even in the 1840s and 1850s, Lincoln's painful awareness of his own vulnerabilities, widely known in political circles, combined with his deep sense of a family curse connected to his mother's illegitimate birth, should have kept him from White House ambitions.

Even his aspirations for lesser office suffered consistent frustration over the course of a decade. He kept his pledge to serve only a single two-year term in the House of Representatives, becoming best known for his impassioned opposition to President Polk's war in Mexico, before returning to Springfield and forgoing a race for reelection he almost certainly would have lost. He sought appointment by the new Whig president, General Zachary Taylor, to a plum patronage position as commissioner of the General Lands Office, but the administration insulted him instead with an offer of the governorship of the wild and inaccessible Oregon Territory—a position that Lincoln readily turned down. He then ran for the U.S. Senate twice, in 1855 and 1858, losing close races both times, and in between made an unsuccessful attempt to win the vice presidential nomination of the new Republican Party. He looked with a combination of bemusement and resentment at the contrasting career of an old rival from Springfield, U.S. senator Stephen Douglas, who had once courted Mary Todd. "With *me*, the race of ambition has been a failure—a flat failure," he wrote. "With *him* it has been one of splendid success. His name fills the nation; and is not unknown, even, in foreign lands."

When he lost the 1858 Senate race to that same Douglas, following a series of remarkably lucid and substantive debates that seized the attention of the nation, he felt ready to abandon politics altogether. He wrote to Dr. Anson Henry, the friend and physician who had treated his breakdown seventeen years before, that "I now sink out of view and shall be forgotten." He told his legal colleague Henry Whitney that he had come to view his entire life as a failure. "I never saw any man so radically and thoroughly depressed, so completely steeped in the bitter waters of hopeless despair," Whitney noted.

Just two years later, this chronic depressive with more defeats than victories in his political résumé and no executive experience whatever somehow won election to the White House to confront the most formidable challenge in presidential history.

"GOD MADE ME ONE OF THE INSTRUMENTS"

One of the key factors that permitted this startling rise involved his instinctive, all but unshakable sense of his own grand destiny. "Mr. Lincoln believed that there was a predestined work for him in the world," recalled his friend Orville Hickman Browning, who in the same year that Honest Abe captured the White House won appointment to the Illinois U.S. Senate seat that Lincoln had long coveted. "Even in the early days he had a strong conviction that he was born for better things than then seemed likely or even possible. . . . While I think he was a man of very strong ambition, I think it had its origin in this sentiment, that he was destined for something nobler than he was for the time engaged in."

One of the earliest samples of his childish handwriting comes from a verse he scrawled in the copybook of a friend: "Good boys who to their books apply / Will make great men by and by." In later life he told an old friend: "You know better than any man living that from my boyhood up my ambition was to be President." Stephen Mansfield, who writes persuasively of Lincoln's spiritual development, notes that "a mystical sense of destiny swirled about him. Nearly everyone who knew him in his youth recalled his certainty that he was made to play a role in important events."

He may have rejected the strict Calvinism of Primitive Baptists such as his father, but he borrowed from their faith a sense of foreordained fate, or "fatalism," as nineteenth-century freethinkers often described it. "I have all my life been a fatalist," he informed his congressional colleague Isaac Arnold. His wife, Mary, noted that he had always been guided by the belief that "what is to be will be, and no cares of ours can arrest nor reverse the decree." One of his favorite, most frequently cited Shakespeare passages came from *Hamlet* (Act 5, Scene 2): "There's a divinity that shapes our ends / Rough-hew them how we will." Herndon reported that Lincoln believed that "men had no free choice" and that each of us counts as no more than "a simple tool, a mere cog in the wheel, a part, a small part, of this vast iron machine, that strikes and cuts, grinds and mashes, all things, including man, that resist it."

In that context, Lincoln remained relentlessly committed to fulfilling, rather than resisting, his destiny as he perceived it. To him, the strange, illogical, often painful patterns of his life story followed some significant and irresistible master plan. Joshua Wolf Shenk concludes: "Far from a passing fancy, Lincoln's fatalism was one of his bedrock beliefs. . . . Lincoln believed that individuals had destinies that had been laid out for them in advance and which they had little, if any, power to affect." Joseph Gillespie, one of his colleagues in the Illinois legislature, described these convictions to Herndon a year after the end of the Civil War and the president's death. "I feel quite sure that there was not a moment when he despaired of success in putting down the rebellion, and he came to believe that he himself was an instrument foreordained to aid in the accomplishment of this purpose as well as to emancipate the slaves."

He saw himself fulfilling a higher purpose not only in his public, political endeavors but in some of his most intimate relationships. When Joshua Speed and his emotional, unstable fiancée went through a turbulent engagement much like Lincoln's own, Abraham's sagacious and calming letters helped guide them to an ultimately satisfying marriage. Regarding that experience, Lincoln wrote to Speed: "I was always superstitious and as part of my superstition, I believe God made me one of the instruments of bringing your Fanny and you together, which union, I have no doubt, He had fore-ordained. Whatever he designs, he will do for *me* yet. 'Stand *still* and see the salvation of the Lord' is my text just now."

That text, from Exodus 14:13, describes the children of Israel trembling in fear at Pharaoh's approaching chariots just prior to their miraculous deliverance at the Red Sea. As Moses promises them, "The LORD shall fight for you, and ye shall hold your peace." It counts as no coincidence, surely, that the episode cited by Lincoln to illustrate his own providential role refers to one of the biblical scenes most frequently referenced by the founders. For revered patriarchs such as John Adams, Thomas Jefferson, and Benjamin Franklin, the splitting of the sea and the safe passage of the Israelites held special significance.

On the prodigiously busy afternoon of July 4, 1776, the Continental Congress passed an additional resolution asking Adams, Jefferson, and Franklin to form a committee that would "bring in a device for a seal for the United States of America." Franklin's suggestion, as edited by Jefferson, described: "Pharaoh sitting in an open Chariot, a Crown on his head and a Sword in his hand, passing through the divided Waters of the Red Sea in Pursuit of the Israelites: Rays from a Pillar of Fire in the Cloud, expressive of the Divine Presence and Command, beaming on Moses who stands on the shore and extending his hand over the Sea causes it to overwhelm Pharaoh. Motto: 'Rebellion to Tyrants is Obedience to God.'"

Congress never officially adopted this design for the seal, but it clearly reflected the thinking of the founders, as well as Lincoln's— affirming the indispensable partnership between God and his people in implementing the process of redemption. Yes, the endangered faithful can initially "stand still and see the salvation of the Lord," as Moses pledges that "the Lord will fight for you." But the next verse in Exodus demands their participation while delivering a mild rebuke from the Almighty: "Wherefore criest thou unto me?" God tells Moses, "Speak unto the children of Israel, that they go forward." To the patriots who risked everything to achieve independence, as to Lincoln in defining his own role in a greater plan for his country, divine assistance arrives only when the human agents of those purposes "go forward" and take the first steps.

This Old Testament notion helped to accommodate the obvious tension between Lincoln's melancholy fatalism and his relentless drive to rise in the world and play his assigned role in history. "That man who thinks Lincoln calmly sat down and gathered his robes about him waiting for the people to call him, has a very erroneous knowledge of Lincoln," wrote Billy Herndon in one of his most frequently quoted observations on his longtime law partner. "He was always calculating, and always planning ahead. His ambition was a little engine that knew no rest."

"THE WHOLE MAN WAS TRANSFIGURED"

That engine rested only briefly after his Senate defeat in 1858 before the "vast iron machine" that shaped the fate of nations began prodding Lincoln in a new, unexpected direction. Illinois Republicans viewed his unsuccessful but spirited campaign as a triumph for their new party: running against a deeply entrenched incumbent with a commanding national profile, Lincoln actually drew 3,821 more votes for Republican candidates for the Assembly than the Democrats won for their nominees. Nevertheless, prior to the passage of the Seventeenth Amendment in 1913, state legislatures made the final decision on selecting U.S. senators, and gerrymandering in Illinois had given the Democrats disproportionate power in Springfield. They therefore reelected Douglas by a margin of 54 to 46. Two days later, a Republican newspaper in the tiny town of Lacon expressed its defiance with an attention-getting banner headline: "ABRAHAM LINCOLN FOR PRESIDENT IN 1860."

That far-fetched notion aimed to get attention more than to launch a credible campaign. But it certainly expressed the local appetite for a rematch between the famous Senator Douglas and the prairie lawyer from Springfield who had lost so narrowly, and the journalistic gambit began to spark bemused discussion. With Douglas the presumed Democratic nominee in the presidential election two years later, it made some sense for Republicans on the national scene to consider the same eloquent orator who had battled him so effectively in their celebrated senatorial debates.

Lincoln dismissed the idea as a passing fancy and wrote to a Republican organizer and ardent admirer, "I must, in candor, say I do not think myself fit for the Presidency. I certainly am flattered, and gratified, that some partial friends think of me in that connection; but I really think it best for our cause that no concerted effort, such as you suggest, should be made." Nevertheless, some of his Illinois associates refused to give up on the idea, and a dramatic encounter forced Lincoln to consider it more seriously.

While working on a trial in Bloomington, Illinois, a few weeks after the election, Lincoln had left the courthouse at dusk of a December day to walk over frozen ground to his rooming house when the editor of the village newspaper grabbed him by the arm and led him to a nearby law office. There Jesse Fell excitedly reported that he had just returned from a trip to the East Coast, where numerous Republicans demanded to know: "Who is this man Lincoln, who is opposing Douglas?" It became obvious that Honest Abe's reputation had already spread far beyond the borders of Illinois, so Fell concluded that he could become a serious presidential candidate. He asked Lincoln to provide a biographical sketch for circulation around the country to fuel interest in his potential campaign.

The recently defeated candidate thanked him for the honor and conceded that he would like to be president. At the same time, he cited well-known Republican leaders including Senator William Henry Seward of New York and Governor Salmon P. Chase of Ohio, who possessed far superior qualifications and seemed likely to claim the nomination. Lincoln set aside Jesse Fell's request for autobiographical notes, but he did begin accepting some of the many invitations that came in to deliver speeches around the country. In the last five months of 1859 he spoke away from home some twenty-three times, traveling to Ohio, Indiana, Wisconsin, and Kansas and later to three New England states, drawing warm responses and respectable crowds wherever he went.

Encouraged by those reactions, Lincoln finally responded to Jesse Fell's year-old appeal for biographical information by forwarding a meager 606-word statement. The accompanying note explained: "Here is a little sketch, as you requested. There is not much of it, for the reason, I supposed, that there is not much of me." In his terse review of his life, the hesitant candidate made only vague, passing reference to his sole claim to national attention: the epic debates with Stephen Douglas. "I was losing interest in politics," he wrote, "when the repeal of the Missouri Compromise aroused me again. What I have done since then is pretty well known."

Against all logic, Lincoln's reluctance to press his own case for the presidential nomination set up a crucial victory for his supporters. In December 1859, the Republican National Committee met in

New York City to decide on a site for the party convention less than five months later. Partisans of each of the major candidates battled for the home-state advantage, with Seward loyalists arguing for Buffalo, Chase backers insisting on Cleveland or Columbus, advocates of Senator Simon Cameron of Pennsylvania pushing for Harrisburg, and campaigners for Representative Edward Bates of Missouri leading the charge for St. Louis. In the midst of this confusion, Norman Judd, one of the masterminds behind Lincoln's stealth campaign, made the case for Chicago as neutral ground because Illinois offered no "leading candidate." In the final balloting, the compromise choice of the budding metropolis on Lake Michigan bested St. Louis by a single fateful vote.

At the end of February 1860, when Honest Abe made the exhausting twelve-hundred-mile rail journey to New York City for an important speech, party insiders continued to dismiss him as a presidential possibility. He prepared a long, scholarly discourse addressing growing talk of southern states leaving the Union and arguing that the framers of the Constitution believed the federal government retained the right to keep slavery from the territories. At the Great Hall of Cooper Union, with the prominent newspaper editor Horace Greeley seated on the platform behind him and a crowd of fifteen hundred (who paid 25 cents each for admission) waiting in front of him, the lanky visitor from the hinterlands approached the podium. Initially, observers noted that the new suit he had bought for the occasion fit him poorly. "When Lincoln rose to speak, I was greatly disappointed," remembered one member of the audience. "He was tall, tall, oh, how tall! And so angular and awkward that I had, for an instant, a feeling of pity for so ungainly a man. I said to myself, 'Old fellow, you won't do; it's all very well for the wild West but this will never go down in New York.'"

But as Lincoln launched into his lengthy address, the impression changed immediately, almost miraculously. "The whole man was transfigured," the skeptical listener remembered. "I forgot his clothes, his personal appearance, and his individual peculiarities. Presently, forgetting myself, I was on my feet like the rest . . . cheering this wonderful man." William Cullen Bryant, celebrated poet and editor of the *New York Evening Post*, declared the Cooper Union address to be the best political speech he had heard in his life. The rival *New York Tribune*, Greeley's paper, reached similarly effusive conclusions. "Mr. Lincoln is one of Nature's orators," the esteemed editor proclaimed, "using his rare powers solely and effectively to elucidate and to convince, though their inevitable effect is to delight and electrify as well." The result amounted to "one of the happiest and most convincing political arguments ever made in this city. . . . No man ever before made such an impression on his first appeal to a New York audience."

"THE TASTE *IS* IN MY MOUTH, A LITTLE"

The reception for this speech (published in its entirety across the country) dramatically enhanced Lincoln's national reputation, yet failed to place him in the front rank of Republican presidential contenders. On the eve of the May convention, *Harper's Weekly* published images and biographies of all eleven Republicans who had been mentioned as potential nominees; Lincoln's name appeared dead last on the list, and the rustic now billed as the "Rail Splitter Candidate" received by far the briefest and most perfunctory review.

That same week, delegates from every state, traveling from as far away as Maine, Florida, and California, boarded special trains to transport them to the rising but raw lakeside metropolis that took enormous pride in hosting its first-ever nominating convention. Already bursting with 110,000 residents and reveling in its status as the continent's fastest-growing city, Chicago had constructed a two-story temporary wooden structure known as the "Wigwam" to accommodate the festivities. The rickety building measured 180 by 100 feet and could hold up to ten thousand delegates and spectators, while more than twice that number jammed the streets to monitor the proceedings. As an act of civic pride, the town's most influential newspaper, the *Chicago Press and Tribune*, endorsed Lincoln as the "favorite son" of Illinois, but nonetheless expressed the common view that Senator Seward would be the all but certain nominee. The most prominent alternatives to the front-runner were Ohio governor Salmon P. Chase (a former senator himself, praised by the *Tribune* for his "inflexible honesty and marked executive ability") and the canny political boss of the key swing state of Pennsylvania, Senator Simon Cameron. Others considered in the thorough analysis at the opening of the convention included U.S. senators William Fessenden of Maine and Ben Wade of Ohio, former senator William Dayton of New Jersey, House members Edward Bates and Francis Preston Blair of Missouri, and even seventy-five-year-old Supreme Court justice John McClean. Home-state contender Abraham Lincoln drew mention mostly for the sake of dismissing his chances since he lacked "the ripe experience of Seward, the age and maturity of Bates and McLean, or the fire of Fessenden and Wade."

Nevertheless, he deployed a tireless cadre of volunteer managers, most of whom knew and admired Lincoln from legal circles in Illinois. Under the leadership of Judge David Davis, a smooth, elegant, and implacable three-hundred-pound force of nature, they worked through crowded days and nights from their two-room headquarters in the Tremont Hotel. According to the traditions of the era, the candidate himself stayed away from the convention and remained at home in Springfield, but he sent regular letters and telegrams to his deputies to fine-tune strategy. "My name is new in the field; and I suppose I am not the *first* choice of a very great many," he acknowledged. "Our policy, then, is to give no offense to others—leave them in a mood to come to us, if they shall be compelled to give up their first love." Senator Lyman Trumbull, a political ally who had bested Lincoln in his first Senate race, in 1855, wrote to the dark-horse candidate to inquire after the seriousness of his improbable White House aspirations. Honest Abe honestly replied: "As you request, I will be entirely frank. The taste *is* in my mouth, a little."

The Lincoln loyalists made sure that the delegates had a different taste in their mouths after the convention began, providing free liquor to the most important state delegations despite the candidate's well-known personal aversion to alcohol and long-expressed sympathy for the temperance cause. Upholding sacred political traditions that have persisted through the nominating conventions of the twenty-first century, delegates celebrated long into the night, strategizing and negotiating while happily sharing bottles, cigars, and electoral analysis.

The core argument for Honest Abe's nomination came down to electability: he could compete in the key swing states—Pennsylvania, Indiana, and Illinois—while his better-known rivals could not. The newly organized Republican Party had run its first presidential candidate four years earlier, rallying behind the explorer and military hero John C. Frémont. In a closely fought and spirited campaign against the well-entrenched Democrats, the dashing and youthful Frémont lost

THE FRONT-RUNNER: William Henry Seward (1801–1872), governor of New York, U.S. senator, and later secretary of state.

"Opposition to Gov. Seward cannot concentrate on any candidate ... he will be nominated." —New York Tribune editor Horace Greeley, May 1860

the three pivotal states to former Pennsylvania senator and secretary of state James Buchanan and with them the election. While Republicans in every part of the country opposed the extension of slavery into the territories, few voters outside the Northeast shared the impassioned abolitionist sentiments that had become popular in New England and upstate New York. Senator Seward, the undeniable front-runner for the nomination, inspired his followers with his moral clarity on the slavery issue but frightened more cautious voters who worried over the possibility of disunion and civil war; after all, Seward's best-known oration dramatically cited an "Irrepressible Conflict" that threatened to split the nation in two.

Nevertheless, the senator's supporters remained supremely confident on the night before the balloting. One of Seward's friends cabled the candidate as he waited anxiously for scraps of news at his gracious home in the upstate village of Auburn, New York. "We have no doubt of a favorable result tomorrow," the telegram read. In Chicago, the New York delegation got a head start on its celebrations with a brass band playing patriotic favorites and champagne for all comers. Horace Greeley, determined to block Seward's nomination at all costs, expressed his resignation in a midnight dispatch. He wrote that "opposition to Gov. Seward cannot concentrate on any candidate . . . he will be nominated."

Greeley himself, like other moderates and pragmatists in the party, preferred the sixty-seven-year-old former congressman Edward Bates of St. Louis, a former slave owner who emphasized intersectional accommodation. For one thing, he offered brighter prospects for flipping closely divided states from the Democratic to the Republican column, and even raised the possibility of competing for the nine electoral votes of his slave-state home base, Missouri. Lincoln promised similar advantages in all-important Illinois, qualifying as the only candidate who could credibly challenge Stephen Douglas in his home state. He also boasted well-advertised roots in swing-state Indiana, where he spent most of his boyhood, while his advocates made a special point of wooing Pennsylvania's delegates in the likely event that their "first love," favorite son Senator Simon Cameron, failed to gain traction on the first ballot. Most important, Lincoln's distinctly limited role in national politics had earned him far fewer enemies than his high-profile competitors. Bates, for instance, had participated in the short-lived Know-Nothing Party with its anti-immigrant, anti-Catholic platform. Lincoln, on the other hand, always expressed solidly pro-business, pro-immigration positions that made him far more acceptable to the German American communities that represented an important anti-slavery constituency in Pennsylvania, Ohio, Missouri, and Wisconsin.

"THE ENERGY OF INSANITY"

In addition to their determined efforts at persuasion, the tireless Judge Davis and his conniving comrades clearly outdid the cadres behind Bates, Seward, Chase, and the rest when it came to ensuring a pro-Lincoln atmosphere in the convention hall through manipulation of the surging local crowds. A burly lawyer named Ward Hill Lamon, who had ridden the circuit with Lincoln and later served as his White House bodyguard, concentrated on recruiting enthusiastic Chicagoans with booming, robust voices to pack the galleries. The resulting preponderance of Honest Abe enthusiasts left the competing campaigns amazed and frustrated, giving rise to widespread charges that Lamon (or someone else in the Lincoln high command) had printed up counterfeit tickets and arranged early admission to make sure that the Rail Splitter's advocates far outnumbered backers for Seward or anyone else.

When Norman Judd, one of the convention's principal organizers, placed Lincoln's name in nomination and praised "the man who can split rails and maul Democrats," the multitudes exploded with raucous cheers and furious stamping that literally shook the bunting-draped rafters of the flimsy Wigwam. The crowds in the galleries joined with enthusiasts on the floor to make a noise that struck some observers as "infernal" but energized the Lincoln backers, who heard it as heavenly. No one present could forget or deny the impact of this electrifying and infectious energy. Journalist Murat Halstead reported: "Imagine all the hogs ever slaughtered in Cincinnati giving their death squeals together, a score of big steam whistles going, and you conceive something of the same nature." As the yelling and banging finally began to subside, one voice carried above the din, declaring: "Abe Lincoln has it, by the sound now. Let us ballot."

The resulting tally put the tall, long-limbed lawyer from Illinois in a surprisingly strong position with 102 delegates, good for second place. Seward led, as expected, with 173½ votes, but still fell far short of the 233 needed for nomination. Cameron, Chase, and Bates all placed well behind, each scoring between 48 and 51 votes. On the second ballot, which followed immediately, the votes of the also-rans began to shift toward the two front-runners, with Seward gaining 11 delegates to stand at 184½, while Lincoln picked up 79 votes (mostly from Pennsylvania) to move into a virtual tie for the lead with 181.

Before the third ballot began, it became obvious that momentum would carry Honest Abe to the nomination unless some sudden shift occurred to interrupt his progress. Newspaper editor Thurlow Weed, Senator Seward's longtime friend and political manager, desperately tried to turn aside the Lincoln surge by rushing to wavering state delegations with last-minute deals. To Weed's chagrin, he discovered that Judge David Davis had already secured agreements with some of these waverers to make Lincoln their second choice. He had conducted these freewheeling negotiations over two nights of booze-soaked, dusk-to-dawn negotiations despite a one-sentence written order from the candidate: "Make no contracts that bind me."

Unbound, the delegates proceeded to stampede toward Lincoln. When the Ohio delegation announced the shift of four votes from Chase to Lincoln, it put Abe over the top and, as Halstead witnessed the resulting jubilation, thousands of voices bellowed "with the energy of insanity." Hearing the festive commotion, a guard who had been assigned to the roof of the Wigwam with a noisy ceremonial cannon looked down through an open skylight and gestured to ask what had happened. From the stage, a party official yelled up to him: "Fire the salute—Old Abe is nominated." The shot went off to notify the surrounding city of the historic moment. Halstead reported that "the entire city could hardly contain itself. . . . There were bands of music playing, and joyous cries on every hand." Lincoln delegates poured out onto the clogged streets "like drunkards, unable to manage themselves."

Meanwhile, the distant candidates waited for news. When Senator Seward received the cable announcing Lincoln's nomination and the disappointing result of his own decades of planning and service, his poker face showed no emotion. According to friends who tried to comfort him, he drily observed of his victorious rival, "Well, Lincoln will be elected and has some of the qualities to make a good president."

Lincoln himself received regular updates in Springfield at the newspaper offices of the *Illinois State Journal*. When a breathless messenger boy ran all the way from the telegraph office to hand him a one-sentence cable, he stared at it in silence for almost three minutes before sharing it with his gathered friends and colleagues. The message simply declared: "Mr. Lincoln, you are nominated on third ballot." The candidate stood up and quietly received the congratulations of the little group around him, patiently shaking hands before preparing to walk home. A larger crowd had begun to assemble outside, delirious over the success of the local hero. Another telegram arrived, proclaiming: "We did it—glory to God."

The Republican nominee for the nation's highest office then took his leave. "Well, gentlemen," he announced, "there is a little woman at our house who is probably more interested in this dispatch than I am. . . . I will take it to her."

"BALLS OF UNEARTHLY LIGHT OVER OUR HEADS"

The campaign that followed proceeded to its inevitable, anticlimactic result, given the hopeless divisions in the Democratic Party. The northern Democrats nominated Senator Stephen A. Douglas, as expected, while Democrats from the southern states convened their own pro-slavery convention and chose the sitting vice president of the United States, thirty-nine-year-old John C. Breckinridge of Kentucky. Former Whigs and Know-Nothings, mostly from border states that cared more about compromise to preserve the Union than about advancing any agenda on the slavery issue, selected a fourth candidate. They nominated Senator John Bell of Tennessee to represent the hastily organized Constitutional Union Party.

In the end, Bell carried Tennessee, Kentucky, and Virginia for 39 electoral votes. Breckinridge won the states of the Deep South, plus the slave state of Delaware, for 72 electoral votes. Douglas triumphed only in Missouri, while splitting the electoral votes of New Jersey for a sad total of only 12. Lincoln carried the rest of the northern states and, unexpectedly, prevailed in the far western states of California and Oregon. He received only 39.8 percent of the national popular vote—in part because ten southern states didn't even allow his name on the ballot—but the Electoral College gave Lincoln 180 votes, well above the necessary 152.

Despite the often-repeated contention that Lincoln won the election of 1860 only because three other candidates divided the votes against him, the Republican nominee actually carried an absolute majority in fifteen states, which provided 169 electoral votes—17 more than he needed for victory. Nevertheless, his victory struck many, if not most, Americans as far-fetched and bizarre. Despite the long campaign and the intensive press attention to every aspect of Lincoln's life and character, the idea of this untutored, wilderness rustic actually ascending to the presidency seemed otherworldly, even preposterous. Some contemporaries, such as the Brooklyn poet Walt Whitman, associated the election of Lincoln with spectacular, unprecedented, seemingly supernatural cosmic events.

On July 20, 1860, after the conventions and in the midst of the four-way campaign for the presidency, astonished observers from Vermont to Virginia, from the Great Lakes to the Atlantic, experienced an exceedingly rare astronomical phenomenon known as a meteor procession—only four of which have been identified in Earth's history. As the Smithsonian Institution describes it, a meteor procession occurs "when a meteor grazes the Earth's atmosphere and fragments into smaller meteors all traveling in the same paths." The celebrated landscape artist Frederic Edwin Church, a leading member of the Hudson River School, painted a vivid, even lurid depiction of what he saw on that eerie night from his home near the Catskill Mountains in his startling canvas "The Meteor of 1860." Whitman, in *Leaves of Grass*, hailed

> . . . *the strange huge meteor procession, dazzling and clear, shooting over our heads*
> *(A moment, a moment long, it sail'd its balls of unearthly light over our heads,*
> *Then departed, dropt in the night, and was gone;)*

He designated 1860 as the "Year of meteors! brooding year!" and associated its display of fireballs in the firmament with the flaming wreckage of the "19th Presidentiad," which ended by inserting the haunted, haunting figure of Lincoln in the White House.

"THE HIDEOUS, APELIKE FORM OF ABRAHAM LINCOLN"

Whitman revered and admired the new president, but many other contemporaries could scarcely reconcile themselves to the surprising reality of his rise to power. The *Charleston Mercury*, one of the South's most influential newspapers, commented: "A horrid looking wretch he is, sooty and scoundrelly in aspect, a cross between the nutmeg dealer, the horse-swapper and the night-man. . . . He is a lank-sided Yankee of the uncomeliest visage and of the dirtiest complexion. Faugh! After him what white man would be President?"

Senator Willard Saulsbury, Democrat of Delaware, declared on the Senate floor that "I never did see or converse with so weak and imbecile a man; the weakest man I ever knew in high place. If I wanted to paint a despot, a man perfectly regardless of every constitutional right of the people, I would paint the hideous, apelike form of Abraham Lincoln."

Even George B. McClellan, the "Young Napoleon" who would serve as Lincoln's most important general in the first year and a half of the Civil War, identified his commander in chief as a simian being. "The President is nothing more than a well meaning baboon," he wrote to his wife. "I found 'the original gorilla' about as intelligent as ever. What a specimen to be at the head of our affairs now!"

No wonder that hostile contemporaries saw the cursed hand of a malevolent fate as responsible for installing the unworthy Lincoln in his exalted position. In 1861, William Henry Seward, newly appointed as secretary of state, reacted angrily when advisors warned that German Americans would feel "disappointed" if he failed to honor a member of their community with an important diplomatic post. "Disappointment! You speak to me of disappointment!" he railed. "To me, who was justly entitled to the Republican nomination for the presidency, and who had to stand aside and see it given to a little Illinois lawyer! You speak to me of disappointment!"

Charles Francis Adams, son of President John Quincy Adams and grandson of the "Atlas of Independence," similarly recalled Seward's sense of the president's unworthiness for his high office. "He thought Lincoln a clown, a clod, and planned to steer him by indirection, subtle maneuvering, astute wriggling and plotting, crooked paths. He would be Prime Minister; he would seize the reins from a nerveless President."

In dealing with the searing contempt of his detractors, Lincoln's fatalism helped him to prevail. The peculiar story of his nomination only strengthened the sense that he had been selected as an "instrument" of a higher purpose, playing a preassigned role in history's providential plan. If Norman Judd hadn't prevailed by a single vote in securing the convention for Chicago over St. Louis, if Lincoln's scholarly Cooper Union address had failed to connect with his demanding Manhattan audience, if Ward Hill Lamon hadn't distributed counterfeit convention tickets to local Lincoln partisans to sway the emotions of undecided delegates, his chances of nomination and election might have remained remote.

"NOT KNOWING WHEN, OR WHETHER EVER, I MAY RETURN"

As he prepared to leave Springfield for the long rail journey to Washington, the president-elect reviewed the peculiar paths of his life in his first fifty-two years as he tried to discern the ordained direction for the road ahead. In both conversation and correspondence, he pondered his role in destiny and design, searching for the right response as the southern states seceded and the lame-duck Buchanan administration declared itself powerless to stop them.

On January 30, 1861, he quietly stole away from the advisors and office-seekers crowding his home and made a half-day rail journey to Coles County. There he rented a horse and buggy to drive ten more miles to visit his seventy-two-year-old stepmother, Sarah Bush Johnston Lincoln, who survived on the last farm established by his late father. Since his nomination, she had become obsessed with the idea that something awful would happen to her beloved stepson after he became president. She had always viewed Abraham as her pride and soul mate, so he attempted to comfort and reassure her. He also visited his father's grave for the first time, having neglected the funeral ten years before. Belatedly, he ordered a modest stone marker to honor the site before his return to Springfield in the evening.

Ten days later, on a cold, rain-drenched Sunday morning in February, Lincoln and his family gathered at the modest red-brick Great Western Railway station to make their departure for the inauguration. In the waiting room, his friends filed past and shook his hand for final goodbyes. He had informed the press, which covered every move of the president-elect in the midst of national crisis, that he would make no formal farewell address. The reporter Henry Villard noted that Lincoln's face "was pale, and quivered with emotion so deep as to render him almost unable to utter a single word."

A special train awaited him, consisting of a compact locomotive with a single passenger car and another baggage car. The ringing bell signaled the moment of departure, and he made his way onto the rear platform of the train to look out at a forest of rain-slicked black umbrellas, partially concealing the faces of friends who had surrounded and sustained him for twenty-four years. Despite his advertised intention to depart without remarks, the intensity of the moment overcame the president-elect.

"My friends," he began, after several moments of silence, "no one, not in my situation, can appreciate my feeling of sadness at this parting. To this place, and the kindness of these people I owe everything. Here I have lived a quarter of a century, and have passed from a young to an old man. Here my children have been born, and one is buried. I now leave, not knowing when, or whether ever, I may return, with a task before me greater than that which rested upon Washington. Without the assistance of that Divine Being who ever attended him, I cannot succeed. With that assistance I cannot fail. Trusting in Him who can go with me, and remain with you and be everywhere for good, let us confidently hope that all will yet be well. To His care commending you, as I hope in your prayers you will commend me, I bid you an affectionate farewell."

When he turned to enter the train, three cheers rang out from the little crowd, and almost immediately the locomotive pulled away, gathered speed, and chugged out of sight into the thick mist of the gray, damp day. On board his private car, reporters immediately asked the president-elect about his impromptu speech. He sat down and tried to write out its brief lines from memory, struggling with the task in the lurching train, and then finished the job by dictating the rest to his newly hired personal secretary, John Nicolay. As his recent biographer Ronald C. White Jr. observes, "He devoted 63 of his 152 words to sketching the omnipresence of God. The God that Lincoln invoked was more than the creative first force cited by Jefferson. Lincoln appealed to a God who acted in history—who attended George Washington in the past, was able to go with Abraham Lincoln to Washington in the present, and would remain with Lincoln's friends in Springfield in the future."

This was also a God, Lincoln sensed, who had prepared a difficult, even tragic course for him to follow. For a vigorous, physically powerful man who had not yet celebrated his fifty-second birthday or even begun his presidency, the phrase "not knowing when, or whether ever, I may return" seems strikingly, painfully prescient.

AFTER THE BATTLE: President Abraham Lincoln and General George B. McClellan confer at Antietam, Maryland, October 1862.

Secretary of the Navy Gideon Welles recorded in his diary that before the climactic confrontation, the president told his cabinet that he had made "a vow, a covenant, that if God gave us the victory in the approaching battle he would consider it an indication of Divine Will and it was his duty to move forward in the cause of Emancipation."

WAITING FOR A SIGN

Lost Orders and Found Faith

Abraham Lincoln's journey from his comfortable middle-class home in Springfield to the family's new residence at the White House took twelve days, covered 1,904 miles, and carried him on the tracks of eighteen different railroads. Along the way, and amid mounting fears of disunion and war, he addressed large, curious crowds in major cities, offering mostly bland, extemporaneous remarks meant to reassure the anxious public. He often spoke of God and asked for divine assistance in the task of preserving the Republic. In Indianapolis, he referred to himself twice as "an accidental instrument" and urged his listeners to "bear in mind that with you, and not with politicians, not with Presidents, not with office-seekers, but with you, is the question, 'Shall the Union and shall the liberties of this country be preserved to the latest generation?'" In Columbus, he declared that "I turn, then, and look to the American people and to that God who has never forsaken them."

While Lincoln looked to the people for their support, tens of thousands of those citizens got their first look at the president-elect during his draining journey to the capital. The New York diarist George Templeton Strong reported that "the great rail-splitter's face was visible to me for an instant, and seemed a keen, clear, honest face, not so ugly as his portraits." A massive crowd estimated at two hundred thousand greeted Lincoln as he made his way down lower

Broadway in Manhattan. There the poet Walt Whitman got his first glimpse of the president-elect, noting "his look and gait—his perfect composure and coolness—his unusual and uncouth height, his dress of complete black, stovepipe hat pushed back on the head, dark-brown complexion, seam'd and wrinkled yet canny looking face . . . and his hands held behind him as he stood observing the people."

Lurking just beneath the surface of the huge and superficially friendly crowd, Whitman also noted a malevolent air of danger and hostility. "Many an assassin's knife and pistol lurk'd in hip or breast-pocket there, ready, as soon as break and riot came," he reported at the time.

In Trenton, Lincoln addressed the New Jersey state senate, nostalgically recalling his boyhood fascination with books that described Washington's heroic crossing of the Delaware not far from the state capitol in which he stood. In that spirit, he declared himself "most happy indeed if I shall be an humble instrument in the hands of the Almighty, and of this, his almost chosen people, for perpetuating the object of that great struggle."

To succeed in that great struggle, he resolved to hone himself into a more effective instrument for those hands to wield.

"TRYING WITH ALL HIS MIGHT TO UNDERSTAND"

Once established in the White House, Lincoln focused on two significant, simultaneous goals of personal transformation: pursuing a mastery of military science that would facilitate a meaningful role as commander in chief, and plunging into prayer, Bible study, and church worship with a rigor he had previously avoided. The former purpose represented a practical necessity, while the latter filled an acute spiritual need.

After the commencement of hostilities at Fort Sumter and the bloody, humiliating Federal defeat at the First Battle of Bull Run, Lincoln became even more painfully aware of his shortcomings as the civilian leader in charge of the most complex military challenge in the nation's history. The eleven Southern states that left the Union to form the Confederacy chose a proven warrior to lead them: Jefferson Davis, a West Point graduate, had distinguished himself as commander of a crack regiment in the Mexican War and as secretary of war under President Franklin Pierce. Lincoln knew that his own three months of experience as a militia volunteer battling mosquitoes in the Black Hawk War looked comically inadequate by comparison.

He therefore resolved to make himself an expert on the history, theory, and technology of armed conflict. His secretary John Nicolay noted that the president began to haunt the Library of Congress and "gave himself, night and day, to the study of the military situation. He read a large number of strategical works. He pored over the reports from the various departments and districts of the field of war. He held long conferences with eminent generals and admirals, and astonished them by the extent of his special knowledge."

William Howard Russell, an Irishman dispatched by the *Times* of London to cover the great conflict in North America, expressed pity for the backwoodsman from Illinois, who seemed overmatched by the task before him: "The poor President! . . . trying with all his might to understand strategy, naval warfare, big guns, the movement of troops, military maps, reconnaissances, occupations, interior and exterior lines, and all the technical details of the art of slaying. He runs from one house to another, armed with plans, papers, reports, recommendations, sometimes good humoured, never angry, occasionally dejected."

Lincoln's unshakable sense of purpose enabled him to overcome such discouragement; after all, he had risen from poverty to power as the ultimate self-made man. When asked who taught him the intricacies of the law so that he could establish himself as one of his state's most highly paid attorneys, he baldly replied: "I studied with nobody." Just as he had used treasured law books and his own towering intellect to take the place of formal legal training, he now employed all available scholarly materials on the science of war to make up for his lack of military experience.

In the process, he involved himself in day-to-day direction of the war effort to an extent inconceivable to prior commanders in chief.

Previous presidents who had launched major wars—James Madison in the War of 1812 and James K. Polk in the Mexican War—left crucial decisions in the hands of their generals and made few efforts to impose their wishes on faraway fronts. But the development of the telegraph and railroads had made presidential involvement far more feasible, and Lincoln seized that opportunity.

"NO CONTENDING AGAINST THE WILL OF GOD"

For Lincoln, that meant not only the development of sophistication and skill in the study of war but also the deepening of his spiritual strength to fulfill his role in the providential plan. In one of the notes to himself that he scribbled on scraps of paper to record his own philosophical speculations, he wrote in October 1858: "Certainly there is no contending against the Will of God; but still there is some difficulty in ascertaining, and applying it, to particular cases."

To overcome that difficulty after he ascended to the presidency, he made it a point to participate more regularly and conspicuously in the study of Scripture and in public prayer. On the first Sunday after the inauguration, the Lincoln family attended services at New York Avenue Presbyterian Church, turning down an invitation from the more prominent, prestigious First Presbyterian, the "church of the presidents," which featured an array of prominent politicians in its membership. Instead, the new master of the White House chose an "Old School" congregation that favored scholarly exploration of theological issues while scrupulously avoiding contemporary controversies or partisan sermonizing. Impressed with the intellectual rigor and oratorical force of the burly, booming-voiced pastor, Phineas Densmore Gurley, the Lincolns began attending services regularly and invited Reverend Gurley for frequent visits to the executive mansion. The president even sent in a check for his "pew rent" of $50 a year—the first time he had formally affiliated with any religious institution.

These were surprising steps for an unconventional religious thinker who had been notorious as a young man in New Salem for questioning the basic assumptions of Christianity. Shortly after his arrival in that tiny town, he became involved in the local debating society and shocked his neighbors with his radical views, inspired by enthusiastic reading of skeptics such as Revolutionary pamphleteer Thomas Paine and the Scottish poet Robert Burns. According to the recollections of numerous friends, he even penned an agnostic tract of his own, remembered as "his little book on Infidelity," attempting to disprove the divinity of Christ and denying the sacred authority of the Bible. His friend Samuel Hill feared that circulation of this work would wreck young Abe's political aspirations, and so he claimed to have "snatch[ed] it from his hand" when Lincoln least expected it and to have burned the only copy in a tin-plated stove.

Nevertheless, Lincoln's reputation as an "open scoffer at Christianity" still became a dangerous issue in his first race for Congress in 1843. When he ran again three years later, Lincoln confronted the charges against him by publishing an open letter in newspapers throughout the district. While admitting "that I am not a member of any Christian Church," he insisted that "I have never spoken with intentional disrespect of religion in general" and that "I still do not think any man has the right thus to insult the feelings, and injure the morals, of a community in which he may live."

This scrupulously balanced approach worked well with the electorate, despite emitting the unmistakable aroma of a carefully calculated dodge: Lincoln suggested that faith meant little to him, though he found it indispensable for the community at large. As he grew older, battling back from debilitating bouts of intense depression and suffering tragic losses that echoed his grim childhood, he drifted toward prayer and scriptural study with an intimate intensity that clearly transcended political convenience. This was especially true when his son Eddie died before his fourth birthday in 1850, and the cherished favorite of his four boys, Willie, succumbed to typhoid fever at age eleven during the Lincolns' first nightmarish year in the White House.

After both tragedies, substantive and comforting conversations with concerned pastors helped soften Abraham's long-standing reservations about orthodox Christian teaching. His biographer David Herbert Donald notes that "he did not experience a religious conversion," but by the summer of 1862 he looked back on the death of his sons and the other events of a "tragic spring" and "recognized that he underwent what he called 'a process of crystallization' in his religious beliefs." Part of this transformation resulted from his struggle to come to terms with the ongoing ordeal of his wartime presidency. "Since his election he had come increasingly to speak and think in religious terms," Donald writes. "Before 1860 he rarely invoked the deity in his letters or speeches, but after he began to feel the burdens of the presidency, he frequently asked for God's aid." In his First Inaugural Address he pleaded with the seceding states for reconciliation and re-union, expressing the hope that conflict could yet be avoided by "intelligence, patriotism, Christianity, and a firm reliance on Him, who has never yet forsaken this favored land."

Like many other Americans of his time and our own, he questioned the Lord's connection to his painful personal life, while expressing full confidence in the Almighty's direct, ongoing role in shaping the fate of "this favored land." He might anguish over his own afflictions and even at times wonder whether he had been "cursed," but he never doubted that a higher power controlled the great events in which he played an assigned role.

"I AM NOT TO EXPECT A DIRECT REVELATION"

In the troubled, occasionally desperate autumn of 1862, a small delegation of Pennsylvania Quakers visited the president in the White House and prayed earnestly for his strength and success. In subsequent correspondence, he thanked them for their visit, alluding to his "fiery trial" and once again describing himself as "a humble instrument in the hands of our Heavenly Father" who felt powerless to control the course of the current conflict. "If I had had my way, this war would never have been commenced; if I had been allowed my way this war would have been ended before this," Lincoln wrote. "But we find it still continues; and we must believe that He permits it for some wise purpose of his own, mysterious and unknown to us; and though with our limited understandings we may not be able to comprehend it, yet we cannot but believe, that he who made the world still governs it."

On September 13, with battlefield reverses causing an angry wave of public dissatisfaction with his leadership, he received a memorial from "Chicago Christians of All Denominations," who insisted that the Almighty expected the president to change the direction and focus of the war by freeing the slaves. In his reply, the president asked, "What *good* would a proclamation of emancipation from me do, especially as we are now situated? I do not want to issue a document that the whole world will see must necessarily be inoperative, like the Pope's bull against the comet!" While the Chicago Christians claimed divine guidance for their position, Lincoln lamented the fact that he had been granted no such inspiration. "If it is probable that God would reveal his will to others, on a point so connected with my duty, it might be supposed he would reveal it directly to me; for unless I am more deceived in myself than I often am, it is my earnest desire to know the will of Providence in this matter. *And if I can learn what it is I will do it!* These are not, however, the days of miracles, and I suppose it will be granted that I am not to expect a direct revelation."

Amazingly, the same day he wrote these words and despaired of receiving any clear indication of what, exactly, the Almighty meant for him to do, a series of events began to unfold that gave Lincoln precisely the "direct revelation" he desired. Within a week, he recognized and accepted this supernatural sign, and cited it in making the most consequential decision of his presidency.

"THE AUTHENTIC HIGH-WATER MARK OF THE CONFEDERACY"

The signal that altered the course of human history originated from the encampment of the 27th Indiana Volunteers in Frederick, Maryland, just forty miles from the White House. The weary troops had marched from the capital in a desperate, determined attempt to intercept invading Confederates at the darkest moment for the Union cause.

Since the beginning of the war, the huge, well-equipped Army of the Potomac suffered an unbroken string of disappointments and defeats in major confrontations with the Confederates in the crucial eastern theater. Most recently, at the end of August in the conflict's second year, the Confederate commander Robert E. Lee and his brilliant lieutenant Thomas J. "Stonewall" Jackson outmaneuvered the Federal forces at the Second Battle of Bull Run. They inflicted devastating losses, with more than ten thousand Union troops killed or wounded, and sent the badly beaten blue coats scuttling back to their encampments around Washington. This success encouraged Lee to launch a bold invasion of the North, hoping to rally Southern sympathizers as he marched through Union territory in the slave state of Maryland. He ultimately aimed to strike crippling blows by seizing or surrounding the Pennsylvania cities of Harrisburg and Philadelphia, forcing the Yankees to sue for peace.

If nothing else, a prolonged invasion could strengthen the hands of anti-war Democrats who might sweep the fall elections and take over both houses of Congress from Lincoln's struggling Republicans. As the Pulitzer Prize–winning historian Bruce Catton summarized the situation: "This was the authentic high-water mark of the Confederacy. Never again was the South so near victory; never again did the South hold the initiative in every major theater of war."

Most important, Lee's triumphs brought both Britain and France to the verge of formal recognition of the Confederacy. Frustrated by a Union naval blockade that disrupted the supply of American cotton for their profitable textile industries, both European powers openly considered forcing mediation on the warring American factions. After the second Southern victory at Bull Run, the British prime minister, Viscount Palmerston, commented that one more success by Lee would prove that Southern independence had been "permanently established." He proposed to wait only a few weeks more, asking his cabinet to prepare plans for British intervention to end the fighting, with formal recognition to follow. In short order, the globe's family of nations would welcome a new member—the first nation in history explicitly and proudly committed to permanent protection of the institution of slavery.

To counteract the threat, Lincoln defied the wishes of his leading cabinet members and congressional allies to restore overall command to the temperamental and discredited General George B. McClellan, who had been removed due to dithering and indecision some six months before. Despite the widespread distrust of the preening "Young Napoleon," and despite McClellan's scarcely concealed contempt for the president, he enjoyed the confidence of the badly demoralized Union Army. Less than ten days after the disaster at Bull Run, Little Mac set out to block Lee's ragged, hungry but battle-hardened hordes before they could penetrate the Union heartland and shatter the Northern will to continue the war.

THE THREE MOST SIGNIFICANT STOGIES

The 27th Indiana, a volunteer infantry regiment that had fought gallantly for a full year in the war for the Union, took part in that effort, marching into the tidy, church-spired village of Frederick, Maryland, on the cool, clear morning of September 13. The tired troops arrived just a day behind the advancing Confederates and received orders to make camp in a green, empty field just outside the town as the army regrouped. Most of the men took advantage of the break to wander through the tall grass looking for pieces of wood to make fires so they could boil their coffee. Southern troops had camped in the same plot of land only hours before, leaving behind their trash, waste, and smoldering campfires, so the Hoosiers needed to take care to avoid the mess when they stretched out to rest.

By midmorning they sipped their bitter coffee, smoked their pipes, and waited for orders to move out. Then as an aging, forty-six-year-old corporal named Barton W. Mitchell, talked with his friend First Sergeant John McKnight Bloss, he noticed a stuffed package half hidden in the partially trampled grass a few feet from his head. Lying on his back, without bothering to get up, he reached over to grab the envelope and then opened it with interest. To his delight, it contained three fragrant cigars, wrapped in two long papers covered with dense handwriting in a clear but cramped script.

The two soldiers threw aside the wrapping, sniffed the cigars, and began looking for matches to enjoy a smoke. Delayed in their intention to light up, Corporal Mitchell's curiosity got the better of him. He picked up the papers in the grass to give them a closer look and noticed a bold heading that announced, "Army of Northern Virginia, Special Orders 191." The document bore the date September 9, 1862, four days earlier, and mentioned the names of Confederate generals Jackson, Longstreet, Hill, and McLaws—important commanders that every soldier in the Army of the Potomac had heard about. The two crowded pages seemed to spell out in great detail the disposition of the full rebel army and Lee's point-by-point instructions to each commander of his dangerously divided forces in their ongoing invasion of the North.

At this point, Mitchell and Bloss got the idea that they might have found something significant. As Sergeant Bloss later reported in a letter home: "Corporal Mitchell was very fortunate at Frederick. He found General Lee's plan of attack on Md and what each division of his army was to do. I was with him when he found it and read it first. I seen its importance and took it to the Col. He immediately took it to General Gordon, he said it was worth a Mint of Money & sent it to General McClellan."

That unfailingly and often fatally cautious officer at least had the good sense to interrupt a staff meeting to inspect the orders the Hoosier corporal had recovered. McClellan realized the potential significance of what he now held in his hand but questioned the document's authenticity, wondering whether it might not be a clever ruse by wily Confederates to feed him misleading information about their whereabouts and their plans. He asked the members of his staff to inspect the pages, and one of them, General Samuel E. Pittman, quickly recognized the signature at the bottom of the page—"R.H. Chilton, Assist. Adj.-Gen"—as the name of General Lee's chief of staff.

In a strange, preposterously unlikely connection that stunned the gathered Union officers just as it must startle us to this day, Pittman explained that he had been closely acquainted with Chilton in the years just before the war. As it happened, Chilton served at the time as paymaster for the small U.S. Army detachment in Detroit, where

Pittman happened to work as a teller at Michigan State Bank. Pittman therefore became familiar with Chilton's handwriting from innumerable checks and account records that passed through his hands, and he could certify "without doubt" that the script on the intercepted orders matched the scrawl of his onetime friend.

Through this bizarre coincidence, General McClellan could now feel certain of the magnitude of the opportunity fate had inexplicably, unaccountably handed to him. As Bruce Catton summarized the development a hundred years later: "He was the beneficiary of the greatest security leak in American military history—the only one that ever finally affected the outcome of a great war."

In midafternoon, General John Gibbon called on McClellan's tent and found the senior commander absorbed in an uncharacteristic burst of activity, writing orders and barking instructions to subordinates. When he finally made time for the visitor, McClellan pulled the two folded pages out of his pocket and brandished them with flashing eyes. "Here is a paper with which, if I cannot whip Bobbie Lee, I will be willing to go home," he declared with fervor. In the same spirit, the general jubilantly telegraphed his commander in chief: "I have the plans of the Rebels and will catch them in their own trap if my men are equal to the emergency."

Reading those words, Lincoln surely would have worried more over McClellan himself rising to the challenge than he ever would have questioned the fighting spirit of the men. Two months later, the president accurately diagnosed Little Mac's most conspicuous flaw as a leader of men by noting that the great general, for all his abilities, suffered a "bad case of the slows." But with the intercepted orders miraculously in his possession, he moved with unaccustomed determination.

Lee soon noticed the decisive Federal moves and deduced that McClellan had somehow gotten wind of his risky plans and begun to act to take advantage of them. To this day, the blame for the lost orders remains an unsolved mystery, as does the fate of the three most significant stogies in American history. Corporal Mitchell and Sergeant Bloss distinctly recalled that they never got a chance to smoke their prizes of war before handing them up the chain of command, where at some point in the day's frantic proceedings they went missing in action.

But even if some pieces of the puzzle never quite came together, two great armies did—with seventy-five thousand soldiers of the Army of the Potomac hurled against thirty-eight thousand rebels of the tattered but tough Army of Northern Virginia. After twelve hours of fierce fighting around Maryland's Antietam Creek, the two implacable killing machines had completed the bloodiest day of slaughter in American history. By the time the fighting stopped at dusk, nearly six thousand men on both sides lay dead or dying on the field of slaughter, with seventeen thousand more wounded and incapacitated, many with missing limbs. More than twice as many Americans died in one day at Antietam as perished on all battlefields of the War of 1812, the Mexican War, and the Spanish-American War *combined*. As Civil War historian James M. McPherson notes in *Battle Cry of Freedom*, the casualties counted as four times greater than the devastating numbers lost by American forces on the Normandy beaches of D-Day.

As darkness fell, both bleeding armies still held the field, but the next day the badly battered Confederates made a hasty retreat toward Virginia. The headline in the *New York Times* three days later proclaimed, "GREAT VICTORY: THE REBEL ARMY IN FULL FLIGHT OUT OF MARYLAND." Sub-headlines also hailed "The Most Stupendous Struggle of Modern Times" and overestimated "Rebel Losses as High as Thirty Thousand."

Despite Lincoln's increasingly urgent orders that McClellan should pursue the foe, destroy his army, and finish the war, the Young Napoleon reverted to his customary plodding pace and let the Confederates cross the Potomac to slip away and regroup around their capital, Richmond. But Old Abe nonetheless reveled in news of the decisive confrontation he needed, and he interpreted the battle as the signal from on high he required for his plans. This theological context, as much as its strategic significance, made Antietam one of the most consequential military encounters in all of human history.

"AN INDICATION OF DIVINE WILL"

Two months before, Lincoln had drafted his "preliminary proclamation" for freeing the slaves still held by the rebellious states and read it to Secretary of State Seward and Secretary of the Navy Gideon Welles on July 13. They reacted with stunned silence before Seward warned of murderous anarchy throughout the South if the slaves reacted by attacking their masters. A week later, the president read his draft to the entire cabinet, asking for advice on wording but announcing the proclamation as something he felt determined to do. Again Seward advised delay and caution, urging the president to take so momentous a step only after a Union victory to avoid the impression that the government had freed the slaves as "its last shriek of retreat."

Lincoln placed the document he had drafted in a cluttered drawer in his office and waited for a sign. Five days after the victory at Antietam, two days after the triumphal headlines, he announced at a cabinet meeting that he had received the signal he required. Speaking in remarkably personal and spiritual terms at one of the most significant moments of his life, the president revealed that the Lord had fulfilled his part of a fateful bargain and thereby demanded the historic action at hand.

The Secretary of the Treasury, Salmon P. Chase, recorded in his diary a word-for-word transcription of the president's fateful remarks:

> Gentlemen, I have, as you are aware, thought a great deal about the relation of this war to Slavery; and you all remember that, several weeks ago, I read to you an Order I had prepared on this subject, which, on account of objections made by some of you, was not issued. Ever since then, my mind has been much occupied with this subject and I have thought all along that time for acting on it might very probably come. I think the time has come now. I wish it were a better time. I wish that we were in a better condition. The action of the army against the rebels has not been quite what I should have liked. But they have been driven out of Maryland, and

Pennsylvania is no longer in danger of invasion. When the rebel army was at Frederick, I determined, as soon as it should be driven out of Maryland, to issue a Proclamation of Emancipation such as I thought most likely to be useful. I said nothing to anyone; but I made the promise to myself and (hesitating a little)—to my maker. The rebel army is now driven out, and I am going to fulfill that promise.

A few months later, Chase described Lincoln's world-changing announcement in conversation with the artist F. B. Carpenter, who had been commissioned to commemorate the Emancipation Proclamation by painting Lincoln and his cabinet reviewing the document.

"GOD HAS DECIDED THE QUESTION."

Lincoln reviews his initial draft of the Emancipation Proclamation with his cabinet on July 22, 1862 (painting by F. B. Carpenter). He delayed eight weeks until resolving to make the declaration official, waiting until Union success at Antietam, made possible by a chance discovery, stopped Lee's march north. Five days later, the president announced: "God has decided the question in favor of the slaves."

Chase recalled with the painter, just as he had in his diary, that the president paused and then lowered his voice at the very moment he revealed his bargain with the Almighty. Chase asked Lincoln if he had heard the president correctly. Lincoln reportedly replied: "I made a solemn vow before God, that if General Lee was driven back from Pennsylvania, I would crown the result by the declaration of freedom to the slaves."

"SOMETHING SPOOKY"

Newspapers across the continent published the Emancipation Proclamation, announcing the momentous news that it would take effect when Lincoln signed his order on January 1, a hundred days later. The decision produced ecstatic reactions from idealists who had long decried slavery. William Lloyd Garrison judged it "an act of immense historic consequence," while his fellow abolitionist Frederick Douglass, a former slave, declared, "We shout for joy that we live to record this righteous decree." New York editor Horace Greeley conveyed a similar message through a huge front-page headline in his *Tribune* that proclaimed: "GOD BLESS ABRAHAM LINCOLN! . . . It is the beginning of the end of the rebellion; the beginning of the new life of the nation."

Administration critics scoffed at the irony that the Proclamation applied only to slaves held in Confederate territory, leaving the "peculiar institution" unmolested in the four slave states that had remained loyal to the Union. In London, the *Times* ridiculed Lincoln's perceived timidity: "Where he has no power Mr. Lincoln will set the negroes free; where he retains power he will consider them as slaves. This is more like a Chinaman beating his two swords together to frighten his enemy than like an earnest man pressing forward his cause."

Such criticism ignored Lincoln's limited power under the Constitution: he decreed Emancipation in his role as commander in chief, seizing (and liberating) enemy property to suppress a bloody rebellion against the federal Union. If nothing else, the proclamation amounted to a potent blow in the midst of a devastatingly destructive conflict,

316 THE AMERICAN MIRACLE

especially when the president managed to implement his intention of welcoming tens of thousands of freed slaves into the depleted Northern ranks in what had become a fight for freedom. In states that never seceded from the Union, the president claimed no authority to take executive action against slavery; total abolition would have to wait until Lincoln's successful push for passage of the Thirteenth Amendment to the Constitution in the very last weeks of the war.

Nevertheless, the Emancipation Proclamation almost immediately transformed the nature of the conflict "from one to restore the Union into one to destroy the old Union and build a new one purged of human bondage," McPherson wrote. The Northern armies, so often frustrated on the battlefield, suddenly became armies of liberation. Recognizing the change, the governments of Britain and France moved away from their prior intention to recognize the Confederacy and intervene for Southern independence. As the British prime minister now declared: "We must continue merely to be onlookers."

The political impact of Antietam and emancipation also worked greatly to the advantage of Lincoln and his allies. The "Peace Democrats" fell far short of their goal of winning control of both houses of Congress in the November elections: Republicans won a net gain of five seats in the Senate and held on to a twenty-five-member majority in the House of Representatives. They also retained control of seventeen governorships in the nineteen free states of the Union.

This string of historic successes would have been unlikely or impossible without two Union soldiers taking the time to inspect the wrapping for three cigars that the invading Confederates had left behind. Without the lost orders of Antietam there might have been no great battle, and no cue to Lincoln to emancipate the slaves. Instead, an unchecked invasion of Maryland and Pennsylvania likely would have produced political disaster for the war makers in Washington, support for the Confederacy by powers in Europe, and the permanent division of the no-longer-united states.

Despite the failure by Southern officers and investigators to identify culpable parties or explain the loss of Special Orders 191, high-ranking Confederates had no problem in recognizing the hand of God. Major Walter Taylor, a faithful member of General Lee's staff, wrote at the time: "It looks as if the good Lord had ordained that we should not succeed."

Lee himself reached similar conclusions after the war. "Had the Lost Dispatch not been lost, and had McClellan continued his cautious policy for two or three days longer, I would have had all my troops concentrated on the Maryland side, stragglers up, men rested and intended then to attack McClellan," he wrote. "Tho' it is impossible to say that victory would have certainly resulted, it is probable that the loss of the dispatch changed the character of the campaign."

In 1997, some 135 years after Antietam, Harry Turtledove wrote the fascinating alternative-history novel *How Few Remain*, in which a Confederate trooper, not two blue coats, happens to pick up the Lost Dispatch. As a result, the Union Army never catches up with Lee in Maryland and fights him unsuccessfully, on a ground of his choosing, in Pennsylvania, leading to swift Southern victory in the war. "Had those cigars and that order not been lost," Turtledove declared in an author's note, "the world would be a different place today. . . . We are very lucky that the landmass between Canada and Mexico didn't break apart into two countries."

In an interview with the Associated Press, Professor James McPherson made a similar point and identified "something spooky" in the odd story of the Lost Dispatch. "I've never known how to put my feelings about that," he remarked. "My own feeling is that this was a one-in-a-million chance, and there's no way to know how it fell out that it happened."

"I'M A PROPHET TODAY"

Less than ten months after that one-in-a-million chance, "something spooky" similarly characterized Lincoln's otherworldly connection to the next great battle in the war for the Union. Lee made his second desperate attempt to invade the North in the summer of 1863 and stumbled into the largest military confrontation ever fought in the Western Hemisphere. Over the course of three furious days of fighting, 165,000 soldiers converged on a peaceful Pennsylvania farm town of 2,400 and shattered the South's last chance to win the war. During the three days of epic struggle at Gettysburg, the president haunted the telegraph office at the War Department, sending and receiving messages from his generals in the field some seventy-five miles to the north.

On July 3, as Washington prepared for the festive, anxious celebration of Independence Day, the uncertain tide of battle finally turned, and that evening the sweltering capital received the first incomplete reports of a decisive Union victory. On the holiday, the celebrations began by early morning, with cheering crowds accompanied by rockets and firecrackers, as the Marine Band played "The Star-Spangled Banner" in endless repetition. The proclamation issued from the White House declared that the president "especially desires that on this day, He whose will, not ours, should ever be done, be everywhere remembered and reverenced with profoundest gratitude."

The next day, a quiet Sunday, the president and his ten-year-old son Tad called on a severely wounded general just arrived from the battlefield. Daniel Edgar ("Devil Dan") Sickles had been a prominent machine politician, state senator, and man-about-town in New York City before the war. He gained national fame when he murdered the lover of his twenty-two-year-old wife but won acquittal through a groundbreaking plea of temporary insanity. Despite his scandalous history, he managed to raise four regiments for the Union cause and found himself facing some of the enemy's most devastating fire in the second day of the Battle of Gettysburg. A cannonball mangled his right leg, and a military surgeon amputated it in a nearby farmhouse. Demanding immediate transport back to Washington, General Sickles settled into a home not far from the White House, where he smoked cigars and battled the throbbing pain in the stump of his leg. At three in the afternoon, as the wounded hero chatted with Lieutenant Colonel James Rusling from his staff, the president and his boy arrived for their surprise visit.

Lincoln first asked after the general's wounds and requested his eyewitness description of the fighting in Pennsylvania. Later, Sickles inquired about the mood in the capital, and wanted to know whether the president had ever shared the widely reported fear that the Confederates would prevail. Lieutenant Colonel Rusling sat in on the conversation and duly recorded Lincoln's words.

"In the pinch of your campaign up there," Lincoln began,

> when everybody seemed panic stricken, and nobody could tell what
> was going to happen, oppressed by the gravity of our affairs, I went
> into my room one day and locked the door and got down on my
> knees before Almighty God and prayed to him mightily for victory
> at Gettysburg. I told him that this was his war, and our cause his
> cause, but that we couldn't stand another Fredericksburg or Chancellorsville. And I then and there made a solemn vow to Almighty
> God that if he would stand by our boys at Gettysburg, I would
> stand by him. And he did, and I will. And after that, I don't know
> how it was and I can't explain it, but soon a sweet comfort crept
> into my soul that things would go all right at Gettysburg, and this
> is why I had no fears about you.

Sickles registered amazement at this uncomfortably candid recollection of the president's explicit bargaining with God, and changed the subject to another great struggle then unfolding far to the west. He asked Lincoln about the long siege in Vicksburg, Mississippi, twelve hundred miles away, where General Ulysses S. Grant stood a chance of taking the city and clearing the great river to Federal shipping. The president assured him: "I've been praying over Vicksburg also, and believe our Heavenly Father is going to give us victory there too because we need it in order to bisect the Confederacy and have the Mississippi flow unvexed to the sea." As he prepared to go, Lincoln apparently tried to make light of the mystical tone he had adopted during most of their conversation. "General, you will get well," he promised. "I'm a prophet today and I say you will get well, and that we will have glorious news from Vicksburg."

Neither man realized that Vicksburg had already fallen to Union forces on the Fourth of July. And Lincoln's prophecy for the healing of Devil Dan also proved altogether accurate: the general fully recovered and adjusted to the use of his wooden leg, enjoying a flamboyantly active political, diplomatic, and romantic career before his passing at the age of ninety-four.

GENERAL DANIEL EDGAR ("DEVIL DAN") SICKLES: Politician, soldier, diplomat, and, before the war, acquitted murderer of his young wife's lover.

After Sickles lost a leg in battle, Lincoln spoke to him about bargaining with God: "I then and there made a solemn vow to Almighty God that if he would stand by our boys at Gettysburg, I would stand by him. And he did, and I will. And after that, I don't know how it was and I can't explain it, but soon a sweet comfort crept into my soul that things would go all right at Gettysburg, and this is why I had no fears about you." —July 5, 1863

"GOD ALONE CAN CLAIM IT"

Lincoln's private, unheralded role as religious seer not only impressed strangers such as General Sickles but also shocked old friends who remembered the young Abe's once skeptical attitudes. In the grim summer of 1864, when battlefield disappointments led Lincoln and many others to expect crushing defeat in his upcoming campaign for reelection, his cherished comrade Joshua Speed paid a visit to the White House. Speed, product of a wealthy plantation family in Kentucky, had disagreed with Lincoln over the institution of slavery ever since their long-ago days sharing a room over the general store in Springfield. Nonetheless, he remained loyal to the Federal cause and to his friendship with the president and used his home-state prominence to rally pro-Union sentiment in Kentucky during the war.

After arriving in Washington for business in the embattled capital, Speed called on the White House on a sultry summer evening. Ushered upstairs immediately to the president's cluttered private office, he found Lincoln hunched over his desk in the flaring, hissing gaslight, intently studying a heavy-bound Bible.

"I am glad to see you so profitably engaged," the visitor sardonically offered, recalling with a knowing smile their former days in Illinois as radical freethinkers.

"Yes, I am profitably engaged," the president soberly replied.

"Well, if you have recovered from your skepticism, I am sorry to say that I have not," Speed declared.

Putting aside his reading for a moment, Lincoln rose from his chair, looked directly into Speed's face from his towering height, and placed a friendly hand on his shoulder. "You are wrong, Speed," he slowly intoned. "Take all of this book upon reason that you can, and the balance on faith, and you will live and die a happier man."

He expressed similar reverence when he received a delegation of the "Colored People of Baltimore" who presented him with a handsomely ornamented Bible to honor his efforts on behalf of their oppressed race. "This Great Book," he told them in appreciation, "is the best gift God has given to man."

Many biographers suggest that Lincoln sought solace by review-ing the pages of Scripture, but his correspondence and recorded com-ments make clear that he looked more often for guidance, for some unmistakable indication of the Almighty's intentions for the nation and its leader. He repeatedly cast himself as a tool of historic forces and divine will, rather than as an independent actor making signifi-cant decisions on his own.

"In telling this tale I attempt no compliment to my own sagacity. I claim not to have controlled events, but confess plainly that events have controlled me," he told Kentucky newspaper editor Albert G. Hodges in an important letter in April 1864. "Now, at the end of three years struggle the nation's condition is not what either party, or any man devised, or expected. God alone can claim it. Whither it is tending seems plain. If God now wills the removal of a great wrong, and wills also that we of the North as well as you of the South, shall pay fairly for our complicity in that wrong, impartial history will find therein new cause to attest and revere the justice and goodness of God."

By the time of the letter to Hodges, Lincoln had already spent two years grappling to understand the higher purpose of the war and the horrible suffering it engendered. One of the private notes Lincoln made to himself, "not to be seen of men," poignantly probed these questions and foreshadowed the profundities of his Second Inaugu-ral Address. It came to be known as the "Meditation on the Divine Will," a title applied to a random scrap of paper with nine sentences of handwritten text that was discovered by Lincoln's devoted secretaries, John Nicolay and John Hay, shortly after the president's death. Hay, only twenty-three years old when Lincoln wrote out these words and then set them aside, went on to become an acclaimed novelist, diplo-mat, and secretary of state under William McKinley and Theodore Roosevelt. He marveled at the "Meditation," in which "Mr. Lincoln admits us into the most secret recesses of his soul. . . . Perplexed and afflicted beyond the power of human help, by the disasters of war, the wrangling of parties, and the inexorable and constraining logic of his own mind, he shut out the world one day, and tried to put into form his double sense of responsibility to human duty and Divine Power, and this was the result."

Lincoln wrote:

> The will of God prevails. In great contests each party claims to act in accordance with the will of God. Both *may* be, and one *must* be, wrong. God cannot be *for* and *against* the same thing at the same time. In the present civil war it is quite possible that God's purpose is something different from the purpose of either party—and yet the human instrumentalities, working just as they do, are of the best adaptation to effect His purpose. I am almost ready to say that this is probably true—that God wills this contest, and wills that it shall not end yet. By his mere great power, on the minds of the now contestants, He could have either *saved* or *destroyed* the Union without a human contest. Yet the contest began. And having begun he could give the final victory to either side any day. Yet the contest proceeds.

To John Hay, Lincoln's philosophical ruminations, filed away for the president's future reference amid the clutter of personal and official documents, expressed "the awful sincerity of a perfectly honest soul, trying to bring itself into closer communion with its Maker." The date that the president attached to his penetrating paragraph—September 1862—identifies its composition with the weeks surrounding the Battle of Antietam and his corresponding decision to issue the Emancipation Proclamation. It's impossible to determine with any certainty whether he jotted down these intimate reflections before or after learning of the outcome of the great battle, or hearing of the seemingly random discovery of secret orders wrapped around three cigars that determined the result. In his private speculation, as well as remarks to the cabinet, he indicated no doubt as to the Deity's direct engagement in American affairs. He yearned only to shape his own judgments according to a master plan whose existence he consistently acknowledged but whose contours he only vaguely perceived.

THE ASSASSINATION OF LINCOLN: April 14, 1865.

"Our country owed all her troubles to him, and God simply made me the instrument of his punishment." —John Wilkes Booth

12

THE MESSENGER AND
HIS MESSAGE

Lincoln's Vision, Death, and Destiny

The shape of the grand scheme that Lincoln strained to understand came into better focus as the war thundered and staggered to its brutal conclusion and the president prepared his Second Inaugural Address. Though he felt deep-seated foreboding at the prospect of defeat and rejection in his bid for reelection, Union battlefield advances in Georgia and Virginia ensured a Lincoln landslide in November 1864. The incumbent commander in chief received especially overwhelming support from the nearly one million Americans who wore the uniform and had come to revere the president as their steady, sturdy "Father Abraham."

Despite the growing certainty of Union victory, Washington remained very much a city at war. Fifty military hospitals crowded every district of the town and accommodated maimed and dying troops as ceaseless waves of misery swept in from the carnage at the nearby front. Nevertheless, thousands of ordinary citizens jammed the rainy capital determined to celebrate the dawning of Lincoln's second term. Police estimated the huge crowd at thirty thousand to forty thousand people, while the correspondent for the *Times* of London noted that "at least half the multitude were colored people." Barely two years after emancipation, this counted as arguably the largest gathering of African Americans in the nation's history to that time. An inaugural parade featured four smartly uniformed companies of the 45th Regiment of United States Colored Troops, and the emotional crowd applauded every step along their march.

The weather drove the first part of the ceremony indoors to the Senate chamber, but after the swearing in of the new vice president, Andrew Johnson, the rain cleared and the proceedings moved to the steps at the east entrance of the Capitol. The eager multitudes surged forward to cheer their commander in chief and continued roaring despite calls for silence. Finally, as Lincoln's tall figure pushed forward to the podium, all observers noted a sudden change in the heavens that seemed significant, miraculous. As journalist Noah Brooks reported: "At that moment the sun, which had been obscured all day, burst forth in its unclouded meridian splendor, and flooded the spectacle with glory and with light."

"A DIFFERENCE OF PURPOSE BETWEEN THE ALMIGHTY AND THEM"

The presentation that followed, even with Lincoln's high-pitched prairie drawl and his characteristically slow, deliberate delivery, counted as one of the shortest and most celebrated of all inaugural addresses. The eighteen previous speeches had quoted the Bible only once (in the speech by John Quincy Adams), but Lincoln cited Scripture four times, invoked prayer three times, and mentioned God fourteen times in just 701 words. Without exonerating the forces of disunion that he held responsible for the carnage, the president treated the conflict as inevitable: an essential component of an incomprehensible master plan rather than the product of malevolence or conspiracy. "Both parties deprecated war," he recalled; "but one of them would make war rather than let the nation survive; and the other would accept war rather than let it perish. And the war came."

He went on to reflect on the common faith animating the combatants on both sides, despite their irreconcilable differences on the issue of slavery:

Both read the same Bible, and pray to the same God; and each invokes His aid against the other. It may seem strange that any men should dare to ask a just God's assistance in wringing their bread from the sweat of other men's faces; but let us judge not that we be not judged. The prayers of both could not be answered; that of neither has been answered fully. The Almighty has His own purposes.

At the heart of his address, the president offered his astonishing effort to explain those purposes to his fellow citizens. Significantly, he selected the phrase *"American* Slavery" rather than merely blaming "Southern Slavery" for the suffering that his countrymen of every region had been condemned to endure. Mark A. Noll, a distinguished scholar at Notre Dame specializing in the history of American Christianity, saw in this choice a desire "to make a profound public statement about the superiority of divine providence over any partisan grasp of God's will."

The president declaimed:

If we shall suppose that American Slavery is one of those offenses which, in the providence of God, must needs come, but which, having continued through the appointed time, He now wills to remove, and that He gives to both North and South, this terrible war, as the woe due to those by whom offense came, shall we discern therein any departure from those divine attributes which the believers in a Living God always ascribe to Him?

The fatalism that characterized his outlook since adolescence still shaped his sense of himself as a helpless instrument in the hands of a higher power, offering a tentative, lyrical, and poetic plea for a timely end to the slaughter:

Fondly do we hope—fervently do we pray—that this mighty scourge of war may speedily pass away. Yet if God wills that it continue, until all the wealth piled by the bond-man's two hundred and fifty years of unrequited toil shall be sunk, and until every drop of blood drawn with the lash shall be paid by another drawn with the sword, as was said three thousand years ago, so still it must be said, the judgments of the Lord, are true and righteous altogether.

His concluding words resounded then, as they do today, with the gentle character of a benediction:

With malice toward none; with charity for all; with firmness in the right, as God gives us to see the right, let us strive on to finish the work we are in; to bind up the nation's wounds; to care for him who shall have borne the battle, and for his widow, and his orphan—to do all which may achieve and cherish a just, and a lasting peace, among ourselves, and with all nations.

A moment of uncomfortable silence followed his conclusion as many in the damp, shivering audience felt puzzled by the speech's unexpected brevity and intense religious focus. Breaking with tradition, the president offered nothing at all about programs or plans, giving no hints of grand goals that would drive his second administration—as if he knew, somehow, that he would serve only forty-one days of that four-year term.

The famous abolitionist and former slave Frederick Douglass stood near the portico of the Capitol during the ceremony and listened with rapt attention. He had developed profound admiration for Lincoln in the course of the long war, and at the crowded, chaotic, noisy White House reception that opened its doors at eight that evening, the president sought him out and asked his opinion. Douglass demurred, citing the six thousand people waiting to shake the president's hand, but Lincoln demanded an answer. "You must stop a little, Douglass; there is no man in the country whose opinion I value more than yours. I want to know what you think of it?"

In response, the great abolitionist chose his words carefully. "Mr. Lincoln, that was a sacred effort," he simply replied. As he wrote in his diary that night, Frederick Douglass allowed that "the address sounded more like a sermon than a state paper."

THE SECOND INAUGURAL ADDRESS: The president standing at the railing; John Wilkes Booth identifiable on the platform just above, March 4, 1865.

"Fondly do we hope—fervently do we pray—that this mighty scourge of war may speedily pass away." —Abraham Lincoln

Many influential journalists expressed their disappointment and suggested that the president's remarks failed to rise to the majesty of the occasion. The *New York Herald* wrote off the address as "a little speech of 'glittering generalities' used only to fill in the program" and compared Lincoln's plainspoken text unfavorably to the memorable grandiloquence of the most recent utterance by the reigning French monarch, Louis Napoleon. The normally friendly *New York Times* similarly complained that "he makes no boasts about what he has done, or promises of what he will do," while the *Daily Illinois State Register*, one of the president's hometown papers in Springfield, dismissed the speech as "not a very felicitous nor satisfactory performance."

The *New York World* went much further, condemning the president's many biblical references and spiritual speculations as improper violations of the secular focus required by his exalted temporal office. "The President's theology smacks as strong of the dark ages as does Pope Pius IX's politics," the editors jibed, criticizing Lincoln for "abandoning all pretense of statesmanship . . . in this strange inaugural" and instead seeking "refuge in piety." The *Chicago Times*, consistently anti-Lincoln and stridently Democratic, denounced his terse comments as "so slip shod, so loose-joined, so puerile" that "by the side of it, mediocrity is superb."

Other journals absorbed his sentiments sympathetically, and praised the humble, reflective tone Lincoln had adopted for a celebratory occasion on the very verge of final Union victory. The *Washington (D.C.) Daily National Intelligencer* especially appreciated the soaring words of the president's last paragraph, declaring them "equally distinguished for patriotism, statesmanship, and benevolence" and suggesting that they "deserve to be printed in gold."

Lincoln showed scant concern over the decidedly mixed response to his Second Inaugural Address, and sustained an unshakable sense of its permanent importance. Eleven days after the ceremony he wrote to Thurlow Weed, upstate New York newspaper editor and long-time political partner of Secretary of State Seward, prophesying that the speech would "wear as well—perhaps better—than anything I have produced; but I believe it is not immediately popular. Men are not flattered by being shown that there has been a difference of purpose between the Almighty and them. To deny it, however, in this case, is to deny there is a God governing the world."

"BLESS THE LORD, THERE IS THE GREAT MESSIAH!"

That governance brought a rapid sequence of momentous events crowding into Abraham Lincoln's last six weeks of life. On March 20, sixteen days after the draining inauguration ceremonies, Ulysses S. Grant, commanding general of all Union armies, invited the president to join him for an extended visit to army headquarters in City Point, Virginia. The trip would provide the exhausted executive with a welcome escape from the constant strain that marked his residence at the White House, with the ever-present press of relentless office-seekers and nagging annoyance of carping congressional critics. Leaving the turbulent federal city would also enable him to plot strategy with Grant for the final stages of the war and the anticipated occupation of the Confederate capital, Richmond. He traveled by boat with his wife and his son Tad as soon as the James River could be cleared of torpedoes for his safe passage.

They arrived at City Point to a round of dinners and receptions for the top military brass and their fashionable wives, and received the ardent adoration of the masses of men in uniform. The troops hailed Lincoln as a presumptive conqueror, and father figure to all of the hundreds of thousands who had served the Union cause. On April 3, Grant completed a bloody ten-month siege by accepting the surrender of the city of Petersburg; within hours, the Confederate government fled from nearby Richmond just ahead of advancing boys in blue.

After four years of planning, prayer, and frustration, Lincoln wanted to enter the rebel capital together with the victorious troops, even though Secretary of War Edwin Stanton stoutly disapproved. "Allow me respectfully to ask you to consider whether you ought to expose the nation to the consequence of any disaster to yourself in the pursuit of a treacherous and dangerous enemy like the rebel army," he wrote the president. Elated by the rapidly unfolding developments, Lincoln disregarded the secretary's warning. "I will take care of myself," he crisply responded.

After a brief boat ride on a clear, unseasonably warm day, Lincoln disembarked without pomp or pretense in the vanquished, badly damaged city the day after its surrender. A work party of former slaves recognized him as he came ashore, and their leader rushed forward to greet the president with an emotional exclamation. "Bless the Lord, there is the great Messiah! . . . Glory Hallelujah!" he shouted as the workers fell to the ground in front of the hero they viewed as their deliverer.

"Don't kneel to me," Lincoln told them, embarrassed by the

tearful display. "That is not right. You must kneel to God only, and thank him for the liberty you will hereafter enjoy." When word spread of Lincoln's appearance, eager crowds of former slaves surrounded him as he approached the center of town, yelling, "Bless the Lord, Father Abraham's come."

The president and his party returned to Washington at sundown on Palm Sunday, April 9, in the midst of continuing celebrations over the conquest of Richmond. That night, as he settled back into his familiar White House office, he received the great news that earlier in the day General Lee had surrendered his fabled Army of Northern Virginia to General Grant at Appomattox Court House. At dawn the next morning, the thunderous firing of five hundred cannon heralded the victory, by order of the secretary of war. Gideon Wells, secretary of the navy, reported in his diary: "Guns are firing, bells ringing, flags flying, men laughing, children cheering; all, all jubilant."

For most of the day, crowds milled around the White House and clamored for the president to speak. He eventually came out to greet them but declined to make extended remarks because, he told them, "if you dribble it all out of me" he'd have nothing left to say for the more substantive comments planned for the next night. He did, however, oblige his well-wishers by asking the band to play "Dixie," which he described as "one of the best tunes I have ever heard." He jested with the throng that he had received legal authorization from the attorney general for this musical selection and that the rebel song counted as "a lawful prize" of war since "we fairly captured it." Late in the day, caught up in the excitement of the joyful moment, Mary Lincoln wrote: "The crowds around the house have been immense; in the midst of the bands playing, they break forth into singing."

Another happy horde assembled the following evening, April 11, despite the damp, foggy spring weather. Once again they began yelling for Lincoln, who came out to the second-story window above the north door. Reporter Noah Brooks, asked to hold a lamp so that the president could read his prepared remarks, described the scene: "Outside was a vast sea of faces, illuminated by the lights that burned in the festal array of the White House, and stretching far out into the misty darkness. . . . Within stood the tall, gaunt figure of the President, deeply thoughtful, intent upon the elucidation of the generous policy which should be pursued toward the South. That this was not the sort of speech which the multitude had expected is tolerably certain."

Lincoln began by announcing, "We meet this evening, not in sorrow, but in gladness of heart. . . . In the midst of this, however, he from whom all blessings flow, must not be forgotten. A call for a national thanksgiving is being prepared, and will be duly promulgated." He went on to present a series of legal and practical arguments for reintegrating the states of the Confederacy as quickly as possible, with special focus on the situation in Louisiana, where a tentatively functioning pro-Union government had already emerged. Significantly, he also gave his first public endorsement to the bold and still controversial notion that freed slaves deserved at least some limited right to vote. Concerning the elective franchise for "the colored man," the president declared: "I myself prefer that it were now conferred on the very intelligent, and on those who serve our cause as soldiers."

But even that cautious notion provoked an explosion of rage from one of Lincoln's listeners after the president finished his remarks and went back inside the White House. "That means nigger citizenship," snarled the celebrated actor John Wilkes Booth to the two companions who had accompanied him to the executive mansion for the occasion. "That is the last speech he will ever make. By God, I'll put him through."

"THE HANDSOMEST MAN IN AMERICA"

Only twenty-six years old and described by adoring theater critics as "the handsomest man in America" and "a natural genius," Booth hardly fit the standard profile of a presidential assassin. The gunmen who murdered James A. Garfield, William McKinley, and John F. Kennedy, as well as the would-be killers who fired weapons without lethal effect at Andrew Jackson, both Presidents Roosevelt, Gerald Ford, and Ronald Reagan, had all been lonely drifters with long histories of serious mental illness. None of them had achieved stable or successful careers, let alone wealth, national fame, and public adulation. By the time of his twenty-second birthday, however, Booth was earning at least $20,000 a year, the equivalent of at least $500,000 in today's dollars. He had accumulated enough of a fortune to begin investing in land speculation and oil drilling schemes in Pennsylvania, while he simultaneously collected the amorous attentions of a succession of enraptured females. Just two months before his announced intention to kill Lincoln, he became engaged to a princess of Washington society and the daughter of a U.S. senator. Ironically, the girl's powerful papa, John P. Hale of New Hampshire, counted as one of the most ardent abolitionists in Congress and a devoted supporter of Abraham Lincoln. When Booth was killed by pursuing federal soldiers twelve days after the assassination, they found this young lady's photograph in his pocket—together with pictures of four other beauties with whom he had been involved.

Booth's strange life featured other random connections to the president of the United States, undesired by either man. On November 9, 1863, Lincoln had sought relief from the burdens of the war by attending a performance of Charles Selby's *The Marble Heart* at Ford's Theatre. Booth starred as a Greek sculptor in robe and sandals who had achieved the mystical ability to make his statues spring to life. During the performance he delivered an angry line of dialogue while pointing a finger directly at the president in his box, less than twelve feet above the stage. At the time, Lincoln commented to his sister-in-law, "He does look pretty sharp at me, doesn't he?" At another performance, the president's son Tad enjoyed Booth's theatrics so thoroughly, and applauded so lustily, that the popular actor rewarded the boy with the gift of a single rose.

Another Lincoln son, Robert, had a far more significant encounter with another member of the Booth family in the early months of the Civil War. According to Robert Lincoln's own recollection, he waited in a jostling, impatient crowd to board a train late at night at the busy rail station in Jersey City. To his horror, the people behind him inadvertently shoved him off the platform just as the train began to move, and he felt himself falling toward the tracks and, very possibly, to his death beneath the train wheels. Suddenly a strong arm grabbed his coat collar and pulled him back up to the platform. When he turned to thank his rescuer, he recognized the famous, chiseled face of Edwin Booth, older brother of John Wilkes Booth and the most famous actor in the world at the time. Pumping the famous man's hand with emotion and gratitude, young Lincoln declared, "That was a narrow escape, Mr. Booth" and thanked him profusely. Two weeks later, Booth received a letter of commendation from General Adam Bardeau in recognition of his presence of mind and courage, while informing him that the unidentified lad he had pulled from the train tracks happened to be the oldest son of the president of the United States.

Other links binding the Lincolns and the Booths concerned their painful consciousness of illegitimate origins. Lincoln felt personally, perpetually cursed because his mother had been born out of wedlock, while John Wilkes Booth and all of his nine siblings had also entered the world outside the bonds of matrimony. The family patriarch, the British actor Junius Brutus Booth, left his wife behind in London and fled to America with his beautiful mistress, where they produced their talented brood.

Like Lincoln, young Booth felt himself destined for greatness from an early age. When he was fourteen, a Gypsy fortune-teller read his palm and reportedly gasped at his "bad hand." She predicted that the athletic young man would lead a grand, short life but would unavoidably "meet a bad end." His sister Asia Booth remembered that he wrote down the prediction at the time, showed it to his family, and carried it with him for years thereafter.

That cruel prophecy may have influenced Asia to pen a chilling poem about her teenage brother two years later. Supposedly based on a disturbing vision that their mother experienced at the time of John Wilkes's birth and which she frequently discussed with her ten children, the clumsy verses first appeared in June 1854, nearly eleven years before Booth left his decisive mark on history. In retrospect, the speculation as to the baby's fate registers as both haunting and peculiar:

> *Tiny, innocent white baby hand,*
> *What force, what power is at your command,*
> *For evil, or good? Be slow or be sure,*
> *Firm to resist, too pure to endure—*

My God, let me see what this hand shall do
In the silent years we are attending to;
In my hungering Love, I implore to know on this ghostly night
Whether 'twill labour for wrong, or right,
For—or against Thee?

While never positioning himself as consciously for or against God, Booth did develop an early interest in politics, at age sixteen playing an active role in organizing Maryland's Know-Nothing Party—a radical anti-immigrant movement that Lincoln always despised.

Booth also harbored strong feelings about slavery that differed radically from the attitudes of Lincoln. Growing up on the Maryland farm owned by his theatrical family, he aspired to the manners and style of a southern gentleman. Though his scandalous origins and actor's vocation gave him only tenuous access to the aristocracy, he enthusiastically embraced the outlook of the plantation class, describing the institution of "African slavery" as "one of the greatest blessings (both for themselves and for us) that God ever bestowed upon a favored nation." Here he echoed the "this favored land" construction employed by Lincoln in his First Inaugural Address, but to very different purpose.

His writings also suggest that he shared with Lincoln a sense of himself as a significant, preordained tool in service to an implacable, inscrutable destiny. Writing in his diary after the assassination, he averred: "I struck for my country and that alone. A country groaned beneath this tyranny and prayed for this end.... Our country owed all her troubles to him, and God simply made me the instrument of his punishment."

Initially he had hoped that the punishment he planned would serve a real-world purpose. For several months in the summer and fall of 1864 he schemed to kidnap the president rather than to kill him. The idea involved rushing the captured Lincoln from Washington into Rebel territory in Virginia, where the plotters could hold him hostage until Federal authorities agreed to release many (if not all) of the two hundred thousand Confederate prisoners of war then suffering in Northern jails. The evidence suggests that Booth traveled all the way to Montreal for a meeting with agents of the Confederate secret service, who apparently approved of his plot.

Using a fatal combination of charisma and money, he recruited a half dozen Southern sympathizers to help him execute his grand and flamboyantly theatrical scheme. The reelected president scheduled a visit to Ford's Theatre on January 18, and Booth meant to invade his box in the midst of the play with at least five accomplices. They would bind and gag the struggling Lincoln, then lower him onto the stage and carry him out through a side door into a waiting wagon. In his calculations, Booth confidently assumed that the thousand members of the theater audience would feel too stunned by the daring abduction to get out of their seats to stop it.

Fortunately for all concerned, the president canceled his theater plans that night because of a sudden freezing rainstorm, forcing Booth to seethe and scheme for another two months before he got a second chance to apprehend the commander in chief. When he discovered that Lincoln would attend a performance of *Still Waters Run Deep* at the Campbell Hospital just outside the city, the plotters prepared to grab him before he arrived. They would surround his small carriage, subdue the driver, and then gallop away with the kidnapped president lashed to the back of their horses. Booth actually assembled his gang on a desolate, hidden stretch of road and waited in vain for the approach of the presidential carriage. Again, Lincoln frustrated their plans at the last moment when he decided to skip the theatrical performance in order to review a regiment of Indiana volunteers who were returning from the front and to attend a reception in the National Hotel in Washington. Ironically, Booth had recently booked a room for himself in the same establishment.

Embittered by these frustrations and the imminent collapse of the Confederacy, Booth blamed Lincoln for the suffering of the South and made no secret of his loathing for every aspect of the president's existence. "That man's appearance, his pedigree, his coarse low jokes and anecdotes, his vulgar similes, and his policy are a disgrace to the seat he holds," he told his sister.

On March 4, he attended the inauguration and cut a conspicuous figure with his striking good looks, well-tailored clothes, and elegant top hat. Because of the actor's celebrity status, many members of the huge crowd identified him at the Capitol; amazingly, two of the rare surviving photos of the event clearly show Booth's face. He stands in the midst of the dense crowd, jammed onto a ledge overlooking the modest podium. No more than twenty feet away from the commanding figure of the president, he seems to be listening intently as Lincoln delivers his noble speech. Later, Booth snarled to his friend and admirer Samuel Knapp Chester: "What an excellent chance I had to kill the president, if I had wished, on inauguration-day!"

After the capture of Richmond and Lee's surrender, an obsession with the idea of murder began to crowd out any lingering hope that a successful kidnapping could somehow rescue the disintegrating Confederate cause. Booth nourished the notion that killing the three chief figures of the federal executive—the president, vice president, and secretary of state—could throw the Union into chaos and inspire the beleaguered South to new resistance. Like Lincoln under very different circumstances, he waited for fate to send him a sign that would guide his actions.

"GOD AND HIS ANGELS CAME TO MEN IN THEIR SLEEP"

If the end of the war brought dark, desperate ruminations to John Wilkes Booth, the two weeks at the beginning of April amounted to the most fulfilled and joyful days of Abraham Lincoln's difficult life. Senator James Harlan of Iowa perceived a change that seemed soul deep when the president returned from his visit to conquered Richmond. "His whole appearance, poise and bearing had marvelously changed," he reported. "The indescribable sadness which had previously seemed to be an adamantine element of his very being, had been suddenly exchanged for an equally indescribable expression of serene joy as if conscious that the great purpose of his life had been achieved . . . yet there was no manifestation of exultation, or ecstasy. He seemed the very personification of supreme satisfaction. His conversation was, of course, correspondingly exhilarating."

In this new frame of mind, even dreams and omens that would have worried him in the past took on new, more hopeful connotations. Herndon recalled that in their days together in Springfield, Lincoln frequently brooded over "foreboding of his fate" and placed a "somewhat superstitious" value on the messages from his dreams. The future president's law partner remembered that "more than a dozen times" Lincoln told him: "I feel as if I shall meet with some terrible end."

One of the most powerful indications of that grim destiny came to him at a moment of conspicuous public triumph: the night of November 6, 1860, as he learned that he had won the election to his first term as president of the United States. Gathered with other confident Republicans at the state capital in Springfield, they received returns by telegraph till long past midnight and then began celebrating their sweep of northern states that guaranteed Electoral College victory. Fireworks, cannon blasts, and jubilant toasts roused the citizens of the normally quiet town, who for the most part felt too excited by the national victory of their unassuming neighbor to enjoy much in the way of sleep.

Lincoln himself trudged home only in the small hours of the morning and then stretched out on a couch in his bedroom to catch some much-needed rest before his first day as president-elect. Before he could close his eyes he caught sight of a strange vision in the little round mirror that rested atop a bureau on the other side of the room. In that dim light, he saw two faces in the mirror—both of them his own—but one "reflecting the full glow of health and hopeful life" and the other "showing a ghostly paleness." At first he assumed his eyes had played tricks on him after an exhausting day, but each time he stared back at the mirror while struggling for sleep the double image reappeared.

The next day he reportedly discussed the phenomenon with his wife, Mary, who suggested that the two faces signified that he would win two terms, and not just one, as president of the United States. But Lincoln, with the fatalism that shaped his thinking for most of his life, settled upon a less encouraging interpretation. He described his conclusions on several occasions to his longtime legal colleague and trusted bodyguard Ward Hill Lamon, appointed by the president as

U.S. marshal for the District of Columbia. As Lamon recalled in his memoir, Lincoln admitted that the omen from his Springfield bedroom "worried him not a little" and "that he tried to reproduce the double reflection at the Executive Mansion but without success." Yet he remained certain that "the mystery had its meaning, which was clear enough to him. To his mind the illusion was a sign—the life-like image betokening a safe passage through his first term as President; the ghostly one, that death would overtake him before the close of the second."

Lamon specifically recalled a conversation with the president after he learned of his renomination at the Republican convention in Baltimore on June 8, 1864. "His mind then instantly travelled back to the autumn of 1860; and the vanished wraith—the ghostly face in the mirror, mocking its healthy and hopeful fellow—told him plainly that although certain of reelection to the exalted office he then held, he would surely hear the fatal summons from the silent shore during his second term. With that firm conviction, which no philosophy could shake, Mr. Lincoln moved on through a maze of mighty events, calmly awaiting the inevitable hour of his fall by a murderous hand."

Oddly enough, the president seemed to break free of that "firm conviction" of his own impending doom during the last few weeks of his life. He continued to look for meaning in his dreams, but hoped to use those messages for practical purposes. During his stay at army headquarters at City Point, he dreamed of the White House burning, and he sent his wife back to Washington ahead of him to assure himself of the safety of the executive mansion. Earlier, in June 1863, he corresponded with Mary concerning another warning dream he had experienced while she visited Philadelphia with their ten-year-old son. "Think you had better put 'Tad's' pistol away," he wrote. "I had an ugly dream about him."

But his ugliest, most disturbing dream in April 1865 left Lincoln reportedly unperturbed; though he discussed the nightmare with Mary, Lamon, and perhaps a few others, he refused to attach a negative interpretation to it. During the week that culminated with the assassination, Lamon recalls sitting in the White House with the president and his wife and finding Lincoln falling into a "melancholy, meditative mood," speaking in "slow and measured tones" about the importance of dreams. Lamon felt so affected by this portentous discussion that he says he made notes immediately afterward, in order to reproduce as accurately as possible the thinking of the great man in one of their last conversations.

"It seems strange how much there is in the Bible about dreams," the president reflected. "There are, I think, some sixteen chapters in the Old Testament and four or five in the New Testament in which dreams are mentioned. . . . If we believe the Bible, we must accept the fact that in the old days God and His angels came to men in their sleep and made themselves known in dreams."

He went on to describe an arresting vision he had experienced some days earlier, after he "retired very late" to his White House bedroom. He said that "there seemed to be death-like stillness about me. Then I heard subdued sobs, as if a number of people were weeping. I thought I left my bed and wandered downstairs. There the silence was broken by the same pitiful sobbing, but the mourners were invisible. I went from room to room; no living person was in sight, but the same mournful sounds of distress met me as I passed along. It was light in all the rooms; every object was familiar to me; but where were all the people who were grieving as if their hearts would break?"

Determined to find the cause of the mourning, he kept walking till he entered the East Room, where he encountered "a sickening surprise. Before me was a catafalque, on which rested a corpse wrapped in funeral vestments. Around it were stationed soldiers who were acting as guards; and there was a throng of people, some gazing mournfully upon the corpse, whose face was covered, others weeping pitifully. 'Who is dead in the White House?' I demanded of one of the soldiers. 'The President,' was his answer; 'he was killed by an assassin!' Then came a loud burst of grief from the crowd, which awoke me from my dream. I slept no more that night."

Hearing this account, Lamon redoubled his concern over the president's safety. But a few days later Lincoln told him, "Your apprehension of harm to me from some hidden enemy is downright foolishness. . . . In this dream it was not me, but some other fellow, that was killed. . . . As long as this imaginary assassin continues to exercise himself on others I can stand it. Well, let it go. I think the Lord in His own good time and way will work this out all right. God knows what is best."

"MOVING WITH GREAT RAPIDITY TOWARDS AN INDEFINITE SHORE"

Because Ward Hill Lamon first published these reminiscences some twenty years after Lincoln's death, some historians question the reliability of his account of the president's dream of mourning in the White House. But no one challenges the profound importance that Lincoln himself attached to a recurring dream that he experienced on the last night of his life and described to the cabinet on the very morning of the assassination.

He awoke that day—Good Friday—at 7:00 a.m., stepped into his slippers, and read a few pages of the Bible before joining his family for breakfast. He walked over to the War Department to receive the latest telegraphic dispatches; the government expected the imminent surrender of the last Confederate army in the field, with General Sherman's victorious troops in North Carolina pressing hard against the crumbling resistance of General Joseph Johnston. He also met with a line of important visitors who were waiting for him in his office, including Senator John P. Hale of New Hampshire, whom Lincoln had just appointed minister to Spain. The president didn't know that the senator's adored daughter had recently, and secretly, become engaged to the dashing young actor John Wilkes Booth; otherwise Lincoln might well have congratulated him.

At eleven, the president led a cabinet meeting that welcomed General Ulysses S. Grant as its special guest. He had come to Washington to report on Lee's surrender at Appomattox five days before, so the Good Friday meeting took on the air of a celebratory occasion. Several of the cabinet secretaries noted at the time that Lincoln appeared especially engaged, forceful, and optimistic. Secretary of War Stanton remembered the president as "grander, graver, more thoroughly up to the occasion than he had ever seen him." Frederick Seward attended the session in place of his father, Secretary of State William Seward, who had been badly injured in a carriage accident and rested at home. Young Seward reported that each member of the cabinet expressed "kindly feeling toward the vanquished, and hearty desire to restore peace and safety at the South, with as little harm as possible to the feelings or the property of the inhabitants."

As the discussion unfolded, cabinet members asked Grant about the latest news from General Sherman in North Carolina, and the commanding general told them he expected word momentarily of the final Confederate surrender. Lincoln then interjected to Grant: "Well, you *will* hear very soon now, and the news will be important." When the general asked how the president could be so sure of the outcome, Lincoln answered: "Because I had a dream last night; and ever since the war began, I have invariably had the same dream before any important military event occurred." He then mentioned Antietam, Gettysburg, Vicksburg, and other decisive engagements, and described the dream in which "he seemed to be in some singular, indescribable vessel" that was "moving with great rapidity towards an indefinite shore." Since the familiar dream always signaled some momentous occurrence with profound impact on the war, he had no doubt as to its meaning this time.

If any of the assembled cabinet secretaries considered it peculiar, or in any way inappropriate, for the president of the United States to put so much stock in the half-conscious images of his sleep, they maintained a respectful silence. After all, the same president had previously spoken to the same cabinet about bargaining with God to prevail at Antietam.

At the conclusion of the session, Grant took the president aside to express regrets that he and his wife, Julia, would be unable to join the Lincolns at Ford's Theatre that evening for a performance by the celebrated English actress Laura Keene in an uproarious comedy called *Our American Cousin*. While honored by the invitation, the Grants had committed to make a trip to the New Jersey shore to visit their sons. Lincoln understood, and spent part of the day trying to persuade other dignitaries to join his theater party. In the end, he settled for the daughter of a New York senator named Clara Harris and her fiancé,

Major Henry Rathbone, who had served with conspicuous gallantry in the war.

"WE MUST *BOTH* BE MORE CHEERFUL IN THE FUTURE"

Government offices closed at noon that day to honor Good Friday, but the president discovered that so many papers and petitioners had accumulated in his office that he still found no time for lunch. Instead, he ate a single apple and continued to attend to the people's business before he called a halt to go on a promised carriage ride with Mary. They rode in an open carriage to enjoy the fine, fragrant spring weather and drove to the Navy Yard, where the president got out to chat with sailors aboard a ship that had performed heroically in the assault on Charleston Harbor. As they made their way back toward the city, Mary noted his unusually happy mood.

"Dear Husband, you almost startle me with your great cheerfulness," she offered.

"And well may I feel so, Mary," he replied. "I consider *this day*, the war has come to a close. We must *both*, be more cheerful in the future—between the war and the loss of our darling Willie—we have both been very miserable."

Back at the White House he met with old friends from Illinois, and read to them four chapters from *The Nasby Letters*, a popular work of scathing humor by journalist David Ross Locke. Written in the voice of "Reverend Petroleum Vesuvius Nasby," a cowardly, scurrilous, hard-drinking blowhard who defended slavery and the Confederate cause, Locke's work gave Lincoln enormous pleasure with its parody of his implacable opponents. Dinner had been planned early because of the president's theater plans, but the White House attendants had to summon Lincoln four times before he finally said goodbye to his guests. "I'd much rather swap stories than eat," he said.

At dinner, together with Robert and Tad, Mary began complaining of a headache and wondered whether they should cancel their night out. But Lincoln noted that the presidential appearance at Ford's Theatre had been announced in the morning papers and "the people expected it." His closest associates had urged him not to go out to see the play. Lamon, who had been dispatched by the president on a special mission to Richmond over the weekend, pleaded with him to "promise me you will not go out at night while I am gone, particularly to the theatre." Lincoln, who regularly dismissed concerns over his personal safety, only guaranteed that "I promise to do the best I can toward it."

One of his other bodyguards, W. H. Crook, also urged the president to stay at the White House on that evening. Lincoln had previously spoken with him about three different occasions on which he suffered through assassination dreams similar to the one described to Lamon, and Crook offered to accompany him to the theater as extra security. Noting that his hardworking protector had been on the job since eight that morning, the president urged him to go home, even though his replacement, John Frederick Parker, proved more than two hours late showing up for his shift. When Lincoln and his wife boarded their carriage for the short ride to the play, the president turned to his bodyguard and said, "Good-bye, Crook." This registered at the time as odd and disturbing, since Lincoln habitually parted with the words "Good night, Crook."

W. H. Crook eventually spent fifty years serving eleven more presidents as a White House guard, but this farewell remained the most vivid moment in his career. "It was the first time that he neglected to say 'Good Night' to me and it was the only time that he ever said 'Goodbye.' I thought of it at that moment and, a few hours later, when the news flashed over Washington that he had been shot, his last words were so burned into my being that they can never be forgotten."

"USELESS, USELESS"

The presidential party arrived at the theater at eight-thirty with the play already in progress. Actors and audience, who had been expecting the commander in chief, happily interrupted the proceedings to stand and cheer the Lincolns as they made their way to the specially decorated, flag-draped, second-story box. The orchestra, prepared for the occasion, struck up the rousing ruffles and flourishes of "Hail to the Chief."

Bodyguard John Frederick Parker, arriving just in time to make the trip to Ford's Theatre with the president and his lady, took up his assigned station at the back door to the presidential box. Naturally bored, and unable to hear much of the play, he took advantage of the intermission to visit a nearby tavern for some welcome refreshment with Lincoln's coachman. It's unclear whether he ever returned to the theater. He later told family members and federal authorities that the president had released him early from duty, allowing John Wilkes Booth to make his way through the corridors and stairways of the theater (where the famous actor was known to all) and to burst in on the president unimpeded. After the assassination, Parker faced charges for "neglect of duty," but judges dismissed the complaint in June 1865.

For Booth, Parker's absence represented a major stroke of luck—one of many that enabled him to fulfill his deadly intentions. On Friday morning, April 14, he left his room at the National Hotel near Capitol Hill to pick up his mail at Ford's Theatre. While there, he chatted with one of the proprietors, who proudly informed him that the president would attend the performance of *Our American Cousin* that night.

This represented the circumstantial signal—the encouragement of fate—that Booth had waited to receive. He promptly resolved to use the occasion to kill the president, to avenge the suffering of the South, and, he hoped, to rally the remnants of the Confederacy to rise in fresh resistance. He knew the play intimately and planned to shoot Lincoln at the point of the biggest laugh line in the comedy, when audience guffaws might help cover the noise of murder.

He calculated 10:15 as precisely the right moment, and then ordered his two followers, George Atzerodt and Lewis Powell, to make their assigned strikes at the same time. According to Booth's plan, Atzerodt would murder Vice President Andrew Johnson in his hotel room just as Powell slaughtered Secretary of State Seward at home, where he was recuperating from his carriage accident. The idea of coordinated timing—deadly attacks on different targets at precisely the same moment—of course represents a hallmark of modern terrorism, and highlights the obvious terroristic intent of the Good Friday attacks. As it happened, only Booth himself completed his bloody task: Atzerodt lost his nerve and never confronted Johnson at all, while Powell knifed Seward savagely and repeatedly but failed to kill him. The secretary of state wore a metal brace on his lower face to help heal the broken jaw from his carriage accident, and it deflected most of Powell's stabs, saving Seward's life.

At Ford's Theatre, Booth waited for the designated moment and reveled in the most spectacular role he had ever played. The president only intermittently enjoyed the play; relaxing in the walnut rocking chair specially provided to him, he frequently dozed off, as he often did during public performances that ran late in the evening. His wife grabbed his hand to keep him at least somewhat attentive and looked over at the senator's young daughter and her beau seated in the chairs beside them. "What will Miss Harris think of my hanging on to you so?" she whispered.

"Why, she will think nothing of it," he replied.

According to most biographers, these passing sentiments constituted Lincoln's last words.

But another account, given directly by Mary Lincoln to a Springfield pastor some seventeen years later, also deserves consideration, and provides a more evocative and meaningful finale to the president's conscious life. Leading Lincoln scholars such as Allen Guelzo and Wayne Temple consider the later recollection of the president's wife as most likely reliable. The curator of the Abraham Lincoln Presidential Library in Springfield, Dr. James Cornelius, has also suggested that "we believe the words to be substantiated." In *Lincoln's Battle with God*, Stephen Mansfield argues that the touching spiritual sentiments that Mary Lincoln remembered most certainly conformed to the deepening religious faith that played an incontestably powerful role in the president's final years.

According to his wife's testimony on the subject, Lincoln leaned toward Mary and spoke directly into her ear so as not to disturb the others during the play. "We will visit the Holy Land, and see those places hallowed by the footsteps of the Savior," the president reportedly promised. "There is no place I so much desire to see as Jerusalem."

Within seconds of Lincoln's expression of these sentiments, Booth lunged forward from the shadows at the rear of the box and fired the .44-caliber Derringer "pocket cannon" into the back of the president's head from a distance of less than a foot. Lincoln slumped forward immediately as the single bullet lodged right behind his eye; he never regained consciousness.

Booth, as planned, pushed to the edge of the second-story box after slashing with his dagger at Major Rathbone, who tried to stop him. He then leapt onto the stage nearly twelve feet below, an acrobatic maneuver he had made famous with similarly spectacular entrances in some of his most popular productions. This time, however, the spur on his riding boot caught on the bunched flag at the front of the box, and he landed with a painful injury—breaking the fibula in his lower leg—before making his escape. Though some contrarian accounts suggest that he actually injured himself later in the course of his flight from pursuers, contemporaries as well as subsequent generations welcomed the notion that Old Glory herself—in the form of a decorative Treasury Guard flag—intervened to slow the fleeing assassin.

Twelve days later, federal troops surrounded him in a Virginia tobacco barn. His accomplice David Herold agreed to surrender (he was later hanged), but Booth continued to resist, even as the soldiers set the barn ablaze. When Booth kept moving around inside the burning building, a sergeant named Boston Corbett spotted him in the midst of the flames and took a shot. The bullet struck the assassin in the neck, piercing three vertebrae and partially severing his spinal cord. Dragged to the porch of a nearby farmhouse, he died three hours later at the break of day. In his final moments he reportedly pleaded with the soldiers around him to "tell my mother I died for my country." After that, his last words count as an uncontested verdict on his life. "Useless, useless," he said.

In Washington, Lincoln lingered longer, with his powerful frame surviving for nine hours after the bullet entered his brain. A twenty-three-year-old army surgeon named Charles A. Leale had been in the audience for *Our American Cousin* and rushed to the wounded, unconscious president in his box. At first he thought Lincoln had already died, but after finding a faint pulse and performing artificial respiration, he directed volunteers who gently carried the president across Tenth Street to the home of a tailor. In a narrow room at the back of the first floor he lay diagonally across a bed notably too short for him. The leading physicians of the city gathered there in the course of the long, damp, misty night, and all concluded that death was inevitable and imminent. Political allies from Congress and the cabinet also circulated through the jammed, gaslit backroom, along with Lincoln's oldest son, Robert, who sobbed aloud. They crowded the low, too-small bed in hopes of hearing some immortal last words from the president, but he neither woke nor stirred. At several points he seemed to stop breathing, producing an awful, guttural, choking sound, before the end came at 7:22 on Saturday morning. "It is all over," the physicians informed the hysterical Mary Lincoln. "The president is no more."

At the foot of the bed, Secretary of War Stanton solemnly, tearfully intoned his final benediction. "Now he belongs to the ages," he reportedly proclaimed—though some sources suggest that he actually said, "Now he belongs to the angels," and found himself misunderstood for the next 150 years.

"WE GAIN A NATIONAL MARTYR"

Either way, no one could mistake the overwhelming nature of the national mourning that followed the president's death. The next day, Easter Sunday, began Lincoln's transformation from mortal leader to sacred symbol. In sermons across the country, pastors and priests noted the president's death on Good Friday and saw in the tragedy the elements of redemptive sacrifice. A preacher in New York City declared, "We gain a national martyr. May we not have needed this loss." Lincoln's story as a man of humble background, constant sorrows, and abiding kindness served to encourage this messianic understanding of his life and his death. The well-circulated accounts of his publicly discussed premonitions of his own death deepened the supernatural aura surrounding the tragic events.

Nearly everyone in Washington joined the huge crowds that came to honor him as he lay in state in the East Room of the White House—just as his recent dream had anticipated. Even more citizens crowded the Capitol when his casket occupied the rotunda. During the thirteen-day journey back to Springfield, an estimated seven million Americans either lined the tracks to watch the train as it passed or else viewed the coffin in the cities where it stopped; this represented nearly a third of the population of the Northern states that Lincoln led during the war. The crowds along the route displayed hand-lettered signs that declared THE DARKEST HOUR IN HISTORY or HE LIVES IN THE HEARTS OF HIS PEOPLE. In a single day in Philadelphia, 150,000 people waited in line to see his remains. One black mourner in Pennsylvania declared, "He was crucified for us."

By the time of his burial at Oak Ridge Cemetery in Springfield some twenty days after the assassination, he had become, truly, the "Redeemer President." Walt Whitman had originated that phrase in an uncannily prophetic political tract from 1856, at a time when neither Whitman nor his countrymen knew anything of the obscure country lawyer in Illinois. Nonetheless, the poet expressed the national need for a "Redeemer President of These States" who would arise from "the real West, the log hut, the clearing, the woods, the prairie, the hillside." The poet declared that he would be "much pleased to see some heroic, shrewd, fully-formed, healthy-bodied, middle-aged, beard-faced American blacksmith or boatman come down from the West across the Alleghenies, and walk into the Presidency, dressed in a clean suit of working attire, and with the tan all over his face, breast and arms."

From the time he watched Lincoln's arrival in New York City, Whitman recognized that his longed-for redeemer had arrived. He hailed the president-elect for a "religious nature" that was "of the amplest, deepest-rooted, loftiest kind." In sum, he saw in Lincoln "the greatest, best, most characteristic, artistic, moral personality" in American life.

Not surprisingly, after the assassination Whitman became obsessed with "the tragic splendor of his death, purging, illuminating all." His poem "O Captain! My Captain!" gained instant fame around the world, and made reference to the already famous dream Lincoln had described to his cabinet about riding a fast-moving ship to an unknown destination.

> *My Captain does not answer, his lips are pale and still*
> *My father does not feel my arm, he has no pulse nor will,*
> *The ship is anchor'd safe and sound, its voyage closed and done*
> *From fearful trip the victor ship comes in with object won;*
> *Exult O shores, and ring O bells!*
> *But I with mournful tread,*
> *Walk the deck my Captain lies*
> *Fallen cold and dead.*

In 1890, two years before his own death, Whitman still saw the era of Lincoln's presidency and the immeasurable horror of the assassination as the defining American experience. "I hope to be identified with the man Lincoln, with his crowded, eventful years," he wrote, "with America as shadowed forth into those abysms of circumstances. It is a great welling up of my emotion sense: I am commanded by it."

PUNISHMENT FROM PROVIDENCE RATHER THAN PROTECTION

The commandment to come to terms with the Lincoln miracle applied first to Lincoln himself: he strained constantly to understand his role as a tool of the divinity that had long nourished and protected the American experiment. It is easy to see a beneficent providence steering his unlikely ascent: Lincoln alone possessed the gifts, the depth of soul and intellect, to bring about a successful conclusion to the nation's most devastating conflict. In his contribution to a fascinating 1960 collection of essays called *Why the North Won the Civil War*, David M. Potter of Yale and Stanford gives Lincoln's leadership the most conspicuous credit. He writes that "it hardly seems unrealistic to suppose that if the Union and the Confederacy had exchanged presidents with one another, the Confederacy might have won its independence."

But if Lincoln's astonishing rise supports the old idea of divine favor toward the American Republic, how does his heartbreaking fall conform to this traditional sense of providential protection? If you credit a higher power for the blessing of Lincoln's life, how can you fail to blame that deity for the curse of his untimely death?

Yes, his illogical elevation to the presidency at a moment of unparalleled peril may seem unnatural, even *supernatural*. But bizarre coincidences also surrounded the sad, squalid details of his murder. The Booth and Lincoln families interacted in several significant ways before the assassination; on the last morning of his life the president met cheerfully with the father of his assassin's fiancée. Had Lincoln somehow survived the mad conspiracy to take his life, he surely would have probed for a message from God in the nature of the violence against him.

The timing of that violence struck his contemporaries as altogether extraordinary: in the week of his transcendent triumph, at the very moment that his wounded nation needed him for the looming task of Reconstruction, Lincoln disappeared abruptly from the scene. Had he only respected his wife's raging headache and canceled the theater party, or enjoyed the protection of a dutiful, sober bodyguard rather than a tippling young slacker, he might have survived the assassin's evil plots and added immeasurably to the nation's greatness. The random factors that came together to allow Booth to succeed in his evil errand suggest punishment from providence rather than protection.

Yet the context of the president's death indicates that his survival to that point in his life might reflect divine intervention in his behalf more than his ultimate slaying proved its absence. On nearly a dozen occasions since his 1860 election victory he managed to escape unharmed from serious efforts to murder him. Booth himself organized two different expeditions to kidnap Lincoln but saw these schemes thwarted through last-minute changes in the presidential schedule. The assassin also stalked the commander in chief while the war still raged, approaching within pistol range at the president's second inauguration and then again at the last speech from the White House balcony.

Other threats came even closer to success. Before his first inauguration, the president-elect received scores of death threats that ranged from the usual methods (bullets, stabbing, lynching, stoning) to the exotic (poisoned ink and spider-filled dumplings). First-class detective work by Scotsman Alan Pinkerton, who later organized Union intelligence during the Civil War, discovered a credible plot by supporters of secession to murder the would-be "tyrant" as the presidential train passed through Baltimore on the way to the capital city. Secret agents foiled those plans by spiriting Lincoln into town in the middle of the night, and in disguise, hours in advance of his publicly announced schedule.

Other plans against him included the "Yellow Fever Plot" of 1863, in which a prominent Kentucky physician (and later governor of the state) tried to infect him with the dread disease by presenting a gift of fine dress shirts that had been used by dying patients and deliberately contaminated. Later, explosives expert Thomas Haney, a sergeant with the Confederate Torpedo Bureau, received an order to somehow penetrate the White House to blow up the dining room while the Lincolns relaxed at dinner. After careful preparation, he made his nervous way toward the executive mansion to complete his mission when an Illinois cavalry unit detained him by chance and then made their arrest.

On July 2, 1864, the president once more came close to death. Visiting Fort Stevens just outside of Washington, he stood on a parapet and watched with fascination as Jubal Early's Confederate raiders launched a desperate attack. He borrowed a spyglass from a signal officer who remembered that the towering president "stood there with a long frock coat and plug hat on, making a very conspicuous figure." Another officer standing next to Lincoln took a shot in the leg and fell, seriously wounded, after which an ordinary soldier roughly ordered the commander in chief to "get down or he would have his head knocked off." The incident represents the closest exposure of any president of the United States to enemy fire while in office.

During sweltering summer months, the Lincolns generally sought refuge from the stifling confines of the White House in a quaint cottage at the Soldiers' Home, a facility for military retirees in the countryside just outside the city. On a humid night in August 1864, after working late at the executive mansion, the president rode alone on his horse to his summer residence. As he slowed his pace and approached the entrance to the Soldiers' Home, a rifle shot from fifty yards away startled his mount, which immediately took off at what Lincoln described as "break-neck speed [which] unceremoniously separated me from my eight-dollar plug hat, with which I parted company without any assent, express or implied."

He arrived at the Soldiers' Home close to eleven o'clock. When Private John W. Nichols noticed the president was "bareheaded" and asked after the missing top hat, Lincoln casually mentioned the rifle shot and the sudden lunge of his frightened mount that "jerked his hat off."

The next day, Nichols and another solider searched for the missing headpiece and found it with a bullet hole shot straight through it, just inches above where the president's forehead would have fit inside. When presented with the evidence, Lincoln marveled at his close escape but explained that "I can't bring myself to believe that any one has shot or will deliberately shoot at me with the purpose of killing me; although I must acknowledge that I heard this fellow's bullet whistle at an uncomfortably short distance from these headquarters of mine." He suggested that the true origin of the nearly fatal bullet came from a hunter who "fired off his gun as a precautionary measure of safety to his family after reaching his house."

Whatever the true nature of the incident, Lincoln ordered Private Nichols to say nothing about it because "no good can result at this time from giving it publicity." Nonetheless, Secretary Stanton almost certainly heard of the pierced plug hat and immediately ordered additional protection for the president. Mounted, well-armed troops now rode along with the chief executive's carriage when he traveled back and forth between the White House and the Soldiers' Home.

That detachment succeeded in turning away a separate well-planned effort by the Confederate secret service to kidnap Lincoln and hold him for ransom. A preacher, professor, and volunteer spy named Thomas Nelson Conrad, accompanied by his loyal slave William and two partners, slipped through the Federal lines and established themselves in Washington for three months. The team of four finally made their attempt to intercept the president's carriage on a country road outside of town but galloped away at the sight of the heavy guard. Conrad reported to his superiors that his mission resulted in "humiliating failure," but after the war he won appointment as the third president of Virginia Agricultural and Mechanical College—later known as Virginia Tech.

The record of nearly perpetual danger that surrounded the sixteenth president throughout his term of office indicates extraordinary good luck, or preordained protection, that allowed him to survive as long as he did. He died just five days after Lee's surrender granted him the definitive victory that had become the all-consuming purpose of his life. He had achieved, at last, "the serene joy" that Senator Harlan described and had become "the very personification of supreme satisfaction."

For his mourning fellow countrymen who searched for supernatural meaning in his sudden death, this sense of a mission accomplished suggested an angelic dimension. In the Hebrew Scriptures, the most common word for "angel" is *malakh*—literally translated as "messenger" or "one who is sent." Ancient interpretations suggest that such members of the heavenly host come to Earth only for the purpose of specific, limited errands, and then return to the Almighty. If Secretary Stanton did actually bid farewell to his fallen chief by declaring, "Now he belongs to the *angels*," he perhaps spoke more meaningfully than he realized.

"NATIONALITY BECOMES EVEN A KIND OF RELIGION"

While Lincoln's death deprived the nation of his leadership, the timing of that loss served an important public purpose.

As Frederick Douglass hopefully observed: "It may be that the blood of our beloved martyr President will be the salvation of our country." After the death of some seven hundred thousand Americans in an incomparably catastrophic conflict, both sides embraced the hope that the fallen president should represent the final casualty of the war. In her fascinating 2015 book *Mourning Lincoln*, Martha Hodes of New York University notes that the horror of the assassination managed to unite the recently warring regions in their public expressions of grief—even if some in the South feigned or exaggerated their signs of sorrow to avoid retribution and advance their own interests. Nonetheless, many recent Confederates sincerely regretted Lincoln's removal from the scene and looked wistfully at his expressed wish to treat the former rebels with mercy and to "let them down easy." One North Carolina planter commented: "Old Abe with all his apeishness, was a kind-hearted man and disposed to treat us generously." Walt Whitman noted that the sacred meaning of Lincoln's death "belongs to these States in their entirety—not the North only, but the South—perhaps belongs most tenderly and devotedly to the South." In the searing national grief, he saw "a cement to the whole people, subtler, more underlying, than any thing written in constitution, or courts or armies."

Astonishingly, the magnitude of the loss only strengthened the long-standing national belief in divine supervision of the nation's destiny. As historian Mark A. Noll observed, the preachers and religious thinkers of the time "almost universally ... maintained the long-treasured axiom that the United States had enjoyed, and would continue to enjoy, a unique destiny as a divinely chosen people. The war, they held, had decisively reconfirmed this calling."

As an example, Charles Hodge of Princeton Theological Seminary declared that "the first and most obvious consequence of the dreadful civil war just ended, has been the final and universal overthrow of slavery within the limits of the United States. This is one of the most momentous events in the history of the world. That it was the design of God to bring about this event cannot be doubted."

Touching similar themes, one of the leading theologians of the era, Reverend Horace Bushnell, delivered an impassioned address at Yale on July 26, 1865, to honor alumni who had perished in the recently concluded struggle. "The story of this four years' war is the grandest chapter, I think, of heroic fact, and tragic devotion, and spontaneous public sacrifice, that has ever been made in our world," he declared. "So the unity now to be developed, after this war deluge is over, will be no more thought of as a mere human compact, or composition . . . but it will be that bond of common life which God has touched with blood; a sacredly heroic, Providentially tragic unity, where God's cherubim stand guard over grudges and hates and remembered jealousies, and the sense of nationality becomes even a kind of religion."

That distinctly American faith in the mission of the nation took even stronger hold as the people emerged from the shadow of war. As Lincoln died on Good Friday and rose to the status of holy martyr on Easter Sunday, so too the United States would rise from the charnel house of mass slaughter to shining new life. At Gettysburg, the president prayed for a "new birth of freedom." Within weeks of his death, his countrymen saw the nation itself as born again.

On the Glorious Fourth of 1865, less than three months after the assassination, John Williamson Nevin, a prominent seminarian in Pennsylvania, delivered a soaring Independence Day address at Franklin and Marshall College. "Our national deliverance has been wrought out for us, as a world-historical act, by God himself," he declared. "The past stands pledged for the prosperity of what is still to come. God has done great things for us, whereof we are glad; and this, itself, is our best reason for believing that he will do for us, still greater things hereafter."

As he confidently predicted, "He will not forsake the work of his own hands."

"SO EXTRAORDINARY AS TO EXCITE ASTONISHMENT": The original flag that flew over Maryland's Fort McHenry and inspired Francis Scott Key to compose his patriotic verses on September 13, 1814.

"Blest with vict'ry and peace, may the heav'n rescued land praise the power that hath made and preserv'd us a nation." —*The Star Spangled Banner,* Francis Scott Key

13

"THIS FAVORED LAND"

America Is No Accident

Since the days of the Pilgrims, leaders of the new society that arose in the New World have embraced the core concept of a divinely determined destiny. For nearly four hundred years, Americans nourished the notion that God maintained an intimate, protective connection to their singular nation. Only recently, with the emphasis on guilt over gratitude in our teaching of history, has the public grown uncomfortable with the idea that fate favors American endeavors. Today, the merest suggestion that the Almighty plays favorites among the nations of the world strikes contemporary sensibilities as offensive, outrageous, or at least controversial.

Much of that controversy involves a fundamental misunderstanding of the old idea of divine providence in the rise of the Republic. It confuses the reality of American exceptionalism with fantasies about American perfectionism. To argue that a higher power directed the United States to a unique and valuable role in the world isn't the same as insisting that our national saga unfolded without flaw, folly, or failure. The confidence that this nation has been distinctively blessed doesn't mean that it's been exclusively blessed—or that it has provided an unmitigated blessing to each citizen, or to all nations, at every moment in its history.

Today, every schoolchild learns of the consistently tragic mistreatment of the continent's native inhabitants and the brutal exploitation of African slaves, along with countless other examples of Americans falling far short of the founders' high ideals. Of course, integrity demands attention to these dark chapters, but it also requires an appropriate sense of balance. This book focuses on the freakish good fortune and the prodigious good deeds of the United States not as a way to obscure our sins but in order to restore the missing context for consideration of such shortcomings. The founders and builders of this remarkable Republic believed deeply in heavenly favor for their efforts, and the stories told here show that they were neither deluded nor devilish in harboring this conviction. In fact, the preceding pages ought to make clear that many of the most notable personalities in the early history of the country—Franklin, Adams, Jefferson, Madison, Hamilton, Jackson, Houston, and especially Lincoln—enjoyed something like the gift of prophecy.

These stories of prescience and public service don't portray such giants as spotless heroes any more than they expose the United States as an immaculate country. The evidence for divine providence doesn't prove that America is perfect, but it does strongly suggest that America is no accident. An isolated instance of fortunate coincidence or eerie congruence may count as an anomaly. But a long chain of seemingly haphazard but consistently beneficial occurrences suggests something else entirely—a pattern or, more accurately, a design.

And whose design do we credit for America's emergence?

As the preceding accounts demonstrate beyond dispute, the founders whom we honor for the blueprints that served us so splendidly believed with unanimous and unwavering confidence in a larger scheme in which they played a part. They couldn't always make out the contours and details of that master plan, but they never doubted its existence. An honest examination of the nation's origins and development doesn't demonstrate the power of randomness or chance nearly as much as it makes the case for purpose and intent.

A year before the Declaration of Independence officially launched the American experiment, the Continental Congress in Philadelphia emphasized supernatural guidance that had brought the colonies to the verge of nationhood. A formal declaration "Setting Forth the Causes and Necessity of Their Taking Up Arms" proudly hailed the "perfect legislatures" and the "amazing increase of the wealth, strength and navigation" in North America, which counted as "so extraordinary, as to excite astonishment."

It didn't win new fans in England that the Americans reveled in these advantages as a gift from God, rather than as a contribution from their earthly king. In this ringing proclamation of July 6, 1775 (coauthored by Thomas Jefferson), the representatives of the "United Colonies" unhesitatingly acknowledged "as signal instances of the Divine favour towards us, that his Providence would not permit us to be called into this severe controversy, until we were grown up to our present strength, had been previously exercised in warlike operation, and possessed of the means of defending ourselves." At the very beginning of the world-shaking events of the Revolution, these proud patriots affirmed the idea that a divine designer had deliberately engineered the American miracle.

In the next struggle against the motherland, a new anthem sounded similar notes and rallied flagging spirits in the War of 1812. "The Star-Spangled Banner," scribbled by Francis Scott Key while he was held prisoner on a British man-of-war, praised the noble character of "the land of the free and the home of the brave." But its final verse (alas, seldom heard today) also acknowledged the creator of that character:

> *Blessed with vict'ry and peace, may the heav'n-rescued land*
> *Praise the power that hath made and preserv'd us a nation*
> *Then conquer we must when our cause it is just*
> *And this be our motto: "In God is our trust."*

Cynics might insist that the British enemy (the "foe's haughty host" as condemned in Key's lyric) also invoked the deity in their own well-loved anthem, "God Save the King." But that song celebrates the monarch as personification of the tribe ("Send him victorious / Happy and glorious / Long to reign over us") and makes the plea that he should prevail over tribal enemies. American patriotic songs, on the other hand, consecrate the nation as an ideal ("and crown thy good / with brotherhood") or at least an idea, open to anyone who chooses to adopt the national creed. After all, a cantor's son named Irving Berlin emigrated from Russia as a small boy, then produced "God Bless America" as an eve-of-war gift to the "land that I love" and specifically asked for divine direction ("stand beside her / And guide her"), not just favor.

This distinction illuminates an irreducible difference between American exceptionalism and the conviction of all other peoples on Earth that their own heritage counts as worthwhile and special. President Obama and other avatars of enlightened opinion may equate our distinctive nationalism with "British exceptionalism and Greek exceptionalism," but that equation ignores the fact that America alone bases identity on ideas and values more than on birthplace and bloodline. Foreign observers from Alexis de Tocqueville to Josef Joffe have joined homegrown enthusiasts in recognizing the United States as a vehicle chosen by fate for promoting goodness and human advancement far beyond its borders.

So, too, tens of millions of intrepid souls from every corner of the Earth have staked their lives on the unshakable belief that God himself prepared America as a land of refuge and new life. Whatever our current doubts about the nation's present and its prospects, this sense of a divinely directed destiny is never more than a generation or two in the past. Immigrants of every era have sensed something magical, preordained, and powerful in their risky journeys to the New World. For those who choose to begin again in this nation of fresh starts, America can never be an accident. My Ukrainian grandparents certainly felt something purposeful and supernatural in their difficult journey to these shores, just as surely as they recognized the idea that their own marriage, which somehow survived the death of five children and other unimaginable hardships, counted as *beshert*—inevitable, fated, part of the cosmic plan.

IMPOSSIBLE TO WRITE OFF
MINOR MIRACLES

In that same tradition, Americans still commonly recognize the impact of fate or good fortune in shaping their most important relationships. In moments of reflection and candor, most of us will acknowledge elements in life-changing bonds such as marriage that transcend our conscious choice or control. A chance meeting may alter everything, producing offspring and, eventually, grandchildren, impacting a family's future for generations. Even in this age of spreading skepticism, most of us still see the force of destiny operating in our private lives. Why, then, deny the power of providence in the life of our country?

In my case, my personal history helps to inform my sense of our national history. Through an improbable, unexpected, and profoundly lucky combination of circumstances, I stumbled into the most consequential encounter of my existence nearly thirty-three years ago. On an autumn afternoon in 1983, I went to the beach near my home in Santa Monica, California, to clear my mind and get some exercise by splashing in the chilly Pacific. The only other person in the water on that particular stretch of beach looked to be body-surfing, and when I recognized a female form I paddled over on my boogie board to attempt a conversation.

My opening line fell somewhere between clunky and cunningly contrived. "What do you do that allows you to come to the beach on a Tuesday afternoon?" I asked.

The girl answered that she was a writer and a psychologist, and I initially dismissed her as a typical Californian who dabbled in unproduced screenplays. When, however, she described her two published books and I spoke about my own work, she startled me by saying, "Oh, then you're Michael Medved, aren't you?"

It turns out that she had reviewed one of my books for the *Los Angeles Times*—a review that I remembered for its snarky punch lines. We then bantered back and forth about the theme of her first book: *Children: To Have or Have Not?*, which, she said, helped to confirm her inclination never to have kids. "But you're so young," I presumptuously offered. "I'm sure you'll change your mind someday." (As it turned out, the only way I could convince her about the importance of children was to father them with her.) When we met again a few days later, we already felt connected and involved, and we married a bit more than a year later.

It's a preposterous story that reminds me of the fragility of fate every time I think of it. What if I hadn't gone to the beach that afternoon? Or if I'd plunged into the waves an hour earlier or an hour later? We wouldn't have met that afternoon, or perhaps ever. Or what if she hadn't picked out my book from a big, messy pile of recent releases available to writers at the *L.A. Times* and then penned her entertainingly nasty review? Would I have felt the same uncanny sense of connection that seemed to push us together with a force we could neither understand nor control?

After celebrating thirty-one anniversaries and raising three children to adulthood, it's impossible for us to write off the minor miracle of our meeting as random or accidental. From the beginning, the link felt planned and purposeful. It's true that I can't prove the role of destiny in my marriage, but I can't doubt it, either.

Most married couples reach similar conclusions, of course. No one can feel absolute certainty that one union or another fits into a predetermined, eternal scheme, but spouses who believe that their connection was meant to be will naturally treat that bond more respectfully, even reverently. It stands to reason that a match made in heaven enjoys a better chance of survival here on Earth. The conviction that a marriage matters in some ultimate sense, and that it's based on more than ephemeral feeling and convenient coincidence, can help to overcome the strains that inevitably afflict even the happiest couples.

The same logic applies to the old and precious American idea that the country's grandeur reflects intention more than accidents. Just as faith in God-made matches makes for better marriages, so faith in a God-made nation makes for a better nation. The deep devotion that has characterized the citizenry in every generation expresses not just appreciation of America's greatness and goodness but confidence that the national experiment represents God's will in history. In his provocative 2007 book *Americanism: The Fourth Great Western Religion*,

Yale professor David Gelernter notes that "the American Religion incorporates the biblical ideas of a chosen people in a promised land. Those concepts are the source of America's (sometime) sense of divine mission; of her (not invariable but often powerful) feeling of obligation to all mankind; of her democratic chivalry—her nagging awareness of a duty to help the weak against the strong. This 'chivalry' has nothing to do with knights and ladies; it is a deep sense of duty to the suffering."

"A GENIUS FOR GREAT AND UNSELFISH DEEDS"

That unique vision of our abiding national purpose has impressed countless observers around the world, including those with only limited connection to the United States. Shortly after the global horrors of World War II, Pope Pius XII pronounced his own benediction. "America has a genius for great and unselfish deeds," he declared. "Into the hands of America God has placed the destiny of an afflicted mankind."

To critics of the United States, this sense of global mission is dangerous, not divine. The British journalist Clifford Longley, for instance, wrote the essay "The Religious Roots of American Imperialism" in 2002. He condemned "imperialists" who "implacably believed they were doing good, fulfilling God's will, even when they were actually doing harm . . . Nations who believe they are 'chosen' are a potential threat to others. . . . Indeed, in the extreme case, the Chosen People status can grow into a condition of zealous religious nationalism that is potentially fascistic."

In America's case, however, even the most commonly derided examples of "imperialist adventures"—in Cuba and the Philippines at the turn of the last century, or Korea, Vietnam, Iraq, and Afghanistan more recently—never resulted in permanent conquest or colonization. The most telling indictment of American foreign policy over the last century has been not the list of bloody foreign wars that enriched the nation or expanded its power but the list of bloody foreign wars, undertaken for idealistic motives, that actually may have damaged the nation's interests. Overseas involvement of the United States frequently relied on religious rhetoric that emphasized America's divinely designated role in the world, but those missions demanded national sacrifice far more often than they resulted in national gain.

Americans have always understood the generous blessings showered upon their Republic as imposing special responsibilities rather than conferring special privileges. The intimate involvement of the Almighty in establishing and sustaining the United States confronted America with an obligation to conduct herself more nobly than other nations, not an authorization to behave more selfishly or recklessly. In his Farewell Address, George Washington urged his countrymen to "observe good faith and justice toward all nations; cultivate peace and harmony with all. Religion and morality enjoin this conduct; and can it be, that good policy does not equally enjoin it? . . . Can it be that Providence has not connected the permanent felicity of a nation with its virtue?"

Washington emphasized the connection between providential protection and virtue in foreign affairs, but the same logic applies even more forcefully to the nation's conduct regarding its own inhabitants. The idea of America's higher purpose didn't produce the instances of obvious injustice in the Republic's past, nor did it excuse them, but it has inevitably motivated efforts to correct those crimes and to mitigate their negative and unjust impacts.

Every nation on Earth flagrantly mistreated indigenous peoples and participated at some point in ruthless systems of slavery. But the American desire to deserve God's special blessing inspired movements to do better than the rest of the world and to overcome the cruelty—however halting and imperfect those attempts might have been. The abolitionists who campaigned for decades to liberate enslaved Africans frequently cited the evidence of divine favor toward the United States not as the basis for tolerating the "peculiar institution" but as a reason to demand its immediate elimination. After World War II, the commonly accepted concept of America as a symbol of hope and a nation of destiny didn't result in justification or amnesia regarding the harsh, senseless internment of Japanese Americans following Pearl

Harbor. Within a generation, President Reagan signed into law a formal apology with the payment of compensation. Viewing the rise of our country as a divinely directed American miracle doesn't mean the United States counts as flawless. What it does signify is that we're specially called to correct our flaws, and to strive more consciously toward justice and decency than other societies.

ACCOUNTABILITY MORE THAN ARROGANCE

Confidence in divine providence, in other words, fosters accountability more than arrogance. Whenever we've fallen short, the stubborn conviction that the Almighty expects better has spurred efforts toward redemption.

Writing in 2014, David Adesnik of the American Enterprise Institute provided important perspective on widespread misunderstandings regarding American exceptionalism. "Exceptional does mean better in important ways, although these exceptional traits long coexisted with shameful ones, such as one century of slavery and another of segregation," he wrote. "Critics often stumble on the complexity of this point, unable to comprehend how the United States can claim unique virtues if it also committed terrible acts of oppression. They fail to understand how the virtues embodied in the Founding ultimately subverted the forces of oppression."

In response to such arguments, cynics could reasonably insist that the usefulness of a notion hardly proves its validity. The idea of heavenly partiality toward America and Americans could qualify as nothing more than a convenient fiction. The fact that the nation clearly benefited from its much-trumpeted confidence in such favor doesn't mean that it ever actually existed.

But that acknowledgment still leaves contemporary observers with a difficult struggle to provide alternative explanations for America's unprecedented, remarkable run of good fortune. The assumption that it's nothing more than dumb, blind luck doesn't add up; if the breaks operate on behalf of a particular party over more than three centuries, then that luck looks neither dumb nor blind. If fortunate coincidences form a consistent pattern over a broad sweep of history, then there's an indication of something more at work. As previously observed, a pattern of happy accidents is still a pattern.

"A BARGAIN WITH THE DEVIL"

The rejection of deliberate design in our unique history leads inevitably to the twin traps of conspiracy theories and disdain for America, both increasingly popular elements in contemporary culture.

Following the unexpected death of seventy-nine-year-old Supreme Court justice Antonin Scalia in February 2016, Anne Applebaum marveled at the sudden explosion of dark speculation regarding his demise. "In its essence, a conspiracy theory is the modern equivalent of a myth: It's a story that people tell to explain otherwise inexplicable events. The appeal of conspiracy theories is so deep because the human need for meaning is so profound," she wrote in the *Washington Post.* "The human brain is designed to reject the random, the haphazard, the arbitrary. It's just too much for many people to accept that accidents happen, planes crash, ships founder on the rocks and elderly people die in their sleep: A dramatic event must fit into a larger narrative."

Without the narrative of America's providential progress embraced by the founders and nearly all their successors, anxious citizens seek meaning and comprehension in malevolent schemes by the Illuminati, the Bilderbergers, the Skull and Bones Society, or the 1 percent and their dreaded "new world order."

This same need to find a plausible explanation for painful and perplexing present circumstances brings many fearful souls at home and abroad to endorse the grandest conspiracy theory of them all: that the United States of America, as the planet's only surviving superpower, seized control of the international order through its corrupt and oppressive ruthlessness. Instead of the old idea of America as the predestined benefactor of all mankind, this new vision sees the Republic as the planet's chief source of resource rape and human suffering. It views the obvious advantages of the United States as so many ill-gotten gains, not the product of distinctive blessings from destiny or the Deity.

Shelby Steele of Stanford's Hoover Institution identified the origins of this worldview in "a bubble of post-'60's liberalism" that alleged that "America's exceptional status in the world follows from a bargain with the devil—an indulgence in militarism, racism, sexism, corporate greed, and environmental disregard as the means to a broad economic, military and even cultural supremacy in the world. And therefore America's greatness is as much the fruit of evil as of a devotion to freedom." Yet even this ferocious resentment couldn't ignore the persistent centrality of the United States in twenty-first-century civilization. As Dr. Steele wrote in September 2011: "Our national exceptionalism both burdens and defames us, yet it remains our fate. We make others anxious, envious, resentful, admiring and sometimes hate-driven. There's a reason al Qaeda operatives targeted the U.S. on 9/11 and not, say, Buenos Aires. They wanted to enrich their act of evil with the gravitas of American exceptionalism. They wanted to steal our thunder."

In the years since that attempted theft, many worry that the nation's enemies may yet succeed in robbing America of its blessing and its birthright. Even those who accept the thought that the United States once enjoyed a covenant with an all-powerful Protector now fear that fate no longer operates in our favor.

Similar anxieties have afflicted the populace for many generations. After the Martin Luther King Jr. and Robert Kennedy assassinations in the tumultuous, tragic spring of 1968, the novelist John Updike solemnly informed an interviewer that God must have "withdrawn his special blessing for America." But after two decades of struggles, stumbles, and surprisingly consequential leadership, the United States and its Western allies achieved a stunningly complete and completely unexpected victory in the Cold War, and optimistic observers proclaimed the "end of history." If past patterns play out, current proclamations of disaster and decline may look similarly inappropriate and premature.

Nevertheless, many of the serious voices in the nation's current conversation sing arias of gloom and apocalypse, and expect no more miracles in the years ahead. Steve McCann at the *American Thinker* website, a successful businessman, naturalized citizen, and unfailingly elegant writer, offered a column to follow the Fourth of July in 2015 whose title baldly proclaimed: "The United States Is a Dying Country." He followed this funereal pronouncement seven months later with another cheerless dispatch: "The United States at the Point of No Return." Even my friend Peggy Noonan, the marvelous columnist and former White House speechwriter, seems to have signed on to the present mood of disillusionment and doom. Writing in February 2016 about the political rise of Donald Trump and Bernie Sanders, she notes that "we are in some kind of moment" and then invokes the famous formulation of the "Iron Chancellor," Otto von Bismarck: "In Washington there used to be a widespread cliché: 'God protects drunks, children and the United States of America.' I'm in Washington a lot, and I've noticed no one says that anymore."

"ACCORDING TO ALL HUMAN REASONING, A GREAT FUTURE"

But should Americans abandon their long-standing faith in providential protection? In the face of terrorist threats, the stagnation of middle-class incomes, and a polarizing political process that seems for the moment both grating and degrading, to depend on supernatural deliverance would seem childish and naive. Yet our forebears faced circumstances far less favorable while holding fast to the expectation that destiny would rescue and renew the Republic.

After eight years of ceaseless bloodshed and devastating economic dislocation, the American Revolution produced an estimated twenty-five thousand American deaths through battlefield casualties, civil strife, and rampaging epidemics in the cities and countryside. As a percentage of the population, an equivalent body count today would come to more than 2.6 million. Yet as we've seen, the survival of the thirteen colonies, and their ultimate emergence into the United

States, left the citizens who endured all the destruction with no doubt that a higher power had worked his will among them.

In similar terms, the unimaginable horrors of the Civil War only served to confirm the nation's sense of purpose in fulfilling the will of the Almighty. The slaughter and suffering of the conflict may shock the modern conscience but somehow never shook the firm faith of Americans that their unique nation remained specially blessed.

Those who survived found profound purpose, even glory, in what Lincoln called "the fiery trial through which we pass." In the summer of 1865, German and Swiss Americans who had staunchly supported the victorious Union cause gathered at the German seminary in Mercersburg, Pennsylvania, to hear the renowned theologian Philip Schaff address them in their native tongue. In translation, his words declaimed: "A country where so many streams of noble blood have flowed, where so many sacrifices were offered by the government and the people, and where the hand of God so visibly and wonderfully guided events to a happy end—must have, according to all human reasoning, a great future. It has passed through the trial of fire and has now entered into the maturity of manly strength and self-sufficiency."

That confidence in glories yet to come had taken hold with such force in the years following the war for the Union that the phrase "this favored land" assumed its place as part of the popular lexicon of everyday Americans. Deployed by Lincoln in his First Inaugural Address in 1861 (as he called for "a firm reliance on Him who has never yet forsaken this favored land"), it also echoed Andrew Jackson's Farewell Address of twenty-four years before (in which he noted that "Providence has showered on this favored land blessings without number"). In June 1888, the description of the United States of America as "this favored land" made perhaps its most celebrated appearance—in a newspaper poem by a twenty-four-year-old bard describing the single most disappointing at-bat in the history of baseball:

Oh, somewhere in this favored land the sun is shining bright;
The band is playing somewhere, and somewhere hearts are light,
And somewhere men are laughing, and somewhere children shout;
But there is no joy in Mudville—mighty Casey has struck out.

Young Ernest Thayer's final stanza mixed pathos and humor in a way that any American of the era could understand: despite the mourning in Mudville due to the team's heartbreaking, bottom-of-the-ninth loss, no one could doubt that even that stricken (and fictional) village would soon resume its place in "this favored land," complete with light hearts and tuneful bands.

America at the moment may be Mudville: depressed by fleeting distractions, discouraged by TV news concerning economic and political setbacks, appalled at the latest crop of candidates for high office, but still privileged to constitute the world's most favored nation-state and to boast an overwhelmingly optimistic populace. According to Gallup and other prominent polling organizations, big majorities of Americans believe that the nation at large is headed in the wrong direction, but even larger majorities express satisfaction in their own lives. Since economic recovery from the Great Recession began in 2009–10, upward of 80 percent of respondents say they are "very satisfied" or "somewhat satisfied" with their personal situation in the world. A 2016 survey for *USA Today* showed that a commanding 68 percent of young people below the age of thirty-five express confidence they will enjoy greater success than their parents—with even higher numbers among blacks and Latinos.

In other words, despite the dire attitudes among politicians and pundits about the big-picture state of the Union, when citizens look at the world from a more private perspective they see reason to believe that the country in which they actually live out their lives will continue to enjoy the blessings of providence.

"WAKE UP AND SNAP OUT OF IT"

That doesn't mean that we should look for flashy miracles just over the horizon. Like Americans of prior generations, we'll find it difficult to spot signs of divine intervention until history has already moved past the moment of deliverance. This understanding rests on a firm scriptural basis: in Chapter 33 of the Book of Exodus, just before following the Lord's instruction and carving the second tablets of the law, Moses asks God, "Show me now your glory."

But despite the favor the Almighty feels for the man described in the text as the "servant of God," he denies the request. "He said, 'You will not be able to see My face, for no human can see Me and live.' God said, 'Behold! There is a place near Me; you may stand on the rock. When My glory passes by, I shall place you in a cleft of the rock; I shall shield you with My hand until I have passed. Then I shall remove My hand and you will see My back, but My face may not be seen'" (Exodus 33:20–23).

One traditional understanding for this elusive and mystical passage involves the role of the Almighty in history: no one can see God face-to-face as he participates in the events of the moment. But we can view the "back" of the Lord as he passes through time. As Bismarck noted in a similar spirit: "The statesman's task is to hear God's footsteps marching through history, and to try and catch on to His coattails as He marches past."

In the modern era of democratic participation and mass communication, it must be the task of the citizen as well as the statesman to listen for God's footsteps. And that perspective should make the American miracle unmistakable, impossible to miss.

A dictionary definition of "miracle" describes "an extraordinary event manifesting divine intervention in human affairs." The rise of the American Republic qualifies on all counts. As Pulitzer Prize–winning historian Walter A. McDougall unforgettably framed the issue: "The creation of the United States of America is the central event of the past four hundred years." And as the eighty-one-year-old sage Benjamin Franklin observed at the Constitutional Convention: "And if a sparrow cannot fall to the ground without his notice, is it probable that an empire can rise without his aid?"

With that well-earned certainty that "he who made the world still governs it" (in Lincoln's phrase), Americans of today should regain our bearings. Historian Victor Davis Hanson notes that "a nation's health is not gauged by bouts of recession and self-doubt, but by its time-honored political, economic, military and social foundations. A temporarily ill-seeming America is nevertheless still growing, stable, multiethnic, transparent, individualistic, self-critical, and merito-cratic; almost all of its apparently healthy rivals are not." Hanson observes that "America typically goes through periodic bouts of neurotic self-doubt, only to wake up and snap out of it."

David Gelernter similarly urges his countrymen to recapture a sense of their identity and their history: "That is who we are: a biblical republic, striving to live up to its creed. The dominion of ignorance will pass away like smoke and we will know and be ourselves again the moment we choose to be. Why not now?"

WITH GRATITUDE . . .

The publication of this book provides special reasons for gratitude. Naturally, I'm thankful to have completed the task of writing it, but I feel even more grateful to have overcome the cancer that recently put the project in jeopardy.

In mid-December 2014 a routine visit to the dentist's office resulted in a diagnosis of stage 3 throat cancer (appropriate, somehow, for a professional radio host) and led to a course of treatment that included eight weeks of radiation and chemotherapy.

In that context, I first need to thank, publicly and profusely, my dental hygienist, Shirley Stettler, in the office of Dr. Robert Gelb in Bellevue, Washington, whose care for her patients and sharp eyes led her to notice something odd on the side of my neck. That resulted in my timely treatment under the supervision of two outstanding physicians: Dr. Gary Goodman, my oncologist, and Dr. Vivek Mehta, my radiation oncologist, both of Swedish Medical Center in Seattle. With all the talk of trouble in our national health care system, my own experience proved an American miracle of compassion and competence. Thanks to the staff at Swedish, I've been cancer free for nearly a year and managed to return to daily broadcast and to my fascinating and fulfilling work on this book.

One nurse in particular also played a conspicuous role in my recovery: Richelle Braunstein Medved married my wonderful son, Danny, at a joyous family celebration at the end of August 2014, and barely a hundred days later she faced the burden of a seriously sick father-in-law. While dutifully completing her RN (and then, later, her BSN), she gave tirelessly of her time and her healing skill. Alongside Danny and my wife, Diane, she literally camped out at the hospital during the weeks I was there and assisted immeasurably with every aspect of my care. Our daughters, Shayna and Sarah, and my brothers, Harry and Jonathan, also interrupted their busy lives to rally to my support. I've already tried to express appreciation to all my family members, but it ought to be repeated here as part of the milestone of publication.

And when it comes to enabling my continuing radio work, in sickness and in health, all credit goes to my broadcast partners, senior producer Jeremy Steiner ("Pride of Hillsdale College"), associate producer Greg Tomlin ("Rock Star Greg"), and substitute host David Boze. Dave, my talk show colleague and fast friend, did a magnificent job guest-hosting my show during most of the eleven weeks I had to miss; no one else in the radio-TV universe could have come as close to capturing both the style and the substance that I try to convey every day. Mark Davis of Dallas also stepped in to cover for me with exemplary professionalism and skill. As to Jeremy and Greg: I think of both of them as kid brothers more than producers, and Jeremy in particular eased me back to work as quickly as possible with the love and brilliance he's daily displayed in the twenty years we've been privileged to work together.

My executive assistant, Karmen Frisvold, similarly helped to keep my world operating smoothly while I couldn't supervise it personally: a real achievement that she balanced with her own adorable infant son, Keller. She also participated in gathering research for this book, as well as securing visual imagery and arranging the sourcing of each chapter. Mark Giuliano, a virtual member of our family for nearly a decade, also provided first-rate research assistance in time he could steal from his law school education, while his beloved father, the late Dr. Tom Giuliano, inspired me with his courage in facing cancer and offered invaluable medical care and advice.

Unexpectedly, I received additional inspiration from listeners and readers whom I never have met but who reached out to me from every corner of the country. I read all of the e-mails, letters, and cards that came in by the tens of thousands during the recovery period, and I'm appreciative for each one of them. I'd also like to thank all the friends, and friendly strangers, who remembered me in their prayers. I not only believe in the power of prayer but felt it personally. I can't prove that it worked on my body, but I know how powerfully it worked on my spirit.

At my publisher, Crown Forum, I was privileged to once again benefit from my superb editor, Mary Reynics, who provided encouragement, understanding, and crucial guidance in helping this book find its form—until interrupted for the arrival of her own first child, Joseph. During her maternity leave, the formidable David Kopp took over and provided sage advice, with the help of intrepid editorial assistant Julia Elliott. Tina Constable, publisher of Crown Forum, has been passionately supportive of this project from the beginning. And my agent, Richard Pine, has now worked with me for (gulp!) more than forty years, and a total of thirteen books. Why not forty more years?

And speaking of that idea, I'd need at least that much time to express my appreciation to my partner in everything, Dr. Diane Medved. She not only played the primary role in enabling my recovery but also barely left my side until I managed to struggle back to normal life. She postponed progress on her own sixth book to help with proofreading, rewriting, and incomparably insightful advice on *The American Miracle*. Combining brilliance, beauty, grace, humor, strength, faith, and limitless energy and generosity of spirit, she remains the most magnificent human being I've ever been fortunate enough to encounter. As the preceding pages make clear, a pattern of happy accidents is still a pattern, and I perpetually praise the patterns that brought us together more than thirty years ago. I look forward to all the fresh chapters that await our continued collaboration.

Seattle, April 2016

SOURCES

CHAPTER 1: THE GLORIOUS FOURTH

BOOKS

Bigelow, John F., George B. Cheever, and Wilbur Fisk Tillett. *The Hand of God in American History*. Nashville: Cokesbury, 1923. Kindle edition, 2014.

Ellis, Joseph J. *First Family: Abigail and John Adams*. New York: Random House, 2010.

Hitchens, Christopher. *Thomas Jefferson: Author of America*. New York: HarperCollins, 2005.

Kaplan, Fred. *John Quincy Adams: American Visionary*. New York: HarperCollins, 2014.

McCullough, David. *John Adams*. New York: Simon & Schuster, 2001.

McDougall, Walter A. *Freedom Just Around the Corner*. New York: HarperCollins, 1983.

Meacham, Jon. *Thomas Jefferson: The Art of Power*. New York: Random House, 2010.

Raynor, L. M. *Life of Thomas Jefferson*. Boston: Lilly, Wait, Colman & Holden, 1834.

Webster, Daniel. *Speeches and Forensic Arguments.* Boston: Perkins and Marvin, 1830.

ARTICLES

Battin, Margaret P. "July 4, 1826: Explaining the Same-day Death of John Adams and Thomas Jefferson." *Historically Speaking,* July/August 2005.

Butterfield, L. H. "July 4 in 1826." *American Heritage Magazine,* June 1955.

Cohen, Richard. "The Myth of American Exceptionalism." *Washington Post,* May 9, 2011.

"A Date with Destiny? The Thomas Jefferson–John Adams Anomaly." *Macronicity* blog, May 8, 2013.

Edel, Charles N. "A Realist in the White House." *Wall Street Journal,* December 12, 2014.

Guelzo, Allen C. "Democracy and Nobility." *Weekly Standard,* January 12, 2015.

Romano, Andrew. "Oliver Stone in the Tyranny of Obama's 'Exceptional' America." *Daily Beast,* October 17, 2013.

Soloveichik, Meir. "God's Providence and the United States: A Thanksgiving Reader on Judaism and the American Idea." Rabbi Elchanan Theological Seminary, December 2014.

"The Story of the Fourth of July." ConstitutionFacts.com, retrieved September 28, 2014.

"What's So Great About America." *Wall Street Journal,* November 15, 2010.

SPEECHES

Coolidge, Calvin. "Inaugural Address." Washington, D.C., March 4, 1925.

Washington, George. "First Inaugural Address." New York, April 30, 1789.

INTERVIEWS

McDougall, Walter A. Interview in the *Washington Post*, April 26, 2004.

CHAPTER 2: BLOWN BLESSEDLY OFF COURSE

BOOKS

Bunker, Nick. *Making Haste from Babylon.* New York: Random House, 2010.

Gragg, Rod. *The Pilgrim Chronicles: An Eyewitness History of the Pilgrims and the Founding of Plymouth Colony.* Washington, D.C.: Regnery, 2014.

Hodgson, Godfrey. *A Great and Godly Adventure.* New York: PublicAffairs, 2006.

Mann, Charles C. *1491: New Revelations of the Americas Before Columbus.* New York: Vintage Books, 2006.

Marshall, Peter, and David Manuel. *The Light and the Glory.* Grand Rapids, MI: Baker Book House, 1977.

Miller, Perry. *Errand into the Wilderness.* New York: Harper & Row, 1956.

Morgan, Edmund S. *The Founding of Massachusetts.* New York: Bobbs-Merrill, 1964.

ARTICLES

Gaskill, Malcolm. "The Pilgrims Are Us." *Wall Street Journal,* November 29/30, 2014.

CHAPTER 3: REVOLUTIONARY REVELATIONS

BOOKS

Bobbrick, Benson. *Angel in the Whirlwind: The Triumph of the American Revolution.* New York: Simon & Schuster, 1997.

Commager, Henry Steele, and Richard B. Morris. *The Story of the American Revolution as Told by Participants.* New York: Da Capo, 1958.

Hibbert, Christopher. *Redcoats and Rebels: The American Revolution Through British Eyes*. New York: Avon Books, 1990.

Kidd, Thomas S. *God of Liberty*. New York: Basic Books, 2010.

McCullough, David. *1776*. New York: Simon & Schuster, 2005.

Palmer, Dave R. *George Washington's Military Genius*. Washington, D.C.: Regnery, 2012.

Scheer, George F., and Hugh F. Rankin. *Rebels and Redcoats: The American Revolution Through the Eyes of Those Who Fought and Lived It*. New York: Da Capo, 1957.

Wood, W. J. *Battles of the Revolutionary War: 1775–1781*. New York: Da Capo, 1995.

CHAPTER 4: INDISPENSABLE, INDESTRUCTIBLE

BOOKS

Barton, David. *The Bulletproof George Washington*. Aledo, TX: Wall-Builder Press, 1990.

Brookhiser, Richard. *George Washington: Founding Father*. New York: Simon & Schuster, 1996.

Flexner, James Thomas. *Washington: The Indispensable Man*. New York: Back Bay Books, 1974.

Freeman, Douglas Southall. *Washington*. New York: Collier Books, 1968.

Larson, Edward J. *The Return of George Washington*. New York: Harper-Collins, 2014.

Lillback, Peter A. *George Washington: Sacred Fire*. Bryn Mawr, PA: Providence Forum Press, 2006.

Novak, Michael, and Jana Novak. *Washington's God*. New York: Basic Books, 2006.

Randall, Willard Sterne. *George Washington: A Life*. New York: Henry Holt, 1997.

CHAPTER 5: "AN ASSEMBLY OF DEMIGODS"

BOOKS

Bowen, Catherine Drinker. *Miracle at Philadelphia: The Story of the Constitutional Convention, May to September 1787.* New York: Back Bay Books, 1986.

Cheney, Lynne. *James Madison: A Life Reconsidered.* New York: Viking, 2014.

Chernow, Ron. *Alexander Hamilton.* New York: Penguin Books, 2005.

Collier, Christopher, and James Lincoln Collier. *Decision in Philadelphia: The Constitutional Convention of 1787.* New York: Ballantine Books, 1986.

Hamilton, Alexander, John Jay, and James Madison. *The Federalist: A Commentary on the Constitution of the United States.* New York: Modern Library, 1941.

Lefer, David. *The Founding Conservatives: How a Group of Unsung Heroes Saved the American Revolution.* New York: Sentinel, 2013.

Meese, Edwin, III. *The Heritage Guide to the Constitution.* Washington, D.C.: Regnery, 2005.

Thach, Charles C. *The Creation of the Presidency.* Baltimore: Johns Hopkins Press, 1969.

Vile, John R. *The Constitutional Convention of 1787: A Comprehensive Encyclopedia of America's Founding.* Santa Barbara, CA: ABC-CLIO, 2005.

ARTICLES

Jeter, Derrick G. "Founding Father's Friday: Daniel of St. Thomas." DerrickJeter.com, July 5, 2013.

TRANSCRIPTS

Franklin, Benjamin. "Request for Prayers at the Constitutional Convention." July 28, 1787.

CHAPTER 6: PROVIDENTIAL PURCHASE

BOOKS

Burgan, Michael. *The Louisiana Purchase.* Mankato, MN: Compass Point Books, 2002.

Cerami, Charles A. *Jefferson's Great Gamble: The Remarkable Story of Jefferson, Napoleon and the Men Behind the Louisiana Purchase.* Naperville, IL: Sourcebooks, 2004.

Din, Gilbert C., and John E. Harkins. *The New Orleans Cabildo: Colonial Louisiana's First City Government 1769–1803.* Baton Rouge: Louisiana State University Press, 1996.

Furstenburg, François. *When the United States Spoke French.* New York: Penguin Press, 2014.

Handlin, Oscar. *Chance or Destiny: Turning Points in American History.* Boston: Little, Brown, 1954.

Hitchens, Christopher. *Thomas Jefferson: Author of America.* New York: HarperCollins, 2005.

Kluger, Richard. *Seizing Destiny.* New York: Random House, 2007.

McDougall, Walter A. *Freedom Just Around the Corner.* New York: HarperCollins, 1983.

Meacham, Jon. *Thomas Jefferson: The Art of Power.* New York: Random House, 2010.

Robert, Andrew. *Napoleon: A Life.* New York: Viking, 2014.

ARTICLES

Hamilton, Alexander. "Purchase of Louisiana." *New York Evening Post,* July 1803.

CHAPTER 7: AMERICAN AGINCOURT

BOOKS

Arthur, Stanley Clisby. *The Story of the Battle of New Orleans.* Henderson, NV: HardPress, 2012.

Brands, H. W. *Andrew Jackson: His Life and Times*. New York: Doubleday, 2005.

Drez, Ronald J. *The War of 1812, Conflict and Deception: The British Attempt to Seize New Orleans and Nullify the Louisiana Purchase*. Baton Rouge: Louisiana State University Press, 2014.

James, Marquis. *The Life of Andrew Jackson*. New York: Bobbs-Merrill, 1938.

Meacham, Jon. *American Lion: Andrew Jackson in the White House*. New York: Random House, 2008.

Meyers, Marvin. *The Jacksonian Persuasion: Politics and Belief*. Stanford, CA: Stanford University Press, 1960.

Remini, Robert V. *The Battle of New Orleans: Andrew Jackson and America's First Military Victories*. New York: Penguin, 1999.

Smith, Elbert B. *Magnificent Missourian: The Life of Thomas Hart Benton*. Philadelphia: Lippincott, 1938.

Ward, John William. *Andrew Jackson: Symbol for an Age*. New York: Oxford University Press, 1962.

ARTICLES

McWilliams, James. "How the Battle of New Orleans Birthed the American Character." *New Yorker*, January 8, 2015.

"September 4, 1813: Andrew Jackson in a Gun Fight." Pastnow.word press.com, September 4, 2013.

"Ursulines of New Orleans. Arrival of Postulants from France a Century Ago. Our Lady of Prompt Succor. The Battle of New Orleans." *Records of the American Catholic Historical Society of Philadelphia*, volume 23.

CHAPTER 8: "BIG DRUNK" AND LONE STAR LUCK

BOOKS

Fehrenback, T. R. *Lone Star: A History of Texas and Texans*. Boulder, CO: Da Capo, 2000.

Lester, Charles Edwards. *The Life of Sam Houston.* New York: J. C. Derby, 1855.

William, Davis C. *Lone Star Rising: The Revolutionary Birth of the Texas Republic.* New York: Free Press, 2004.

Yoakum, Henderson K. *The History of Texas from Its First Settlement in 1685 to Its Annexation to the United States in 1846.* Charleston, SC: Nabu Press, 2011.

ARTICLES

"Battle of San Jacinto." Texas State Library, tsl.texas.gov, retrieved August 25, 2015.

"San Jacinto, Battle of." Texas Historical Association, tshaonline.org.

"'This Glorious Achievement': Thomas J. Rusk's Account of the Battle of San Jacinto." Daughters of the Republic of Texas Library at the Alamo, drtlibrary.wordpress.com, April 30, 2010.

LETTERS

Rusk, Thomas Jefferson. "Official Report of the Battle of San Jacinto." Head Quarters Army of Texas, April 22, 1836.

CHAPTER 9: GOLDEN TIMING

BOOKS

Brands, H. W. *The Age of Gold: The California Gold Rush and the New American Dream.* New York: Anchor, 2003.

Crocker, H. W., III. *Don't Tread on Me: A 400-Year History of America at War, from Indian Fighting to Terrorist Hunting.* New York: Crown Forum, 2006.

Greenberg, Amy. *A Wicked War: Polk, Lincoln and the 1846 U.S. Invasion of Mexico.* New York: Vintage Books, 2012.

Haynes, Sam W., and Christopher Morris. *Manifest Destiny and Empire: American Antebellum Expansionism.* College Station: Texas A&M University Press, 1997.

Hittell, John S. *Bancroft's Pacific Coast Guide Book.* San Francisco: A. L. Bancroft, 1822.

———. *Discovery of Gold in California.* New York: Century, 1891.

———. *Mining in the Pacific States of North America.* New York: John Wiley, 1862.

Howe, Daniel Walker. *What Hath God Wrought: The Transformation of America, 1815–1848.* New York: Oxford University Press, 2007.

Kluger, Richard. *Seizing Destiny.* New York: Random House, 2007.

Merry, Robert W. *A Country of Vast Designs.* New York: Simon & Schuster, 2009.

Ohrt, Wallace. *Defiant Peacemaker: Nicholas Trist in the Mexican War.* College Station: Texas A&M University Press, 1997.

Singletary, Otis A. *The Mexican War.* Chicago: University of Chicago Press, 1960.

ARTICLES

Donlick, Edward. "Kickoff Time for the Forty-Niners." *Wall Street Journal,* August 9/10, 2014.

SPEECHES

Hittell, John S. "Marshall's Gold Discovery." Lecture delivered to the Society of California Pioneers, San Francisco, January 24, 1893.

CHAPTER 10: THE MIRACLE OF LINCOLN

BOOKS

Burlingame, Michael. *The Inner World of Abraham Lincoln.* Champaign: University of Illinois Press, 1994.

Donald, David Herbert. *Lincoln.* New York: Simon & Schuster, 1995.

Egerton, Douglas R. *Year of Meteors: Stephen Douglas, Abraham Lincoln, and the Election That Brought on the Civil War.* New York: Bloomsbury, 2010.

Epstein, Daniel Mark. *Lincoln and Whitman: Parallel Lives in Civil War Washington.* New York: Random House, 2004.

Mansfield, Stephen. *Lincoln's Battle with God: A President's Struggle with Faith and What It Meant for America.* Dallas: Thomas Nelson, 2012.

Shenk, Joshua Wolf. *Lincoln's Melancholy: How Depression Challenged a President and Fueled His Greatness.* New York: Houghton Mifflin, 2005.

Thomas, Benjamin P. *Abraham Lincoln, a Biography.* New York: Alfred A. Knopf, 1952.

White, Ronald C., Jr. *A. Lincoln: A Biography.* New York: Random House, 2009.

ARTICLES

Guelzo, Allen C. "Abraham Lincoln and the Doctrine of Necessity." *Journal of the Abraham Lincoln Association* 18, no. 1 (1997).

"People & Ideas: Abraham Lincoln." PBS.org, retrieved November 5, 2015.

CHAPTER 11: WAITING FOR A SIGN

BOOKS

Catton, Bruce. *The Army of the Potomac: Mr. Lincoln's Army.* New York: Doubleday, 1962.

The Century Illustrated Monthly Magazine. New York: Scribner, April 1909.

Cowley, Robert. *What Ifs? of American History.* New York: Berkley Books, 2004.

Donald, David Herbert. *Lincoln.* New York: Simon & Schuster, 1995.

———. *Why the North Won the Civil War: Six Authoritative Views on the Economic, Military, Diplomatic, Social, and Political Reasons Behind the Confederacy's Defeat.* New York: Simon & Schuster, 1996.

Hodes, Martha. *Mourning Lincoln.* New Haven, CT: Yale University Press, 2015.

McPherson, James M. *Battle Cry of Freedom: The Civil War Era.* New York: Oxford University Press, 2003.

Turtledove, Harry. *How Few Remain: A Novel of the Second War Between the States.* New York: Del Rey, 1997.

ARTICLES

"The Lost Orders." National Park Service, NPS.gov, retrieved February 23, 2016.

Piper, John. "Abraham Lincoln's Path to Divine Providence." Desiring God.org, February 12, 2008.

"Religious Quotations by Abraham Lincoln." AbrahamLincolnOnline .org, retrieved February 22, 2016.

Steber, Beth. "The Lost Document That Changed the Course of American History: How Robert E. Lee's Secret Civil War Battle Plans Were Found Wrapped Around Cigars Under a Locust Tree—and Ended Up in Union Hands." Associated Press, September 15, 2012.

Sullivan, Christopher. "Did Battle, and US Future, Hang on Thread of Fate?" Associated Press, September 15, 2012.

SPEECHES

Lincoln, Abraham. "Address to the New Jersey State Senate." Trenton, New Jersey, February 21, 1861.

LETTERS

Lincoln, Abraham. "Letter to Thurlow Weed." Washington, D.C., March 15, 1865.

CHAPTER 12: THE MESSENGER AND HIS MESSAGE

BOOKS

Donald, David Herbert. *Lincoln*. New York: Simon & Schuster, 1995.

Epstein, Daniel Mark. *Lincoln and Whitman: Parallel Lives in Civil War Washington*. New York: Random House, 2004.

Mansfield, Stephen. *Lincoln's Battle with God: A President's Struggle with Faith and What It Meant for America*. Dallas: Thomas Nelson, 2012.

Selzer, Adam. *Ghosts of Lincoln: Discovering His Paranormal Legacy*. Woodbury, MN: Llewellyn, 2015.

Stauffer, John. *Giants: The Parallel Lives of Frederick Douglass and Abraham Lincoln*. New York: Hachette, 2008.

White, Ronald C., Jr. *A. Lincoln: A Biography*. New York: Random House, 2009.

———. *Lincoln's Greatest Speech: The Second Inaugural*. New York: Simon & Schuster, 2002.

ARTICLES

Boyes, Christina. "5 Failed Assassination Attempts on President Lincoln You Didn't Know About." Travel Thru History, travelthroughhistory.tv, February 27, 2015.

Burlingame, Michael. "When Black Americans Lost Their Moses." *Wall Street Journal*, February 6, 2015.

Dreisbach, Daniel. "Lincoln's 700 Words of Biblical Meditation." Liberty Law Site, LibertyLawSite.org, March 4, 2015.

Lepore, Jill. "'Mourning Lincoln' and 'Lincoln's Body.'" *New York Times*, February 4, 2015.

Lozada, Carlos. "Grief, Fear, Glee: How American Reacted to Lincoln's Killing, 150 Years Ago." *Washington Post*, April 1, 2015.

Noll, Mark A. "'Both . . . Pray to the Same God': The Singularity of Lincoln's Faith in the Era of the Civil War." *Journal of the Abraham Lincoln Society* 18, no. 1 (1997).

Reynolds, David S. "Lincoln and Whitman." *History Now: The Journal of the Gilder Lehrman Institute*, GilderLehrman.org, retrieved March 4, 2016.

Stashower, Daniel. "The Unsucessful Plot to Kill Abraham Lincoln." *Smithsonian*, February 2013.

White, Ronald C., Jr. "Lincoln and Divine Providence: Response." *Seattle Pacific University Magazine* 29, no. 3 (2006).

———. "War and the Will of God." *Christianity Today*, August 8, 2008.

Yoder, Edwin M., Jr. "Booth on Stage: Echoes and Memories of the Actor-Assassin." *Weekly Standard*, June 8, 2015.

SPEECHES

Lincoln, Abraham. "Last Public Address." Washington, D.C., April 11, 1865.

———. "Second Inaugural." Washington, D.C., March 4, 1865.

CHAPTER 13: "THIS FAVORED LAND"

BOOKS

Gelernter, David. *Americanism: The Fourth Great Western Religion*. New York: Doubleday, 2007.

Joffe, Josef. *The Myth of America's Decline: Politics, Economics and a Half Century of False Prophecies*. New York: Liveright, 2014.

ARTICLES

Adesnik, David. "Obama, Putin and American Exceptionalism." *inFocus*, Summer 2014.

Applebaum, Anne. "Donald Trump's Campaign of Conspiracy Theories." *Washington Post*, February 18, 2016.

Dickinson, John, and Thomas Jefferson. "A Declaration by the Representatives of the United Colonies of North-America, Now Met in Congress at Philadelphia, Setting Forth the Causes and Necessity of Their Taking Up Arms." July 6, 1775. Government Printing Office 1927, House Document 398.

Gelernter, David. "What Is the American Creed?" *Wall Street Journal*, July 1, 2012.

Guelzo, Allen C. "'That Glorious Consummation': Lincoln on the Abolition of Slavery." Gilder Lehrman Institute, gilderlehrman.org, retrieved February 2, 2016.

Hanson, Victor Davis. "The American 21st Century." Townhall.com, December 30, 2010.

Kissinger, Henry A. "Otto von Bismarck, Master Statesman." *New York Times*, March 3, 2011.

Longley, Clifford. "The Religious Roots of American Imperialism." *Global Dialogue* 5 (Winter/Spring 2003).

McCann, Steve. "The United States Is a Dying Country." *American Thinker,* July 17, 2015.

Noll, Mark A. "'Both . . . Pray to the Same God': The Singularity of Lincoln's Faith in the Era of the Civil War." *Journal of the Abraham Lincoln Society* 18, no. 1 (1997).

Noonan, Peggy. "Trump, Sanders and the American Rebellion." *Wall Street Journal,* February 11, 2016.

Page, Susan, and Jenny Ung. "Poll: Millennials Still Optimistic About Success and the American Dream." *USA Today,* March 14, 2016.

"Satisfaction with Personal Life." Gallup.com, retrieved April 22, 2016.

Steele, Shelby. "Obama and the Burden of Exceptionalism." *Wall Street Journal,* September 1, 2011.

INDEX

Abell, Elizabeth, 278
Adair, John, 168, 171, 172, 175, 180
Adams, Abigail, 4, 6, 12, 52
Adams, Charles Francis, 297
Adams, Henry, 131–132
Adams, John, 2–5, 20, 52, 54, 88, 120, 126, 239, 283–284, 297, 360
  death of, 10–13, 16–18, 24
  Jefferson, Thomas and, 2–4, 6, 8
Adams, John Quincy, 2–4, 6, 10–12, 15–17, 24, 131, 236, 239, 297, 326
Adams, Louisa, 12
Adams, Thomas, 10, 11
Adesnik, David, 367
Agincourt, Battle of, 175
Alamo, the, 213–214, 220, 222, 223
Algonquin Indians, 77
Allen, Robert, 195
"America the Beautiful," 21
Americanism: The Fourth Great Western Religion (Gelernter), 364–365
Ames, Fisher, 143
Andrew Jackson: Symbol for an Age (Ward), 182
Angel in the Whirlwind (Bobrick), 56
Annapolis, Maryland, 91, 92
Antietam, Battle of, 300, 312, 313, 316, 317, 323, 343
Applebaum, Anne, 368
Appomattox Court House, 332, 342

Armstrong, John, 155
Arnold, Isaac, 282
Arnold, Matthew, 164
Arthur, Stanley Clisby, 176
Articles of Confederation, 90–92, 95, 97, 98, 102, 117, 121, 131
Atzerodt, George, 346, 347
Avezac, Louise d', 158

Bacon, Leonard Woolsey, 28
Baines, George Washington, 227
Baldwin, Abraham, 110, 111
Bancroft, George, 20–21
Bangs, Isaac, 52
Barataria Bay pirates, 159–161, 166–168, 180
Barbé-Marbois, François, 135, 138–140, 145
Bardeau, Adam, 335
Bates, Edward, 287, 289, 291, 292, 293
Bates, Katharine Lee, 21
Battin, Margaret P., 16–17
Battle Cry of Freedom (McPherson), 312
Beauharnais, Josephine de, 135, 141
Bedford, Gunning, 103–104
Bell, John, 295
Benedict, Abner, 59–60
Benton, Jesse, 150–152
Benton, Jessie, 152
Benton, Thomas Hart, 150–152, 183
Berthier, Alexandre, 137

Bible, the, 1–2, 9, 24, 31, 52–53, 283, 284, 372–373
Bigler, Henry W., 255
Bill of Rights, 118
Billings, William, 70
Bismarck, Otto von, 370, 373
Black Hawk War, 275, 303
Blair, Francis Preston, 289
Bloss, John McKnight, 309–311
Bobrick, Benson, 55, 56
Bonaparte, Joseph, 137, 142
Bonaparte, Lucien, 137, 142
Bonaparte, Napoleon, 8, 89, 122, 123, 127–140, 141–146, 154, 155, 179, 212, 240, 242
Booth, Asia, 335–336, 337
Booth, Edwin, 335
Booth, John Wilkes, 208, 324, 329, 333–338, 342, 346–348, 352
Booth, Junius Brutus, 208, 335
Borneman, Walter R., 259
Boston, Massachusetts, 30, 50–52, 54
Bowen, Catherine Drinker, 113
Braddock, Edward, 77–82
Bradford, William, 26, 33, 35–37, 39, 40, 45, 47
Brandywine, Battle of, 83
Brannan, Samuel, 256
Breckinridge, John C., 294, 295
Brooklyn, Battle of, 48
Brooklyn, New York, 59, 61, 62, 64–66, 68
Brooks, Noah, 326, 332
Browning, Orville Hickman, 282
Bryant, William Cullen, 287
Buchanan, James, 238, 239, 243, 244–246, 251, 252, 291, 298
Buckner, Alexander, 205
Bull Run, First Battle of, 302
Bull Run, Second Battle of, 308
Bunker, Nick, 31
Bunker Hill, Battle of, 58, 68
Burnet, David, 215, 216, 223
Burns, Robert, 305
Bushnell, Horace, 356–357
Butler, William O., 248

Calhoun, John C., 194, 247
Calvinism, 21, 31, 44
Cameron, Simon, 287, 289, 293
Campbell, James, 111–112
Carpenter, Francis B., 277, 314–315
Carroll, Charles, 3

Carroll, William, 168, 171, 194, 197, 200
Castlereagh, Lord, 154
Casualties
    in Battle of New Orleans, 164
    in Battle of San Jacinto, 220–221
    in Civil War, 308, 312, 355, 370
    in French and Indian War, 80
    in Haiti, 133
    in Napoleonic Wars, 89
    in Revolutionary War, 61, 62, 68
    in War of 1812, 173–175
Catton, Bruce, 308, 311
Cerami, Charles, 146
Champlain, Samuel de, 37
Chance or Destiny (Handlin), 134, 135, 146
Chase, Salmon P., 286–289, 292, 293, 313–315
Cherokee Indians, 154, 188–191, 193, 196, 200, 201–203, 226
"Chester" (Billings), 70
Chester, Samuel Knapp, 338
Chilton, R. H., 310–311
Choctaw Indians, 154, 163
Church, Frederic Edwin, 295–296
Civil War, 8, 229, 262, 267, 277, 296, 300, 302–319, 323, 325–328, 330–333, 336, 338, 342–343, 351, 355, 370–371
Claiborne, William, 159–160, 165
Clark, William, 127
Clay, Henry, 271
Clinton, Henry, 54
Coahuila y Tejas, Mexico, 209, 210
Columbus, Christopher, 28
Comanche Indians, 209
Concord, Battle of, 49
Confederation Congress, 91–92, 97, 98, 100, 110, 117, 120
Connecticut Plan, 102, 112
Conrad, Thomas Nelson, 354–355
Constitution of the United States, 95, 97, 142, 143, 146, 315
    Bill of Rights, 118
    opponents to, 115–116
    ratification of, 116–119
    signing of, 88, 114–116
    slavery and, 99
    Thirteenth Amendment, 316
    three-fifths clause, 99
Constitutional Convention, 90–91, 94–121, 234, 373
    Connecticut Plan, 102, 112

executive branch, 97, 99, 100
Franklin's speech to, 105–107
Great Compromise, 112, 113
New Jersey Plan, 100–101
proportional representation issue, 100–102, 108–111
secrecy of, 98, 112, 114
setting agenda, 96–97
slavery and, 99, 119
on verge of dissolution, 102–104
Virginia Plan, 96–98, 100–102, 110, 115
Continental Army, 48–53, 55, 56, 58–69, 83, 101
Continental Congress of 1776, 3, 6, 53, 54, 58, 69, 82, 234, 360–361
Cooke, Henry, 173
Coolidge, Calvin, 21
Cooper Union address (Lincoln), 287–288, 297
Corbett, Boston, 348
Cornelius, James, 347
Couto, Don José Bernardo, 250
Craik, James, 85, 86
Creek Indians, 153, 154, 191–192
Crockett, Davy, 183, 187, 213
Crook, W. H., 345
Custis, George Washington Parke, 84–86
Custis, Jacky, 84

Davies, Samuel, 82
Davis, David, 289, 292, 293
Davis, Jefferson, 303
Dayton, Jonathan, 106–107
Dayton, William, 289
Declaration of Independence, 2, 3, 6, 7, 11, 20, 54, 56–58, 96, 101, 102, 116, 120, 131, 236, 360, 361
Decrès, Denis, 138
Defiant Peacemaker (Ohrt), 249
Delaware River, 75, 302
Delgado, Pedro, 219
Dermer, Thomas, 38
Dickinson, Mrs. A. M., 214
Dinwiddie, Robert, 76
Dirty Shirts, 148, 167, 172, 173, 181
Donald, David Herbert, 274, 305–306
Donelson, Andrew Jackson, 236
Dorchester Heights, Massachusetts, 50–52, 68
Douglas, Stephen A., 281, 285, 286, 291, 294, 295

Douglass, Frederick, 315, 328, 355
Drez, Ronald, 179
Dubourg, Guillaume, 175, 176

Eagleton, Thomas, 280
Early, Jubal, 353
Ellsworth, Oliver, 92, 103, 110
Emancipation Proclamation, 315–316, 323
Executive branch of government, 97, 99, 100

Featherstonhaugh, George William, 15
Federal Convention, 91, 93, 98, 100 (*see also* Constitutional Convention)
Federalist, The (Hamilton, Madison, and Jay), 117, 120–121
Fell, Jesse, 286
Ferguson, Patrick, 83–84
Fessenden, William, 289
Few, William, 107, 110, 119–120
Fitzgerald, Richard, 82
Flexner, James Thomas, 75
Ford, Gerald, 333
Ford's Theatre, Washington, 334, 337, 344–347
Fort Sumter, 229, 302
Founding fathers, 20, 24, 56 (*see also* Constitutional Convention)
1491 (Mann), 38, 45
Fourth of July, 1826 (the Glorious Fourth), 1, 3, 4, 7, 9–13, 16–17, 20, 24, 236
Franklin, Benjamin, 20, 54, 78, 112, 283–284, 360
Constitutional Convention and, 96, 101, 105–107, 109, 111, 114–116, 119, 373
Freaner, James, 246, 247, 251
Frémon, Charles, 152
Frémont, John Charles, 152, 290–291
French and Indian War, 77–82, 124
French Revolution, 89, 137

Garfield, James A., 333
Garrison, William Lloyd, 315
Gaskill, Malcolm, 30
Gates, Horatio, 124
Gelernter, David, 364–365, 374
George II, King of England, 77
George III, King of England, 68, 83, 94
statue of, 56–58, 68
Gerry, Elbridge, 99, 115–117
Gettysburg, Battle of, 229, 317–320, 343, 357

Gettysburg Address, 275
Ghaemi, Nassir, 270
Ghent, Treaty of (1814), 178, 179
Gibbon, John, 311
Gibbs, Samuel, 170, 171
Gillespie, Joseph, 283
Gist, Christopher, 75–76
Gleig, Robert, 164, 174
"God Bless America," 362
Gold, 233, 251, 253–263
Goliad, Texas, 214, 220, 223
Gordon, William, 50
Gorges, Fernando, 42
Graham, Mentor, 278
Graham, Michael, 61–62
Grant, James, 57, 62, 69
Grant, Mark, 18
Grant, Ulysses S., 319, 330–331, 332, 342, 343
Graydon, Alexander, 67
Great Compromise, 112, 113
Greeley, Horace, 287, 288, 290, 291, 315
Guadalupe Hidalgo, Treaty of (1848), 233, 234, 250–253, 257, 258, 261
Guelzo, Allen, 347
Guild, Jo C., 194–195
Gurley, Phineas Densmore, 304

Haiti (Saint-Domingue), 124, 127–128, 131–134, 136, 137, 146, 156, 158
Hakluyt, Richard, 27
Hale, John P., 334, 342
Halstead, Murat, 292–294
Hamilton, Alexander, 20, 127, 360
    Constitutional Convention and, 101, 104, 107, 121
    The Federalist by, 117
    Jefferson, Thomas and, 123
    on Louisiana Purchase, 123–124
    pen name Publius, 117
    in Revolutionary War, 126
Hamlet (Shakespeare), 282
Hancock, John, 54, 116, 118
Hand, Edward, 65
Handlin, Oscar, 134, 135, 146
Haney, Thomas, 353
Hanks, Dennis, 272, 273
Hanks, Elizabeth, 272
Hanks, Henry, 272
Hanks, John, 271
Hanks, Lucy, 268
Hanson, Victor Davis, 373–374

Hariot, Thomas, 38
Harlan, James, 338
Harris, Clara, 343, 347
Harrison, William Henry, 237, 242
Hay, John, 322
Helvoet Sluys, Netherlands, 124, 134–135, 146
Henry, Anson, 278–279
Henry, Patrick, 118
Henry V (Shakespeare), 175
Herndon, Billy, 267–268, 276–277, 282–284, 339
Herold, David, 348
Hessian mercenaries, 54, 61, 62, 64–65
Hill, Samuel, 305
History of American Christianity, A (Bacon), 28
History of the United States (Bancroft), 20–21
Hittell, John Shertzer, 255, 259–260
Hodes, Martha, 355–356
Hodge, Charles, 356
Holmes, John, 8
Homer, 189, 190
Hopkins, Elizabeth, 32
Hopkins, Oceanus, 32
Horseshoe Bend, Battle of, 154, 185, 191, 192, 199
House of Representatives, 97, 99, 102, 109, 112, 144, 149, 177, 194, 205–208, 265, 276, 281, 316
Houston, Eliza Allen, 195–200, 202, 205, 226
Houston, Elizabeth Paxton, 188, 190, 192, 204
Houston, Major Samuel, 188, 190
Houston, Margaret Moffette Lea, 224–228
Houston, Sam, 360
    background of, 187–190
    Cherokee Indians and, 188–190, 193, 196, 200–203, 226
    children of, 226
    death of, 229
    as governor of Tennessee, 194–200
    indestructibility of, 186, 193
    as Indian agent, 193–194
    Indian names for, 189, 203
    Jackson, Andrew and, 184–185, 194, 195, 202, 206, 208, 237
    marriage to Eliza, 195–200, 202, 205, 226

marriage to Margaret, 225–226
mental state of, 200
physical appearance of, 188, 200–201
portrait of, 186
as president of Texas Republic, 209, 224
religion and, 188, 226–227
San Jacinto, Battle of, 216–222, 224, 230, 240, 245
secession and, 228–229
as senator, 226
Stanbery, William and, 204–207
Tiana, relationship with, 202, 209
trial of, 206–208
in War of 1812, 154, 190–192
wounded, 191–193, 198, 199, 220, 221, 224
Howe, Lord Richard "Black Dick," 63
Howe, William, 51, 52, 54, 58, 60–64, 68, 83

Iliad, The (Homer), 189, 190
Indian Prophecy, or Visions of Glory, The (Custis), 84–86
Indians (*see* Native Americans)

Jackson, Andrew, 200, 204, 265, 360
assassination attempt on, 182–184, 333
background of, 149–150, 181
Benton brothers and, 150–152, 183
death of, 185
Farewell Address of, 371
health of, 182, 185
Houston, Sam and, 184–185, 194, 195, 202, 206, 208, 237
indestructibility of, 181, 182–184
Native Americans and, 152–154, 185
New Orleans, Battle of, 148, 149, 161–168, 170, 171, 174–181, 193, 235, 240, 263
nickname of, 153
physical appearance of, 153, 157, 182
pirates and, 160–161, 166, 168, 180
portrait of, 184
in Revolutionary War, 181–182
Texas and, 209, 210
Trist, Nicholas and, 236–238, 263
in War of 1812, 154–155, 158–180, 190–192
Jackson, Rachel, 155, 157
Jackson, Robert, 181–182
Jackson, Thomas J. "Stonewall," 308
James, Marquis, 202

James I, King of England, 29, 43
Jamestown Colony, 29–30, 42
Japanese Americans, 366–367
Jay, John, 117
Jefferson, Martha, 235
Jefferson, Thomas, 20, 55, 56, 88, 90, 159, 265, 283–284, 299, 360
Adams, John and, 2–4, 6, 8
on Constitutional Convention, 120
death of, 9–11, 12–13, 16–18, 24, 236
Declaration of Independence and, 3, 7, 131, 143, 236, 361
Hamilton, Alexander and, 123
inaugural address of, 7
Louisiana Purchase and, 124, 139, 142–146, 209
as minister to France, 120, 126
New Orleans and, 130, 131
slavery and, 8
Trist, Nicholas and, 9–10, 234–236, 263
western exploration and, 126–127
Jefferson's Great Gamble (Cerami), 146
Jenifer, Daniel of St. Thomas, 108–110, 119
Joffre, Josef, 362
Johnson, Andrew, 326, 346, 347
Johnson, Lyndon Baines, 227
Johnson, Paul, 145–146, 260
Johnston, Joseph, 342
Johnston, Matilda, 273
Jones, Christopher, 34–35, 46
Judd, Norman, 287, 292, 297
"July 4, 1826: Explaining the Same-Day Deaths of John Adams and Thomas Jefferson" (Battin), 16–17

Kansas-Nebraska Act, 227
Keane, John, 162, 164, 180
Keene, Laura, 343
Kennedy, John F., 20, 333
Kennedy, Robert M., 369
Key, Francis Scott, 206, 358, 361
King, Martin Luther Jr., 20, 369
Kings Mountain, Battle of, 84
Kinsley, Mark, 22
Kluger, Richard, 259

Lafayette, Marquis de, 83, 90, 94
Lafitte, Jean, 159–160, 167–168
Lafitte, Pierre, 159
Lamar, Gazaway Bugg, 217

Lamar, Mirabeau Buonaparte, 217, 224
Lambert, John, 174
Lamon, Ward Hill, 292, 297, 339–342, 345, 352
Lansing, John, 117
Larson, Edward J., 95
Leale, Charles A., 349
Leaves of Grass (Whitman), 296
Leclerc, Charles Emmanuel, 128, 130, 132
Leclerc, Paulette, 132
Lee, Henry, 94
Lee, Richard Henry, 117
Lee, Robert E., 84, 308, 309–311, 315–317, 332, 338, 342, 355
Lee, William, 95
Leipzig, Battle of, 154
Leonard, Abiel, 52
Leonidas, 61
Lewis, Meriwether, 127
Lexington, Battle of, 49
Life of Sam Houston, The, 230–231
Life of Thomas Jefferson, The (Rayner), 12–13
Lincoln, Abraham, 20, 22, 228, 360, 373
  ambition of, 282, 284
  assassination of, 267, 323, 341, 342, 345, 348–349, 351, 352, 356
  birth of, 268
  burial of, 350
  character and personality of, 271, 276–281, 338–342, 350
  childhood and youth of, 269–274, 282, 304–305
  Civil War and, 267, 277, 296, 300, 302–304, 306–307, 309, 311, 312, 316–320, 322, 323, 325–328, 330–333, 336, 342–343, 351, 355
  death of mother of, 272
  death of sons of, 305, 306
  death threats and plots against, 336–338, 346, 352–355
  debates with Stephen Douglas, 281, 286
  education of, 273
  emancipation of slaves and, 300, 307, 313–316, 323
  fatalism of, 282–284, 297, 327, 339–340
  father, relations with, 274, 298
  First Inaugural Address of, 306, 336, 371
  in House of Representatives, 265, 276, 281

  illegitimate birth of mother of, 268, 281, 335
  in Illinois legislature, 275–276, 278
  in Illinois militia, 275, 303
  inheritance of, 267–268, 270–271
  marriage of, 276
  McClellan, George B. and, 296–297, 300, 309
  mental health of, 270, 277–280
  mourning for, 349–350, 355–356
  photographs and paintings of, 264, 300, 314
  physical appearance of, 274, 279, 287, 296, 301–302
  poems by, 271, 272, 279–280, 282
  pre-presidential career of, 265–266
  presidential election of 1860 and, 285–297, 339
  presidential election of 1864 and, 321, 325, 340
  reading by, 273
  religion and, 270, 282, 299, 302, 304–306, 313–315, 319–323, 326–328, 330, 347, 350, 352
  Rutledge, Ann and, 277–278
  Second Inaugural Address of, 322, 325–330, 338
  Senate defeats and, 281, 285, 289
  sense of destiny of, 267, 282–284, 299, 306, 322, 336, 339–340
  speeches by, 266, 275, 287–288, 297, 299, 301, 306, 322, 325–330, 333, 336, 338, 352, 371
  Trist, Nicholas and, 263
Lincoln, Captain Abraham, 271
Lincoln, Eddie, 305, 306
Lincoln, Mary Jane, 270
Lincoln, Mary Todd, 276, 278, 281, 282, 294, 331, 332, 339, 340, 344, 346, 347, 349
Lincoln, Mordecai, 271
Lincoln, Nancy Hanks, 268, 271, 272, 281, 335
Lincoln, Robert, 334–335, 344, 349
Lincoln, Sarah, 268, 273
Lincoln, Sarah Bush Johnston, 272–273, 298
Lincoln, Tad, 318, 331, 334, 340, 344
Lincoln, Thomas, 269–274, 282, 298
Lincoln, Thomas junior, 269
Lincoln, Willie, 305, 306, 344
Lincoln's Battle with God (Mansfield), 347

Lincoln's Melancholy (Shenk), 270
Line Jackson, New Orleans, 148, 164–168, 171, 172, 175, 178
Livingston, Edward, 158, 235
Livingston, Robert, 130–131, 139–142, 143, 147, 158
Locke, David Ross, 344
Long Island, Battle of, 60–62, 68, 69
Longley, Clifford, 365
Loring, Elizabeth Lloyd, 68
Louis XIV, King of France, 125
Louis XV, King of France, 77, 125
Louisiana Purchase, 122, 123, 136, 138–146, 155, 158, 179, 209, 240, 263
Luce, Ed, 15

MacDougall, Duncan, 173
Madison, James, 5, 20, 103, 141, 178, 234, 360
    Constitutional Convention and, 90, 95–98, 101, 106–108, 110, 113–116, 119, 120, 143, 304
    death of, 98
    The Federalist by, 117, 120–121
    as secretary of state, 131, 136, 139, 143
    Trist, Nicholas and, 236, 263
Making Haste from Babylon (Bunker), 31
Manifest Destiny, 234, 238–240, 247, 251
Mann, Charles C., 38, 45
Mansfield, Stephen, 282, 347
Marshall, John, 233, 240, 253–257, 260
Martin, Joseph Plumb, 64
Martin, Luther, 103, 104, 109, 111, 115–116
Martin, Martha, 196, 198
Martin, Robert, 196
Mason, George, 93–94, 99, 115, 117
Mason, Richard, 257
Massachusetts Bay Colony, 30, 38
Massasoit (Indian chief), 41, 43, 44
Mayflower, 26, 31, 32, 34–36, 46
Mayflower Compact, 34
McCandless, Wilson, 177
McCann, Steve, 370
McClean, John, 289
McClellan, George B., 296–297, 300, 309–312, 317
McCulloch, Ben, 219
McCullough, David, 66
McDougall, Walter A., 24–25, 373
McEwen, Mrs. Robert, 196–197
McEwen, Robert, 196

McGrady, John, 209
McKinley, William, 322, 333
McPherson, James M., 312, 316
McWilliams, James, 180
"Meditation on the Divine Will" (Lincoln), 322–323
"Meteor of 1860, The" (Church), 296
Meteor procession, 295–296
Mexican War, 233, 241–246, 248, 262, 303, 304, 312
Michaux, André, 127
Mississippi River, 124–126, 129, 162, 170, 180, 185, 216, 319
Missouri Compromise, 8, 227, 286
Mitchell, Barton W., 309–311
Monmouth, Battle of, 83, 86
Monongahela, Battle of, 72, 79–82
Monroe, James, 5, 7, 8, 144, 194
    death of, 17–18
    as envoy to France, 139, 140, 158
    as secretary of state, 155
    War of 1812 and, 155–156, 174
Montgomery, Lemuel, 191
Monticello, Virginia, 234–236
Mormons, 255–256
Morris, Robert, 96
Morton, Thomas, 38, 39
Mount Vernon, Virginia, 74, 78, 81, 84, 94, 95
Mourning Lincoln (Hodes), 356

Nasby Letters, The (Locke), 344
Native Americans, 18, 29, 35–47, 74, 75, 77, 79–81, 85–86, 152–154, 185, 255, 271, 360 (*see also* specific tribes)
Nevin, John Williamson, 357
New England Triptych (Schuman), 70
New Jersey Plan, 100–101
New Orleans, Battle of, 148, 149, 161–181, 193, 235, 240, 263
New Orleans, Louisiana, 125–127, 131, 133, 135, 136, 139, 140, 143, 144, 155–159, 192, 274
New Salem, Illinois, 274–275, 280, 304–305
Nichols, John W., 354
Nicolay, John, 299, 303, 322
Noll, Mark A., 327, 356
Noonan, Peggy, 370

"O Captain! My Captain!" (Whitman), 351
Obama, Barack, 15–16, 266, 362

Ohrt, Wallace, 249
Oolooteka (Indian chief), 189, 193, 201–203
Osage Indians, 202, 203
O'Sullivan, John T., 238–240, 247
Our American Cousin (Taylor), 343, 346, 349

Page, John, 55–56
Paine, Thomas, 305
Pakenham, Sir Edward Michael, 161, 167, 169–173, 178–180
Paris, Treaty of (1763), 124, 125
Parker, John Frederick, 345, 346, 352
Paterson, William, 100–102, 111
Patuxet, Massachusetts, 37, 41–43
Paul III, Pope, 42
Peace, Friendship, Limits and Settlement, Treaty of (1848) (*see* Guadalupe Hidalgo, Treaty of)
Peacefield, Quincy, 3–4
Peale, Charles Willson, 72
Penn, William, 112
Percy, Lord Hugh, 62, 67
Philadelphia, Pennsylvania, 50, 53, 54, 88, 90–116
Pichon, Louis-André, 136
Pierce, William, 105, 110, 119–120, 303
Pilgrims, 30–47
Pinckney, Charles Cotesworth, 110–111, 121
Pinkerton, Alan, 353
Pittman, Samuel E., 310–311
Pius IX, Pope, 177, 330
Pius XII, Pope, 365
Plymouth Colony, 26, 30, 34, 40, 43–46
Plymouth Rock, 36
Polk, James K., 184, 207, 224, 232, 239, 240
  death of, 261
  gold rush and, 258–260
  last annual message to Congress of, 257–258
  Mexico and, 238, 241–253, 261–262, 304
  Trist, Nicholas and, 238, 243, 245–248, 252, 261–262
Polk, Sarah, 261
Pope, Alexander, 189
Potter, David M., 351
Powell, Lewis, 346
Presidential elections
  1800, 119

1820, 8
1860, 228, 285–297, 339
1864, 321, 325, 340
Princeton, Battle of, 82
Proportional representation, 100–102, 108–111
Puritans, 30
Putnam, Israel "Old Put," 68

Quasi War, 126
Quimby, Robert, 164

Raguet, Henry, 218
Raleigh, Sir Walter, 29, 30, 33, 38
Randolph, Edmund, 95, 111
  Constitutional Convention and, 96, 97, 101, 107, 108, 115, 118
Randolph, John, 144
Rathbone, Henry, 343, 348
Raven, The (James), 202
Rawdon, Lord Francis, 54, 69
Rayner, B. L., 12–13, 17
Reagan, Ronald, 20, 265, 333, 367
Red Sticks, 153, 185, 191
Reed, Joseph, 50, 53, 58
Remini, Robert V., 168–169, 178
Return of George Washington, The (Larson), 95
Revolutionary War, 17, 19–20, 48–72, 75, 82–84, 86, 89–90, 93, 95, 104, 112, 124, 126, 133, 138, 210–211, 302
Richmond, Virginia, 331, 332, 338
Roanoke Colony (Lost Colony), 29, 38, 46
Roberts, Andrew, 145
Rochambeau, Donatien-Marie-Joseph de, 133
Rodriguez Canal, New Orleans, 164, 170
Roman Republic, 89, 99
Roosevelt, Franklin D., 20, 265, 333
Roosevelt, Theodore, 20, 265, 322, 333
Royal Navy, 51, 53, 154, 161, 162
Rush, Benjamin, 101
Rusk, Thomas Jefferson, 223
Rusling, James, 318–319
Russell, William Howard, 303
Rutledge, Ann, 277–278, 279
Rutledge, John, 114
Rutledge, Robert, 278

Samoset, 40–41, 43
San Francisco, California, 256, 259, 260

San Jacinto, Battle of, 216–222, 224, 230, 245

Sanders, Bernie, 370

Santa Anna, Antonio López de, 212–223, 245

Saratoga, Battle of, 124

Saulsbury, Willard, 296

Scalia, Antonin, 368

Schaff, Philip, 371

Scheldt River, 134, 146

Schuman, William, 70

Scott, Winfield, 242–246, 248, 262

Scripps, John Locke, 269

Seal of the United States of America, 284

Secession, 8, 228–229

Seizing Destiny (Kluger), 259

Senate, 97, 102, 109, 112, 144, 149, 178, 252–253, 281, 285, 289, 316

Serle, Ambrose, 58

Seven Years' War, 77, 124

Seward, Frederick, 342–343

Seward, William Henry, 286–294, 297, 313, 330, 343, 346, 347

Shakespeare, William, 175, 282

Shawnee Indians, 271

Shays, Daniel, 93

Shays' Rebellion, 93, 94

Shenk, Joshua Wolf, 270, 279, 283

Sherman, Roger, 102, 109–112

Sherman, Sidney, 217

Sherman, William Tecumseh, 342, 343

Sickles, Daniel Edgar "Devil Dan," 318–321

Slavery, 8, 18, 19, 99, 119, 227, 239, 247, 270, 283, 291, 308, 321, 326–327, 336, 360, 366
    emancipation of slaves, 300, 307, 313–316, 323

Smallpox, 73–74, 182

Smith, Erastus "Deaf," 218, 220

Smith, John, 42

Spartacus, 89

Spartans, 61

Special Orders 191 (Lost Dispatch), 310–311, 316–317, 323

Speed, Fanny, 283

Speed, Joshua, 264, 277, 279, 283, 321

Springfield, Illinois, 276, 280

Squanto (Tisquantum), 34, 41–47

Stanbery, William, 204–207

Stanton, Edwin, 331, 342, 349, 354, 355

"Star-Spangled Banner, The," 206, 318, 358, 361

Stedman, Charles, 67

Steele, Shelby, 369

Steele, William, 107

Stevenson, Andrew, 207, 208

Strong, George Templeton, 301

Stuart, John Todd, 276, 278

"Suicide's Soliloquy, The" (Lincoln), 279

Sumner, Charles, 262

Sutter, Johann Augustus, 254, 255, 257

Sutter's Mill, Coloma, California, 233, 240, 253–255

Talleyrand, Charles Maurice de, 131, 136–140

Tallmadge, Benjamin, 63, 66

Taylor, Walter, 316–317

Taylor, Zachary, 242, 281

Tea Party, 119

Tecumseh, 153

Temple, Wayne, 347

Ten Commandments, 119

Thanksgiving, 31, 44, 47

Thayer, Michael, 371–372

Thermopylae, 61

Thirteenth Amendment to the Constitution, 316

Thomas, Benjamin, 269

Thornton, William, 162, 163, 167, 168, 171

Three-fifths clause, 99

Tiana, 202, 209

Tocqueville, Alexis de, 362

Touissant Louverture, 128, 129, 131

Trail of Tears, 193

Travis, William Barrett, 214

Trenton, Battle of, 75

Trist, Eliza, 234

Trist, Nicholas Philip, 9–10, 266
    background of, 234–235
    in Cuba, 237–238, 244
    death of, 262
    Guadalupe Hidalgo Treaty and, 233, 234, 250–252, 257, 258, 261
    Jackson, Andrew and, 236–238, 263
    Jefferson, Thomas and, 9–10, 234–236, 263
    Lincoln, Abraham and, 263
    Madison, James and, 236, 263
    in Mexico, 243–251
    personality of, 237
    photograph of, 232
    Polk, James K. and, 238, 243, 245–248, 252, 261–262

Trist, Nicholas Philip (*cont'd*)
    Scott, Winfield and, 244, 262
Trist, Virginia Jefferson Randolph, 10,
    235, 237–238, 246, 262–263
Troupe, George, 177
Trumbull, John, 51
Trumbull, Lyman, 289
Trump, Donald, 370
Turtledove, Harry, 317
27th Indiana Volunteers, 307, 309–310
Tyree, Will, 199

Ursuline convent, New Orleans, 169,
    176–177

Valley Forge, 49, 104
Van Buren, Martin, 91, 184, 237
Veracruz, 242, 246
Vicksburg, Mississippi, 319, 343
Victor-Perrin, Claude, 134, 135
Villard, Henry, 298
Villeré, Gabriel, 162–163, 180
Virginia Plan, 96–98, 100–102, 110, 115
Voltaire, 125

Wade, Ben, 289
Walker, Arda, 182, 184
Walker, Robert, 252
Wampanoag Indians, 38, 43, 45
War for Independence (*see* Revolutionary
    War)
War of 1812, 8, 145, 150, 153–155, 158–
    180, 190–192, 242, 304, 312, 361
War of 1812, The: Conflict and Deception:
    The British Attempt to Seize New
    Orleans and Nullify the Louisiana
    Purchase (Drez), 179
Ward, John William, 182
Washington, Augustine, 73
Washington, burning and occupation of,
    154, 155, 165
Washington, George, 20, 48, 92, 100, 111,
    132, 214, 265, 299
    adopted children of, 84
    background of, 73–74
    Constitutional Convention and, 90, 94–
        96, 98, 104, 107, 114, 116, 119, 120
    courage of, 77
    death of, 84
    Farewell Address of, 366
    First Inaugural Address of, 70–71, 120
    in French and Indian War, 77–82
    health of, 73–74, 78–80, 182
    indestructibility of, 73–75, 78, 80–87
    marriage of, 84
    physical appearance of, 73, 74, 80, 182
    portrait of, 72
    retirement from army of, 94
    in Revolutionary War, 49–56, 58, 60–
        68, 70, 75, 82–84, 86, 95, 104, 302
    slaves owned by, 95
    in Virginia militia, 74–78
    wilderness treks by, 74–77, 85
Washington, Jane, 73
Washington, Lawrence, 73–74
Washington, Martha, 84
Washington, Mary Ball, 78
Washington, Mildred, 73
Waterloo, Battle of, 145
Webster, Daniel, 13–15, 24
Weed, Thurlow, 293, 330
Weems, Parsons, 86
Weightman, Roger, 5
Weimer, Peter L., 254–255
Welles, Gideon, 300, 313, 332
Wellington, Duke of, 161, 242
Wellington's Heroes, 148, 161, 167, 171,
    181
West, Benjamin, 94
White, John, 29
White, Ronald C. Jr., 299
Whitman, Walt, 295, 296, 302, 350–351,
    356
Whitney, George, 10
Whitney, Henry C., 276, 281
Why the North Won the Civil War (Potter),
    351
Wilkinson, James, 92
Williams, Roger, 39
Williams, Willoughby, 199–200
Wilson, James, 101, 105, 108, 110, 113,
    115, 118
Wilson, Woodrow, 20, 265
Wilton, Joseph, 56
Winslow, Edward, 35–37, 40
Winthrop, John, 38
World Parliament of Religions, 28

"Yankee Doodle," 69
Yellow fever, 132, 234, 353
You, Dominique, 159, 166, 168
Young, Brigham, 256

ABOUT THE AUTHOR

MICHAEL MEDVED's daily three-hour radio program, *The Michael Medved Show*, reaches five million listeners on more than three hundred stations coast to coast. He is the author of twelve other books, including the bestsellers *The 10 Big Lies About America*, *Hollywood vs. America*, *Hospital*, and *What Really Happened to the Class of '65?* He is a member of *USA Today*'s board of contributors, a former chief film critic for the *New York Post*, and for more than a decade, cohosted *Sneak Previews*, the weekly movie-review show on PBS. Medved is an honors graduate of Yale with departmental honors in American history. He lives with his family in the Seattle area.

READ MORE FROM NATIONALLY SYNDICATED
TALK-RADIO HOST AND BESTSELLING AUTHOR
MICHAEL MEDVED:

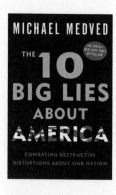

Uncover the truth behind the ten biggest lies that millions of Americans believe about our country, and gain the ammunition to fire back and defend our nation.

If every American benefits from the productivity of the free market, why do so many people doubt our business system? Learn the devastating rebuttals to the most widely circulated smears against capitalism.

Explore Medved's extraordinary journey from punk liberal activist to lovable conservative curmudgeon as he reveals why the Right is right.